For Wladimiro della Porta and Vittorio Diani, in memoriam

SECOND EDITION

SOCIAL MOVEMENTS

AN INTRODUCTION

**DONATELLA DELLA PORTA
AND MARIO DIANI**

Blackwell
Publishing

© 1999, 2006 by Donatella della Porta and Mario Diani

BLACKWELL PUBLISHING
350 Main Street, Malden, MA 02148–5020, USA
9600 Garsington Road, Oxford OX4 2DQ, UK
550 Swanston Street, Carlton, Victoria 3053, Australia

The right of Donatella della Porta and Mario Diani to be identified as the Authors of this Work has been asserted in accordance with the UK Copyright, Designs, and Patents Act 1988.

First edition published 1998
Second edition published 2006 by Blackwell Publishing Ltd
4   2008

Library of Congress Cataloging-in-Publication Data
Della Porta, Donatella, 1956–
      Social movements : an introduction / Donatella della Porta and Mario Diani. – 2nd ed.
          p.   cm.
      Includes bibliographical references and index.
      ISBN 978-1-4051-0282-7 (pbk. : alk. paper)
      1. Social movements.   I. Diani, Mario, 1957–   II. Title.
      HN17.5.D45 2006
      303.48′4 – dc22

                                                                          2005011636

A catalogue record for this title is available from the British Library.

Set in 10 on 12.5 pt Dante
by SNP Best-set Typesetter Ltd, Hong Kong
Printed and bound in Singapore
by Markono Print Media Pte Ltd

The publisher's policy is to use permanent paper from mills that operate a sustainable forestry policy, and which has been manufactured from pulp processed using acid-free and elementary chlorine-free practices. Furthermore, the publisher ensures that the text paper and cover board used have met acceptable environmental accreditation standards.

For further information on
Blackwell Publishing, visit our website:
www.blackwellpublishing.com

CONTENTS

Preface to the Second Edition   vii

1   The Study of Social Movements: Recurring Questions, (Partially) Changing Answers   1
   1.1   Four Core Questions for Social Movement Analysis   5
   1.2   What is Distinctive about Social Movements?   20
   1.3   On This Book   29

2   Social Changes and Social Movements   33
   2.1   Social Structure, Political Cleavages, and Collective Action   36
   2.2   States, Markets, and Social Movements   42
   2.3   Knowledge, Culture, and Conflicts   47
   2.4   Structural Transformations, New Conflicts, New Classes   52
   2.5   Summary   62

3   The Symbolic Dimension of Collective Action   64
   3.1   Culture and Action: The Role of Values   67
   3.2   Culture and Action: The Cognitive Perspective   73
   3.3   Problems and Responses   85
   3.4   Summary   87

4   Collective Action and Identity   89
   4.1   How Does Identity Work?   93
   4.2   Multiple Identities   98
   4.3   Does Identity Facilitate Participation?   100
   4.4   How Is Identity Generated and Reproduced?   105
   4.5   Summary   113

5   Individuals, Networks, and Participation   114
   5.1   Why Do People Get Involved in Collective Action? The Role of Networks   117

5.2 Do Networks Always Matter?   121
5.3 Individuals and Organizations   126
5.4 Individual Participation, Movement Subcultures,
and Virtual Networks   131
5.5 Summary   134

6 Social Movements and Organizations   135
6.1 Organizational Dilemmas in Social Movements   140
6.2 Types of Social Movement Organizations   145
6.3 How Do Social Movement Organizations Change?   150
6.4 From Movement Organizations to Social Movement Networks   156
6.5 Summary   161

7 Action Forms, Repertoires, and Cycles of Protest   163
7.1 Protest: A Definition   165
7.2 Repertoires of Action   168
7.3 The Logics and Forms of Protest   170
7.4 Strategic Options and Protest   178
7.5 Factors Influencing Repertoire Choice   181
7.6 The Cross-National Diffusion of Protest   186
7.7 Cycles of Protest, Protest Waves, and Protest Campaigns   188
7.8 Summary   191

8 The Policing of Protest and Political Opportunities for Social
Movements   193
8.1 The Policing of Protest   197
8.2 Political Institutions and Social Movements   201
8.3 Prevailing Strategies and Social Movements   206
8.4 Allies, Opponents, and Social Movements   210
8.5 Discursive Opportunity and the Media System   219
8.6 Summary   221

9 Social Movements and Democracy   223
9.1 Social Movement Strategies and Their Effects   226
9.2 Changes in Public Policy   229
9.3 Social Movements and Procedural Changes   233
9.4 Social Movements and Democratic Theory   239
9.5 Social Movements and Democratization   245
9.6 Summary   248

Notes   250

References   261

Index of Names   329

Index of Subjects   341

PREFACE TO THE SECOND EDITION

Many things have happened since the first edition of this book appeared in January 1999. Only a few months later, in November of the same year, what would have become known as "the battle of Seattle" drew public opinion's attention worldwide towards the sustained challenge that broad coalitions of very heterogeneous actors were mounting against neoliberal globalization and its main institutional protagonists, such as the IMF or the WTO. All of a sudden, neoliberalism turned from being regarded as the only possible path to development, on the basis of the TINA (There Is No Alternative [to free market]) dogma and the so-called "Washington consensus," into a highly disputed and increasingly unpopular option. Leading financiers, economists, and policymakers as well as political leaders across the left–right spectrum were confronted with the claim that another world was indeed possible.

Time will tell whether the last few years have actually seen the emergence of a new major political force, in the shape of the global justice movement(s) active across the five continents. We think they have, as we shall try to point out throughout this book, but we might be wrong. Whatever the case, the last years have certainly seen new problems arising for social movement analysts, and therefore also for a book like ours. The first edition of *Social Movements* was strongly embedded in, and reflective of, the experience of the "new social movements": that is to say, the movements which had developed since the late 1960s on issues such as women's rights, gender relations, environmental protection, ethnicity and migration, peace and international solidarity – with a strong (new) middle-class basis and a clear differentiation from the models of working-class or nationalist collective action that had historically preceded them. While there are surely continuities between those movements and the current wave of global justice campaigns, there are also many suggestions that the overall patterns of collective action they display is significantly different from those we had grown accustomed to. After many years "in the doldrums," to borrow Leila Rupp and Verta Taylor's felicitous expression, working-class action seems to be back with a vengeance; over all, mobilizations by the dispossessed (be they unskilled workers on precarious employment in the US, populations affected by famine and disease in West Sudan, or local communities threatened by new dams in India) have gained increasing attention and visibility. Basic survival rights and social entitlements seem to play a more balanced role in contemporary mobilizations, alongside more postmaterial ones, related to quality of life, than was the case in the recent past.

It is not for us to discuss here whether the oblivion in which collective action on social inequality has been left in the past decades was due to its actual diminished relevance, or to oversights on the part of most social movement researchers (surely not all, as people like Colin Barker or Paul Bagguley in the UK or Judith Stepan-Norris, Maurice Zeitlin, Rick Fantasia, Kim Voss, or Giovanni Arrighi in the US have constantly reminded us). Either way, the consequence for this new edition of *Social Movements* has been that the context within which we had located our work appeared to us, after only five years, very different. Our first response has been that of changing most of the examples of collective-action processes with which we start each chapter of the book. In this new edition they mostly refer to instances of conflicts or personal experiences of activism, somehow linked with global justice campaigns or perhaps mobilizations on a transnational scale. Adapting our conceptual framework has been, unsurprisingly, far more difficult. At the end, we have gone for a "minimalist" solution: instead of trying to formulate a radically new approach, inspired by the new phenomena, we have shown how established analytical categories could be used and – when necessary – modified to account for recent developments.

The degree to which we have been successful is obviously a matter for the readers to evaluate. There is no doubt, however, that we are as usual indebted to many people who, in different ways, have made this a better book than it would have been otherwise. At Blackwell, Susan Rabinowitz first and later Ken Provencher have proved both patient and supportive editors, while Hank Johnston has presented us with an exceptionally thorough and helpful review of our first draft. Three anonymous colleagues reviewed our proposal for the second edition, again providing valuable insight and advice. Among members of our "inner circle," we would like first of all mention Chuck Tilly for his relentless, critical appreciation. Thanks also to Massimiliano Andretta, Delia Baldassarri, Colin Barker, Bob Edwards, Olivier Fillieule, Marco Giugni, Doug McAdam, John McCarthy, Hanspeter Kriesi, Lorenzo Mosca, Friedhelm Neidhardt, Alessandro Pizzorno, Herbert Reiter, Chris Rootes, Dieter Rucht, David Snow, and Sidney Tarrow. Finally, Christina Tischer proved a very reliable assistant with the bibliography of the book, while Sarah Tarrow did nothing to damage her reputation as an outstanding language editor on chapters 2 and 7–9.

Acknowledgments

Parts of sections 5.2 and 5.3 previously appeared in M. Diani, "Networks and Participation," in *The Blackwell Companion to Social Movements*, edited by D. Snow, S. Soule, and H. Kriesi (Oxford: Blackwell, 2004), pp. 339–59. The publishing press *il Mulino* graciously granted permission to reproduce materials that originally appeared in M. Bianchi and M. Mormino, "Militanti di Se Stesse. Il Movimento delle Donne a Milano," in *Altri Codici*, edited by A. Melucci (Bologna: il Mulino, 1984), pp. 159–60.

THE STUDY OF SOCIAL MOVEMENTS: RECURRING QUESTIONS, (PARTIALLY) CHANGING ANSWERS

In the late 1960s, the world was apparently undergoing deep, dramatic transformations – even a revolution, some thought. American civil rights and antiwar movements, the Mai 1968 revolt in France, students' protests in Germany, Britain, or Mexico, the worker–student coalitions of the 1969 "Hot Autumn" in Italy, the pro-democracy mobilizations in locations as diverse as Francoist Madrid and communist Prague, the growth of critical Catholicism from South America to Rome, the early signs of the women's and environmental movements that would shape the new politics of the 1970s: all these phenomena – and many more – suggested that deep changes were in the making.

Accordingly, the study of social movements developed at an unprecedented pace into a major area of research. If, at the end of the 1940s, critics lamented the "crudely descriptive level of understanding and a relative lack of theory" (Strauss 1947: 352), and in the 1960s complained that "in the study of social changes, social movements have received relatively little emphasis" (Killian 1964: 426), by the mid-1970s, research into collective action was considered "one of the most vigorous areas of sociology" (Marx and Wood 1975). At the end of the 1980s commentators talked of "an explosion, in the last ten years, of theoretical and empirical writings on social movements and collective action (Morris and Herring 1987: 138; see also Rucht 1991a).

Today, the study of social movements is solidly established, with specialized journals, book series, and professional associations. The excitement and optimism of the roaring 1960s may be long gone, but social and political events over the last four decades have hardly rendered the investigation of grassroots activism any less relevant or urgent. To the contrary, social movements, protest actions, and, more generally, political organizations unaligned with major political parties or trade unions have become a permanent component of Western democracies. It is no longer possible to describe protest politics, grassroots participation, and symbolic challenges as "unconventional." Instead, references to a "movement society" seem increasingly plausible (Neidhhardt and Rucht 2002; Melucci 1996; Meyer and Tarrow 1998b).

To be sure, there has been considerable fluctuation in the intensity of collective action over this period, as there has been in its degree of radicalism, its specific forms, and its capacity to influence the political process. However, forecasts that the wave of protest of the late 1960s would quickly subside, and that "business as usual," as represented by interest-based politics, organized according to traditional political divisions, would return in its wake, have largely been proved wrong. In different ways, and with a wide range of goals and values, various forms of protest have continued to emerge in recent years (Kriesi et al. 1995; Beissinger 2002; Titarenko, McCarthy, McPhail, and Augustyn 2001; Smith and Johnston 2002; Fillieule and Bennani-Chraibi 2003; Giugni 2004). Not only that: at the start of the new millennium, possibly for the first time since 1968, the wave of mobilizations for a globalization from below (often identified as the global justice movement), seems to have the potential for a global, generalized challenge, combining themes typical of class movements with themes typical of new social movements, like ecology or gender equality (Arrighi, Hopkins, and Wallerstein 1989; Fox and Brown 1998; Brecher, Costello, and Smith 2000; Walton and Seddon 1994; Pianta 2001b; Wieviorka 2003; della Porta, Andretta, Mosca, and Reiter 2005; Wood 2004; Tarrow 2005).

In truth, associating expressions like "global justice movement" with unitary, homogeneous actors would be very misleading. The initiatives against neoliberal globalization are very heterogeneous, and not necessarily connected to each other. They address a range of issues, from child labor's exploitation by global brands to deforestation, from human rights in developing countries to military interventions by Western powers. And they do so in a myriad of forms, from individual utterances of dissent and individual behavior to mass collective events, and from a variety of points of view. Looking at them well illustrates what doing "social movement analysis" actually means. In their research practice, most of the people who study social movements focus either on individuals, organizations, or events, in the best instances trying to capture the interdependence between them.

First, opposition to neoliberal globalization can be looked at as the ensemble of individuals expressing opinions about certain issues, advocating or opposing social change. Globalization has surely raised fears and hopes in equal measure, but the balance has distributed unequally across countries and socioeconomic areas. Repeatedly, public opinion surveys indicate diffuse worries about the impact of globalization on people's lives, both economically and politically. Although this may be more diffused a concern in western Europe than the USA or even more so elsewhere, globalization is undoubtedly at the core of public opinion's interest these days (Inglehart 1999; Grand and Kull 2002; Noland 2004). Those who are skeptical and often hostile to it represent a distinct and vocal sector of public opinion. Their views are forged and reinforced in dialogue with a range of prominent opinionmakers and public figures, exposing the costs and faults of globalization from a Western/Northern as well as an Eastern/Southern perspective, such as Indian writer Arundhati Roy, Philippine sociologist Walden Bello, Australian journalist John Pilger, or economist and Nobel laureate Josef Stieglitz. Books like Naomi Klein's *No Logo* (1999) may be safely credited with the same impact that Rachel Carson's *Silent Spring* (1962) or the Club of Rome's report on *The Limits to Growth* (Meadows, Randers, and Behrens 1972) had on the spread of environmental concerns back in the 1960s and 1970s.

Oftentimes, individual opinions and concerns turn into various forms of political and social participation. Moral and philosophical worldviews and deeply felt convictions are then paralleled by specific attempts by individuals to stop threatening developments, redress instances of injustice, promote alternative options to the managing of social life and economic activity. A possible way of looking at the global justice movement is, then, by focusing on those individuals who actively express their opposition to neoliberal control of global transformations. By signing petitions calling for the cancellation of developing countries' debt, contributing money to the activities of organizations like Attac or Greenpeace, mobilizing to stop the building of dams in India or deforestation in Brazil, protesting at police behavior in Genoa in July 2001, attempting to stop ships exporting toxic waste to developing countries or trains carrying military equipment in preparation for the 2003 attack on Iraq, individual citizens may contribute to the campaigns against neoliberal globalization. They may do so, however, also through actions which affect individual lifestyles and private behavior as much – and possibly more – than the public sphere. Throughout the West, the recent years have seen the spread of fair-trade organizations and practices. By consuming certain products or choosing to do business only with banks committed to uphold moral and ethical standards, individuals may try to affect the balance of economic power on a broad scale (Micheletti, Follesdal, and Stolle 2003; Forno and Ceccarini forthcoming).

However, antiglobalization can hardly be reduced to sets of individuals with similar views and behavior. Rather than concentrating on individual characteristics, it may also be interesting to concentrate on the properties of events featuring conflictual interactions between powerholders and their opponents; as well as events in which individuals and organizations identifying with a cause meet to discuss strategies, to elaborate platforms, and to review their agendas. Global justice activists have been particularly good at staging events or disrupting opponents' events, with a strong emotional impact on public opinion and participants alike. Already before Seattle, periodical meetings by international bodies associated with the neoliberal agenda, such as the World Trade Organization, the International Monetary Fund, the World Bank, or the G8, have provided the opportunity for a string of highly visible, very well-attended demonstrations trying to both disrupt the specific gatherings and draw people's attention to alternative agendas (Podobnik 2004). Events promoted by global justice activists, most notably the World Social Forum gatherings in Porto Alegre and in Mumbai, their European counterparts in Florence (2001), Paris (2003), or London (2004), the corresponding meetings in the South, such as the African Social Forum that met first in Bamako, Mali, in January 2002, have all confirmed the vitality and strength of the "movement of movements" (Pianta 2001a). On February 15, 2003, hundreds of antiwar events across the globe generated what has probably been the biggest coordinated political demonstration in history, with opponents of the attack on Iraq taking to the streets in millions across five continents (Walgrave and Rucht forthcoming). Below the global level, critics of globalization have promoted thousands of events, ranging from confrontational demonstrations to presentations of reports or press releases, from religious vigils to squatting in military buildings. Located anywhere from the national to the very local levels, those events also support popular views about the existence of a distinctive antiglobalization movement.

Other times, by "global justice movement" we mean, first and foremost, the organizations operating on those issues. The opposition to neoliberal globalization has been conducted by broad coalitions of organizations, usually with a transnational basis (Bystydzienski and Schacht 2001; Bandy and Smith 2004). Some – probably most – of them had a long history of political and social activism, well spread over the political spectrum. In Seattle as well as in Genoa or elsewhere, established political parties were involved in the demonstrations, mostly if not exclusively from the left; so were trade unions, farmers, and other workers' organizations; ethnic organizations representing both native populations and migrant groups; consumers associations challenging multinational companies; religious organizations and church groups; environmental groups; women's associations; radical autonomous youth centers (Italy's "centri sociali'); and the like. But the criticism of neoliberal globalization has also produced specific organizations, among which Attac, who advocate the so-called Tobin tax to reduce financial gains in the international stock market; People's Global Action, a coalition of hundreds of groups in the North and the South; or the Rete Lilliput, a network of groups, associations, and individuals active in Italy on environmental, fair trade, and social justice issues. The role of organizations that are not directly political is particularly worth mentioning. The spread of fair-trade practices is facilitated by the existence of extended networks of cooperatives and small retail operators in the West, who try somehow to reach a balance between ethic-driven public action and market requirements. The reproduction of countercultural networks linking radical activists from all over the place is likewise facilitated by the existence of alternative cafes, bookshops, social and cultural centers, offering meeting points – as well as at times accommodation – to people identifying with radical milieus. From a totally different perspective, the network of Islamic schools, mosques, and other institutions offering support to funda mentalist versions of Islam may also be regarded as providing the organizational infrastructure for the diffusion of that particular version of the opposition to Western globalization (Fillieule and Bennani-Chraibi 2003; Lubeck and Reifer 2004; Langman 2004). Whatever their specificity, organizations secure continuity to collective action even when the potential for spontaneous, unmediated participation somehow subsides. They also provide resources and opportunities for action to escalate when opportunities are more favorable; as well as sources for the creation and reproduction of loyalties and collective identities. While recognizing the importance of organizations operating within movements, we should not make the mistake of identifying the latter with the former. So far, the global justice movement has been less exposed to this risk than other movements, e.g., environmentalism, where big transnational organizations like Greenpeace, WWF, or Friends of the Earth have often ended up stealing the show – if perhaps unwillingly.

1.1 Four Core Questions for Social Movement Analysis

As the example of global justice campaigning suggests, studying social movements means focusing on at least some of the dimensions we have just introduced, as well as, most importantly, on how ideas, individuals, events, and organizations are linked to each other in broader processes of collective action, with some continuity over time. Given their complex, multidimensional nature, it is no surprise that social movements may be approached in reference to very diverse intellectual questions. In this book, we shall focus on four sets of them, broadly articulated. We shall try to relate them to the broader theoretical and practical concerns that have inspired the analysis of grassroots political action and cultural resistance since the 1960s.

The first set of questions refers to the relationship between structural change and transformations in patterns of social conflict. Can we see social movements as expressions of conflicts? And what conflicts? Have there been changes in the main conflicts addressed by social movements? And along what lines?

Another set of questions has to do with the role of cultural representations in social conflict. How are social problems identified as potential objects of collective action? How do certain social actors come to develop a sense of commonality and to identify with the same "collective we"? And how can specific protest events come to be perceived as part of the same conflict? Where do social movement cultures and values originate from?

A third set of questions addresses the process through which values, interests, and ideas get turned into collective action. How does it become possible to mobilize and face the risks and costs of protest activity? What are the roles of identities and symbols, emotions, organizations, and networks, in explaining the start and persistence of collective action? What forms do organizations take in their attempts to maximize the strength of collective challenges and their outcomes?

Finally, it has frequently been asked how a certain social, political, and/or cultural context affects social movements' chances of success, and the forms they take. What does explain the varying intensity over time of collective violence and other types of public challenges against powerholders? Do the traits of political systems and their attitudes towards citizens' demands influence challengers' impact in the political arena? How do protest tactics and strategies change over time, and why?

While these questions certainly do not reflect entirely the richness of current debates on collective action and social movements, they have surely played a significant role in shaping discussions over the last decades. Indeed, the 1960s were important because they saw not only an increase in new forms of political participation, but also a change in the main conflictual issues. Traditionally, social movements had focused mainly on issues of labor and nations: since the 1960s, "new social movements" have emerged instead centered on concerns such as women's liberation, environmental protection, etc. These changes in the quantity and quality of protest prompted significant innovations in social scientists' approach to those questions. The principal theoretical models available at the time for the interpretation of social conflict – the Marxist model and the structural-functionalist model –both came to be regarded as largely inadequate.

In Europe, scholars confronted with the new wave of protest often relied on Marxism. However, their attempts to explain developments in the forms of conflict in the 1960s had encountered a number of problems. The social transformations which occurred after the end of the Second World War had put the centrality of the capital–labor conflict into question. The widening of access to higher education or the entry en masse of women into the labor market had created new structural possibilities for conflict, and increased the relevance of other criteria of social stratification – such as gender relations. Indeed, even the most superficial observer of the 1960s could not help noticing that many of the actors engaged in those conflicts (youth, women, new professional groups) were only partially related to the class conflicts, which had constituted the principal component of political cleavages in industrial societies (Rokkan 1970; Tilly 2004a). Marxist interpretations were not, however, undermined only by doubts about the continued existence of the working-class in postindustrial society: the logic of the explanatory model was also under attack. Critics rejected the deterministic element of the Marxist tradition – the conviction that the evolution of social and political conflicts was conditioned largely by the level of development of productive forces and by the dynamics of class relations. They also espoused the tendency, particularly strong among orthodox Marxists, to deny the multi-

plicity of concerns and conflicts within real movements, and to construct, in preference, outlandish images of movements as homogeneous actors with a high
level of strategic ability (see e.g. Touraine 1977, 1981).

In contrast, American scholars often saw collective action as crisis behavior.
Having reduced collective phenomena to the summary of individual behaviors,
psychologically derived theories defined social movements as the manifestation
of feelings of deprivation experienced by individuals in relation to other social
subjects, and of feelings of aggression resulting from a wide range of frustrated
expectations. Phenomena such as the rise of Nazism, the American Civil War,
or the movement of black Americans, for example, were considered to be aggres-
sive reactions resulting either from a rapid and unexpected end to periods of economic well-being and of increased expectations on a worldwide scale, or from
status inconsistency mechanisms (Davies 1969; Gurr 1970). From a somewhat
different but compatible point of view, the emergence of political extremism was
also associated with the spread of mass society in which integrative social ties
based in the family or the community tended to become fragmented (Kornhauser 1959; Gusfield 1963). Isolation and displacement produced individuals
with fewer intellectual, professional, and/or political resources, who were particularly vulnerable to the appeal of antidemocratic movements of the right and
the left.[1]

To some extent, these problems were shared by the most famous version of
structural-functionalist approach, that of Neil Smelser (1962), that saw social
movements as the side-effects of overrapid social transformation. According to
Smelser, in a system made up of balanced subsystems, collective behavior reveals
tensions which homoeostatic rebalancing mechanisms cannot absorb in the short
term. At times of rapid, large-scale transformations, the emergence of collective
behaviors – religious cults, secret societies, political sects, economic Utopias –
has a double meaning, reflecting on the one hand the inability of institutions and
social control mechanisms to reproduce social cohesion; on the other, attempts
by society to react to crisis situations through the development of shared beliefs
on which to base new foundations for collective solidarity.

Smelser's value-added model of collective behavior consists of six steps: structural conduciveness, i.e. a certain configuration of social structure that may
facilitate or constrain the emergence of specific types of collective behavior;
structural strain, i.e. the fact that at least some trait of the social system is experienced by a collectivity as a source of tension and problems; growth and spread
of generalized belief, i.e. the emergence of a shared interpretation by social
actors of their situation and problems; precipitating factors, i.e. stressful events
that induce actors to take action; mobilization, i.e. the network and organizational activities that transform potential for action into real action; operation of
social control, i.e. the role of social control agencies and other actors in shaping the evolution of collective behavior and its forms (Smelser 1962; see also
Crossley 2002, ch. 2).

Some scholars regard as unfortunate that Smelser's work ended up being strongly associated with the crisis of the functionalist paradigm. Despite its problems, his was a major attempt to connect in an integrated model different processes that would have later been treated disparately, and to firmly locate social movement analysis in the framework of general sociology (Crossley 2002: 53–5). However, given the dominant cultural climate in the years that followed its publication, Smelser's contribution came to be subsumed under the broader set of approaches viewing social movements as purely reactive responses to social crisis and as the outcome of mal-integration, and became the target for the same criticisms. Let us see now how the criticism of Marxist and functionalist approaches were elaborated in relation to the four questions we have identified earlier.

1.1.1 Is social change creating the conditions for the emergence of new movements?

Given the importance of Marxism in European intellectual debates, it is no surprise that European social sciences were the most eager to explain the rise of the movements of the 1960s and the 1970s in explicit critique of the Marxist models of interpretation of social conflict. Criticism addressed both the most structuralist currents of Marxist thinking, deriving class conflict directly from the mode of production, and those interested in the formation of class consciousness (or class in itself). Certainly, scholars of the new movements were not the only ones to be aware of these problems. The same difficulties had been raised by those who had studied the labor movement with the aim of explaining the formation of a collective actor, challenging the widespread idea of an almost automatic transformation of structural strains in conscious behavior (Thompson 1963).

Often departing from a Marxist background, scholars associated with the so-called "new social movements" approach[2] made a decisive contribution to the development of the discussion of these issues by reflecting upon the innovation in the forms and contents of contemporary movements. Scholars of new movements agreed that conflict among the industrial classes is of decreasing relevance, and similarly that representation of movements as largely homogeneous subjects is no longer feasible. However, there were differences of emphasis in relation to the possibility of identifying the new central conflict which would characterize the model of the emerging society, defined at times as "postindustrial," "post-Fordist," "technocratic," or "programmed." An influential exponent of this approach, Alain Touraine, was the most explicit in upholding this position: "Social movements are not a marginal rejection of order, they are the central forces fighting one against the other to control the production of society by itself and the action of classes for the shaping of historicity [i.e., the overall system of meaning which sets dominant rules in a given society]" (Touraine 1981: 29). In the industrial society, the ruling class and the popular class oppose each other, as they did in the agrarian and the mercantile societies, and as they will do, according to Touraine, in the programmed society, where new social classes will replace capitalists and the working class as the central actors of the conflict.[3]

The break between movements of the industrial society and new movements was also stressed in the 1980s by the German sociologist Claus Offe (1985). In his view, movements develop a fundamental, metapolitical critique of the social order and of representative democracy, challenging institutional assumptions regarding conventional ways of "doing politics," in the name of a radical democracy. Among the principal innovations of the new movements, in contrast with the workers' movement, are a critical ideology in relation to modernism and progress; decentralized and participatory organizational structures; defense of interpersonal solidarity against the great bureaucracies; and the reclamation of autonomous spaces, rather than material advantages.

Another contribution to the definition of the characteristics of new movements in the programmed society came from Alberto Melucci (1982, 1989, 1996). Drawing upon the image proposed by Jürgen Habermas of a colonization of lifeworlds, Melucci described contemporary societies as highly differentiated systems, which invest increasingly in the creation of individual autonomous centers of action, at the same time requiring closer integration and extending control over the motives for human action. In his view, new social movements try to oppose the intrusion of the state and the market into social life, reclaiming individuals' right to define their identities and to determine their private and affective lives against the omnipresent and comprehensive manipulation of the system. Unlike the workers' movement, new social movements do not, in Melucci's view, limit themselves to seeking material gain, but challenge the diffuse notions of politics and of society themselves. New actors do not so much ask for an increase in state intervention, to guarantee security and well-being, but especially resist the expansion of political administrative intervention in daily life and defend personal autonomy.

It would be misleading to speak of the new social movements approach without acknowledging that its principal exponents have considerably modified their positions over time. Already in the late 1980s, Offe (1990) recognized the influence of traditional-style political action on the practices of the movements. Melucci increasingly concentrated on the mechanisms by which certain representations of the world and of individual and collective identities are produced and transformed over time (1989; on this point see Bartholomew and Mayer 1992). Moreover, he went as far as to declare the debate about the "newness" of contemporary movements to be outdated or irrelevant (see for example Melucci 1994).

Nevertheless, this perspective had – and still has – several merits. First, it drew attention to the structural determinants of protest, reevaluating the importance of conflict, at a time when nonclass conflicts were often ignored. Compared with Marxists, new social movement theorists had two specific advantages: they once again placed actors at the center of the stage; and they captured the innovative characteristics of movements which no longer defined themselves principally in relation to the system of production. Nor should we forget the existence of the notable area of research largely inspired by their original hypotheses (Maheu 1995).

Despite the influence of the "new social movements" perspective, attention to the relationship between social structure and collective action is by no means restricted to it. Marxism has continued to inspire numerous analysts of collective action who still assign the concept of social class a central role (see for example Barker and Dale 1999; Lavalette and Mooney 2000; Cleveland 2003). In many senses, structural approaches strongly influenced by Marxism can be regarded as the predecessors of the current thriving research on global justice phenomena. Broadly inspired by Immanuel Wallerstein's "world system theory" (1974, 2004), scholars have attempted to locate the new wave of popular mobilization in developing countries as well as within the Western world in the context of much larger processes of economic restructuring on a global scale, and from a long-term historical perspective (Arrighi, Hopkins, and Wallerstein 1989; Silver and Slater 1999, ch. 3; Moody 1997; Reifer 2004).

In explicit critique of analyses suggesting the demise of social conflict and its individualization, and most explicitly the end of conflict about distributive stakes, scholars from this perspective regard the crisis of the workers' movement in the 1980s and 1990s, following financial restructuring at the global level, as a largely conjunctural phenomenon. Systemic failure to meet the expectations of the working class from developing countries will fuel a new wave of sustained class conflicts, that will also reflect the growing feminization of the labor force and its stronger ethnic dimension, following mass migration dynamics (Arrighi and Silver 1999). The increasing relevance of "global justice" as a central concern (Andretta, della Porta, Mosca, and Reiter 2002, 2003) seems to support these arguments. Moreover, and rather unexpectedly, social movements have developed in the South, bridging frames and organizational structures with their Northern counterparts. Especially in some geographical areas (such as Latin America and the Far East), social movement research developed, often within a Gramscian approach, stressing the role of cultural hegemony.

Another important attempt to relate social-structural change to mass collective action has come from Manuel Castells (1983, 1996). In an earlier phase of his work, Castells has contributed to our understanding of the emergence of urban social movements by stressing the importance of consumption processes (in particular of collective consumption of public services and public goods) for class relations, by moving the focus of class analysis from capitalist relations within the workplace to social relations in the urban community (Castells 1983). Later, Castells linked the growing relevance of conflicts on identity both in the West –

e.g. the women's movement – and in the South – e.g. Zapatistas, religious fundamentalisms, etc. – to the emergence of a "network society," where new information technologies play a central role.

Yet another original effort to link structural analysis and social movement analysis has been inspired by French sociologist Pierre Bourdieu. Researchers engaged in the analysis of cultural habits (or the cultural predispositions produced by processes of socialization) as well as their structural determinants have used Bourdieu's insights to explore specific instances of political conflicts, stressing their cultural meanings within the specific fields to which individuals belong. Going beyond economic interests, some scholars explained indeed social movement activism as following needs and desires that derive from values and norms that are typical of specific cultures (or fields). In this sense, action is not rational, but reasonable (Bourdieu 1980: 85–6; Eckstein 2001; Sommier 2003). From a different angle, and with explicit reference to general theory à la Smelser, Crossley (2002) has used Bourdieu's key concepts of habitus, structure, and agency to propose a new theoretical model, able to integrate the insights from European and American approaches over the years. In doing so he has proceeded in parallel with other theoretical work in the broader framework of structuration theory (Sewell 1992; Livesay 2003).

A major criticism of new social movements theory has been that it took as foundational characteristics of new social movements certain traits that were not necessarily new and far from generalizable – such as activists' middle-class origins, or loose organizational forms (D'Anieri, Ernst, and Kier 1990; Calhoun 1993; Rootes 1992; Rüdig 1990; Koopmans 1995; Tarrow 1994; della Porta 1996a: ch. 1). Structural approaches in general have also been faulted for failing to specify the mechanisms leading from structural tensions to action. In fairness, this criticism does not apply to Melucci's work, and only partially to Touraine's; while it is surely appropriate for scholars like Offe or Castells, or world-system theorists, whose focus is clearly not on micro or meso processes. Whatever the case, the approaches presented here must be regarded first of all as theories of social conflict; more specifically, of the impact of structural transformations on stakes and forms of conflict. And it is fair to say that the questions more directly related to the development of collective action have been more cogently addressed by other intellectual traditions.

1.1.2 How do we define issues as worthy objects, and actors as worthy subjects of collective action?

In the 1950s and 1960s, students of collective behavior tended to classify under the same heading phenomena as diverse as crowds, movements, panics, manias, fashions, and so on. Two problems arose from this. On the one hand, although

many of them defined movements as purposeful phenomena, students of collective behavior placed more attention on unexpected dynamics – such as circular reactions – rather than on deliberate organizational strategies or, more
generally, on strategies devised by actors. As James Coleman recalled (1990: 479),
the hypothesis that situations of frustration, rootlessness, deprivation, and social
crisis automatically produce revolts reduces collective action to an agglomera-
tion of individual behaviors. Functionalism ignores the dynamics by which feelings experienced at the (micro) level of the individual give rise to (macro)
phenomena such as social movements or revolutions.

One response to these theoretical gaps has come from symbolic interaction-
ists close to the so-called "Chicago School," credited with having developed the
analysis of collective behavior as a specialist field within sociology. The concept
of collective behavior – contrasted with that of collective psychology – indicated
the shift of attention from the motivation of individuals to their observable
actions. Already in the 1920s, the founders of this approach – among them Robert
E. Park and Ernest W. Burgess – had stressed that collective phenomena do not
simply reflect social crisis but rather produce new norms and new solidarities,
and viewed social movements as engines of change, primarily in relation to
values systems. Subsequently, other students of collective behavior were to make
reference to the tenets of the Chicago School, focusing their attention on situations of rapid change in social structures and prescriptions (Blumer 1951; Turner
and Killian 1987[1957];[4] Gusfield 1963). Tendencies towards large-scale organizations, population mobility, technological innovation, mass communications, and
the decline of traditional cultural forms were all considered to be emerging conditions pushing individuals to search for new patterns of social organization.
Collective behavior was in fact defined as behavior concerned with change
(for example, Blumer 1951: 199), and social movements as both an integral part
of the normal functioning of society and the expression of a wider process of
transformation.[5]

Rooted in symbolic interactionism, the contemporary school of collective
behavior sees particular relevance in the meaning actors attribute to social structures; and the less structured the situations faced by the individual, the more relevant this aspect appears to be. When existing systems of meaning do not
constitute a sufficient basis for social action, new norms emerge, defining the
existing situation as unjust and providing a justification for action (Turner and
Killian 1987: 259). As an activity born outside preestablished social definitions,
collective behavior is located beyond existing norms and ordered social relations.
The study of collective behavior thus concentrates on the transformation of
institutional behaviors through the action of emergent normative definitions.
These definitions appear when the traditional normative structure comes into
conflict with a continually evolving situation.[6] Change, in fact, is conceived of as
part of the physiological functioning of the system: social movements are accom-

panied by the emergence of new rules and norms, and represent attempts to transform existing norms.[7]

The genesis of social movements is in the co-existence of contrasting value systems and of groups in conflict with each other. These are regarded as distinctive parts of social life (Killian 1964: 433). Changes in the social structure and in the normative order are interpreted within a process of cultural evolution through which new ideas emerge in the minds of individuals. When traditional norms no longer succeed in providing a satisfactory structure for behavior, the individual is forced to challenge the social order through various forms of nonconformity. A social movement develops when a feeling of dissatisfaction spreads, and insufficiently flexible institutions are unable to respond.

The sociology of social movements owes many of its insights to students of the collective behavior school. For the first time, collective movements are defined as meaningful acts, driving often necessary and beneficial social change. Observations of processes of interaction determined by collective action moreover constitute important foundations for those who, in more recent times, have taken on the task of understanding movement dynamics. The emphasis on empirical research has led to experimentation with new techniques, providing through various methods of field research a valid integration of archive data. Since the 1980s, the interactionist version of the theory of collective behavior has stressed the processes of symbolic production and of construction of identity, both of which are essential components of collective behavior. This has led to a lasting research program, as demonstrated by the work of scholars such as Joe Gusfield (1963, 1981, 1994), and which has become at the same time very influential and diversified (Snow, Rochford, Worden, and Benford 1986; Snow and Oliver 1995; Melucci 1989, 1996; Eyerman and Jamison 1991; McPhail 1991; Johnston and Klandermans 1995). In a parallel effort, Rochon (1998: 179) has shown how movements develop new ideas and values, working as agents of cultural change, with the "task of translating the chronic problem as described by the critical community into an acute problem that will attract media attention is the province of social an political movements."[8]

In the 1990s, however, some researchers grew dissatisfied with a view of the role of culture in collective action that they regarded as too strategic and rationalistic (in particular scholars like Snow and Benford [1988, 1992], who were conversant with resource mobilization theory), and started to reemphasize again the part played by emotions in the production and reproduction of social movements. In their view, symbolic production is not only (or mainly) strategically oriented, but it involves more feelings and emotions. Moral shocks developing when deeply held rules and norms are broken are often the first step in individual mobilization; and, indeed, protest organizations work at transforming fear into moral indignation and anger (Jasper 1997: 107–14). Movements produce condensing symbols and rhetoric oriented to raise various types of emotions in what has been defined as a libidinal economy of movements. As Jasper (1997: 220) observes, "virtually all the pleasures that humans derive from social life are found in protest movements: a sense of community and identity; ongoing companionship and bonds with others; the variety and challenge of conversation, cooperation and competition. Some of the pleasures are not available in the routines of life."

It is worth noting at least two main problems generated by the collective behavior perspective. On the one hand, despite viewing movements as purposeful phenomena, many students of collective behavior placed most attention on unexpected dynamics – such as circular reactions – rather than on deliberate organizational strategies or, more generally, on strategies devised by rational, strategic actors. On the other hand, focusing on the empirical analysis of behavior, they were often limited to a description – albeit detailed – of reality, without devoting much attention to the structural origins of conflicts which subsequently well up in particular movements. While structuralist approaches like the new social movements dealt with the latter shortcoming, organizational perspectives like resource mobilization theory addressed the former. To its basic tenets we now turn.

1.1.3   How is collective action possible?

In deliberate contrast to conceptualizations of social movements as irrational, largely reactive phenomena, American sociologists in the 1970s started to reflect on the processes by which the resources necessary for collective action are mobilized. In their view, collective movements constitute an extension of the conventional forms of political action; the actors engage in this act in a rational way, following their interests; organizations and movement "entrepreneurs" have an essential role in the mobilization of collective resources on which action is founded. Movements are therefore part of the normal political process. Stressing the external obstacles and incentives, numerous pieces of research have examined the variety of resources to be mobilized, the links which social movements have with their allies, the tactics used by society to control or incorporate collective action, and its results. The basic questions addressed relate to the evaluation of costs and benefits of participation in social movement organizations.

In early contributions in this vein, Mayer Zald (Zald and Ash 1966; McCarthy and Zald 1987a, 1987b), Anthony Oberschall (1973; 1980), and Charles Tilly (1978) defined social movements as rational, purposeful, and organized actions. Collective action derives, according to this perspective, from a calculation of the costs and benefits, influenced by the presence of resources – in particular by organization and by the strategic interactions necessary for the development of a social movement. In a historical situation in which feelings of unease, differences of opinion, conflicts of interest, and opposing ideologies are always present, the emergence of collective action cannot be explained simply as having been caused by these elements. It is not enough to discover the existence of tensions and structural conflicts: we also have to study the conditions which enable discontent to be transformed into mobilization. The capacity for mobilization depends on the material resources (work, money, concrete benefits, services) and/or nonmaterial resources (authority, moral engagement, faith, friendship) available to the group. These resources are distributed across multiple objectives according to a rational calculation of costs and benefits. Beyond the existence of tensions, mobilization derives from the way in which social movements are able to organize discontent, reduce the costs of action, utilize and create solidarity networks, share incentives among members, and achieve external consensus. The type and nature of the resources available explain the tactical choices made by movements and the consequences of collective action on the social and political system (McCarthy and Zald 1977; Edwards and McCarthy 2004).

The existence of solidarity networks once again questioned a widely spread assumption at the time, namely, that movement recruits are mainly isolated and rootless individuals who seek to immerse themselves in the mass as a surrogate for their social marginalization. According to rational approaches, mobilization can thus be explained as being more than the gratification of pursuing a collective good; it also promotes the existence of horizontal solidarity links, within the collective, and vertical links, integrating different collectives. On the basis of a wide range of empirical research, one can therefore foresee that "participants in popular disturbances and activists in opposition organizations will be recruited primarily from previously active and relatively well-integrated individuals within the collectivity, whereas socially isolated, atomized, and uprooted individuals will be underrepresented, at least until the movement has become substantial" (Oberschall 1973: 135). Accordingly, scholars of resource mobilization concentrate their attention on how collective actors operate, how they acquire resources and mobilize support, both within and outside their adherents' group.

Recently, research on social movement organizations has extended its attention to the relations between organizations and the dynamics going on in organizational populations. Increasingly sophisticated network studies have looked at the interactions between the organizations and individuals identified with social movements (Diani and McAdam 2003), with a critical dialogue with research on social capital (Diani 1997), and an increasing attention for the transnational dimension and the connections between organizations operating at that level (Caniglia 2001; Smith 2004a). Concepts and methods borrowed from organizational ecology have been applied to the study of the factors behind organizations' chances of survival, again with reference to both the national (Minkoff 1993, 1999; Edwards and Marullo 1996) and the global spheres (Boli and Thomas 1999; Johnson and McCarthy 2005).

The definition of social movements as conscious actors making rational choices is among the most important innovations of the resource mobilization approach. However, critics have charged it with indifference to the structural sources of conflict and the specific stakes for the control of which social actors mobilize (Melucci 1982; Piven and Cloward 1992). Its emphasis on the resources controlled by a few political entrepreneurs, at the cost of overlooking the self-organization potential by the most dispossessed social groups, has also been criticized (Piven and Cloward 1992). Finally, it has been noted that in its explanation of collective action this approach overdoes the rationality of collective action, not taking the role of emotions adequately into account (Ferree 1992; Taylor and Whittier 1995; Jasper 1997). In fact, as some of the most influential proponents of this approach recently admitted, "early resource mobilization models exaggerate the centrality of deliberative strategic decisions to social movements" (McAdam, Tarrow, and Tilly 2001: 7), overemphasizing similarities between social movements and interest politics.

1.1.4   What determines the forms and intensity of collective action?

The most cogent and systematic response to this question has come from the perspective usually defined as "political process" (Tilly 1978; McAdam 1982). This approach shares with resource mobilization theory a rational view of action – so much so that they are sometimes treated as a unified perspective – but pays more systematic attention to the political and institutional environment in which social movements operate. The central focus of "political process" theories is the relationship between institutional political actors and protest. In challenging a given political order, social movements interact with actors who enjoy a consolidated position in the polity.[9] The concept which has had the greatest success in defining the properties of the external environment, relevant to the development of social movements, is that of "political opportunity structure." Peter Eisinger (1973) used this concept in a comparison of the results of protest in different American cities, focusing on the degree of openness (or closure) of the local political system. Other empirical research indicated important new variables, such as electoral instability (Piven and Cloward 1977), the availability of influential allies (Gamson 1990 [1975]), and tolerance for protest among the elite (Jenkins and Perrow 1977). Sidney Tarrow integrated these empirical observations into a theoretical framework for his study of protest cycles in Italy, singling out the degree of openness or closure of formal political access, the degree of stability or instability of political alignments, the availability and strategic posture of potential allies (Tarrow 1983: 28), and political conflicts between and within elites (Tarrow 1989a: 35).

   To these variables others have been added, relating to the institutional conditions which regulate agenda-setting and decision-making processes. Characteristics relating to the functional division of power and also to geographical decentralization have been analyzed in order to understand the origins of protest and the forms it has taken. In general, the aim has been to observe which stable or "mobile" characteristics of the political system influence the growth of less-institutionalized political action in the course of what are defined as protest cycles (Tarrow 1989a), as well as the forms which these actions take in different historical contexts (Tilly 1978). Comparative analysis has improved our understanding of the central theme represented by the relationship between social movements and the institutional political system (Kitschelt 1986; della Porta 1995; Kriesi et al. 1995; Rucht 1994; Giugni 2004).

The "political process" approach has succeeded in shifting attention towards interactions between new and traditional actors, and between less conventional forms of action and institutionalized systems of interest representation. In this way, it is no longer possible to define movements as phenomena which are, of necessity, marginal and anti-institutional, expressions of dysfunctions of the system. A more fruitful route towards the interpretation of the political dimension of contemporary movements has been established.

One should not ignore, however, some persistent areas of difficulty. On the one hand, supporters of this perspective continue to debate delicate problems such as the choice of the most appropriate indicators to measure complex institutional phenomena. First, the lack of consensus on the relevant dimensions of the concept of political opportunities (McAdam 1996) has resulted in their exponential growth (della Porta 1996c). Early studies of political opportunities focused on a small number of variables. Since the 1980s, however, a number of case studies and cross-national comparisons have added new variables to the original set (see, in particular, Brand 1985; Kitschelt 1986; Rucht 1989; Kriesi 1991). This has expanded the explanatory power of the concept, but reduced its specificity. The concept runs the risk of becoming a "dustbin" for any and every variable relevant to the development of social movements. Most of the concept's problems arise from the way in which it has been developed, picking up variables from a variety of studies on a variety of movements. This accumulation of heterogeneous variables reflecting different authors' concerns and ideas has resulted in a concept which, to quote Sartori (1970, but also 1990), denotes much but connotes little. Particularly in international comparative studies, it is impossible to handle the large number of variables and properly assess their explanatory power. Focus on structural variables might shift attention away from how norms and values, referring in particular to movements goals (or discursive opportunities), influence movement strategies as well as their chances of success (Goodwin and Jasper 2004a).

A second problem arises when we wish to distinguish between "objective" reality and its social construction (Berger and Luckmann 1966). Some changes in the political opportunity structure do not have any effect on a social movement unless they are perceived as important by the movement itself. Structural availability must be filtered through a process of "cognitive liberation" in order to unleash turmoil (McAdam 1986). For protest to emerge, activists must believe that an opportunity exists, that they have the power to bring about change; and they must blame the system for the problem. Looking at structural opportunities without considering the cognitive processes which intervene between structure and action can be very misleading (Gamson and Meyer 1996, Diani 1996). It is important, therefore, to analyze activists' understandings of available opportunities, the lenses through which they view potential opportunities for their movements (McAdam, McCarthy, and Zald 1996). Perceptions of state response may be particularly influenced, for instance, by its more dramatic manifestations, such as repression, causing the less visible responses, such as negotiation, to be overlooked (della Porta 1996c).

The political process approach has also been criticized externally, from various perspectives. Scholars like Piven and Cloward (1992) have criticized political process (and resource mobilization) theorists for dismissing mal-integration (or breakdown) theory for a claim it never made, namely, that rapid social change brought about by urbanization processes, large-scale economic crises, etc., generates collective action. But, breakdown theory actually focused on collective violence and disruptive behavior, and not on the broader range of forms of contention that theorists like Tilly include in their studies (Piven and Cloward 1992). Political process theorists have also attracted criticism for their tendency to adopt a kind of "political reductionism" (Melucci 1987, 1989). In effect, its proponents have paid little attention to the fact that many contemporary movements (of youth, women, homosexuals, or minority ethnic groups) have been affected at least as much by their cultural context as by their political one (Melucci 1996; Rupp and Taylor 1987, 2003; Rochon 1998). Lastly – as we have already noted when introducing resource mobilization theories – rationalist approaches to the study of collective action have tended to neglect the structural origins of protest. Other scholars, often associated with the new movements approach, have explored this area.

Faced with some relevant transformations in the two main sources of opportunities for movements – the nation-state and the political parties – research developed in two main directions. On the one hand, and especially in Europe, attention focused on the role played by movements, not just within the political system, but also within the public sphere. In this direction, the discursive opportunities – i.e., the presence of dominant public discourses on certain controversial issues, which are likely to affect movements' chances of success – have been stressed (Koopmans and Statham 1999). Moreover, more and more attention has been paid to transnational opportunities, or, to put it a better way, to a multilevel opportunity structure for movements (della Porta and Tarrow 2005). The development of the European Union as an arena for movement demands has been discussed in more depth (Imig and Tarrow 2001; Balme, Chabannet, and Wright 2002). Considering movements as part and parcel of the political system, recent studies have also focused on their effects, especially in terms of policy process and policy decisions (della Porta 2004c; Giugni, McAdam, and Tilly 1999; Giugni 2004).

1.1.5 Are these questions specific of social movement analysis?

Before systematically addressing the questions outlined in the preceding section, it is worth asking whether they are peculiar to social movement research. Our response is: not necessarily. In many cases it makes more – or at least as much – sense to talk about collective action at large, rather than social movements. Collective action broadly refers to individuals sharing resources in pursuit of collective goals – i.e., goals that cannot be privatized to any of the members of the collectivity on behalf of which collective action has taken place.[10] Such goals may be produced within movements, but also in many contexts that normally are not associated with movements.

For example, political parties also face the problem of mobilizing their members and providing them with incentives to join and somehow support the organization – if anything through the payment of membership fees; so do interest groups only minding the sectoral – often, very parochial – interests of their specific reference groups (Knoke 1990a; Jordan and Maloney 1997). Likewise, even political parties or narrow interest groups face the problem of adapting their strategies and tactics to changing environments, as the context in which they operate may become more or less favorable – e.g. through changes in the attitudes of powerholders towards specific parties' or interest groups' demands, changes in legal opportunities for interest representation, or changes in the cultural models with which ordinary people make sense of their political and social world (Panebianco 1988). From a different angle, many voluntary organizations do not identify any social or political opponent to protest against, and their strategies focus entirely on service delivery rather than advocacy, political representation, or challenges to dominant norms or lifestyles. Even these organizations, however, still face problems of attracting and keeping members, securing the resources necessary to promote action, elaborating the cultural models necessary to pursue goals along the desired lines, and framing their issues in order to make them as attractive as possible to their prospective supporters/members (Wilson 2000).

As it happens, analyses of collective action and analyses of social movements are inextricably linked. Let us say that the experience of social movements reflects phenomena with more than passing analogies to other instances of political or cultural collective action, taking place within political parties, interest groups, or religious sects. Therefore, when we analyze social movements, we deal with social processes that may also be of interest to researchers who do not define themselves at all as social movement analysts.

Recently there have been several attempts to synthesize scholarship on social movements with the aim of linking it to broader theoretical and/or empirical concerns. Some of these attempts have aimed at integrating social movement theory with general sociological frameworks. A most ambitious development by social movement scholars, openly criticizing the insularity of the social movement studies communities, and which also draws heavily on non Western materials, is the Dynamics of Contention (DOC) program (McAdam, Tarrow, and Tilly 2001). The main suggestion coming from this approach is the possibility of combining the knowledge developed in the fields of social movements with those elaborated on revolutions, democratization, and ethnic conflicts, singling out a field of contentious politics, defined as "episodic, public, collective interaction among makers of claim and their objects when (a) at least one government is a claimant, an object of claims, or a party to the claim and (b) the claims would, if realized, affect the interest of at least one of the claimants" (McAdam, Tarrow, and Tilly 2001: 5). Advocating a dynamic rather than static use of concepts, the scholars involved in this project have tried to single out general mechanisms of contention (see Diani et al. 2003 for a discussion).

1.2 What is Distinctive about Social Movements?

If the core questions addressed by social movement analysts are not necessarily specific, one might wonder whether social movements have an analytical peculiarity which justifies the development of a distinctive field of research. In order to address this question we have to discuss the concept of a social movement.

1.2.1 The concept of a social movement

In a number of pieces, Mario Diani (1992a; 2003a; 2004a; Diani and Bison 2004) has maintained that social movements are a distinct social process, consisting of the mechanisms through which actors engaged in collective action:

• are involved in conflictual relations with clearly identified opponents;
• are linked by dense informal networks;
• share a distinct collective identity.

Conflictual collective action. Social movement actors are engaged in political and/or cultural conflicts meant to promote or oppose social change. By conflict we mean an oppositional relationship between actors who seek control of the same stake – be it political, economic, or cultural power – and in the process make negative claims on each other – i.e., demands which, if realized, would damage the interests of the other actors (Tilly 1978; Touraine 1981: 80–4). Accordingly, addressing collective problems, producing public goods, or expressing support for some moral values or principles does not automatically correspond to social movement action; the latter requires the identification of targets for collective efforts, specifically articulated in social or political terms. In contrast, when collective action focuses exclusively on the behavior and/or the legitimacy of specific individuals, or blames problems on humankind as a whole, on natural disasters or divine will, then it is difficult to speak of social movement processes (Gamson 1992a; Melucci 1996, part I). For example, collective action on globalization issues is conflictual to the extent that organizations like the World Trade Organization or the International Monetary Fund are blamed not because of their officials' misconduct or specific policy mistakes, but as representatives of distinct coalitions of interests.

Dense informal networks. Dense informal networks differentiate social movement processes from the innumerable instances in which collective action takes place and is coordinated, mostly within the boundaries of specific organizations. A social movement process is in place to the extent that both individual and organized actors, while keeping their autonomy and independence, engage in sustained exchanges of resources in pursuit of common goals. The coordination of specific initiatives, the regulation of individual actors' conduct, and the definition of strategies all depend on permanent negotiations between the individuals and the organizations involved in collective action. No single organized actor, no matter how powerful, can claim to represent a movement as a whole. It follows that more opportunities arise for highly committed and/or skilled individuals to play an independent role in the political process than would be the case when action is concentrated within formal organizations.

Collective identity. Social movements are not merely the sum of protest events on certain issues, or even of specific campaigns. On the contrary, a social movement process is in place only when collective identities develop, which go beyond specific events and initiatives. Collective identity is strongly associated with recognition and the creation of connectedness (Pizzorno 1996). It brings with it a sense of common purpose and shared commitment to a cause, which enables single activists and/or organizations to regard themselves as inextricably linked to other actors, not necessarily identical but surely compatible, in a broader collective mobilization (Touraine 1981). Within social movements, membership criteria are extremely unstable and ultimately dependent on mutual recognition between actors; the activity of boundary definition – i.e., of defining who is and who is not part of the network – indeed plays a central role in the emergence and shaping of collective action (Melucci 1996, ch. 3).

For example, recent research on environmentalism suggests that animal rights activism be more distinctive and less identified with environmentalism in Britain than in Italy: as a result, it makes much more sense to regard the two as involved in the same movement process in the latter than in the former (Rootes 2003; Diani & Forno 2003). Likewise, not all networks between like-minded people necessarily reflect social movement processes: for example, the international Zapatista support network is not regarded by many analysts as a social movement because of the lack of a focused identity and the resulting bonds, even though resources of solidarity certainly circulate through it (Olesen 2004).

Collective identity building also entails actors establishing connections between different occurrences, private and public, located at different points in time and space, which are relevant to their experience, and weaving them into broader, encompassing narratives (Melucci 1996). As a result, organizational and individual actors involved in collective action no longer merely pursue specific goals, but come to regard themselves as elements of much larger and encompassing processes of change – or resistance to change. For example, in the case of the global justice movement, participants in events as distant as the "battle of Seattle" and the opposition to the Narmada Valley dam in India may be linked together in the same movement through processes of identity-building based upon organizational networking and supranational communication.

Looking at different combinations of these three elements enables us to contrast social movements to other collective-action processes. Here we provide a few examples; however, we have to keep in mind that no empirical episode of collective action – those that we conventionally define as "environmental movements," "solidarity movements," "disabled movements," or the like – fully corresponds to any pure type. On the contrary, we can normally detect more than one process within any empirical instance of collective action. The exploration of how such processes interact with each other represents a fundamental step of social movement analysis.

1.2.2   Conflictual and consensual collective action

It is not rare to witness broad coalitions of charities and other voluntary associations mobilizing on solidarity issues, for example on social exclusion in domestic politics, or on development or human rights issues in an international perspective, and to refer to them as social movements. In many cases, however, they might be best characterized as "consensus movements." In both social movement and consensus movement dynamics, actors share solidarity and an interpretation of the world, enabling them to link specific acts and events in a longer time perspective. However, in the latter, sustained collective action does not take a conflictual element. Collective goods are often produced through cooperative efforts that neither imply nor require the identification of specific adversaries, trying to reduce the assets and opportunities of one's group or preventing chances to expand them. Prospected solutions do not imply redistribution of power nor alterations in social structure, but focus instead on service delivery, self-help, personal and community empowerment.[11] Likewise, the practice and promotion of alternative lifestyles does not require the presence of opponents defined in social and political terms. Collective actors may fight ethereal adversaries, ranging from bad or conventional taste, in the case of artistic and style-oriented movements, to "the inner enemy" in the case of some religious movements, without necessarily blaming any social actors for the state of things they intend to modify.

However, insisting on the presence of conflict as a distinctive trait of movements need not force social movement analysts away from the investigation of those instances of collective action where a conflict is difficult to identify, such as those oriented to personal change (e.g. the so-called "human potential movement," or many countercultural, alternative lifestyle networks) and those focusing on the delivery of some kind of help or assistance to an aggrieved collectivity (e.g., the so-called "solidarity movement": Giugni and Passy 2001). This perspective implies, instead, that analysts recognize the presence of several social mechanisms or dynamics within each instance of collective action, and focus their efforts on exploring how such mechanisms operate and interact with each other.

1.2.3 Social movements, events, and coalitions

We have a social movement dynamic going on when single episodes of collective action are perceived as components of a longer-lasting action, rather than discrete events; and when those who are engaged in them feel linked by ties of solidarity and of ideal communion with protagonists of other analogous mobilizations. The course of the movement for the control of toxic waste in the United States provides a good example of this dynamic. From a series of initiatives which developed from a local base and in relation to specific goals such as blocking the construction of waste disposal plants in particular areas, the movement gradually developed into a collective force with a national base, concerned with numerous aspects of the relationship between nature and society, and with a much more sophisticated cultural elaboration (Szasz 1994: 69–99).

Identity-building also means that a sense of collective belonging can be maintained even after a specific initiative or a particular campaign has come to an end. The persistence of these feelings will have at least two important consequences. First, it will make the revival of mobilization in relation to the same goals easier, whenever favorable conditions recur. Movements often oscillate between brief phases of intense public activity and long "latent" periods (Melucci 1984b; Taylor 1989), in which self-reflection and cultural production prevail. The trust and solidarity links, activated in the European antinuclear movements during the mobilizations of the second half of the 1970s, for example, represented the base on which a new wave of protests gathered momentum in the wake of the Chernobyl incident in 1986 (Flam 1994d). Second, representations of the world and collective identities which developed in a certain period can also facilitate, through a gradual transformation, the development of new movements and new solidarities. For example, the close relationship existing in several countries between movements of the new left of the early 1970s and successive political ecology movements has been noted on a number of occasions (Dalton 1994; Diani 1995a; Duyvendak 1995).

Reference to other examples of informal networks of collective action, such as coalitions, also illustrates why collective identity is such a crucial feature of social movements. In coalition dynamics, collective actors are densely connected to each other in terms of alliances, and identify explicit opponents, but those links are not necessarily backed by strong identity links. The networks between actors mobilizing on a common goal take a purely contingent and instrumental nature. Resource mobilization and campaigning is then conducted mainly through exchanges and pooling of resources between distinct groups and organizations. The latter rather than the network are the main source of participants' identities and loyalties. Actors instrumentally share resources in order to achieve specific goals, yet do not develop any particular sense of belonging and of a common future during the process. Once a specific battle has been fought, there need not be any longer-term legacy in terms of identity and solidarity, nor attempts to connect the specific campaign in a broader framework.[12]

Associating movements with a distinctive collective identity implies no assumptions about the homogeneity of the actors sharing that identity (in contrast with what is suggested by, for example, Rootes [2000] or McDonald [2002]). We have a social movement identity dynamic to the extent that groups and/or individuals feel part of a collectivity, mobilized to support or oppose social change; that they identify shared elements in their past, present, and future experiences; and that other social or political actors be held responsible for the state of affairs being challenged. Whether a specific collective identity will be inclusive or exclusive, and the degree to which holders of such an identity will share one or several traits, are empirical questions (see chapter 4).

1.2.4 Social movements and organizational processes

Social movements, political parties, and interest groups are often compared with each other, on the assumption that they all embody different styles of political organization (for example, Wilson 1973). At times, they are identified with religious sects and cults (for example, Robbins 1988). However, the difference between social movements and these and other organizations does not consist primarily of differences in organizational characteristics or patterns of behavior, but of the fact that social movements are not organizations, not even of a peculiar kind (Tilly 1988; Oliver 1989). They are networks which may either include formal organizations or not, depending on shifting circumstances. As a consequence, a single organization, whatever its dominant traits, is not a social movement. Of course it may be involved in a social movement process, but the two are not identical, as they reflect different organizational principles.

Indeed, many influential scholars in the field have often used the term "social movement" to mean both networks of interaction and specific organizations: citizens' rights groups like Common Cause, environmental organizations like the Sierra Club, or even religious sects like Nichiren Shoshu (McAdam et al. 1988: 695; see also Lofland 1996). Yet we should not uncritically apply to social movement analysis concepts borrowed from organizational theory: "all too often we speak of movement strategy, tactics, leadership, membership, recruitment, division of labor, success and failure – terms which strictly apply only to coherent decision-making entities (that is, organizations or groups), not to crowds, collectivities, or whole social movements" (Oliver 1989: 4).

Talking of Common Cause or the Sierra Club or Nichiren Shoshu as "social movements" leads one to formulate concepts like "professional social movement" (McCarthy and Zald 1987a) or "single-organization movements" (Turner and Killian 1987: 369–70) to emphasize the obvious differences between these cases and the nature of social movements as informal networks. But categorizing Common Cause as a "professional social movement" does not add very much to the insights provided by concepts like "public interest group" (see, among others, Etzioni 1985). Similarly, a religious organization like Nichiren Shoshu or Hare Krishna may be conveniently analyzed as a "sect." This concept takes into account the greater organizational rigidity and the more hierarchical structure that these organizations display by comparison with social movement networks (Robbins 1988: 150–5). It also recognizes the higher degree of social control that is exerted on members. In contrast, what the terms "public interest group" and "sect" do not really capture are the interaction processes through which actors with different identities and orientations come to elaborate a shared system of beliefs and a sense of belonging, which far exceeds the boundaries of any single group or organization, while maintaining at the same time their specificity and distinctive traits.

The instability of the relationship between organizational and movement identities means that movements are by definition fluid phenomena. In the formation and consolidation phases, a sense of collective belonging prevails on links of solidarity and loyalty which can exist between individuals and specific groups or associations. A movement tends to burn out when organizational identities come to dominate once more, or when "feeling part of it" refers primarily to one's organization and its components, rather than to a broader collective with blurred boundaries (Diani 2003a).

To shift the emphasis from single organizations to informal networks allows us, furthermore, to appreciate more fully the space reserved for individuals within movements. Individual participation is essential for movements, and one of their characteristics is, indeed, the sense of being involved in a collective endeavor – without having automatically to belong to a specific organization. Strictly speaking, social movements do not have members, but participants.[13] The participation of the individual, detached from specific organizational allegiances, is not necessarily limited to single protest events. It can also develop within committees or working groups, or else in public meetings.[14] Alternatively (when the possibility arises) one may support a movement by promoting its ideas and its point of view among institutions, other political actors, or the media. However, the existence of a range of possible ways of becoming involved means that the membership of movements can never be reduced to a single act of adherence. It consists, rather, of a series of differentiated acts, which taken together reinforce the feeling of belonging and of identity (see also Gusfield 1994: 62).

If social movements are analytically different from social movement organizations, any organization which is involved in a social movement dynamic may be regarded as a "social movement organization." This may also hold for bureaucratic interest groups, and even political parties. By saying that political parties may be part of social movements we do not mean to suggest that "social movements" is a broader theoretical category in which several types of organizations (interest groups, community groups, political parties, and so forth) are represented as many subtypes. Rather, we suggest that under certain and specific conditions some political party may feel itself to be part of a movement and be recognized as such both by other actors in the movement and by the general public. This is likely to be the exception rather than the rule, and to be largely restricted to parties whose origins lie in social movements, such as the Green parties (Kitschelt 1989; Richardson and Rootes 1994).

One could reasonably object that no matter how strong their identification with a movement, political parties actually perform specific functions at the level of interest representation and in this sense are different from social movements.

That differences exist at the functional level is beyond question. Yet, the main peculiarity of social movements does not consist of their specific way of performing the function of interest representation. Of course their networks of interaction favor the formulation of demands, the promotion of mobilization campaigns, and the elaboration and diffusion of beliefs and collective identities. These factors all, in turn, contribute to redefining the cultural and political setting in which the action of interest representation takes place. However, when we focus on the function of interest representation in strict terms, we do not look at the way "the movement" performs this function. We look at the way different specific social movement organizations do this. Whether or not they decide to include participation in elections within their repertoire of action is dependent upon several factors, including external opportunities, tactical and/or ideological considerations, and their links to other actors in the movement. The mere fact that they decide to do so, however, will not automatically exclude them from the movement. Rather, they will be part of two different systems of action (the party system and the social movement system), where they will play different roles. The way such roles are actually shaped will constitute a crucial area of investigation (Kitschelt 1989).

It goes without saying that stressing the peculiarity of movements as informal networks does not imply ruling out of social movement analysts' remit the analysis of specific organizations, as some critics have suggested (e.g. Pickvance 1995: 46). Instead, it forces analysts to explicitly recognize, by elaborating specific concepts, the distinction between social movement processes and organizational processes. Rather than looking at groups as diverse as Common Cause or the Nazi party as "movements," applying to them the same label used for networks of multiple organizations, we suggest using a rigorous definition of movements to identify the co-presence and interaction within each of them of both movement and (bureaucratic) organizational processes. For example, recognizing such differences enables us to better specify the distinction between the Nazi party and the Nazi movement, and to explore the interaction between the two processes. We could map the extent and the shape of the links, connecting the various right-wing and paramilitary organizations which provided in the late 1910s and the 1920s the backbone to what was to become the Nazi party (Anheier 2003). We could then document how the NSDAP and its most directly connected organizations came to play an increasingly central role in the right-wing network. Finally, we could illustrate how eventually formal links between the party, its individual members, and its collateral organizations came to almost totally replace the informal links between them through (a) the definition of formal criteria for individual membership in the party, and (b) the domination of the party over any other organization, including the SS. Far from preventing us from analyzing movements which largely overlap with a specific organization, a view of a movement as an informal network of several individuals and organizations would help us to identify the tension between movement and organizational dynamics within complex empirical cases of collective action, and possibly to trace its evolution over time.[15]

1.2.5 Social movements and protest

Until the early 1970s debates on social movements emphasized their noninstitutionalized nature (Alberoni 1984). Even now, the idea is still very popular that social movements may be distinguished from other political actors because of their adoption of "unusual" patterns of political behavior. Several scholars maintain that the fundamental distinction between movements and other social and political actors is to be found in the contrast between conventional styles of political participation (such as voting or lobbying political representatives) and public protest (Rucht 1990a, 1995).

There are some objections to considering protest a core feature of social movements. First, public protest plays only a marginal role in movements concerned with personal and cultural change, in religious movements, and the like. Cultural conflict and symbolic challenges often take forms, such as the practice of specific lifestyles, the adoption or certain clothes or haircut, the adoption of rituals, that can only be regarded as protest if we stretch the concept to a very considerable degree (Snow 2005). Moreover, even in the political realm it is increasingly debatable whether protest can still be considered an "unconventional," or even violent or "confrontational," activity. Various forms of political protest have increasingly become part of the consolidated repertoire of collective action, at least in Western democracies. In general, protest seems no longer restricted to radical sectors, but rather an option, open to a much broader range of actors when they feel their relative position in the political process to come under threat (e.g., Dalton 1996).

At the same time, however, protest still differentiates social movements from other types of networks, like those referred to as "epistemic communities" (Haas 1992; Keck and Sikkink 1998). These communities are organized around networks of individuals and groups with specific scientific and/or managerial competences in distinct policy areas. Like social movements, their members share a common frame of reference and take sides on conflictual issues. The forms of structural ties and exchange of resources within those networks are, however, different from those that tend to characterize social movements. Epistemic communities involve actors usually endowed with decision-making power and certified knowledge, as well as, often, electoral accountability. Instead, social movement actors usually occupy a peripheral position in decision-making processes, and need to mobilize public opinion to maintain their pressure capacity.

Even if some forms of protest are "normalized," social movements tend to invent new disruptive forms of action – challenging the state on issues of law and order. As the new wave of global justice collective mobilization at the turn of the century has confirmed, social movement politics is still to a large extent "politics in the streets." The use of protest as a major source of pressure has relevant effects on the structure and strategy of social movements.

1.3 On This Book

Looking at recent global justice mobilizations, in this chapter we have, first of all, identified four key questions that have attracted the attention of analysts of social movements since the 1960s. These refer to how changes in the social structure in Western countries, most specifically the passage from an industrial to a postindustrial mode of social organization, might affect the forms of collective action (section 1.1.1); how cultural and symbolic production by social actors enables the identification of social problems as worthy objects of collective action and the construction of collective identity (section 1.1.2); how organizational and individual resources make collective action not only possible but also successful, at least potentially (section 1.1.3); how the forms of action adopted by social movements, their developments over time, and their clustering in broader waves of contention are all affected by the traits of the political and social systems in which social movements operate (section 1.1.4).

For each of these questions we have also identified some of the most influential answers provided by social movement scholars over the years. This has enabled us to introduce, if briefly, the most influential approaches that have characterized the field in the last decades: particularly, if not exclusively, the new social movements, collective behavior, resource mobilization, and political process approaches. While none of these perspectives is reducible to any of the issues we identified, they do address some more neatly than others. The new social movements perspective can be regarded first and foremost as a theory of how the stakes and the central actors of social conflict are modified under changing structural conditions; the collective behavior approach mainly theorizes the role of symbolic production in shaping collective action and the conditions for the emergence of new issues and/or identities; resource mobilization theory explores the conditions leading to the emergence of collective action among people who might have more than one good reason not to engage in it; finally, the political process approach looks at the forms of collective action and their variation across different political regimes and different points in time.

In the second part of the chapter, we showed how social movements may be regarded as distinctive social and political processes. In particular, we identified their distinctiveness in their consisting of informal networks, linking individual and organizational actors engaged in conflictual relations to other actors, on the basis of a shared collective identity (section 1.2.1). This has enabled us to differentiate social movements from a number of other related processes and phenomena. These include collective actions oriented to nonconflictual goals, such as in the field of charity work (section 1.2.2); coalitions mobilizing on specific issues or events for instrumental reasons (section 1.2.3); political organizations such as parties and traditional interest groups (section 1.2.4); and protest repertoires (section 1.2.5).

As we have repeatedly argued, the questions we have identified are neither restricted to nor specific of social movement analysis, and can be of interest to a much broader spectrum of social and political analysts. At the same time, they are surely central to social movement research as it has developed since the 1960s, hence our decision to organize the rest of the book around such questions. We start with a discussion of the structural bases of contemporary movements (chapter 2). By this we refer on the one hand to the mechanisms by which new social groups and new interests take shape, while other groups and interests which previously held center stage see their relevance declining; and on the other, to the impact which structural changes such as the growth and contraction of public welfare, and the expansion of higher education, have on forms of political participation and, in particular, on noninstitutional participation. The impact of globalization processes is particularly relevant to our discussion.

There follow two chapters dedicated to symbolic production. Chapter 3 shows how cultural elaboration facilitates the definition of social problems as the product of asymmetries of power and conflicts of interest, and the identification of their causes in social and political factors which are subject to human intervention. In chapter 4 we show how the creation and reinforcement of symbols also represents the base for the development of feelings of identity and solidarity, without which collective action cannot take place.

A third important level of analysis consists of the organizational factors which allow both the production of meaning and the mobilization of resources necessary for action. We take into consideration both informal networking and the more structured component of the organizational dimension. Chapter 5 deals in particular with the analysis of individual participation. We look at the mechanisms behind individual decisions to become engaged in collective action and to sustain their commitment over time, but we also look at how individuals create, through their participation, several opportunities for the development of networks that keep social movements and oppositional milieus together. Chapter 6 concentrates on certain properties of movement organizations, discussing the factors – internal and external – which influence the adoption of certain organizational models, and the consequences which follow for mobilization.

The fourth crucial dimension is the interaction between movements and the political system. Movements represent innovative, sometimes radical, elements both in the way in which the political system works, and in its very structure. The characteristics of the political system offer or deny essential opportunities for the development of collective action. It is also, if not exclusively, in reference to the political system that we can evaluate the impact of protest movements and their consequences in the medium term. In chapter 7, we reconstruct some of the properties of protest cycles which have marked the history of recent decades, and the repertoires of collective action which were formed within these. In chapter 8, we present certain aspects of the relationship between the configurations of political opportunities and the development of mobilization. In chapter 9 we discuss, finally, the problem of the effects of movements. While the center of our analysis is represented by political change, we will nonetheless try to pay attention also to the impact of movements on the social and cultural spheres.

The issues with which we are concerned are undoubtedly central to the analysis of collective action. Our treatment, however, is anything but comprehensive. First, the studies to which we refer have been largely inspired by the experience of "new social movements" and, more recently, of the "global justice movement." In our analysis, there is no lack of reference to works dedicated to working-class conflict or, even more obviously, to ethnonationalist movements, or to mobilizations which developed in the last century, but we focus on contributions which have analyzed phenomena such as nationalism (Johnston 1991a; Jenson 1995) or working-class solidarity in America (Fantasia 1988) by borrowing concepts from analysts of "new" movements; or which have become essential reading for all those concerned generally with collective action (such as Tilly 1978). We are not concerned in any systematic way with the enormous body of literature dedicated to collective phenomena which are somehow related to "new" social movements.[16]

More generally, our work is not a reconstruction of the "state of the art" in this field, or capable of recognizing the worth of all significant contributions in this line of research. Fortunately, in the last few years important works have been published, thoroughly and comprehensively covering social movement research from a methodological (Klandermans and Staggenborg 2002) and more general perspective (Snow, Soule, and Kriesi 2004b). This book is instead an attempt to present certain central problems of recent debates. We have chosen, in addition to essential studies relating to the analysis of movements, a selection of other works which, for various reasons we feel to be useful illustrations of our line of argument. From this point of view, we have paid particular, though not exclusive, attention to studies which have combined theoretical analysis and empirical research (understood in its widest and most inclusive sense: Diani and

Eyerman 1992; Klandermans and Staggenborg 2002). Among the best-known works we have concentrated on those which to some extent have broken with the previous dominant strands of theorizing and research. In order to make our treatment more coherent, we have chosen to introduce the issues covered by each chapter with examples drawn from a particular movement, focusing our attention in a selective way on the relevant research.

Several reasons forced us to devote only scattered attention to many perspectives, which nevertheless contained indications of considerable interest to the questions we posed. These are partly practical, from lack of space, to our difficulty in controlling a particularly extensive literature. However they are also partly theoretical. They reflect the heterogeneity of the conceptual instruments with which movements and collective action have been analyzed up to now. The range of social and political contexts in which movements develop makes it even more problematic to elaborate models which are capable of dealing with such a high level of variation among "local" conditions for action. It is certainly true that overcoming these difficulties is a central concern for students of movements; but to incorporate all these lines of thinking would have required an attempt to translate concepts and theories into a homogeneous language, which still seems a very distant goal, not only for the two of us, but for the scientific community as a whole (see also McAdam, Tarrow, and Tilly 1996, 2001).

SOCIAL CHANGES AND SOCIAL MOVEMENTS

In the mid-nineties France saw the "return of the social question," with an (uneasy) alliance between the public sector, unemployed, and marginally employed. In 1995, the extended strike of the *cheminots* (public transport workers) unexpectedly gained large support in public opinion: it "brought millions into the street in remarkable demonstrations of solidarity across the country, and forged direct organizational and symbolic links between the labor movement and various groups of excluded, including illegal immigrants, unemployed workers, and the homeless, as well as the lycée and university students and an intelligentsia that had been widely dismissed as apathetic and uninterested" (Fantasia and Stepan-Norris 2004: 556). Various marginal groups mobilized in the so-called "mouvements de sans" on behalf of the "have-nots": migrants without legal residence permits, homeless people, the unemployed. Analysts described a coalition between the "moral left" of the middle class that mobilized on human rights, and the "social left" that mobilized the workers. In particular, the unemployed protested in 1997 against a reform that reduced the funding for unem- ployment compensation and centralized its management. In 1994, the group Agir contre le chomage! (AC!; in English, Act Against Unemploy- ment!) organized five marches starting from the provinces and converging in Paris, demanding a reduction in working hours in order to create new jobs, as well as more investment "against exclusion." During and after the marches, the unemployed organized at the local and national levels. In the winter of 1995–6, groups of unemployed staged a campaign of "job req- uisitions": with well-publicized blitz actions, they marched into factories and commercial enterprises with job vacancies, leaving their CVs. The fol- lowing winter there would be weekly demonstrations and a series of occu- pations of local employment agencies – the ASSEDICS – as well as of the Ecole Normale Supérieure, the town halls, and the headquarters of the

Socialist Party, demanding the special Christmas doles that had been abolished by the reform.

The unemployed also protested at the European level: French, German, Spanish, and Italian unemployed converged in European Marches against unemployment, job insecurity, and exclusion in 1997; two years later, 30,000 mobilized on the same issues at the EU summit in Cologne, united as the European Network of Unemployed (ENU). The resources for these protests came from a heterogeneous, transnational coalition involving Trotskyite and Catholic groups, new social movements and trade unions – among the latter, the French Confédération Générale du Travail, the Italian Confederazione Generale Italiana del Lavoro, and the German magazine *Express* (close to the German unions). Notwithstanding the high costs of mobilization, the emerging debate on the social dimension of the EU was perceived as a window of opportunity. With few exceptions, the organizations participating in the march did not reject European integration, but instead asked for a different social and political EU (Chabannet 2002). AC! declared: "A 'social France' was never given spontaneously by capitalists and governors . . . In a similar way, a social Europe will come only from active and united intervention of European workers" (in Salmon 1998: 218).

It was during this cycle of protest that the French unemployed formed collective resources for mobilization. Although the unemployed are considered politically apathetic, with very little propensity for collective action, the movement organizations "succeeded in modifying, at least for a certain period, the unemployed's perception about their own mobilization potential. They encouraged the unemployed to express collective claims and convinced thousands of them to mobilize" (Royall 1998: 362). In fact, they provided a space for aggregation, socializing people who were often isolated (Mauer 2001), and increased their relational skills and savoir faire (Maurer and Pierru 2001). Mobilization provided a challenge to the image of unemployment as an individual problem and consequently the social stigma attached to it.

Moreover, the unemployed attracted allies. If the traditionally unemployed have found support on the left of the political spectrum, in the French case they mobilized against what was perceived as "treason" by the left and by the Socialist national government elected in May 1997, accused of having shifted from "a socialism with a human face to liberalism with humanitarian undertones" (Bourneau and Martin 1993: 172). Nevertheless, the unemployed succeeded in winning support in public opinion: not only were the Christmas doles reintroduced, but sympathetic media coverage changed the public image of the unemployed: from poor people queuing for charity, to rebels struggling for their rights (Salmon 1998; Maurer and Pierru 2001: 388). Acting in an institutionalized field, with welfare-state institutions focusing on the issue of unemployment (Fillieule 1993b), the protestors addressed the political issue of the recognition of the unemployed themselves – winning a symbolic battle when their organization was invited to meet President François Mitterrand.

This account of the mobilization of the French unemployed stresses some of the main dimensions that have structured the debate on the interaction between societal characteristics and social movements. First of all, it indicates that movements usually refer to a base that, in various ways, is defined by some social features. Although in American social movement research, criticism of breakdown theory (see chapter 1) has for long time (and with few exceptions, among which Piven and Cloward 1992) diverted attention from structural grievances (Buechler 2004), there is no denying that the socioeconomic structure of a society influences the type of conflicts that develop in it. Since the 1970s, indeed, European social movement scholars especially have focused on new conflicts in Western democracy: the ecological movement or the women's movement were the typical objects of this stream of research. Social movements have been considered indeed as the bearers of postmaterialistic values, while the class cleavage on which the labor movements had mobilized seemed to be pacified. The "return" of movements of the poor represents a useful starting point for the discussion of the relationship between changes in the social structure and collective action.

Social change may affect the characteristics of social conflict and collective action in different ways. It may facilitate the emergence of social groups with a specific structural location and potential specific interests, and/or reduce the importance of existing ones, as the shift from agriculture to industry and then to the service sector suggests. As the account on the French unemployed indicates, however, structural tensions do not directly translate into mobilization: the misery of the unemployed deters protest, more than facilitating it. Societal conditions also have important influences upon the distribution of resources that are conducive to participation in collective action, such as education, and/or facilitate the articulation of interests. The shift to smaller factories and offshore production of industrial activities has played against workers' capacity to act as a class, while women's increasing access to higher education and the job market has facilitated the development of new ties between them and their emergence as a new collective actor.

Keeping in mind these kinds of effects, we shall focus on three types of transformation which have interested Western societies since the Second World War: in the economy, in the role of the state, and in the cultural sphere. Without attempting to cover the innumerable processes which make up what is usually regarded as the transition to postindustrial (or postmodern, disorganized, post-Fordist, and so on) society (Amin 1994; Lash and Urry 1987; Castells 1996 1997; Kumar 2005), we shall limit ourselves to mention those processes of change that have been explicitly cited in the social movement literature as affecting social movements. We shall then discuss the broader implications of these changes for the analysis of innovations in forms of collective action. In particular, we shall address two problems: how does the experience of "new" movements affect our understanding of concepts like "class conflict" and "class action"? and how should we interpret the overwhelming presence of members from the so-called "new middle class" in social movements at the end of the twentieth century? In the next section we shall indeed focus on changes in the social structure and their reflection in political cleavages (2.1); then on the social impacts of changes in the political sphere (2.2), and on the effects of cultural changes on social movements (2.3). We shall conclude by discussing the hypothesis of new social movements as actors of new class conflicts (2.4).

2.1　Social Structure, Political Cleavages, and Collective Action

The effects of socioeconomic characteristics upon social and political conflicts have often been addressed by looking at political cleavages; that is, at the main politicized conflict lines (Lipset and Rokkan 1967). Political cleavages have traditionally been associated with a model of collective action in which actors: (1) fought against each other in order to protect material or political interests; and (2) defined themselves (as members of a class, a faction, or a national group) in relation to these interests.

Structural interpretations of social movements in industrial society have normally associated them with two fundamental processes. The first relates to the emergence of the market; the second to the creation of the nation-state and of modern citizenship (Rokkan 1970; Lipset and Rokkan 1967; Giddens 1990). The advent of the market economy resulted in the centrality of conflicts between capital and labor, but also produced another cleavage, opposing urban and agrarian social sectors. The construction of nation-states is an outcome of territorially based conflicts which set the central areas of new states against peripheral areas; as well as of conflicts between the emerging lay state and those who denied its legitimacy, supporting instead the temporal power of ecclesiastical structures (church–state conflict). The principal conflicts which have characterized contemporary societies have developed around these tensions: the consolidation of cleavages and their institutionalization have produced for political systems (and, in particular, their party systems) a configuration that has remained stable until the last decades of the twentieth century (Rokkan 1970; Bartolini and Mair 1990).[1] In this evolution, new social movements, such as the ecology movement, seemed to represent an innovation, lacking a specific social base and being largely indifferent to the goal of conquering the state.

Structure affects collective action not only by creating forms of dependence between social groups, and thus the potential for conflicting interests. Consolidated forms of the organization of social life (from economic to political action, from family life to associations) also influence the make-up of collective actors. Collective action on the part of particular social groups is in fact facilitated when these groups are: (1) easily identifiable and differentiated in relation to other social groups; (2) endowed, thanks to social networks among their members, with a high level of internal cohesion and with a specific identity. Collective action will depend therefore on the simultaneous presence of specific categorical traits and of networks which link the subjects sharing such traits (Oberschall 1973; Tilly 1978). From this perspective, the central question for the analysis of the relationship between structure and action will be whether social changes have made it easier to develop such social relationships and feelings of solidarity and of collective belonging, to identify specific interests, and to promote related mobilization. The move towards capitalism not only created aggregates of individuals joined together by the fact that they possessed the means of production (the capitalists) or their own labor force (the proletariat); it also created systems of social relationships which facilitated the development of an internal solidarity in these aggregates and their transformation into collective actors. The integration of the capitalist class was facilitated by its limited size, the overlapping of family ties and relationships of an economic nature, and by access to – and control of – communications. Many of the structural changes described in the following pages – for example those relating to transformations in the organization of work and in the localization of productive activities – have important consequences for the organization of interaction within social groups.

2.1.1 Economic change, social fragmentation, and movements

The working class was a central actor in the conflicts of the industrial society not only because of its size or the relevance of its economic function, but also as a consequence of a wider range of structural factors. In the Fordist factory, a large number of workers performed similar tasks within large productive units, where labor mobility was limited. These factors certainly facilitated identification of a specific social actor and reinforced internal cohesion. The concentration of the proletariat in large productive units and in urban areas produced dense networks in which a specific class identity developed along with a capacity for collective mass action (Thompson 1963; Lodhi and Tilly 1973; Snyder and Tilly 1972; Calhoun 1982; Lash and Urry 1987; Fantasia 1988; Urry 1995).

The bases of the industrial conflict have been weakened by modifications affecting the conditions described above. Within industry, the ways in which work is organized have changed. Automated technologies and small work groups have replaced the Fordist conveyor-belt approach and the related mass-worker model. Collective solidarity derived from the carrying out of the same duties has been weakened as a result. Starting in the 1980s, production began to move from large factories to smaller ones as corporations shifted production offshore and began to rely on suppliers to produce component parts of their products, rather than producing them themselves. This brought about a significant decentralization of production processes within a geographical area and led to the growth of the hidden and informal economy (Castells 1996: chs. 2–3; Amin 1994). Also the physical closeness of the factory and the neighborhoods inhabited by the working classes, which once represented a source of solidarity, is now broken (Lash and Urry 1987; Hirsch 1988).[2]

The importance of some productive sectors changed as well, with a noticeable decline in industrial work in favor of administrative and service occupations. Highly qualified work in the tertiary sector has grown throughout the world, creating a professional new middle class, which is very different from traditional clerical workers in industry or public bureaucracies. The change has affected both the private sector, with a marked increase in "producer services," and the public sector, with a strong expansion of "social services" related to education, health, and social care (Castells 1996: 208–20). The new middle class is, however, far from a homogeneous group; indeed, there appear to be considerable differences in terms of social rewards within it. The status of the new professionals is not always comparable with that of the traditional middle-class professionals (lawyers, doctors, and so on). In the new producer service sector (such as advertising, marketing, communications) precarious and low-paid forms of work are fairly widespread and constitute marked discrepancies between the cultural capital which individuals have at their disposal, and the recognition – in terms of earnings as well as of social prestige – which is obtained from these.[3]

Unemployment also increased in many countries, and came to be considered as a structural feature of capitalist economies. The relationship between the employed and the unemployed has also changed, in more general terms: entry into the labor market is delayed more and more, excessively prolonging a nonadult lifestyle; increasingly fewer sectors of the population can count on stable and protected forms of work. If it is difficult to determine effectively the level of unemployment, and its structural determinants, in developed countries, the incidence of precarious and temporary work has risen enormously (Castells 1996: ch. 4). Growing inequalities emerge not only between the North and the South (Pianta 2001b), but also within the North, even in the most modern global cities (see Sassen 2000). Poverty is also more and more widespread: according to the UN Human Development Report of 1999, at the turn of the century 80 countries have a per capita income which is lower than 10 years ago; 1.2 billion people live in conditions of extreme poverty, even by the World Bank's ridiculously low threshold of one dollar a day.

Demographic pressure and other difficulties in an increasing number of areas in the southern hemisphere have triggered significant migrations towards the stronger economies, promoting the expansion in Western societies of a subproletariat with a strong ethnic character (Castells 1996: ch. 4, especially 233–4). While by no means a new phenomenon (O'Sullivan See 1986; Olzak 1992), the scale of migrations towards the end of the twentieth century has certainly increased the potential for racial conflicts within Western democracies and created opportunities for the resurgence of extreme right groups (Hainsworth 1992; Wrench and Solomos 1993; Wieviorka 1995; Koopmans 1996a, 1997).

Another fundamental force of change has consisted of the massive entry of women into the paid labor force. Within Western societies, the phenomenon has been particularly pronounced in the service sector, which suggests a relationship between dematerialization of the economy and increased opportunities for women (Castells 1997: 163). This process has affected lines of differentiation and criteria for interest definition within social groups, which were previously perceived as homogeneous. Continuing wage differentials between men and women represent, for example, an obvious source of division and potential conflict within the salaried classes (Castells 1997: 169). At the same time, the combined impact of women's growing economic independence and professional commitments has shaken the base of patriarchalism both at home and within the professions and created opportunities for the development of even deeper gender conflicts in the private sphere (Walby 1997).

These processes have weakened the structural preconditions that had facilitated the emergence of a class cleavage, particularly in the working-class model of collective action. Overall, the size of social groups which lack full access to citizenship and its entitlements has grown, whether because they are migrants (legal or illegal), because they are employed in the hidden economy, or engaged in low-paid work. The sense of general insecurity has been further reinforced by the growth of individual mobility, principally horizontal: and thus more people tend to change jobs several times in the course of their life – whether out of choice or out of necessity (Esping-Andersen 1993; Castells 1996). The multiplication of roles and of professions and of the related stratifications, and the (re)emergence of ethnicity or gender-based lines of fragmentation within socioeconomic groups have made it more difficult to identify specific social categories.

The greater frequency of job changes and the weaker links with territorial communities have also made relationships among those who once shared the same structural condition more unstable and fragmentary. Work seems to be gradually losing its collective nature, a process Manuel Castells has defined as "individualization of labor" (1996: 265). It is more difficult to deduct actors' interests from their structural position, and to organize their protection on that basis (Dalton 1988: ch. 8).

The first effect of these changes has been a weakening of the labor movement. If the decline of strike activities could be interpreted as a sign of institutionalization of the industrial relations and depoliticization of the industrial conflicts, especially in the nineties, the decline in union membership has been quoted as an indicator of an unavoidable crisis of the labor movement. Also in the service sector, a fragmented social base is hard to organize, especially with the growing flexibilization of the labor market and the connected increasing insecurity. And the more and more numerous unemployed and migrants were also difficult to mobilize.

At the beginning of the new millennium, however, conflict on labor issues again seems to be on the rise, although in new forms: the unemployed protest, even if sporadically; workers have organized in the South, where unions often increased their membership (Norris 2002: 173 ff.); grassroots networks linked workers transnationally (Moody 1997). New grassroots unions emerged (see below), and traditional unions started to invest more on the mobilization of the workers – for instance, the AFL-CIO now invest as much as 30 percent of their budget in organizing (as opposed to the usual 5 percent) (Fantasia and Stepan-Norris 2004: 570). While labor demobilized in the private sector, in the public sector (as in the example of the French *cheminots*) workers voiced their opposition to neoliberal reforms that cut social services (Eckstein 2001). As Piven and Cloward (2000) noticed, in the United States there has been a return to old forms of secondary action such as community boycotts, sympathy strikes, and general strikes. In France (but also in Italy and Spain) the turn of the millennium has been characterized by general strikes against pension reform, privatization of public services, cuts in public health and education. In these actions, the trade unions were joined by various movements, bridging labor issues with global justice, defense of the environment, peace, and gender equality. The development of a frame of global injustice has indeed been perceived as another recent tendency in the labor movement. The NAFTA free-trade agreements produced increasing transnational campaigns of Canadian, US, and Mexican workers (Ayres 1998; Evans 2000). The dockers of Seattle, who had already taken part in a transnational strikes started by the dockers in Liverpool (Moody 1997), also supported the protest against the WTO, extending their solidarity from the local to the international level (Levi and Olson 2000). In these waves of mobilization, the labor movement met other movements – environmentalist, feminist, urban, etc. (della Porta, Andretta, Mosca, and Reiter 2005). Moreover, increasing inequalities stimulated the rise of solidarity movements with marginal groups in the North (Giugni e Passy 2001), as well as protest by marginal groups themselves (Simeant 1998; Kousis and Tilly 2004; Chris Tilly 2004).

2.1.2 *Economic globalization and social conflict*

Structural processes also influence the territorial dimension of conflict. Traditionally, social movements have organized at the national level, targeting national governments. As the example of the French unemployed illustrates, today's national protests are more often accompanied by transnational ones, in a process of scale shift (McAdam and Tarrow 2005). But the relationship between economic activities and geography has changed too, in the sense that such activities are increasingly transnational in both "strong" and "weak" sectors. Thus the importance of the multinationals has grown: the emphasis on the international division of labor has facilitated the transfer of activities with high environmental risks to the poorest areas. Decentralization of production went hand in hand with the centralization of economic control, with the merging of firms into larger and larger corporations.

While the process of global interdependence has its roots in the distant past (Wallerstein 1974; Tilly 2004a: ch.5), the technological revolution of the 1980s contributed to intensifying "both the reality of global interdependence, and also the awareness of the world as one single unit" (Robertson 1992: 8). In the economic system, growing interdependence has meant the transfer of production (in economic theory, the "delocalization of production processes") to countries with lower wages; a strengthening of multinational corporations; and especially the internationalization of financial markets, to the extent that some speak of an "economy without borders." Global economic interdependence has been a factor in pushing large numbers of people from the South and East of the world to its North and West, but also in transforming the division of international labor by deindustrializing the North (where the economy is increasingly service oriented) and industrializing some areas in the South (in particular in Latin America and Central Asia and now also in eastern Europe), where the economy used to be based on the export of raw materials.

The contractual capacity of trade unions has been significantly weakened by the threat of moving production to locations with lower labor costs (Castells 1996: ch. 2). Economic globalization has also raised specific problems around which actors, both old and new, have mobilized. In the world's North, it has brought unemployment and especially an increase in job insecurity and unprotected working conditions, with frequent trade-union mobilization in the agricultural, industrial, and service sectors. In the South, too, the neoliberalist policies imposed by the major international economic organizations have forced developing countries to make substantial cuts in social spending, triggering fierce protests (Walton and Seddon 1994; Eckstein 2001; Ayuero 2001). Again, already weak political regimes have often allowed the private exploitation of natural resources as well as development projects with major environmental impact. Native populations have mobilized against the destruction of their physical habitat – for instance, via the destruction of the Amazon forests or the construction of big dams, often sponsored by IGOs such as the World Bank or the IMF (Passy 1999).

2.2   States, Markets, and Social Movements

Politics and the state have experienced equally relevant changes. State action is capable of producing collective actors in at least two ways: by fixing the territorial limits of political action (i.e. setting borders); and by facilitating or blocking the development or the growth of certain social groups – depending on the priorities of public policy, and in particular on the destination of public spending.

2.2.1   Territorial boundaries and social conflicts: the transnationalization of protest

Traditionally, political action in the industrial society presupposed a specific concept of space and territory, which translated into the model of the nation-state. Having the monopoly of the legitimate use of force in a certain area, the state fixed its borders, and thus the "natural" limit of the complex of much wider relationships conventionally defined as society. Social relationships were, in the first place, relationships internal to a particular nation-state.[4] There were, admittedly, many communities within states that were endowed with specific institutions and forms of self-government, but they were considered to be largely residual phenomena, destined to disappear as modernization processes advanced (Smith 1981).

Relevant collective actors were, at that time, those social groups able to influence the formulation of national policy: for example, groups with central economic and professional roles, or organized labor. Political and class conflict tended to be seen as conflict between social groups defined on a national scale, and concerned with the control of national policymaking. The existence of conflicts between the center and the periphery that were not based on class issues did not belie this perception: minority nationalities, groups bearing a particular cultural, historical, and/or linguistic identity, defined their strategies and their own images in reference to a central state and to the dominion which the state exercised on their territory, and they often aimed at building their own nation-states. In this case, the goal was not concerned with national policy but rather with the modification of the borders of the nation-state. However, actors did define themselves in terms of the state and its borders.

The correspondence of nation-state and society is nowadays weaker than it was in the past. In this sense, economic globalization has called into question not only the role of the nation-state, less and less capable of governing within its own borders, but also, in more general terms, the capacity of politics to intervene in the economy and regulate social conflict. Global capitalism has in fact breached the longstanding historical alliance among capitalism, the welfare state, and democracy (Crouch 2004). The shift from Keynesian-driven economics – with the state playing an important role in governing the market – to neoliberal capitalism implied a reduction of labor protection as well as workers' rights (Brecher, Costello, and Smith 2000). To prevent hemorrhages of capital, even left-wing governments have espoused the liberal concepts of flexibilization of the workforce and cuts in social spending.

Overall, the capacity of the state to regulate behavior within a certain territory has clearly lessened. First, the importance of territorial political structures within single states has grown. In most cases this has been intertwined with the consolidation of various forms of territorial decentralization (Keating 1988; Sharpe 1988; Bukowski, Piattoni, and Smyrl 2003). In some cases, moves towards autonomy have led to the emergence of genuine subnational entities, often in places where historical traditions of autonomy were strong, but even where they were weak (for instance, in Spain). At the same time, the growing interdependence among states and the strengthening of some IGOs have weakened the idea of the states as the only relevant units in the international system. The devolution of regulatory power to IGOs such as the EU has unsettled national boundaries (Bartolini 2004).

Globalization is not only a matter of new technologies but also of the political tools set in place to regulate and reproduce the mode of production through the proliferation of international governmental and nongovernmental organizations (U. Beck 1999; Boli and Thomas 1999). While the national political context still filters the impact of international shifts on national politics, growing economic interdependence went hand in hand with "a significant internationalization of public authority associated with a corresponding globalization of political activity" (Held and McGrew 2000: 27). From this perspective, the international system based on the nation-state seems to be mutating into a political system composed of overlapping multilevel authorities with low functional differentiation and scant democratic legitimacy. In the political system, globalization has brought a transnationalization of political relationships. In fact, recent research into international relations has highlighted a pluralization of relevant actors (Nicholson 1998: 131 ff.). Since the second world war, and increasingly in recent years, we have seen growth in the number of international governmental organizations with both a worldwide scope of action (like the United Nations) and a regional one (like the European Union, but also Mercosur in Latin America and NAFTA in North America); with military objectives (NATO or the now defunct Warsaw Pact) or with the declared aim of fostering economic development (the IMF, World Bank, or WTO) (Princen and Finger 1994: 1).

International organizations have contributed to the spread of international regulations and norms, which in some cases supersede national sovereignty. As has often been pointed out, "no official authority controls states in the contemporary world system, but many are subject to powerful unofficial forces, pressures and influences that penetrate the supposed hard shell of the state" (Russett and Starr 1996: 62). Furthermore, while the majority of intergovernmental organizations function as a meeting place and discussion forum where decisions are taken unanimously and then ratified by national organs, a growing number of international organizations make decisions on a majority basis that bind all member states (ibid.). International governmental organizations have been both tools for economic globalization, through policies liberalizing trade and the movement of capital, and a way to govern processes that can no longer be handled at the national level.

This does not mean that the state has lost its centrality. Analysts of the recent impressive growth of Far East economies point, for example, to the role of the state as a facilitator of development (Castells 1996: 89). But undoubtedly the presence of simultaneous moves toward the constitution of supranational and subnational authorities has brought about significant changes in the construction of collective actors. For example, in the case of minority nationalities within multicultural states, the presence of supranational entities tends to change the criteria according to which actors define themselves, as well as their strategies. European integration has certainly contributed to the remobilization of ethnic minorities in western European states, providing them with a new interlocutor and new goals: from the construction of new states following the breakup of those already in existence, there has been, increasingly, a move towards the renegotiation of relationships between central and peripheral regions of a state, within a "regional Europe." At the same time, we have seen a shift from nationalist identities with a strong ethnic component, to identities that combine reference to the nation with greater attention to multiculturalism and the cohabitation of diverse cultural groups (Johnston 1991b; Melucci 1996). The struggle for self-government of indigenous peoples addresses not only specific rights, but also the very political rights of nonterritorially bounded communities (Brysk 2000; Yashar 1996).

Moreover, not only has globalization weakened the power of politics over economics, it has generated transnational conflicts on the policies of international institutions, producing different results depending on the organization and field of intervention involved. In particular, opposition has arisen to the neoliberalist policies of the so-called international financial institutions (such as the IMF or the WB), which wield strong coercive power through the threat of economic sanctions and conditionalities on international credit. More generally, in addition to the acquisition of power by these largely nonrepresentative, nontransparent bodies, criticism has centered on their manifest democratic deficit. Similar considerations may hold for other international organs, for example, in the sphere of the United Nations, or for other types of policy enacted by the European Union itself, from environmental issues to human rights. In all of these cases, new opportunities have emerged for mobilization and campaigns conducted on a transnational scale (Tarrow 1995; Chatfield et al. 1996; Marks and McAdam 1998). As governance began to involve multiple territorial levels, protestors also started to develop multilevel strategies (Imig and Tarrow 2001a and 2001b; della Porta and Tarrow 2004; della Porta 2004b; della Porta and Caiani 2006; see also chapter 8 below).

2.2.2   State and classes: the conflicts around the welfare state

The state does not influence the formation of collective actors only through the definition of territorial boundaries to political action. It is well known that the role of the state in the economy has increased progressively in the course of the twentieth century, peaking in the 1970s, and then, even if unequally in cross-national comparison, declining with social expenditures at the turn of the century (Crouch 1999). However considered, the state has moved from being a guarantor of the market to managing economic activities through public enterprise; moreover, the welfare state has contained social inequalities (for a global discussion, see Rose 1988). This has led some observers to hold that the principal social cleavage is no longer based on the control of the means of production, but relates, rather, to the procurement of the means of survival either in the private market or through public intervention (Saunders 1987, quoted in Crompton 1993: 103–4; see also Taylor-Gooby 1986; Papadakis and Taylor-Gooby 1987). Certainly, criteria for allocation of public resources, often those concerned with the satisfaction of basic needs such as housing or transport, have represented a significant area for collective action, in particular, for social groups from an urban context (Dunleavy 1980; Castells 1983; Lowe 1986: Pickvance 1977, 1985, 1986).

Processes of a political nature, rather than based on market dynamics, affect the existence of certain social groups. As mentioned, the field of unemployment is heavily influenced by state institutions that affect the number of unemployed as well as their conditions. After the Second World War, the phenomenon has become more marked, with the development of the welfare state, as well as of neocorporatist patterns of interest representation (see chapter 8 below). In recent decades, social movements have criticized the model of the interventionist state, as well as that of the state as mediator between the forces of production. Various factors have converged towards a further widening of the potential for conflict. First, as the active role of the state in the distribution of resources has become increasingly evident, the opportunities for mobilization to protect ever more heterogeneous social groups and interests have also grown. Second, while the expansion of social rights has certainly brought greater opportunities for those from the lowest social classes, it has also entailed considerable fiscal redistribution. This has been considered, in the medium term, as particularly heavy for the middle classes, as well as insufficient to cover the growing costs of the welfare state, particularly in the context of an ageing population. The result has been a universal welfare crisis that is at the same time fiscal and political. The explicitly political nature of the criteria for the allocation of social resources has, in fact, stimulated mobilization among the middle classes, not only in the form of antitax movements, but also from a perspective which is globally critical of the welfare state (Fabbrini 1986; Brissette 1988; Lo 1982, 1990).

More recently, however, the global justice movement has mobilized mainly in defense of the welfare state. In differing ways in various countries, trade-union organizations have joined in protest, accusing neoliberal globalization of subordinating citizens' rights to the free market, thus increasing the inequalities both between the North and South and within their own countries. The forerunners of the Seattle protests can in fact be found, at least in part, in the world of work. As mentioned, in various ways, depending on the prevailing patterns of interest representation in various countries, the 1990s saw a transformation of labor action. While, in general terms, the union federations in European countries accepted privatization, deregulation, and the "flexibilization" of labor, opposition grew in other sectors both inside and outside unions. In France, Italy, and Germany, for example, protest extended particularly to public services, expressing opposition to privatization and its effects on domestic work conditions and the global efficiency of services. Accused of defending old privileges, the public-sector unions often sought consensus in public opinion by claiming to defend public against private values, service against goods.

Apart from public transport, opposition to neoliberal economic policies extended particularly to education and health. In these areas, in countries with pluralist patterns of industrial relations (with various representative organizations competing with each other), new unions highly critical of the various forms of privatization arose and expanded – from Coordonner, Ressembler, Construire (CRC), and Solidaire, Unitaire, Démocratique (SUD-PTT) in France (Béroud, Mouriaux, and Vakaloulis 1998: 49; Sommier 2003), to Cobas in Italy (della Porta 2005c). In the so-called neocorporative countries, with occupational representation confined to a single union, public-sector unionists took the most radical positions (for instance, first the OETV and then Ver.di in Germany). It was no coincidence that these unions were the most involved in the protest campaigns against neoliberal globalization (della Porta 2005c, 2005d).

To summarize: the growth of the role of the state has multiplied the number of social actors whose existence and opportunities seem to be linked at least partially to political decision-making mechanisms. At the same time, the processes of globalization which we have just described, have undermined the capacity of consolidated political actors to effectively mediate between the various interests. Changes in the criteria for defining actors and for determining the stakes to play for, have promoted the multiplication of collective identities and of mobilized interests and, therefore, also their segmentation.

2.3   Knowledge, Culture, and Conflicts

Social movements also react to changes in the value system and the culture in general. We shall discuss in a later chapter the *discursive opportunities* for movements (see chapter 8), and their effects on values, knowledge, and attitudes. But in this section we want to single out some general cultural changes that have often been mentioned in relation to movements, looking in particular at the conception of the public and the private, the growth of movement counterculture, as well as the development of global culture.

2.3.1   Shifting boundaries between the public and the private

In the past, the expansion of the role of the state has contributed to the modification of the boundaries between the public and the private. The state has intervened with growing frequency in areas relating to private life, in particular, through the provision of social services and the action of welfare agencies. The principal form of support offered to citizens has been, however, accompanied by increased control over aspects of life that previously would have been left to the autonomous regulation of social actors. The extension of the public health service, for example, has favored the standardization of therapeutic methods and the treatment of crucial events in the experience of individuals, such as maternity. A tendency towards the bureaucratization and rationalization of the private sphere has followed (Habermas 1976, 1987; Melucci 1989, 1996).

In this way, definitions of criteria for determining normality and deviance in areas which were previously left to the regulation of other institutions (such as the church or the family), have become the object of public intervention. Thus the premises have been created for the rise of new conflicts whose protagonists are new social groups – for example, professionals and users of social services, or managers with responsibility for the coordination and running of public agencies (Hoffman 1989). In many cases, protest has related not only to the efficiency of services but also to their impersonality and their tendency to create and reproduce deviance and marginality instead of combating them.[5] Similar concerns are expressed by movements that criticize private groups of professionals (for example, certain sectors of the medical establishment, pharmaceutical companies, and so on) accused of subordinating care for service users to organizational and economic logics (Scotch 1988; Desario 1988; J. Gamson 1989; Chesler 1991; Oliver and Campbell 1996).

In the industrial society, a (relatively) clear distinction between public and private allowed people to define citizenship rights as a complex of civil opportunities (relating, for example, to freedom of expression and association), political opportunities (relating to the right to vote, for example), and social benefits (relating to access to minimum levels of well-being and education) without any further qualifications (Marshall 1976). These rights, in fact, referred to the citizen as understood generically – usually male, adult, Western. Mobilization aimed at extending rights of citizenship entailed provision of the same set of entitlements to social groups which had been excluded: illiterate and nonaffluent people, but also women and ethnic minorities (Barbalet 1988).

Towards the end of the twentieth century, however, various factors have revealed the problematic nature of this notion of citizenship. Not only has it been pointed out how Marshall's model was hardly applicable in countries other than Britain (Giddens 1983; Barbalet 1988), but also a series of structural processes have undermined previously taken-for-granted understandings. With the consolidation of the presence of women in the public sphere (in both professional and political terms), the contradiction has become clear between rights formally recognized as universal, and existing forms of organization of family and professional life which have restricted women's enjoyment of those rights. Immigration waves to Western countries have made the problem more urgent of how to articulate citizens' rights in such a way as to allow for the existence of different cultural groups. Particularly, the growing number of nonnational residents pushed for an adaptation of the very notion of citizenship rights, with the effects of various degrees of protection for different "shades" of citizenship (Bonazzi and Dunne 1994; Soysal 1994; Cesarani and Fulbrick 1996).

Numerous initiatives have also been launched in defense of the rights of children and more generally of minors. On some occasions, these mobilizations have taken on a broad political meaning. The most visible event so far has probably been the "White March" that in October 1996, in Belgium, gave voice to public outrage at the protection offered by some state bodies to a group of criminal pedophiles. With the parents of the murdered children among its chief promoters, the march was the peak in a wave of mass protests which questioned the legitimacy of the Belgian elites as a whole. In this case, identification with a relatively specific cause – no matter how emotionally charged –

provided the basis for mobilizations with a far broader political impact (Cartuyvels et al. 1997; Tondeur 1997; Rihoux and Walgrave 1997; Walgraave and Maassens 2000).

All these examples suggest that, although the nation-state and modern citizenship rights took their inspiration from universal identities, other possible sources of collective identity and of conflict have not disappeared. Other criteria regularly appear alongside those of a functionalist or universal type, to define collective actors. These are based on "ascribed" traits such as gender, ethnic origin, or age. In consequence, citizenship appears to be less a set of endowments, and more a process of a conflicting nature, where what is at stake are the criteria defining what a citizen is.[6] The fact that the state has widened its scope for intervention only makes the political nature of those asymmetries and inequalities more obvious.[7]

2.3.2 Cultures and countercultures

Growing differentiation in lifestyles represents another source of "problematization" of social identities. In a world in which class allegiances seem fragmented and political ideologies are in crisis, cultural consumption, use of one's free time, ways of organizing one's emotional life, eating habits, or styles of clothes can all represent a powerful factor for diversification and, in the final analysis, of new stratification, among social groups (Bourdieu 1984; Eder 1993). In many cases, it is simply an issue of individual consumer behavior, no different from other fashion phenomena. In other cases, however, lifestyle becomes the stake in conflicts regarding the legitimacy of emerging cultural forms or the defense of traditional ones.

Youth movements and other oppositional countercultures provide examples of how individual lifestyle may take up an antagonistic character. The emergence of punk at the end of the 1970s had elements which could easily be reduced to fashion, but also a powerful symbolic antagonism, in the sense of breaking away from consolidated canons of decorum and good taste. In other words it also had a distinctive countercultural flavor. Similar remarks may apply to other forms of youth cultural experience, from rap to rave.[8] More recently, alternative cultures and lifestyles have been nurtured in the Italian and Spanish squatted youth centers, as well as in the radical wing of the antiroad movement in the UK (Doherty 1998; della Porta, Andretta, Mosca, and Reiter 2005). In the late twentieth century, various sectors of social movements have indeed reserved considerable space to action concerning consumer goods and cultural elaboration. Women's, squatters', or youth movements have promoted the construction of alternative networks offering autonomous opportunities for support and social contacts to their participants (Melucci 1984a; Lyons 1988; Taylor and Whittier 1992).

In other cases, collective action on lifestyles has been concerned with the defense of values and traditions which, it was held, were threatened. Movements such as the American Moral Majority or those against the introduction of divorce in Italy in the early years of the 1970s also chose the private sphere and the criteria by which one can define a particular lifestyle as ethically desirable as their favored terrain for political mobilization (Wood and Hughes 1984; Wallis and Bruce 1986; Oberschall 1993: ch. 13).

The growing importance of lifestyle has also led to consumerism becoming a specific object of collective action. The consumer has been increasingly identified as a political, and not simply as an economic, actor. Consumer organizations have addressed their mobilization attempts to the public in general. Structures for the production and distribution of alternative goods, for example in the food sector, have been created; campaigns and mobilizations in favor of consumers have also been launched. They have taken forms ranging from quasi-countercultures (for example, in the alternative networks promoting and distributing organic food in the early stages of environmental movements) to classic public interest-group action (for example, in the form of mass professional organizations like Common Cause) (McFarland 1984; Forbes 1985; Gronmo 1987; Mayer 1989; Pinto 1990; Ranci 1992). Fair trade and boycotts have grown enormously in recent years, with a particularly successful trend among young people (Micheletti 2003; see also chapter 7 below).

Although not always connected with each other, all these activities, from different points of view, draw our attention once again to the new importance assumed by collective action concerned with the defense of certain models of behavior and moral codes, rather than with the conquest of political power or the protection of economic interests. Various transformations in the private sphere and in forms of cultural production appear to have increased potential for conflicts of a symbolic nature. The variety of life experiences to which the individual has access is a result of the multiplication of group allegiances. Each of these can provide relationship and identity resources essential in turning some of the possible sources of inequality into a public debate, defining them as social problems rather than individual difficulties. As Pierre Bourdieu observes, indeed, "Each society, at each moment, elaborates a body of social problems taken to be legitimate, worthy of being debated, of being made public and sometimes officialized and, in a sense, guaranteed by the state" (1992: 236; emphasis in the original). Typically, on the issue of unemployment, mobilization efforts are thwarted by the widespread feelings among the unemployed that their economic difficulties derive from individual failures. A precondition for protest is the shift to a conception of unemployment as a problem of society which requires public authorities to intervene.

None of these specific social problems have succeeded, however, in becoming the primary source of identity, able to represent the central criteria for the organization of action, comparable with that of class or national allegiance in the industrial society (see, for example, Melucci 1996). In parallel, the map of adversaries against which collective energies can, from time to time, be mobilized is equally varied: mass media, technoscientific elites, educational and social welfare institutions, entrepreneurial classes which control mass consumption, and so on. In this situation of uncertainty, instead of representing the preconditions for action concerned with economic or political goals, the definition of collective identity tends to become an autonomous problem, an object of collective action as such (although this may also apply to class conflict: Pizzorno 1978). The same thing can be said about the search for lifestyles and ways of acting which are ethically desirable and appropriate. These needs do not result inevitably in the development of social movements. For example, dissatisfaction with the contemporary urban lifestyle does not necessarily lead to support for environmental movements; it can take a variety of forms, from political engagement in a traditional political party to, quite simply, the transformation of individual consumer behavior, a sense of personal alienation, or deviant behavior. Yet the growth of needs linked to identity represents potential for conflict around which movement action can, under favorable conditions, develop.

2.3.3 Between the global and the local

Identities are increasingly defined within a process of accelerated cultural globalization. Globalization has produced significant cultural changes in today's world, a growing interdependence in which social actions in a given time and place are increasingly influenced by actions that occur in distant places. As Giddens suggested (1990: 64), globalization implies the creation and intensification of a "worldwide social relationship which links distinct localities in such a way that local happenings are shaped by events occurring miles away and vice versa." The shortening of space and time in communication processes affects the production and reproduction of goods, culture, and the tools for political regulation. Indeed, globalization has been defined as "a process (or set of processes) which embodies a transformation in the spatial organization of social relations and transactions – assessed in terms of their extensity, intensity, velocity and impact – generating transcontinental or interregional flows and networks of activity" (Held et al. 1999: 16).

One of the dangers perceived in globalization is the predominance of a single way of thinking, which apparently emerged from the defeat of "real socialism." The international system had been tied to a bipolar structure in which each of the two blocs represented a different ideology; the fall of the Berlin Wall, which symbolically marked the demise of the Eastern bloc, made capitalism seem the single, dominant model. In cultural terms, "modernization" processes promoted by science and the leisure industry have paved the way for what Serge Latouche has called "the westernization of the world" (1989), i.e., the spread on a global scale of Western values and beliefs. Although the scenario of a single "McDonaldized" world culture (Ritzer 1996: 2000) is an exaggeration, there is an undeniable increase in cultural interactions with the exportation – albeit filtered through local culture – of Western cultural products and values (Robertson 1992). The metaphor of a "global village" stresses that we are targeted in real time by messages sent from the most faraway places. The spread of satellite TV and the internet have made instantaneous communication possible, easily cross-ing national boundaries.

While national and subnational identities do not fade, the impact of values from other cultures and the growth of interaction between cultures increase the number of identifications that interweave into and compete with those anchored in the territory. Globalization is not only "out there" but also "in here" (Giddens 1990: 22): it transforms everyday life and leads to local resistance oriented to defending cultural traditions against the intrusion of foreign ideas and global issues. The resurgence of forms of nationalism, ethnic movements, religious mobilizations, and Islamic (and other) fundamentalism(s) are in part a reaction to this type of intrusion. While cultural globalization risks causing a loss of national identity, new technologies also provide a formidable array of tools for global mobilization, easing communication between worlds once distant, with a language that defies censorship. Increased perception of issues as global also heightens people's willingness to mobilize at a transnational level. Through the presence of transnational networks of ethnocultural communities, local tradi-tions also become delocalized and re-adapt to new contexts (Thompson 1995).

2.4 Structural Transformations, New Conflicts, New Classes

The processes of structural change, which we discussed briefly in the preceding pages, contribute in various ways to the weakening of the bases of traditional social conflicts and their recent reemergence in new forms. It is more debatable whether it is possible to establish a global characterization of new conflicts on this basis. The transformations we have discussed – and even more so the inter-pretations that different scholars have provided of them – seem to point in diver-gent and sometimes contradictory directions.

2.4.1 Still classes?

Various of the changes we have mentioned point at two common elements. First, there is a marked increase of activities linked to the production of knowledge and to symbolic manipulation, and the identification in the control of those activities as a major stake of conflict. The development of an advanced administrative/service sector in fact reflects the growing relevance in the economic sphere of information-processing, compared with the transformation of natural resources. The same expansion of areas of state intervention, which leads to the multiplication of identities and of politically based interests, makes ever more essential the role of decision-makers and communicators able to develop efficient syntheses between heterogeneous concerns and values.

Second, many recent transformations have produced the potential for conflicts which cut across conventional distinctions between the private and public spheres. Evidence of this includes the influence that certain styles of scientific knowledge and certain ways of organizing it have on the psychophysical well-being of the individual (for example, in the field of therapies and the health services). Alternatively, one may think of the public and collective relevance of individual consumer behavior and ways of life, which previously would have been relegated to the private sphere. Or, again, one might consider the importance of ascribed traits such as ethnicity or gender in conflicts concerning the extension and full realization of citizens' rights.

These processes point at a specific area of nonmaterial conflicts. Their stake is represented by the control of resources which produce meaning, and which allow actors to intervene not only on their own environment but also on the personal sphere, and above all on the link between these two levels. Rather than economic or political power, contemporary social conflict has, according to this view, more to do with the production and circulation of information; social conditions for production and the use of scientific knowledge; and the creation of symbols and cultural models concerned with the definition of individual and collective identities. This thesis has been formulated in a number of ways and with various levels of theoretical generalization (Touraine 1981; Lash and Urry 1987; Melucci 1989, 1996; Eder 1993), although somewhat diverse conclusions have been drawn as far as the relationship between structure, conflict, and movement is concerned.

In order to try to make sense of what is undoubtedly a highly diversified debate we must first of all keep in mind that those who investigate the relationship between structure, class, and collective action sometimes move from rather different points of departure, and use the same terms in quite different ways. To begin with, we must note the difference between a "historical" and a "structural" (Eder 1995) or "analytical" (Melucci 1995) concept of class. In the first meaning, class is a historical product of capitalist society (referring in other words to the working and the capitalist class, and to the specific structural processes which produced and reinforced their identity). In the second, a class is a group of people with similar "relationships within which social resources are produced and appropriated" (Melucci 1995: 117). The inequalities in power and status, peculiar to postindustrial society, might well not be conducive to the reproduction of industrial class conflict, but still provide the structural roots for the emergence of new collective actors. The tension between these two different approaches has affected recent debates on the persistence of class as a factor shaping conventional political behavior, and in particular, electoral participation (Dalton et al. 1984; Dalton 1988; Heath et al. 1991; Clark and Lipset 1991; Franklin et al. 1992; Pakulski and Waters 1996; Wright 1996; Manza and Brooks 1996; Szelenyi and Olvera 1996).[9]

A second issue among those who still recognize the relevance of structural interpretations regards the existence of a hierarchical structure of different types of conflicts, and the possibility of identifying core conflicts comparable to those which according to dominant interpretations shaped the industrial society. The most coherent attempt to identify the core conflicts of postindustrial (or "programmed") society has been Alain Touraine's.[10] According to him, the category of social movement fulfills a fundamental task, both in defining the rules by which society functions and in determining the specific goal of sociology: "The sociology of social movements" writes Touraine (1981: 30), "cannot be separated from a representation of society as a system of social forces competing for control of a cultural field." That is, the way in which each society functions reflects the struggle between two antagonistic actors who fight for control of cultural concerns which, in turn, determine the type of transforming action which a society performs upon itself (Touraine 1977: 95–6). It is in relation to the concept of historicity – defined by the interweaving of a system of knowledge, a type of accumulation, and a cultural model – that different types of society can be identified, along with the social classes which accompany them. Touraine identifies four types of society, each featuring a distinctive pair of central antagonistic actors: agrarian, mercantile, industrial, and "programmed" (a term which he prefers to "postindustrial" society). A particular trait of the programmed society is the "production of symbolic goods which model or transform our representation of human nature and the external world" (Touraine 1987: 127; 1985). It is the control of information that constitutes the principal source of social power. In consequence, conflicts tend to shift from the workplace to areas such as research and development, the elaboration of information, biomedical and technical sciences, and the mass media. The central actors in social conflict are no longer classes linked to industrial production but groups with opposing visions concerning the use and allocation of cognitive and symbolic resources. In contrast with Marxism, classes are not defined only in relation to the system of production (see, for example, Miliband 1989), and class action is, in fact, the "behavior of an actor guided by cultural orientations and set within social relations defined by an unequal connection with the social control of these orientations" (Touraine 1981: 61). As for Pierre Bourdieu, the cultural sphere is the main place for the exercise of social domination. However, Touraine differs from the deterministic approach of his French colleague in that he conceives social movements as struggling to influence the cultural sphere (Girling 2004).

Mobilizations by social movements address, therefore, the defense of the autonomy of civil society from the attempts of public and private technocratic groups to extend their control over ever-widening areas of social life.[11] If Touraine's formulation places the analysis of conflicts and movements in the center of his general theoretical model, other scholars have still paid attention to the structural dimension, but without attempting to identify new dominant cleavages. Originally influenced by Touraine, Alberto Melucci held to be improbable the emergence of new conflicts with a centrality comparable to that of the capital–labor conflict of the industrial society.[12] Melucci has never denied the persistent importance of traditional conflicts based on inequalities of power and wealth, and of the political actors, protagonists of these conflicts. However, he has identified the peculiarity of contemporary conflicts in processes of individualization which still have their roots in structural dynamics, yet of a different kind – for example, the pervasive influence of caring institutions over the self, the globalization of communications and life experiences, the growth of media systems. And he has denied the possibility of reducing responses to these differentiated structural tensions to any sort of unified paradigm of collective action. The latter – itself in a variety of forms – is, rather, just one of innumerable options open to individuals struggling for an autonomous definition of their self.

2.4.2 New middle classes for new social movements?

The relationship between structural change and new conflicts has also been viewed from another perspective. A number of scholars have stressed the fact that social change has produced a new social stratum – the so-called new middle class. According to this point of view, this class is able, as a result of the resources it controls and of its position, to play a central role in new conflicts. For some time, analyses of postindustrial society have revealed, in parallel with the growth of the administrative/service sector in society, the emergence of social groups which stand out, because of their level of education, the roles they play, and their specific social location, from the traditional middle classes (Bell 1973; Gouldner 1979; Goldthorpe 1982; Lash and Urry 1987; Scott 1990). The new middle class, according to these analyses, is constituted from sectors of the population that tend to be employed in the service sector: they are highly educated, yet are not comparable with managers or traditional professionals. As a result of their technical and cultural competence and of their economic-functional position, members of the new middle class are more likely to mobilize in conflicts of the new type we have just described: that is, to fight against technocrats, public and private agencies engaged in the dissemination of information and in the construction of consensus, the military and the apparatus responsible for social control. This argument has been presented on numerous occasions in recent years, and several investigations have confirmed the persistent presence of the new middle class among sympathizers and activists of the new movements.[13]

However, it is unclear whether the link between the new middle class, new movements, and new types of conflict effectively demonstrates the existence of a specific structural base for these types of conflict. The presence *en masse* of the new middle class in protest movements could, in fact, simply reflect the traditional inclination of the intellectual middle class to participate in any type of conflict (Bagguley 1992, 1995a; Pakulski 1995) – their greater confidence in their own rights and capacity to speak up and participate in political life (Bourdieu 1984). From this perspective, the reference to specific structural contradictions at the base of new conflicts somewhat loses consistency. It is, rather, the case that belonging to the middle class, on the one hand, facilitates the taking up of concerns which are generically favorable to public involvement; and on the other, puts at one's disposal individual resources and competences which can be spent in various types of political action.

In effect, comparative analysis of political participation has revealed on numerous occasions that variables of a sociodemographic type tend to explain with equal efficacy both unconventional participation (particularly widespread among movement sympathizers and activists) and conventional participation. There is, for example, a strong correlation between two factors that are usually regarded as indicators of the new middle class – youth and a high level of education – and various types of political attitudes and/or political participation (Barnes et al. 1979; Jennings et al. 1990; Opp 1989: ch. 7; Norris 2002: 201 ff.). Intellectuals have traditionally constituted the leadership of ethnic movements (Smith 1981). Furthermore, some comparisons between political ecology movements and more traditional environmentalist currents show that activists from the new middle class are present in equal measure in both sectors, in spite of the fact that it is difficult to identify conservationist groups as new social movements (Diani 1995a: 58).

Rather than on peculiar class dynamics, the undeniable relationship between membership in the new middle class and involvement in contemporary protest movements might well be dependent on yet other factors. For example, it might be the outcome of the enormous rise in access to higher education, which again originated in the 1960s. More specifically, higher education might not only provide people with distinctive intellectual skills; it might also foster the growth of an egalitarian and anti-authoritarian set of values, which are overrepresented among at least some sectors of the new middle class (Rootes 1995). Alternatively, youth radicalism might be related to generational experiences, as the current members of the new middle classes have all been exposed to that particular combination of social conditions, consisting of the end of the Cold War and the spread to the middle classes of unprecedented economic prosperity (Pakulski

1995: 76; Braungart and Braungart 1986, 1992). Or there might be lifecycle effects, as younger people's political involvement might be dependent on their biographical availability, given their more uncertain status, their still unsettled professional life, and their greater independence from family and community linkages (Piven and Cloward 1992; Crook et al. 1992: 146–7; *contra* Inglehart 1985, 1990a).

Moreover, the notion of middle class risks comprising quite heterogeneous social sectors: those who work in the sector of culture and personal services and those who fulfill managerial or other technocratic functions risk remaining unclear; the sectors of the new middle class which are closer to the problems of the management of organizations (managers) and those who, instead, draw their legitimacy and their status from being controllers of professional resources, independent of specific organizational structures (professionals) (Kriesi 1993: 31–2). In particular, the process of globalization is supposed to produce new cleavages between "winners" and "losers" *within* the middle class (Kriesi 2003). To evaluate appropriately the importance of the new middle class in social movements, it is useful, therefore, to differentiate between its internal components. Taking inspiration from Wright (1985), who regards classes as defined by different combinations of "assets in the means of production, organizational assets and skills or credentials," Hanspeter Kriesi has identified the distinctive characteristic of the new middle class in the fact that it exercises some control over organizational resources and/or over professional skills, but does not possess the means of production (Kriesi 1993: 28; see also Kriesi 1989b).[14] In particular, it is necessary to look at three different sectors of the new middle class: alongside the "sociocultural specialists"[15] are managers and those who fulfill clearly technical roles. This last group includes administrative and commercial personnel from public and private organizations, technical specialists – some highly qualified and others less so – and those working in "protective services" (the police, the army, civil protection organizations, and the like).

Awareness of the various components of the new middle class and evaluation of their impact on political participation, alongside that of those belonging to the traditional classes (the old middle class and the working class) help to interpret more accurately the relationship between class condition and (new) forms of participation. According to a survey in the Netherlands, managers and sociocultural professionals are indeed more prone than any other socioeconomic group to mobilize in new movements, even when controlling for variables which, in theory, correlate, such as education and salary levels (Kriesi 1993: 196 ff.). Furthermore, this tendency is stronger among people under 40 years of age, a fact that supports the hypothesis of a link between movements and recent transformations of the middle classes (1993: 198). This appears even more significant if one considers that in general, class position explains movement participation better than participation in traditional party politics; and that this emerges from

a context in which the impact of class variables on politics appears, to many analysts, in decline (see also Dalton 1988: ch. 8; *contra* Heath et al. 1991).

These data are consistent with what has emerged from the analysis of environmentalist militancy (Cotgrove and Duff 1980; Jamison, Eyerman, and Cramer
1990; Dalton 1994: ch. 5; Diani 1995a). Those filling the highest positions in
groups engaged in this kind of activity are not only highly educated and – in the
broadest sense – members of the middle class, but also bring specific competences to bear on the work of the group. The case of environmentalism and,
more generally, of new movements analyzed by Kriesi, shows both the continuity and the discontinuity in the relationship between the educated middle classes
and political participation. The central position of intellectual groups in collective action – a constant trait in modern society – has not been challenged by
recent developments. At the same time, however, the competences and the
overall profile of the middle-class activists seem to adapt themselves to what is
at stake in "new" conflicts.

Analyses of the link between individual class location and political behavior
have certainly brought to light a series of relevant characteristics of new forms
of political participation. They have, in particular, provided important information about old and new social movement activists and sympathizers. In doing so,
however, they have postulated a direct link between the structural position of
individuals and collective action that is by no means clear-cut. In fact, while it is
possible to look at classes as aggregates of subjects who occupy analogous positions in the system of social stratification, in terms of the resources they control,
the prestige they enjoy, and their social opportunities, this is not necessarily an
appropriate strategy when dealing with the problem of collective action.[16]

Alternatively, it is advisable to analyze classes as collective actors with a specific identity and self-awareness, and linked to other social groups by relationships of a cooperative or conflicting nature. In this perspective, class exists only
in circumstances where people mutually recognize and are recognized as part of
a distinctive social group, if specific interests and solidarity between the occupants of particular social positions have been identified, and if, on this basis, specific forms of collective action are to be promoted (Thompson 1963; Tilly 1978;
Touraine 1981; Fantasia 1988; Urry 1995).

This perspective maintains that structural changes (for example, in the
economy or in the private sphere) provide a basis for the development of new
political identities, and new criteria for the organization of conflict, only in cases
where these are the object of explicit political action (Bartolini and Mair 1990;
Kriesi et al. 1995). As Martin Lipset and Stein Rokkan (1967) observed, a cleavage is in fact a politicized interest. The major class distinctions of industrial
society operated as criteria for the organization of political conflict because class
mobilization had been made possible by extended networks linking class-based
organizations and class communities among themselves as well as to sectors of

other social groups with a more ambiguous location, in particular the middle classes. In this way, two clear-cut antagonists – working class and bourgeoisie – had finally emerged out of the complex structure of preindustrial society. Likewise, for a new cleavage to emerge, based on the new middle class – however defined – and/or providing a stable political articulation to the new structural tensions we have just discussed, specific political organizations and systems of both individual and group relationships have to develop. However, to date, this seems to have occurred only very partially.

In the first place, it is still unclear to what extent the new middle class/service class will be able to consolidate as a specific collective actor, and develop a relatively stable collective identity. The question is particularly appropriate, given the multiplicity of social positions and roles in which what is defined as the new middle class is actually fragmented; and given that frequent mobility – between social positions as well as locality – is regarded as one distinctive trait of postindustrial society (hardly a property conducive to the establishment of the networks needed to turn an aggregate into a collective actor) (Crook et al. 1992: 117; Eder 1995; Urry 1995; Melucci 1995, 1996).

The relationship between new middle class and traditional middle class seems to be equally ambiguous (Offe 1985).[17] Many observers have referred to traditional middle-class groups as social sectors "threatened by modernization and by change." According to this reading – which is popular among scholars of the anti-nuclear movements (Rüdig 1990; Flam 1994d; see also Klandermans and Tarrow 1988; Pichardo 1997) – contemporary social movements also organize, in part, the protest of those social groups (such as shopkeepers or, in general, the autonomous petite bourgeoisie) who see their status threatened by socioeconomic transformation. New and old middle classes often build alliances in citizens' committees organized against "locally unwanted land uses" (della Porta 2004c).

From this perspective, opposition to nuclear power, and indeed to other dangerous plant, is not only the sign of a progressive shift towards battles around "postindustrial" conflicts such as those relating to the control of development. It also shows the diffidence of the traditional middle classes towards activities and technical competences that are outside their traditional domain, such as high-tech applications; the signs of moral revolt against the subordination of "traditional" values to the imperatives of efficiency and modernity; the reaction to the threat which derives from living with a potential source of environmental damage. Similar considerations could be applied to the propensity of the middle-classes to mobilize in opposition to situations perceived to be threatening to their own prestige and social decorum, such as in the case of protests against crime and urban deviance, or those against migrants. These traits are not restricted to movements with a clear right-wing connotation; in contrast, many "new" social movements (including, but not exclusively, environmentalism) also seem to present more than sporadic characteristics typical of traditional, defensive middle-class moral protest (Eder 1993, 1995).

In other words, conditions favoring the return of various forms of status politics seem to have been reproduced. In these, the central role is taken by social groups brought together by certain levels of prestige and specific moral codes (Turner 1988; Eder 1993). Telling against the more structural version of the middle-class thesis, the attention paid by the middle class to its own group identity and positioning is certainly not a characteristic exclusive to recent mobilizations (Calhoun 1993; D'Anieri et al. 1990). As the historical experience of the anti-alcohol movement reminds us (Gusfield 1963), the middle class has distinguished itself over time by its continual attention to moral codes, socially acceptable rules of conduct, and principles defining the "good life." Reasons for this attitude are to be found in the historically ambiguous positioning of the middle classes between the industrial bourgeoisie and the working class. Indeed, the petite bourgeoisie came to focus on symbolic production and on the defense of its own social status as a result of its uncertain place in the class system. For similar reasons, they may have felt the need to differentiate themselves from the principal social groups, and particularly from those – the industrial proletariat, throughout the twentieth century – which most closely threatened their prestige (Turner 1994; Calhoun 1993; Oberschall 1993: ch. 13; Eder 1993, 1995). At the same time, there are reasons to argue that substantial differences separate many recent examples of lifestyle politics from the traditional version of status politics. As Featherstone (1987) notes, reference to values and lifestyles does not necessarily characterize distinctive groups with specific identities and long-established structures. Actors involved in collective action may actually share little, apart from the common reference to a given set of values and preferences (see also Wood and Hughes 1984; Crook et al. 1992, esp. p. 144; Urry 1995).

The relationship between new middle class and working class is not any clearer, nor has it been the subject of massive in-depth investigation. In the case of the Netherlands study by Kriesi, it seems, for example, that even belonging to the working class can facilitate mobilization in new movements, particularly as far as younger people are concerned. Thus there would appear to be at least a partial convergence in the new movements of those social groups which were already particularly active in "historical" opposition movements: there is a certain continuity, in other words, between "old" and "new" forms of class opposition. Also in the global justice movement, a heterogeneous social base has been highlighted as an innovative feature or an enhancement by comparison to movements of the past (Epstein 2000; Gill 2000; Ayres 2004; Piven and Cloward 2000; Andretta, della Porta, Mosca, and Reiter 2002 and 2003).

In sum, if there is ample evidence suggesting the emergence of new structural conflicts, the forms of these conflicts and their capacity to persist over time is far from obvious. We would like to close our discussion by mentioning a few further reasons for caution. First, there is no evidence that the material and redistributive dimension has lost all significance in conflicts in which contemporary, nonworking-class movements are protagonists (Brooks and Manza 1994: 562–3). For example, mobilizations for the development of collective services in urban areas and for urban renewal have certainly been determined by powerful concerns with collective and nonmaterial goods, such as those associated with the quality of life. However, they have also focused on the redistribution of material resources, placing the social groups most penalized by transformations in industrial activity and by processes of urban renewal in opposition to economic groups which were the protagonists and promoters of these processes (Castells 1977, 1983, 1997; Lowe 1986; Feagin and Capek 1991; Bagguley 1994). These struggles have often seen the emergence of new alliances between working-class and community groups (Brecher and Costello 1990). Furthermore, new forms of collective action have emerged based on conditions of particular unease, concerned, for example, with the struggle against "new poverties." Movements and mobilizations of homeless people have developed (Cress and Snow 1996); initiatives supporting the unemployed and marginal groups have sprung up everywhere, often in close collaboration with the voluntary sector (Bagguley 1991, 1995b; Pearce 1993). In all these cases, the conflict has been concerned, once again, not only with a general notion of the quality of life, but with the allocation of material rewards among different social groups. Attention to social justice and material conditions (such as poverty) became – as often mentioned – central in the recent wave of protest against neoliberal globalization.

One should also note that, according to many observers, contemporary movements do not necessarily demonstrate a radical ongoing transformation in the stakes of collective action as well as in its actors. Movements of recent years should rather be regarded as a manifestation of the difficulties representative systems have in dealing with the new demands which social change inevitably produces. From this perspective, "new movements" are not necessarily the reflection of global structural transformations, or forerunners of the rise of new criteria to determine the structure of political conflicts. They are, rather, the next in a long series of manifestations of the cyclical nature of political protest.[18] This objection is a serious one, particularly when aimed at inappropriate or hurried generalizations concerning elements of "newness" revealed in recent years. It is important to be aware that not all examples of collective action in recent decades are automatically of the new type. The 1960s and 1970s have seen not only the rise of new political phenomena but also the revival of initiatives taken by "old" collective actors such as the working class and ethnolinguistic minorities. The latter's capacity for mobilization has manifested itself in a variety of forms in recent years (Smith 1981; Melucci and Diani 1992; Breuilly 1993; Connor 1994).

At the same time, however – as Alberto Melucci, in particular, has remarked on several occasions (1988, 1994, 1995, 1996) – the question of the newness of contemporary phenomena of collective action should be treated on an analytical rather than on an empirical level. Looking at the empirical characteristics of a given historical social movement (from the environmental movement [Jordan and Maloney 1997] to the women's movement [Roseneil 1995; Walby 1997] to the working-class movement [Calhoun 1982]) will inevitably lead to the discovery of a mix of both "new" and "old" actors, "new" and "old" conflicts (not to mention "new" and "old" repertoires of action: chapter 7, this volume). However, what really matters is – according to Melucci – assessing the newness of certain specific processes in terms of their centrality to the systemic properties of advanced societies. For example, emphasis on the collective identity of a social group is by no means restricted to contemporary movements. But what renders this process peculiar, and therefore "new," in postindustrial society is its centrality, due to the current dominance of symbolic production, and of the social relationships which shape it (for a critique of Melucci's argument see Pickvance 1995).

2.5 Summary

In this chapter we have asked ourselves whether looking at the social structure and at changes in this may provide a useful key to the interpretation of collective action. We have examined a series of recent modifications to the social and political structure, and their innovative potential in relation to consolidated lines of conflict structuring. The transformation of the economic sphere – in particular, the move to a more or less advanced service and administrative sector and the decentralization of industrial production – has undermined not only the numerical consistency of the working class but also the living and working conditions which facilitated class action. Today we face greater diversity in professional roles and interests. On the political side, the legitimacy of the state is called into question both by the tendency towards globalization and by that towards localization, but also by a retreat of the state in the face of the market. Furthermore, the capacity of the state to create and reproduce social groups through public intervention has led to an increasing number of demands which are fragmented and increasingly difficult to mediate. New potential for conflict originates therefore in the increasingly blurred borders between the public and the private spheres, particularly from the multiplication of criteria to define rights of citizenship and the growing capacity for intervention among public and private institutions, in areas of private life such as physical and mental health. Conflicts developed around the definition of new identities with particular attention to cultural issues, lifestyles, knowledge.

Mobilizations and movements have developed in recent years around interests involving actors who can be associated in various ways with the transformations which we have just reviewed. Scholars such as Touraine have identified the central conflicts in postindustrial society in struggles for the control of symbolic production. Others have emphasized the high level of involvement of new middle-class members in new conflicts, as a result of their particular professional position and of the intellectual resources which they control. However, the flexibilization of the labor market has produced increasing poverty in the North and the South; and the attack on the welfare state by dominant neoliberalist and free-market economic policies has produced the return of protest on "materialistic" issues of social justice.

It is important, however, to remember that collective action does not spring automatically from structural tensions. In this respect it is still doubtful that a new political cleavage, with the capacity to structure conflicts similar to that demonstrated by the capital–labor or the center–periphery cleavages in industrial society, has emerged, let alone been consolidated. Numerous factors determine whether or not this will occur. These factors include the availability of adequate organizational resources, the ability of movement leaders to produce appropriate ideological representations, and the presence of a favorable political context. The rest of our book is dedicated to the mechanisms which contribute to an explanation of the shift from structure to action.

THE SYMBOLIC DIMENSION OF COLLECTIVE ACTION

On November 6, 2000, *Business Week* devoted a special section to global justice campaigns. It wrote: "Many of the radicals leading the protests may be on the political fringe. But they have helped to kick start a profound rethinking about globalization among governments, mainstream economists, and corporations that, until recently, was carried on mostly in obscure think-tanks and academic seminars" (quoted in Bircham and Charlton 2001: 390). At the World Economic Forum in Davos, an annual meeting of the great and the good, finance guru George Soros said: "This protest movement is plugging into something that is widely felt. . . . by their disruption they have created a concern that was not there before" (ibid.).

These statements reflect dramatic changes in both the public visibility of "globalization" as an issue, and attitudes toward it. Until the 1990s, for public opinion worldwide and for many political actors, both in the institutions and at the grassroots, globalization was still a largely meaningless word. A decade later, it had become the key concept for anybody discussing social and political change.

The recent growth of the relevance of globalization in public discourse and the media (Andretta, della Porta, Mosca, and Reiter 2002: ch. 1) has seen an increasing number of actors – intellectuals, public agencies, private corporations, religious leaders, political activists, national and international nongovernmental organizations – attempting to define it, to stress the risks attached to it, as well as to highlight its promises (Nederveen Pieterse 2000; Ayres 2004). Although they are increasingly acknowledging its attendant problems, transnational business actors and international financial institutions are still the most unconditional supporters of globalization (Anheier, Glasius, and Kaldor 2001: 9–10). Deregulation and the resulting free trade of capital and goods are portrayed as the necessary preconditions for the start of sustained development processes outside the Western world. Far from only protecting powerful interests, economic globalization will generate diffuse well-being among the majority of the world population, thus also facilitating the spread of democratic practices. Accordingly, restrictions on financial and goods trade should be vehemently opposed, and major economic powers are fully justified in playing an active political role, including military action, in those countries where the freedom of markets and access to key resources is under threat.

Critics of neoliberal globalization can by no means be reduced to the so-called antiglobalization movement, or movement for a globalization from below. They also include to a varying extent transnational institutions and agencies, such as the FAO or UNESCO, skeptical experts, mainstream media, churches, etc. However, even those civil-society actors most frequently associated with the movement (radical activist networks, religious organizations, industrial and farmers' unions, community activists, environmental groups, left-wing political parties) still define the issue and represent the main goals and strategies of the movement in very different ways. In its identification of globalization as an overarching theme, this movement has been able to link together many other specific issues and concerns: questions of environmental preservation and social justice; questions of workers' rights in developed countries and rights of developing countries to obtain easier access to Northern markets, an outcome that the mix of protectionist policies and nationalism among the Northern labor movement had made difficult to achieve in the recent past; equilibrium between local community rights and traditions and aspirations to global, universalistic cultures.

There are several points worth noting in the above example. First, issues do not have an independent life outside of people's efforts to characterize them as such. Many of the problems that the antiglobalization movement faces nowadays were already there well before the word "globalization" started circulating (Tilly 2004a; Wallerstein 1974, 2004). Hunger and disease in non-Western countries, war, imperialism, and colonialism had been tackled by sustained collective action innumerable times in the postwar world, not to mention earlier cases such as the human rights and antislavery movements, or nationalistic movements with a transnational basis (Hobsbawm 1994: ch. 15; D'Anjou 1996; Hanagan 1998b). That they now come under the heading of globalization cannot be explained exclusively by the growing interdependence between nation-states and supranational bodies. One also has to look at how social actors have elaborated definitions of those issues that link them to a broader process, called globalization.

Second, the emergence of issues is not an obvious process. In contrast, it originates from sustained symbolic and cultural conflict between different actors. At one level, globalization becomes either a catchword to synthesize all the positives and gains one can get from the removal of commercial barriers and the global triumph of the free market; or a catchword for all the evils, misery, and exploitation that total dominance by market forces can generate. At another level, however, there are substantive differences in ways that actors define globalization despite being broadly favorable or critical of it. Even pro-market forces express different degrees of support; critics may oppose globalization in its entirety – as happens, say, among right-wing nationalist organizations – or rather favor a democratic, grassroots version of it.

Third, movements can also be regarded as the expression of specific values. Social movements not only aim at specific policy changes or the replacement of specific political elites, but at broader transformations in societal priorities, in the basic mechanisms through which a society operates. Within the new global movement we find the strong influence of values related to both the historical experience of the left and to religious experience. However, the question remains, what factors matter most? Is it values that shape social movement activity? Or is it instead movement actors' capacity to represent their concerns in ways that motivate people to act and broaden support for their cause? This dilemma reflects two different views of the relationship between culture and collective action.

Historically, the role of culture in collective action has been subsumed under the heading of ideology. Ideology is usually conceived as "a relatively stable and coherent set of values, beliefs, and goals associated with a movement or a broader, encompassing social entity, [. . .] assumed to provide the rationale for defending or challenging various social arrangements and conditions" (Snow 2004: 396). Think, e.g., of the debates between Marxist thinkers and political leaders arguing that culture – in particular, revolutionary culture – would stem from the development of productive forces and the appropriate material conditions; and those assigning ideology a more active role in encouraging activists and masses to act (e.g. Gramsci). Think also of the attention paid by social psychologists in the 1950s or 1960s to personalities attracted to ideological thinking (e.g. Kornhauser 1959; for a discussion see Snow 2004: 381).

The last few years have seen a deepening of the discussion of the role of culture in social movements. The broad framework is provided by the debate on structure and agency (Bourdieu 1977, 1990; Giddens 1984; Emirbayer and Mische 1988): social actors act in the context of structural constraints, which not only have to do with material resources but also with cultural ones. Actors' interpretations of their situation, their preconceptions, their implicit assumptions about social life and its guiding principles, about what is worthy or unworthy, all drastically constrain their capacity to act and the range of their options. At the same time, through action, agents also try – and sometimes succeed – in modifying the cultural structures in which they are embedded. Social agency is indeed at the same time oriented on the reproduction of its constraining structures, and the creation of new ones. This duplicity can be found even in the experience of social movements, which by definition should be the most oriented towards change (Sewell 1992; Crossley 2002; Livesay 2003).

This debate has also brought about a reassessment of the role and characteristics of ideology. Although the term has remained popular over the years (Turner and Killian 1987; Oliver and Johnston 2000; Zald 2000), it has come under growing criticism since the 1980s, for implying unrealistic levels of ideological coherence and integration, of ideological proximity among social movement participants, of correlation between ideas and behavior (see Snow 2004: 396 ff. for a summary; Melucci 1989, 1996 for a classic version of this critique).

The major critique has probably been that this notion of ideology collapses two quite different aspects of culture: values and the interpretative tools – habits, memories, prejudices, mental schemata, predispositions, common wisdom, practical knowledge, etc. – that enable people to make sense of their world (Swidler 1986). The two aspects do not necessarily operate in the same direction. For example, those who mobilize most readily and intensely are not necessarily those with the strongest values but those whose interpretation of the situation provides a clear rationale for acting (in terms of their perception not only of the opportunities to act, but also of the available alternatives or of the emotional pressure exerted on them). In what follows we address these two aspects separately, starting with values.

3.1 Culture and Action: The Role of Values

We may think of social action as driven largely by the fundamental principles with which actors identify. According to this perspective, values will influence how actors define specific goals, and identify strategies which are both efficient and morally acceptable. Moreover, values will provide the motivations necessary to sustain the costs of action. The more intense one's socialization to a particular vision of the world, the stronger the impetus to act. The characteristics of a given system of values will shape the components of action.

How is this model articulated in the case of collective action in movements? How, in other words, is it possible to describe values as the central explanatory variable in the case of actions which, by definition, call into question at least some of the (culturally legitimized) assets of power in a given society? On the one hand, we can relate collective action to lack of social integration in the system, or, alternatively, to the inability of the system to reproduce and reinforce its fundamental values. The tradition of research into movements prior to the

1960s, which largely focused on revolutionary movements of the right and the left in the first half of the century, paid great attention to interpretations of this type (Kornhauser 1959). Nowadays, according to this perspective, the emergence of global justice movements could be interpreted as evidence of the failure of society to instill free-market values among its members, most notably the younger generation. Not infrequently, for instance, schools are blamed by business for their hostility towards entrepreneurial culture, and neoliberal politicians (including recent recruits like Tony Blair: Beck 1999) have often criticized schools on the very same ground.

On the other hand, we could also interpret collective action as evidence of the emergence of trends towards social reintegration rather than disintegration; as proof, in other words, of the formation and consolidation of new value systems. From this point of view, the success of global justice activism could be linked to the spread of new values, combining in equal measure attention to social justice, human rights, environmental preservation. In recent times, the link between the emergence of new conflicts and the value dimension has been stressed with considerable force in the context of various forms of "new politics," connected with environmental issues, feminism, peace, and civil rights (Dalton 1988; Kriesi 1993: 60 ff.; Rohrschneider 1988; Norris 2002). In the most ambitious formulation of this model, the rise of "new" political movements from the 1970s onwards is associated with more general processes of value change (Inglehart 1977, 1990a, 1990b; Clark and Inglehart 1998). Inglehart's argument is based on two assumptions. According to what he defines as the "scarcity hypothesis" (Inglehart 1990a: 56), there is a hierarchy of needs, and needs of a higher order (relating, for example, to the intellectual and personal growth of the individual) are conceivable only when those of a lower order (relating, for example, to physical survival) have been satisfied. Moreover, according to the "socialization hypothesis" (Inglehart 1990a: 56), there is a continuity in adult life which leaves broadly unaltered both the fundamental principles and the order of priorities established in the formative years leading to maturity.

The experiences and lifestyles of those born in the West in the period following the Second World War, and who became adults in the 1960s or later, have been very different from those of preceding generations. In particular, they have enjoyed unprecedented levels of affluence, easier access to higher education, and reduced exposure to the risks of war. In Inglehart's view, this situation is likely to produce conditions which are particularly favorable to changes in needs and basic orientations. In particular, a gradual weakening of the system of "material" values and their replacement by "postmaterial" values is likely to set in. While the former reflects concerns relating to economic well-being and personal and collective security, the latter are oriented, rather, towards the affirmation of expressive needs. They would, in other words, prioritize individual achievement in private, and an expansion of freedom of expression, democratic participation, and self-government in the public domain.

In order to understand fully this phenomenon, it seems essential to characterize the 1960s as one of those rare moments in history which produced the conditions for a radical change in perspective. From this standpoint, one might argue that social transformations and events of particular relevance and impact, such as the fading away of the Cold War and generalized economic growth, produced an irreversible change in conceptions of social and political life, and that a new generation[1] of citizens (and, in many cases, of militant politicians) was formed. It would thus be possible to speak of a 1960s generation, just as one speaks of generations when referring to the events of 1848, of the post-Victorian era, or of the Great Depression of the 1920s and 1930s (Braungart and Braungart 1986: 217; Jamison and Eyerman 1994). The 1960s generation would have passed on – at least in part – these new conceptualizations to younger groups, even though political contexts subsequently differed greatly.[2]

The emergence of postmaterial values has been documented by an impressive amount of survey data collected in the USA and in key European countries from the beginning of the 1970s.[3] Since then, the gap between the number of people holding materialist values (i.e., in the basic formulation of the survey questionnaires, identifying "maintaining order in the nation" and "fighting rising prices" as their top policy priorities out of a list of four) and those holding postmaterialist values (i.e., assigning priority to "giving people more say in important government decisions" and "protecting freedom of speech") has narrowed substantially, even though materialists are still in the majority. Furthermore, the younger cohorts of the population have been shown to be consistently more sensitive to postmaterialist values than older cohorts (Inglehart 1990b: 75).

The empirical evidence relating to value change has generated a notable number of analyses of the new politics, the emergence of green parties, and the characteristics of activists and supporters of new movements (see e.g. Rohrschneider 1988, 1993b; Dalton 1988, 1994). They have demonstrated that those with postmaterial values are strongly disposed to support new forms of collective action or to take part in some way in protest activities (Inglehart 1990b). In particular, it has been suggested the situation has led to the development of new cleavages and the related processes of political realignment along materialist vs. postmaterialist lines (Dalton 1988; Jennings et al. 1990).

Inglehart's theses have provoked considerable debate. Suggestions that the growth of postmaterialist values might not be a sign of profound change but rather a transitory phenomenon, the consequence of an unrepeatable historical conjunction such as that which took place in the 1960s, have been dismissed by data showing that generational replacement actually results in a steady increase of postmaterialists among Western – and not only Western – publics (Abramson and Inglehart 1992; Inglehart 1990b; de Graaf and Evans 1996; Inglehart 1997, 1999; Inglehart and Baker 2000; Inglehart and Norris 2003).

The link between postmaterialist orientations and new social movements has also been questioned. Hostility towards the politics of "law and order" is certainly a distinctive characteristic of these movements. They have certainly mobilized on a number of occasions in support of freedom of expression and direct democracy. But they have equally promoted other mobilizations (for example against war, nuclear energy, or environmental pollution) which is difficult to consider independently from preoccupations with personal and collective security, or, in other words, from purely "materialist" concerns (Brooks and Manza 1994: 558–63).

Likewise, the value distance between the materialist and the postmaterialist camp might be at least partially an outcome of the way questions are posed, as they require people to choose between items measuring one or the other basic orientation.[4] When the possibility of a co-existence of the two value orientations is taken into account, more complex configurations may emerge. For example, in their study of grassroots activists in the Greater Vancouver area, Carroll and Ratner (1996) found that a political-economy representation of social conflict – broadly inspired by "materialist" concerns – often co-existed with a representation emphasizing the importance of identity struggles that was closer to a "postmaterialist" point of view. Moreover, an exclusive focus on the materialist vs. postmaterialist distinction might somewhat conceal another important distinction, opposing authoritarian and libertarian attitudes, which does not overlap with the former (Steel et al. 1992). Despite a substantial correlation between postmaterialism and support for new movements, the quota of postmaterialists embracing authoritarian, right-wing values (for example, opposing welfare spending, or advocating authoritarian policies of nature protection) is far from insignificant (Steel et al. 1992: 350–1; Middendorp 1992; Inglehart 1997: 48).

It is also necessary to ask to what extent postmaterialism can be said to represent the basis of a new political divide. In this context, it is important to take account of the relationship between the materialist–postmaterialist dimension and the more general identification with left and right. Given the tendency of new social movements to identify themselves with the left, the materialist–postmaterialist split might be said to be simply a reworking of the left–right division, thus denying the existence of new and different political perspectives. As yet, there is no conclusive evidence to support or refute this hypothesis. It is certainly the case that both party supporters and trade unionists in the "old" left tend to be postmaterialists, as do new left and new movement activists and sympathizers (Inglehart 1990a: ch. 11; 1990b: 90).

On the other hand, it is far from clear what the left–right dimension refers to in strict terms. At the very minimum, it can be deconstructed into two independent dimensions, one measuring orientations to socioeconomic issues, the other, orientations to libertarian versus authoritarian attitudes. Postmaterialism has sometimes been found to be a poor predictor of both types of orientations (Middendorp 1992; see also Kriesi 1993). With regard to the relationship between general left orientations and movements, it is only certain sectors of the left – from the noncommunist tradition – which seem to be clearly sympathetic to the new movements (Inglehart 1990a: ch. 11). Furthermore, while a generic identification with the left provides an adequate explanation for interest in the issues raised by the new movements, postmaterialism offers a better explanation of the willingness of individuals to participate in these movements (1990a). One might also argue that, rather than postmaterialism being the basis for a new political cleavage, the opposite interpretation could well be true. In other words, where a new cleavage has emerged for specific historical reasons (like in Germany, where the Greens have become a major political player), then this may well have been organized around the materialist vs. postmaterialist divide; where, however, this has not been the case (for example, in the USA), then postmaterialist values may not be associated with any specific political faction (Trump 1991).

Doubts about the relationship between movements and postmaterialism have been reinforced in recent years by two very different developments. On the one hand, the emergence of the antiglobalization movement has raised doubts about the link between postmaterialism and progressive politics. Admittedly, the shortage of surveys explicitly measuring attitudes towards this movement, and/or participation in it, renders it difficult to compare it with the new social movements. It is certainly true that a certain degree of overlap exists when it comes to mobilizations on peace/environmental/human rights issues. On such issues, the correlation to postmaterialism is well demonstrated (Norris 2002). And it is also true that surveys conducted among participants in major gatherings such as Genoa or the Florence European Social Forum suggest that many respondents (about 20 percent) refuse to locate themselves on the left–right cleavage. At the same time, however, global justice movements also address issues that are clearly materialist, related to basic working and living conditions, although they are often defined in a way which combines material interests with issues of sustainability, environmental protection, and the like. Moreover, the great majority of those who still regard the left–right distinction as meaningful identify with the left of the political spectrum: about 25 percent of activists interviewed at the European Social Forum in Florence located themselves on the extreme left side of the left–right continuum and 50 percent at the left, with an additional 10 percent choosing the center-left (della Porta, Andretta, Mosca, and Reiter 2005). Finally, while available data (Inglehart 1997; Norris 1999) suggest a positive relation between postmaterialism and democracy in both old and new democracies, they also suggest that postmaterialists are in favor of open global markets (again, this evidence is difficult to interpret as it could mean both a democratic and nondemocratic globalization).

The last few years have also brought about a totally different example of the link between values and collective action. Whereas the discussion had focused on values (in particular, value change) and participatory democratic politics, the reemergence of ethnic and tribal conflicts in many areas of the world, and most particularly the spread of fundamentalism (well before September 11 and not restricted to Islam: Moaddel 2002; Bennani-Chraïbi and Fillieule 2003; Woodberry and Smith 1998), has set a dramatically different intellectual agenda. Samuel Huntington's (1993, 1996) well-known "clash of civilization" thesis and cognate arguments, suggesting a fundamental conflict between Islam and the West, have assigned values a very different role than the one implied by postmaterialist theorists. They propose a view of social movements as deeply embedded in strongly held sets of values, which represent the stake for fundamental conflicts, susceptible of orienting future relations between major areas of the world.

However, empirical tests of this thesis suggest a more complex picture: contrary to expectations, Norris and Inglehart (2002) found attitudes towards democracy to be very similar in the two camps; but they also found deep and irreconcilable differences in the definition of private lifestyles, especially in gender relations and sexual freedom. This holds true despite the substantial presence of conservative Christian values in important Western countries, most notably the United States (Woodberry and Smith 1998). Norris and Inglehart's conclusion that "The central values separating Islam and the West revolve far more centrally around Eros than Demos" (2002: 3) brings further support to the argument of a gradual shift in priorities from "public politics" to "personal politics," and is not necessarily in contradiction with arguments about postmaterialist values in the West.

A more fundamental objection to the theory of value change addresses the relationship between values and action. If people's values can explain their fundamental sensitivity to particular questions and problems, their impact need not necessarily go beyond this level. In his study of civil rights activists in the US in the 1960s, McAdam (1986), for instance, found that prospective activists' commitment to values of freedom and equality was a poor predictor of their actual participation. Looking at survey data from several west European countries, Fuchs and Rucht (1994) found no correlation between broad support for environmentalism and participation. The decision to act – and, specifically, to act collectively – depends not only on basic internalized principles and/or attitudes but on a complex evaluation of the opportunities and constraints for action. Values are articulated through specific goals and are associated with strategies of appropriate conduct. It is thus necessary to interpret the external situation as favorable to action, or at least as requiring the mobilization of the individual, rather than withdrawal or conformity. And it is essential to be able to transform individual values into collective ones, identifying elements of convergence and solidarity with others sharing the same values (Klandermans 1988; Melucci 1989, 1996; Gamson 1992a).

In other words, it is necessary to have a view of reality which links the values domain with the strategic and solidaristic domain in a coherent fashion. Attention must also be paid both to the cognitive dimension of action, as we shall do in the following sections of this chapter, and to the relationship between action and collective identity – a theme which we consider in the next chapter.

3.2 Culture and Action: The Cognitive Perspective

3.2.1 Collective action as cognitive praxis

The idea that culture, and specifically its impact on collective action, can be reduced to values has been controversial for quite some time. In particular, it has been observed that "culture influences action not by providing the ultimate values toward which action is oriented, but by shaping a repertoire or 'tool kit' of habits, skills, and styles from which people construct 'strategies of action'" (Swidler 1986: 273). That is to say, culture provides the cognitive apparatus which people need to orient themselves in the world. This apparatus consists of a multiplicity of cultural and ideational elements which include beliefs, ceremonies, artistic forms, and informal practices such as language, conversation, stories, daily rituals (Swidler 1986: 273). The content of cultural models, of which values are a key component, is of secondary importance here in relation to the vision of culture as a set of instruments that social actors use to make sense of their own life experiences (see also Eyerman and Jamison 1991).

In relation to the study of collective action, this standpoint allows us to consider problems which an analysis focusing exclusively on values would have neglected. It helps us to reflect on why systems of analogous values are, in certain circumstances, able to support collective action but fail to provide adequate motivation in others. For example, the mobilizing capacity of environmental and antinuclear movements was significantly higher in Germany than in France in the 1980s, despite the levels of postmaterialism being fairly similar in the two countries. Second, the flexibility and skills of actors in adapting to different environmental conditions emerge very clearly. An important precondition for the success of movements lies in their activists' ability to reformulate their own values and motivations in order to adapt them in the most efficient manner to the specific orientations of the sectors of public opinion which they wish to mobilize (Snow et al. 1986; Tarrow 1994). In the context of this need for flexibility and adaptability, strong identification with certain norms and values can even represent an obstacle to actors' freedom, limiting their capacity for action (Kertzer 1988; Swidler 1986; Lofland 1995).

Therefore, it is always possible to interpret the experience of social movements as the unceasing production and reproduction of cultural codes (Melucci

1989, 1991; Benford and Hunt 1992; Hunt and Benford 1994; Benford 1993). Some observers have come to equate movements with a form of drama "in which the protagonists and antagonists compete to affect audiences' interpretations of power relations in a variety of domains" (Benford and Hunt 1992: 38; see also Melucci 1984b, 1989; Sassoon 1984a, 1984b; Gusfield 1994; Rupp and Taylor 2003). One does not need, however, to accept all the theoretical implications of this argument to recognize that social movement activity largely consists of practices more or less directly linked to symbolic production; and that this element is not a precondition for conflict but, rather, one of its constituent parts.

3.2.2 Interpretative frames and ideology

Among scholars interested in symbolic aspects of collective action, the notion of the schema of interpretation, or frame, borrowed from the theoretical work of Erving Goffman (1974) has proved very influential. Frames have been defined as schemata of interpretation that enable individuals "to locate, perceive, identify and label occurrences within their life space and the world at large" (Snow et al. 1986: 464). A frame thus "is a general, standardized, predefined structure (in the sense that it already belongs to the receiver's knowledge of the world) which allows recognition of the world, and guides perception . . . allowing him/her to build defined expectations about what is to happen, that is to make sense of his/her reality" (Donati 1992: 141–2; see also Johnston 1991a, 1991b, 1995a, 2002).

Frame analysis allows us to capture the process of the attribution of meaning which lies behind the explosion of any conflict. In fact, symbolic production enables us to attribute to events and behaviors, of individuals or groups, a meaning which facilitates the activation of mobilization. There are three stages to this process, corresponding to the recognition of certain occurrences as social problems, of possible strategies which would resolve these, and of motivations for acting on this knowledge. Snow and Benford (1988) define these steps as the "diagnostic, prognostic, and motivational" dimension of framing. We shall illustrate them drawing mainly from documents presented at various meetings of the World and the European Social Forum in the last few years.

Diagnostic element

In the first place, appropriate interpretative frames allow the conversion into a social problem, potentially the object of collective action, of a phenomenon whose origins were previously attributed to natural factors or to individual responsibility (Melucci 1989, 1991; Snow et al. 1986). Social problems do in fact exist only to the extent that certain phenomena are interpreted as such by people.

Problems emerge, grow, and disappear, only to reemerge periodically, transformed to a greater or lesser extent (Blumer 1971; Hilgartner and Bosk 1988, Best 1989; Gusfield 1963, 1981; Downs 1972; Rubington and Weinberg 2003).

Diagnosing a problem always entails identifying the actors who are entitled to have opinions on it. This is always a highly contentious process. Various social actors (state agencies, political parties, groups with hostile interests, media operators) try to affirm their own control of specific issues, imposing their own interpretation of these, to the detriment of representations proposed by social movements. Therefore, the latter must, in the first place, claim the legitimacy to deal with particular problems in ways compatible with their own broader orientations (Gusfield 1989; Shemtov 1999). It is through symbolic conflict that certain actors succeed in being recognized as entitled to speak in the name of certain interests and tendencies. In the case of mobilizations on global issues, interpretations of the conflict have stressed the extreme heterogeneity of the actors involved in such campaigns, implicitly suggesting their entitlement to speak on behalf of the human kind: " Social forces from around the world have gathered here at the World Social Forum in Porto Alegre. Unions and NGOs, movements and organizations, intellectuals and artists . . . women and men, farmers, workers, unemployed, professionals, students, blacks and indigenous peoples, coming from the South and from the North" (from the preparatory document of the First World Social Forum in Porto Alegre, January 2001; cited in Andretta 2003).

Another crucial step in the social construction of a problem consists of the identification of those responsible for the situation in which the aggrieved population finds itself. For the unemployed as well as for members of marginal groups, a powerful restraint to mobilization is the widespread belief that poverty depends upon individual failure (see for instance Gaventa 1982; Maurer 2001). In fact:

> the heat of moral judgment is intimately related to beliefs about what acts or conditions have caused people to suffer undeserved hardship or loss. The critical dimension is the abstractness of the target . . . When we see impersonal, abstract forces as responsible for our suffering, we are taught to accept what cannot be changed and make the best of it . . . At the other extreme, if one attributes undeserved suffering to malicious or selfish acts by clearly identifiable groups, the emotional component of an injustice frame will almost certainly be there.
>
> *(Gamson 1992b: 32)*

Again from the Porto Alegre documents emerges a clear attribution of responsibility: "the neoliberal globalization, promoted, reinforced and defended by a set of IGOs (WTO, WB, IMF, NATO and so on), by a hegemonic super potency (USA), and by dominant social groups (multinational corporations) . . .

According to the first WSF document, the grievances imputed to neoliberal globalization are several: "from the exploitation of workers in conditions of union rights weakness to poverty, to gender, racial and ethnic discrimination, from environmental diseases to the lack of migrant rights and so on" (cited in Andretta 2003).

The recent transnational movements are a good example of the selective nature of interpretative frames. For the most part, they have adopted a frame which reduced a series of disparate social phenomena to a dominant theme, neoliberal globalization. Thus, phenomena which might initially have been thought diverse have been incorporated into the same interpretative frame. Other frames might have been devised. For example, if North–South tensions had been represented through an anticapitalist frame only, this would not have made alliances to moderate middle-class sectors, concerned with ethical questions, so easy. Each of the frames summarized earlier accounts for specific interpretations, as plausible as the other. But none of them would have worked so well.

On the other hand, opponents of antiglobalization movements have attempted to deny the existence of the "globalization question" – for example, by emphasizing the positive consequences of the liberalization of markets. They have pointed at the growth of overall income and welfare in developing countries; the statistics suggesting that the market share of developing countries is higher than before; the rise of people above the poverty level; the growth of a prosperous middle class. Apart from denying the issue, they have also attempted to reverse the responsibility: economic deprivation is the product of corrupt national governments whose policies will remain disastrous until they are not exposed to close scrutiny from international institutions such as WTO or IMF; moreover, by calling for protectionist measures, "no-global" protestors are actually helping strong corporate powers in the North (both business and unions) by denying poor countries the chance to compete on the global market – a charge which no-global activists happily refute (see also Haydu 1999, Einwohner 2002, for other examples of counterframing by movement opponents).

The identification of social problems and those responsible for them is, inevitably, highly selective. The highlighting of one particular problem leads to the neglect of other potential sources of protest or mobilization which appear not to fit the interpretation of reality adopted. For example, for a long time, the preeminence within Western society of representations of conflict according to a functional/class or national dimension has made the identification of other sources of conflict – such as gender differences – very difficult. Cultural development places actors in the position of being able to choose, from among various possible sources of frustration and revenge, those against which they should direct all their energies, not to mention their emotional identification. The process can, in this sense, be seen as a reduction of social complexity. At the same time, however, once solid interpretative frames have been established, the possibility of identifying other potential conflicts becomes limited and other ways of representing the same theme are needed. In this sense, the construction of reality, created by relatively marginal actors responsible for mobilizing movements, is inextricably linked to asymmetries of power.

Prognostic element

The action of interpreting the world goes beyond identifying problems, however. It involves seeking solutions, hypothesizing new social patterns, new ways of regulating relationships between groups, new articulations of consensus and of the exercise of power. There is often a strong utopian dimension present in this endeavor. The symbolic elaboration of a movement is thus not necessarily limited to the selection, on the basis of the parameters of instrumental rationality, of "practical" goals in a given social and cultural context. Rather, it opens new spaces and new prospects for action, making it possible to think of aims and objectives which the dominant culture tends instead to exclude from the outset. In this sense, it is possible to conceive of movements as media through which concepts and perspectives, which might otherwise have remained marginal, are disseminated in society. Michel Foucault (1977) noted, for example, that over time not only what is thought changes, but what *can* be thought or conceived of as well. This applies to every phase of insurgency in collective action: it is, in fact, in these circumstances that spaces which were previously inconceivable unexpectedly appear, enabling action to take place (Alberoni 1984; Melucci 1989, 1991).

Various prognostic elements might be present within the same movement. For example, critics of globalization adopt very diverse views regarding the alternatives. Some of them have an approach that Anheier et al. (2001) define as "rejectionist": they express an overall refusal of globalization as a manifestation of global capitalism. Overall, however, this is a very diverse front, consistent with the fact that opposition to capitalism has historically come from very different origins. Leftist organizations and anticapitalist social movements may stress the exploitative practices of global free markets and call for an overthrow of capitalism. Nationalist opponents may found their opposition to capitalism on very different grounds, stressing the threat to national sovereignty by transnational powers, and thus calling for protectionist economic policies and stricter limitations to the circulation of goods and people. Religious fundamentalists may target first of all the spread of individualistic, American-dominated worldviews and lifestyles and the resulting threats to the identity and moral values of specific populations. Whatever the origins of the criticism, political intervention in the global arena by either military superpowers or the UN is to be condemned as imperialistic intervention into local affairs.

Another critical position comes from those whom Anheier et al. (2001) define as "alternatives." Many grassroots groups, countercultural networks, groups searching for viable alternatives to dominant economic practices and lifestyles, do not aim so much to destroy capitalism as to be able to "opt out" of it; namely, to promote experiments in local sustainable economic development, projects in the area of sustainable, GM-free agriculture, alternative and socially responsible trade. From this perspective, the political element is relatively peripheral by comparison to other critical stances. Political intervention in conflicts around the world may be useful as long as it is under the control of civil-society organizations and is based exclusively on nonviolent means; for example, think of peace actions and conflict resolution initiatives in contentious areas such as Israel or the Balkans in the 1990s.

Yet another widespread attitude towards globalization, encompassing both international nongovernmental organizations (INGOs), representatives of international institutions, governments, as well as many social movements, could be characterized as "reformist" (Anheier et al. 2001). While the growing circulation of people, goods, and information across regional and national boundaries is regarded in positive terms, what comes under criticism – even fierce criticism – is the form of such processes to date. Accordingly, a whole range of measures are required to reduce the power of transnational business and financial operators and to increase the role of economic as well as political institutions in regulating flows of exchanges. Active measures to redress social injustice and inequality are in order. The more active political participation of international institutions may be accepted as long as it is explicitly aimed at enforcing human rights and protecting local civil societies in nondemocratic countries, rather than protecting Western states and business special interests.

To sum up, no-global movements are not just anticapitalist, which would make them, in many people's eyes, "outmoded"; nor purely altruistic in the traditional sense (similarly outmoded); and not even purely reactionary forces (even more outmoded). The attempt to find new ways of defining the world, summarized by the slogan "Another world is possible," does not go much further than defining an ultimate goal with which anybody can easily identify. It is still an open debate whether the antiglobalization movement should best be seen as a movement with multiple, loose frames rather than a dominant one (a feature that some, e.g. Westby 2002, attribute to most movements anyway); or whether we can nonetheless identify some relatively homogeneous core ideas, as others (e.g. Andretta 2003) suggest.

Motivational element

On another level, symbolic elaboration is essential in order to produce the motivation and the incentives needed for action. The unknowable outcomes and the costs associated with collective action can be overcome only if the actors are convinced (intuitively even before rationally) of the opportunity for mobilizing and of the practicability and the legitimacy of the action. It is therefore important that frames do not only address the level of social groups and of collective actors, but link the individual sphere with that of collective experience. At the same time, they must generalize a certain problem or controversy, showing the connections with other events or with the condition of other social groups; and also demonstrate the relevance of a given problem to individual life experiences (Benford and Snow 2000: 619; Williams 2004: 105). Along with the critique of dominant representations of order and of social patterns, interpretative frames must therefore produce new definitions of the foundations of collective solidarity, to transform actors' identity in a way which favors action. Gamson (1992b) captures this multiplicity of dimensions when he identifies three central components of the collective construction of the terms: injustice, agency, and identity frames. As motivational framing strongly connects with identity-building, we shall discuss this point in greater detail in the next chapter, when dealing with the role of identity.

Master Frames

Differences between frames and ideology should be easier to catch now. Framing is more flexible a cultural product than ideology, at the same time more specific and more generic than the latter. It does not require a whole coherent set of integrated principles and assumptions but provides instead a key to make sense of the world. In many cases, frames originate from ideologies – for instance, when blue-collar workers experiencing degraded urban living conditions draw on Marxist ideology to suggest that environmental urban crisis could be read as an outcome of the spread of mechanisms of capitalist exploitation from the factory and the labor market to its surrounding community. In other cases, however, frames can affect ideologies. For example, in early nineteenth-century society, generic representations of industrial machines and working conditions as evil were not restricted to working-class organizers but shared with actors with very different viewpoints and goals, such as charitable organizations or churches. Nevertheless, they provided working-class activists with a set of images and symbols that they could use to elaborate more articulated political ideologies.

Differences between ideologies and frames do not prevent us from thinking of frames as capable of delivering broad interpretations of reality. This is particularly true of master frames. The expression reflects the fact that movements and conflicts do not develop in isolation but tend rather to be concentrated in particular political and historical periods (Tilly, Tilly, and Tilly 1975; Tarrow 1989a, 1998). This has consequences at the level of symbolic elaboration, and the discourse of a single movement (or the organization of a movement) must be placed in relation to the general orientations of a given period. If it is possible to identify conjunctions which are particularly favorable to the development of collective action, the dominant visions of the world in that period will inform – or at least influence – the representations produced by the movements taken together.[5] Thus a restricted number of master frames (or dominant interpretative frames: Snow and Benford 1989, 1992) will emerge, to which the specific elaborations of the various organizations or movements can be reduced, more or less directly.

In the early 1970s in Italy, social movements defined conflict in terms of class struggle. At that time, various types of conflict were often interpreted and classified in the light of the Marxist model. The women's movement was first seen from the perspective of emancipation and conquest of equal opportunities rather than as an affirmation of gender differences. In the same way, representations of youth movements often connected their collective action with their social position and their precarious status. At a more directly political level, the rapid transformation of the student movement into little groups organized to resemble – or to caricature – the Leninist party can also be considered proof of Marxism's cultural domination. Models of counterculture and political proposals such as that of the environmentalists, which had little in common with representations of a class nature, were accorded little space in the development of the movements, although they were also present (Lumley 1990). It was only after the salience of dominant cleavages was drastically reduced in the 1980s that collective action was framed under different cultural models such as environmentalism (Diani 1995a). Likewise, Noonan's (1995) analysis of mobilizations by Chilean women shows that their activism in the years before Pinochet was largely framed in terms of motherhood, due to the combination of social movements' heavy Marxist framing and conservative antifeminist feelings. It was only when a "return to democracy" frame, less charged in terms of class conflict, established itself in the social movement sector in the 1980s that space for new feminist frames reemerged.

In contrast, in the USA, interpretative frames linked to the role of individuals, to their rights and aspirations for personal and civic growth, acquired considerable weight after the start of the protest wave of the 1960s. The resulting cultural climate facilitated the spread of movements profoundly different from those which had developed in Italy. At a more directly political level, movements mobilized for freedom of expression (such as the Free Speech Movement), or full citizenship for African Americans, or against American involvement in Vietnam (McAdam 1988b; Eyerman and Jamison 1991: ch. 5). The presence of alternative and countercultural movements was also more evident. These were not limited to strictly communitarian and other world-rejecting forms, typical of the hippy movement and various religious currents of neo-orientalist derivation. They also showed some overlap with broader attempts to support practices designed to encourage inner growth and individual realization, as in the case of the human potential movement.[6]

More recently, opposition to neoliberal globalization has operated, according to some observers, as a master frame (Andretta 2003). The idea that the growing interdependence of economic life and the resulting reduction of barriers to the circulation of capital threaten the living conditions of the large majority of the world's population has brought together farmers of the South, affected by the dominance of multinational agribusinesses and the spread of genetically modified organisms, with trade unionists of the North, who see global liberalization and the resulting fall in corporate tax revenue as a major blow to the modern welfare state. Concerns for the obstacles posed to the free circulation of people, in stark contrast to the free circulation of goods and financial assets, for the profits globalization is often bringing to corrupted authoritarian regimes in Southern countries (Tilly 2004a: ch.5), and for the rising indifference to human rights even in Western democracies, following 9/11, all create a common ground between activists of radical libertarian movements in the West and charities working in developing countries. The indifference to environmental preservation displayed by the very same actors that in developing countries lead economic growth along authoritarian lines, oblivious to workers' rights, and the open hostility demonstrated by right-wing governments in the West, most notably the Bush administration in the US, toward environmental standards, create a common ground for Western environmentalists and the broad coalitions opposing environmental destruction and social exploitation in developing countries (Rothman and Oliver 1999; Doyle 2002). Of course, it remains to be seen whether the overall capacity of the frame to connect so many different experiences is also matched by a corresponding capacity to articulate issues and strategies in local contexts (Tarrow 2005). Still, antineoliberal globalism seems to represent a powerful unifying symbol for many, very diverse, actors worldwide.

3.2.3 Sense-making activities: linking values and frames

Under what conditions are frames successful? Resonance is shaped by credibility and salience (Benford and Snow 2000: 619). Frames should be credible, both in their content and in their sources. Incoherent messages, or messages coming from actors with a shaky reputation, or who are unknown, are unlikely to elicit the same reception as messages from actors with an established public image.[7] Frames should also be salient, i.e. touch upon meaningful and important aspects of people's lives, and show a high "narrative fidelity" (Benford and Snow 2000). Most important, they should resonate not only with their targets, but with the broader cultural structure in which a movement develops (Williams 2004: 105–8).

Successful frames emerge through a variety of ways and forms of cultural production that it would make little sense to try and systematically present here. To put it very simply, and perhaps rather simplistically, the basic precondition for success is that processes of "frame alignment" take place between movement activists and the populations they intend to mobilize. In other words, what is necessary is a "linkage of individual and SMO interpretative orientations, such that some set of individual interests, values and beliefs and SMO activities, goals and ideology are congruent and complementary" (Snow et al. 1986: 464; see also Gamson 1988; Gamson and Modigliani 1989). Collective action thus becomes possible at the point at which mobilizing messages are integrated with some cultural component from the population to which they are addressed.

A major form of frame alignment is what Snow and associates call "frame bridging." This happens when representations by movement organizers incorporate interpretations of reality produced by sectors of public opinion which might otherwise remain separated from each other. Frame bridging can take place at different levels. For example, critiques of the excesses of neoliberal globalization need not necessarily take an anticapitalist or anti-imperialist form. They may also be shared by actors who do not object to globalization *per se*, but to the lack of regulation over global economic actors and to its implications for democracy (reformers, in Anheier et al.'s terms [2001]). One example comes from the bestselling book, *The Silent Takeover*, by business and management expert-*cum*-writer Noreena Hertz (2001). Its recognition that business activities may be as beneficial as pernicious and its author's standing as an academic and business consultant can make its points accessible to both critical sectors of the business community and left-wing critics of globalization (although some of the latter might regard people like Hertz as opponents rather than fellow campaigners). On a different level, numerous examples of frame bridging can be found in the documents produced by organizations in the global justice movement. For example, the World Trade Union Organization, a network of unions which also comprises the European Trade Unions, connects social and environmental justice as follows: "The international institutions must contribute to the balanced economic and social development of all countries, with trade and the use of natural resources taking place in the framework of sustainable development policies that respect the environment, in both producer and consumer countries" (cited in Andretta 2003).

Another important form of frame alignment is what Snow et al. (1986) call frame extension. It allows the specific concerns of a movement or organization to relate to more general goals, in contexts where the connection might not be at all evident. Let us think for example of ATTAC, the network originally born in France from the input of leftist intellectuals such as Ignacio Ramonet (Ancelovici 2002). Given ATTAC's original and major goal of introducing a tax on financial transactions (the Tobin Tax, so called after its proponent, economist

James Tobin), it could easily be perceived as a single-issue organization with a relatively limited domain of action. Hence, frame extension is of the utmost importance for ATTAC or similar organizations. This results in messages articulating the connection between financial globalization and the broad range of problems it generates: "Financial globalization increases economic insecurity and social inequalities. It bypasses and undermines popular decision-making, democratic institutions, and sovereign states responsible for the general interest. In their place, it substitutes a purely speculative logic that expresses nothing more than the interests of multinational corporations and financial markets . . . collected for the most part by industrialized countries, where the principal financial markets are located, [the money originating from the Tobin tax] could be used to help struggle against inequalities, to promote education and public health in poor countries, and for food security and sustainable development" (cited in Andretta 2003).

Frame alignment broadly relies on a dynamic relationship between the development of a movement and the cultural heritage of both the country in which it operates and its institutions.[8] First, movements make reference to cultural currents which, while well rooted in a given country, are somehow overshadowed (Alberoni 1984). This applies to progressive and conservative movements alike. For example, the new right in the US has drawn inspiration largely from the authoritarian, communitarian, illiberal traditions of American society. While liberal culture was, in the 1960s and the early 1970s, able to limit the impact of the new right on public discourse, these currents have remained alive in broad sections of public opinion, and since the 1980s have resurfaced to exert a very important role in public discourse – especially with the Bush administrations (Wallis and Bruce 1986; Bruce 1988; Oberschall 1993: ch. 13; Herman 1997; Blee 2002; Woodberry and Smith 1998; Kniss and Burns 2004).

Second, emerging movements draw on their own traditional heritage and on that of the broader oppositional movements in a given country, presenting them, however, from a new perspective. Western ethnonational movements of the 1960s and 1970s were often successful in linking traditional themes of peripheral nationalism, such as territory or language, which were previously perceived to be predominantly a conservative issue, with radical, anti-establishment perspectives typical of youth countercultures, or with antimilitarist and antinuclear struggles of the period. The critique of the distortion of capitalist development provided a common base for challenges to the economic subordination of "internal colonies" and for solidarity with third-world anticolonialist movements (Touraine, Dubet, Hegedus, and Wieviorka 1981; Touraine, Dubet, Wieviorka, and Strzelecki 1983; Beer 1980; Melucci and Diani 1992; Connor 1994). Likewise, activists of no-global movements drew on several different recent traditions of collective action such as environmentalism, social justice, and internationalism, and somehow managed to integrate them, or at least to identify some shared themes that sounded plausible enough to motivate people to act.

Social movements' frames are often elaborated in reference to elements which form part of the institutionalized culture of a given people. In that context, religion plays a very important role. Even in advanced industrial democracies the role of religion as a source of symbols and identity is far from negligible (Platt & Williams 2002; Young 2002; Williams 1999 and 2002; Inglehart and Norris 2005). Rhys Williams (2004: 107–8) has recently summarized the reasons why religion plays such an important role in the US: the inherent challenge one can find in any religious message, despite its specific contents, and the reluctance to simply accept the world as it is; the availability of religious symbols and language to a very broad range of social groups, from the most established to the most dispossessed; the capacity of most religions – with the possible exception of the most sectarian ones – to speak for the majority of the population and sound legitimate even to those who are not religious themselves (think of the Pope in the anti-Iraqi war initiatives).

For example, the "Churches of the World" network articulates its opposition to neoliberal globalization in the following terms: "We are part of the prophetic ecumenical fellowship looking critically at globalization. And since biblical references are used, amongst other things, to justify globalization, our task is to challenge that in the light of our own reading of the Bible" (cited in Andretta 2003). In the US, religious congregations have also been a context in which to transmit messages to audiences not particularly receptive of explicitly political messages. For example, religious groups campaigning for human rights in central America used religious congregations to spread the outrage and indignation for the murders of prominent religious personalities such as Archbishop Romero in El Salvador (Wood 2003; Nepstad 2001, 2004).

Another well-known example comes from Martin Luther King. In contrast to other leaders of the Afro-American civil rights movement in the 1960s, King was careful in his speeches not to emphasize the differences between blacks and whites. In fact, he tended to avoid the construction of "polemical identities." Instead, he used references to the themes and the values of the heritage of the white American elites of that period, such as the relationship between individual liberty and a sense of responsibility towards the community (McAdam 1994: 38). It was precisely these values, rather than antagonistic values, which provided him with a base from which to argue the full legitimacy of the demands of the civil rights movement (McAdam 1994; Eyerman and Jamison 1991: 166–74).

In different ways, these examples of symbolic re-elaboration remind us that collective action is both a creative manipulation of new symbols and a reaffirmation of tradition. The insurgence of a new wave of mobilization does not, in fact, represent simply a signal of innovation and change, in relation to the culture and the principles prevalent in a given period. It is also, if to a varying extent, a confirmation of the fundamental continuity of values and historic memories which have, in recent times, been neglected or forgotten (see also Stamatov 2002; Jansen 2003).

Reference to the past can operate both as an obstacle and as an opportunity for action. It can represent an obstacle in that long-established ways of thinking and value systems can noticeably reduce the range of options available to the actor (Lofland 1995; Johnston and Klandermans 1995). Too strong an identification with tradition, or, in the same way, an excessive distance between the culture of the activists and sympathizers in a movement, and the rest of society, can in certain cases reduce the efficiency of symbolic re-elaboration (Swidler 1986). It can, in particular, make the processes of realignment of interpretative frames, crucial for the success of mobilization, very difficult. On the other hand, the ability to refer to one's cultural heritage puts the cognitive and value-related resources at the disposal of actors. On the basis of these resources, it is possible to found alternative projects and an alternative political identity. In the absence of references to one's own history and to the particular nature of one's roots, an appeal to something new risks seeming inconsistent and, in the end, lacking in legitimacy.

3.3 Problems and Responses

Recently, the role of frames has also been the subject of considerable discussion. Analyses of collective action centered on the concept of interpretative frames – just as those which focus on the role of organizational resources or of political opportunities – are not exempt from *ad hoc* explanations. At any moment it is possible to uncover the existence within a given society of a multiplicity of cultural models. It is not, therefore, difficult for those studying any movement enjoying a certain success, to identify the cultural elements with which the specific interpretative frame of the movement is aligned. This poses the problem of for mulating systematic hypotheses concerning the relationship between symbolic production activities and the success of attempts at mobilization set up by movement organizations. It is therefore necessary to link the properties of different modes of categorization of reality to the specific nature of the movements and the conflicts which these represent. But it is essential to identify, as a preliminary step, classification criteria for interpretative frames (see Eyerman and Jamison 1991; Diani 1996 for some examples).

The explanatory capacity of frames *vis-à-vis* alternative interpretations of collective action has also been controversial. Is it more important, for the success of a social movement, to have good communicators, or to operate in favorable political conditions, such as divided political elites? For example, in their investigation of conflicts on nuclear power in the 1970s and 1980s in several Western countries, Koopmans and Duyvendak (1995) argued that for all the importance of communication, it was a favorable configuration of opportunities that ultimately helped some antinuclear movements and not others to win the discursive battle. Other studies, however, suggested the opposite. Cress and Snow's (2000) analysis of success of 15 homeless organizations in different US cities suggests that the way in which the homelessness issue was framed actually affected those organizations' chances of securing political recognition or concrete relief. The same applies to a recent study of suffrage organizations in the US from 1866 to 1914 (McCammon 2001; Hewitt and McCammon 2004). Of course, in evaluating these results we have to take into account the different units of analysis. While in a comparison between nations it is difficult to identify the impact of framing strategies, more fine grained explorations of specific cases might well assign symbolic factors a greater weight.

The framing perspective on collective action has also come under fire from researchers, most interested in cultural dynamics, including the original proponents of the concept (Benford 1997; Benford and Snow 2000; Goodwin and Jasper 2004a; Mische 2003). In many instances frames have indeed been treated as static cognitive structures; very little attention has been paid, according to critics, to the way frames are generated and evolve over time, usually in a dialogical relationship between different actors. In the last decade, numerous studies have tried to address this problem by focusing on the dynamic elements of discursive practices. In a major study of conflicts on abortion in the US and Germany, Ferree, Gamson, Gerhards, and Rucht (2002) have illustrated the contentious nature and the multiple spheres involved in the processes whereby abortion issues become the object of conflicting public discourses. Steinberg (1999) has documented the transformations in the rhetorical forms adopted by nineteenth-century English cotton-spinners as their mobilizations evolved over time (see also Ellingson 1995; Polletta 2002; McCaffrey and Keys 2000). Mische (2003) has moved one step further, illustrating how discursive and conversational dynamics not only create new representations of experience, but also constitute relations between social actors (see also Somers 1992). Main advocates of the frame approach have placed greater emphasis on framing practices rather than on frames *per se*, and on the processes through which frames are transformed (Snow 2004: 393–6; see also Cadena-Roa 2002).

The dynamic role of cultural production has also been noted by researchers from a different background than cultural sociology, and closer to the value perspective to culture than to the frame perspective. In his broad investigation of cultural change, with prevalent but not exclusive reference to the US, Rochon (1998) has stressed its dynamic and process-oriented elements. Rather than being generated, *à la* Inglehart, by macrostructural transformations (such as growth of education or rising affluence) affecting the way individuals conceive of their own situation and life projects, value change is a critical struggle in which multiple actors are involved. For critical values to establish themselves, the role of critical communities is essential. It is from such communities – that may include from time to time activists, artists, intellectuals, and the like – that social movements emerge as major agents of cultural change (see also Melucci 1989, 1996; Rupp and Taylor 2003; Williams 2004: 99).

Another related issue is whether frames – and in particular framing skills – should be treated as a particular type of resource, subject to strategic use by skilled political entrepreneurs. Several passages in the original formulations of the framing perspective indeed suggest a view of this kind (Snow et al. 1986; Gamson 1990, 1992a). The most forceful critique of this position has come from theorists who have recently brought back the study of emotions into social movement analysis. From their point of view, cultural interpretations conducive to collective action do not so much originate from cognitive processes and strategic framing as from collective processes with a strong emotional dimension. It is often explicit confrontation with anger and injustice, or direct experience of collective solidarity, rather than political entrepreneurs' skillful manipulation, that move people to collective action (Goodwin, Jasper and Polletta 2001 and 2004; for illustrations: Barker 2001; Berezin 2001).

3.4 Summary

There are at least two ways of looking at the relationship between collective action and culture. The first stresses above all the role of values. Action is thus seen to originate from the identification of social actors with certain sets of principles and concerns. Interpretations of movements in recent decades, based on these premises, have insisted in particular on the shift from materialist values to postmaterialist values. More recently, however, the growing relevance of fundamentalist religious movements (not only within Islam but also within Christianity) has drawn analysts' attention to another, very different version of the relationship between values and collective action.

The second approach, which we have dealt with here, underlines instead the cognitive elements of culture. In this context, mobilization does not depend so much on values as on how social actors assign meaning to their experience: i.e., on the processes of interpretation of reality which identify social problems as "social" and make collective action sound like an adequate and feasible response to a condition perceived as unjust. Action is facilitated by "frame alignment," in other words, by the convergence of models of interpretation of reality adopted by movement activists and those of the population which they intend to mobilize.

Movements' cultural production implies a relationship which involves both conquering and revitalizing aspects (or at least some aspects) of a given population's traditions. This is both an impediment and a resource for action. It is also worth noting that explanations of collective action, centered on the concept of the "interpretative frame," often carry the risk of *ad hoc* explanations. One way out of this difficulty lies in linking various types of interpretative frames developed by actors with certain perceptions of the political opportunities provided by the environment. Recently, the framing perspective has been criticized for its excessive dependence on cognitive elements, to the detriment of the emotional elements of collective action. In the next chapter, which looks at mechanisms for production of identity, we shall see how the cultural and symbolic dimensions are linked to the subjective experience of the individual.

COLLECTIVE ACTION
AND IDENTITY

I think it's made me stronger. I think it's made me really clear about who I am . . . I almost feel my life has a theme. It's not just like I'm this little ant out there living and working with all the other ants on the anthill. There are things that I care really, really deeply about, and that sort of infuses my whole life with meaning. And I've retained that, and I think I always will.

–Radical feminist activist, Columbus, Ohio, USA,
quoted in Whittier (1995: 95)

Until two years ago, I was a woman who belonged to a man. Then I met the women of the collective, and slowly I have acquired the ability to develop new and different relationships with people. Today, I feel myself to be equal in my relationship with this man and in my relationships with the women of the collective.

–Martina, member of a women's collective, Milan, Italy,
quoted in Bianchi and Mormino (1984: 160)

After Greenham I realized how in fact I was putting myself down on occasions. Simply because there were men around I wasn't verbalizing my thoughts enough. I wasn't coming forward . . . the men were dominating, and I was allowing them to dominate me.

–Carola Addington, Greenham Common activist, UK,
quoted in Roseneil (1995: 146)

We are not a unionist movement, nor do we have anything to do with unionism. They have their organizations and we have ours. We are offering an alternative by and for women.

–Laura, worker and activist, Managua, Nicaragua,
quoted in Bandy and Bickam-Mendez (2003: 179)

> If someone asks me, "Who are you?" I'm a radical feminist . . . And I see radical feminism as my life's work, even though I'm spending most of my days, most of my weeks, most of my years, doing something else.
>
> *–Employee of a public interest organization, Columbus, Ohio, USA, quoted in Whittier (1995: 95)*

> For me, being part of a women's group is an essential influence not only on my way of life but also on my thinking. It is important to know yourself. The collective has died and been reborn many times over, along with my own aspirations. Wherever I go, I will always find a women's group.
>
> *–Irma, Member of a women's collective, Milan, Italy, quoted in Bianchi and Mormino (1984: 159)*

> There was the miners' strike and a lot of miners' wives used to come down . . . And there was the American Indian from the Indian reservation . . . And there were delegations from South Africa. And we were just dead ordinary working-class women from the inner cities and we were talking to people who were directly involved in struggles from all over the world.
>
> *–Trisha, Greenham Common activist, UK, quoted in Roseneil (1995: 149)*

> This [visit] gives us more confidence to continue with our struggle, for we see that we're not alone. . . . We hope each of you [North American labor and community organizers on a visit to Mexico] will continue forward with love, for your brothers and sisters, for communities like ours. This is the same struggle all around the world.
>
> *–Hortensia, worker and activist, Tijuana, Mexico, quoted in Bandy and Bickam-Mendez (2003: 179)*

Irma and Martina were part of the Ticinese Collective, a group of women active in Milan around the end of the 1970s and the beginning of the 1980s (Bianchi and Mormino 1984). Trisha and Carola were among the women who took part in the occupation of the Greenham Common area, where cruise missiles where located in Britain between 1983 and 1991 (Roseneil 1995). Hortensia and Laura were active in the mobilization of female workers of *maquilas*, small industrial units producing all sort of goods for export, usually under appalling working conditions, in Central America (Bandy and Bickam-Mendez 2003). The two anonymous quotes[1] belong to women who were involved in the radical feminist movement in the American city of Columbus, Ohio, between the 1970s and the early 1990s (Whittier 1995, 1997). The characteristics of these movements were different, and so was the political and cultural context in which they developed. And yet, for all the differences, these quotations reveal more than random commonalities. They all appear representative, in their own ways, of the relationship between collective and individual experience in social movements. In particular, they tell us about the intersection of collective involvement and personal engagement which characterizes so much collective action (Melucci 1989, 1995; Rupp and Taylor 1987; della Porta 1992; Calhoun 1994a; Goodwin, Jasper, and Polletta 2001; Downton and Wehr 1997; Passerini 1988).

On the one hand, these stories are about personal change: they testify to the new sense of empowerment, and to the strengthening of the self, which originate from collective action. Fighting the cruise missiles in the context of a "women only" campaign, Carola became aware of how much she had undervalued her potential in the past, especially in situations with a strong male presence. For Trisha, being at Greenham Common opened up spaces for contacts and experiences that her working-class origins would have denied her otherwise. For Laura, action in the workplace means developing an original experience of interest representation from a gender perspective, thus reaffirming her autonomy from the male models reflected in unions' practice. For Martina, joining a self-awareness group signified transforming her private life, without developing a strong commitment to public engagement. Even in her case, however, it was the nature of collective experience which made her personal growth possible.

On the other hand, these stories are about the continuity in one's life that a sense of collective belonging provides. For Irma as well as for the Columbus women, being a feminist provided a linkage between different life stages and different types of experiences. The linkage is not necessarily between different points in time; it is also – as Trisha's and Hortensia's quotations suggest – between people acting in different localities and on different specific issues, but united by a common set of values and aspirations.

These stories are, in other words, about identity: in particular, about the relationship between identity and collective action (Pizzorno 1978; Cohen 1985; Melucci 1989; Calhoun 1991, 1994a; Mach 1993; Stryker, Owen, and Whyte, 2000; Horton 2004; Hunt and Benford 2004). In speaking of identity we are not referring to an autonomous object, nor to a property of social actors; we mean, rather, the process by which social actors recognize themselves – and are recognized by other actors – as part of broader groupings, and develop emotional attachments to them (Melucci 1989, 1996; Polletta and Jasper 2001; Goodwin et al. 2001: 8–9). These "groupings" need not be defined in reference to specific social traits such as class, gender, ethnicity, sexual orientation, or the like, nor in reference to specific organizations (although they often get defined in those terms). Collective identities may also be based on shared orientations, values, attitudes, worldviews, and lifestyles, as well as on shared experiences of action (e.g., individuals may feel close to people holding similar postmaterialist views, or similarly approving of direct action, without expressing any strong sense of class, ethnic, or gender proximity). At times, identities may be exclusive, and rule out other possible forms of identification (as in the case of religious sects expressing a wholesale rejection of the mundane world). Other times (actually, most of the time), however, they may be inclusive and multiple, as individuals may feel close to several types of collectivities at the same time.

Building or reproducing identities is an important component of the processes through which individuals give meaning to their own experiences and to their transformations over time. It is worth noting the complexity of the relationship between the individual dimension and the collective dimension in identity-building. On the one hand, through the production, maintenance, and revitalization of identities, individuals define and redefine individual projects, and possibilities for action open and close. The individual stories we just reported show us precisely that "identities are often personal and political projects in which we participate" (Calhoun 1994a: 28). On the other hand, the construction of identity and the rediscovery of one's self cannot be reduced simply to psychological mechanisms; they are social processes (Berger and Luckmann 1966; Moscovici 1981; Billig 1995).

In the following pages we discuss some characteristics of identity construction. We show, first, that identity production is an essential component of collective action, through the identification of actors involved in conflict, the facilitation of trusting relationships among them, and the establishment of connections linking events from different periods. Consistent with what has long been asserted by both sociological (Touraine 1981; Pizzorno 1978; Melucci 1989, 1996) and sociopsychological (Moscovici 1979; Drury and Reicher 2000; Howard 2000) perspectives on collective action, we regard identity as neither a thing one can own, nor a property of actors, but as the process through which individual and/or collective actors, in interaction with other social actors, attribute a specific meaning to their traits, their life occurrences, and the systems of social relations in which they are embedded.

Subsequently, we confront some of the paradoxes which a concept as fleeting as that of identity inevitably creates. First, social identification is simultaneously static and dynamic. On the one hand, reference to identity evokes the continuity and the solidity of allegiances over time. On the other, identity is also open to constant redefinitions. Links postulated by social actors with certain historical experiences and with certain groups appear, in fact, always to be contingent. They are the fruit of symbolic reinterpretations of the world which are inevitably selective and partial (Calhoun 1994a; Melucci 1996). Moreover, identities are forged and adapted in the course of conflict, and their boundaries can be modified quite drastically in the process (Bernstein 1997; Drury and Reicher 2000; Drury, Reicher, and Stott 2003). As a result, in spite of their relative stability, even feelings of identification can be – and in fact are – subject to recurring modifications.

A second paradox is represented by the presence of multiple identities – or, in other words, individuals' feelings of belonging to several different collectives, sometimes defined in reference to very diverse criteria. From a certain point of view, identity operates as an organizing principle in relation to individual and collective experience: for example, it helps actors to identify their allies and their adversaries. At the same time, however, the definition of lines of solidarity and of opposition is often anything but clear: the rise of feminist movements has created, for example, new lines of identification which have often revealed themselves to be in contrast with those which preceded them (for example, those of class). Rather than uprooting these older lines of identity, new identities co-exist with them, generating tensions among actors' different self-representations,[2] or between activists who identify with the same movement yet belong to different generations (Whittier 1995, 1997; Schnittker, Freese, and Powell 2003). Although an idea of similarity is surely behind the concept of collective identity (e.g. Berezin 2001: 84), this homogeneity is rarely if ever multidimensional. Actors who are similar in some traits/attitudes/experiences may differ substantially in other dimensions (Simmel 1955, Diani 2000a). One has also to note, though, that multiple identities need not necessarily be in a tense relation to each other.

4.1 How Does Identity Work?

Identity construction should not be regarded simply as a precondition for collective action. It is certainly true that social actors' identities in a given period guide their subsequent conduct. Action occurs, in fact, when actors develop the ability to define themselves, other social actors, and the "enjeu" (stake) of their mutual relationship (Touraine 1981). At the same time, however, identity is not an immutable characteristic, preexisting action. On the contrary, it is through action that certain feelings of belonging come to be either reinforced or weakened. In other words, the evolution of collective action produces and encourages continuous redefinitions of identity (Fantasia 1988; Hirsch 1990; Melucci 1995; Bernstein 1997; Goodwin et al. 2001; Drury et al. 2003).

Let us look more closely at the mechanisms by which action "constitutes" identity. This happens, first, through the definition of boundaries between actors engaged in a conflict. In contrast to macrostructural approaches to the analysis of social conflicts, the sociology of action has drawn attention to the problematic nature of the structure–action nexus, stressing that conflict cannot be explained exclusively in the light of structural relationships and the contrasting interests which these have determined. It originates, rather, in the interaction between structural tensions and the emergence of a collective actor that defines itself and its adversaries on the basis of certain values and/or interests (Touraine 1981). Collective action cannot occur in the absence of a "we" characterized by common traits and a specific solidarity. Equally indispensable is the identification of the "other" defined as responsible for the actor's condition and against which the mobilization is called (Gamson 1992b). The construction of identity therefore implies both a positive definition of those participating in a certain group, and a negative identification of those who are not only excluded but actively opposed (Touraine 1981; Melucci 1996; Taylor and Whittier 1992; Robnett 2002; Tilly 2004a). It also includes a relationship with those who find themselves in a neutral position. It is with reference to "protagonists, antagonists, and audiences" (Hunt, Benford, and Snow 1994) that movement identities are formed and come to life.

In the second place, the production of identities corresponds to the emergence of new networks of relationships of trust among movement actors, operating within complex social environments.[3] Those relationships guarantee movements a range of opportunities (see chapter 5 below). They are the basis for the development of informal communication networks, interaction, and, when necessary, mutual support. They seem to be an essential replacement for the scarcity of organizational resources; furthermore, information circulates rapidly via interpersonal networks, compensating at least in part for limited access to the media; trust between those who identify with the same political and cultural endeavor enables those concerned to face with greater efficacy the costs and the risks linked to repression; finally, identifying themselves – and being identified – as part of a movement also means being able to count on help and solidarity from its activists (Gerlach and Hine 1970; Gerlach 1971).

The presence of feelings of identity and of collective solidarity makes it easier to face the risks and uncertainties related to collective action. In the case of the workers' movement, close proximity of workplaces and living spaces facilitated the activation and the reproduction of solidarity (see chapter 2 above). Socialist subcultures constructed "areas of equalities" where participants recognized themselves as equal, and felt they belonged in a common destiny (Pizzorno 1996). In postindustrial society, however, direct social relationships founded on territorial proximity have become weaker. While this has not necessarily meant the disappearance of community relations, on the whole, systems of social relations are more distantly connected than they were in the past to a defined territorial space. Their borders extend now to encompass entire national and supranational communities (Wellman et al. 1988; Giddens 1990; Castells 1996; Sassen 1998; Vertovec and Cohen 2003). As a result, collective actors are now less likely than in the past to identify themselves in reference to locality. Collective identity is less dependent on direct, face-to-face interactions which develop in the local community and in everyday spaces. Phenomena of this type had already signaled the shift from premodernity to modernity, and the emergence of public opinion integrated via the printed word (Anderson 1983; Tarrow 1998). But they have undergone a further acceleration with the expansion of the media system and the electronic revolution (Calhoun 1992; Wasko and Mosco 1992; Bennett 2003; Wellman and Haythornwhyte 2002).

To identify with a movement also entails feelings of solidarity towards people to whom one is not usually linked by direct personal contacts, but with whom one nonetheless shares aspirations and values. Activists and movement sympathizers are aware of participating in realities which are much vaster and more complex than those of which they have direct experience. It is in reference to this wider community that the actor draws motivation and encouragement to action, even when the field of concrete opportunities seems limited and there is a strong sense of isolation. It is of course an open issue the extent to which the spread of computer mediated communication may facilitate the diffusion of identities disentangled from references to any specific time and space (see chapter 5, section 5.4 below).

Third, collective identity connects and assigns some common meaning to experiences of collective action dislocated over time and space (see e.g. Lumley 1990; Farrell 1997). At times this takes the form of linking together events associated with a specific struggle in order to show the continuity of the effort behind the current instances of collective action. Let us look for example at the "Call of the European Social Movements," issued before the European Social Forum in Florence in November 2002: "We have come together from the social and citizens movements from all the regions of Europe, East and West, North and South. We have come together through a long process: the demonstrations of Amsterdam, Seattle, Prague, Nice, Genoa, Brussels, Barcelona, the big mobilisations against the neoliberalism as well as the general strikes for the defense of social rights and all the mobilisations against war, show the will to build an other Europe. At the global level we recognise the Charter of Principles of WSF and the call of social movements of Porto Alegre" (cited in Andretta 2003). Here, occurrences which took place at different points in time are brought together as the background of the 2002 meeting, to show continuity between them. Likewise there is an obvious attempt to connect across space mobilizations taking place in all corners of Europe, and to relate them as well to recent developments of collective action on a global scale.

The issue of continuity over time is also important because social movements characteristically alternate between "visible" and "latent" phases (Melucci 1996). In the former, the public dimension of action prevails, in the form of demonstrations, public initiatives, media interventions, and so on, with high levels of cooperation and interaction among the various mobilized actors. In the latter, action within the organizations and cultural production dominate. Contacts between organizations and militant groups are, on the whole, limited to interpersonal, informal relationships, or to interorganizational relationships which do not generally produce the capacity for mass mobilization. In these cases, collective solidarity and the sense of belonging to a cause are not as obvious as they are in periods of intense mobilization. Identity is nurtured by the hidden actions of a limited number of actors. And it is precisely the ability of these small groups to reproduce certain representations and models of solidarity over time which creates the conditions for the revival of collective action and allows those concerned to trace the origins of new waves of public action to preceding mobilizations (Melucci 1996; Rupp and Taylor 1987; Johnston 1991b; Mueller 1994; Whittier 1995).[4]

This linking function of identity does not operate only on the level of collective representations and socially widespread perceptions of certain social phenomena. It also relates the latter to individual experience. In constructing their own identity, individuals attribute coherence and meaning to the various phases of their own public and private history. This is often reflected in their life histories and biographies, i.e., the "[i]ndividual constellations of cultural meanings, personalities, sense of self, derived from biographical experiences" (Jasper 1997: 44). Long-lasting militant careers develop with a constant commitment to a cause, even if articulated in different ways at different times (Downton and Wehr 1997). It is true that any wave of mobilization attracts to social movements people with no previous experience of collective action – at least for biographical reasons. Still, continuity in militancy – the fact that those who have already participated in the past are more likely to become active once again than those who have never done so – has been confirmed by a large number of studies, devoted to both contemporary (McAdam 1988b; Whittier 1995 and 1997; Klandermans 1997: ch. 4; Robnett 2002) and "historic" examples of collective action (Thompson 1963; Gould 1995; Catanzaro and Manconi 1995; Passerini 1988). The "1968 generation," for example, has remobilized in various waves of protest – latest in the global justice campaigns (della Porta 2005e).

Speaking of continuity over time does not necessarily mean assuming that identity persists, let alone that it is fixed. Reference to the past is, in fact, always selective. "Continuity" in this case means rather the active re-elaboration of elements of one's own biography and their reorganization in a new context. In this way, it becomes possible to keep together personal and collective occurrences which might otherwise appear to be incompatible and contradictory. As an example, let us look at a case of radical collective action which would seem to presuppose a drastic personal transformation at the moment of mobilization – that of terrorism. Biographies of Italian terrorists of the 1970s (della Porta 1990) show that they had in many cases moved from militancy in Catholic organizations to armed struggle. In this case, there was clearly a marked break in forms of action and political programs. Nevertheless, there were also elements of coherence in these histories which seem, on the surface, to be so lacking in continuity. One of these was the aspiration to construct social relationships which went beyond the inequalities and the distortions of the present. Also common to both biographical phases was a conception of collective action as the proclamation of absolute truths and the concrete testimony of one's own ideal (and ideological) principles, no matter how distorted.

On the other hand, the outset of each new experience of collective action inevitably means also breaking with the past to some degree. In some cases, the decision to engage in collective action, or join an organization or a project, which is clearly different from what individuals have done up to that point, results in a radical personal transformation. In these cases, people experience genuine conversions, which often mean breaking with their previous social bonds. The transformation of identity can be much more profound in these cases. It will affect not only the political leanings of individuals and their levels of involvement in collective action, but also global life choices and even the organization of everyday life.

The same phenomena are often found among those who join religious movements (Robbins 1988: ch. 3; Snow et al. 1980; Wilson 1982; Wallis and Bruce 1986).[5] Conversion to a cult or a sect often implies a more or less radical transformation of one's identity and loyalties, and this is deeper the more demanding membership criteria in the new group are. For example, joining a group like Hare Krishna implies the acceptance of a highly ritualized lifestyle in which everything has to be in accordance with the sect's precepts (Rochford 1985). Furthermore, the history of conflicts typical of industrial society documents the force of "traditional" political identities and the often exclusive and sectarian nature of collective action. In the century of great ideologies, abandoning political and/or class positions – that is, giving up a certain system of social relationships and of affective identifications in order to adopt another – was always costly. A good example of this is provided in the segmentation of Northern Ireland along religious lines (one could also think of the Israeli–Palestinian conflict for another obvious illustration of this pattern). In Northern Ireland, religious identities have provided criteria for the organization of social relations at all levels, including community and family linkages. Ties cutting across sectarian barriers are infrequent and people involved in them regularly meet with ostracism from their own communities (Bew et al. 1979; McAllister 1983; O'Sullivan See 1986; Maguire 1993). This has rendered the activation of ties with members of the opposing group a very costly and often very dangerous exercise. This applies to social movement organizations too, and has often resulted in failure to cut across sectarian divides. Although many attempts have been made over the last two decades by different types of organizations, from environmentalist to women's (Connolly 2002; Cinalli 2002), to develop new intercultural forms of political participation, even after the Good Friday agreement of 1998, social segregation in Northern Ireland is still high (McGarry 2001).

4.2   Multiple Identities

In modern society, social movements are often represented as "characters" with a strategic capacity for action and bearing a specific cultural role. For these reasons, they are also seen as having a homogeneous and integrated identity. Little attention has been given to the systems of relationships in which actors are involved, and this has prevented the multiplicity of identities and allegiances among militants and movement groups from being recognized. Rather, it has favored the tendency to see identity as the mirror of an underlying objective reality.[6]

In fact, however, collective identification is rarely expressed through the integrated and homogeneous identities which these visions of movements presuppose.[7] As identity is, first, a social process and not a static property, feelings of belonging among groups and collectives which originated from these are, to a certain extent, fluid. A less rigid approach to the question of identity leads us to recognize that it does not always presuppose a strong "collective we" (Lemert 1994; Billig 1995). Identifying with a movement does not necessarily mean sharing a systematic and coherent vision of the world; nor does it prevent similar feelings being directed to other groups and movements as well. Forms of allegiance which are not particularly intense or exclusive can, in certain contexts, guarantee continuity of collective action (Melucci 1984a; Diani 1995a). In reality, it is rare that a dominant identity is able to integrate all the others. More usually, identities have a polycentric rather than a hierarchical structure.[8] But excessive insistence on the role of identity as a source of coherence often leads to neglecting the importance of forms of multiple identity (Calhoun 1994a).

Tensions among various types of identification have to do, first, with the fact that the motivations and expectations behind individuals participating in social movements are, in fact, much richer and more diversified than the public images of those movements, as produced by their leaders, would suggest. By taking part in the life of a movement people often seek answers to their own specific aspirations and concerns. The Milanese women studied by Melucci and his collaborators in the early 1980s, for example, saw their involvement in feminism in many different ways. Some gave pride of place to personal reflection, others gave greater relevance to external intervention. Some valued group action, above all solidarity and affective elements, while others insisted on the importance of developing new forms of interpreting the world (Bianchi and Mormino 1984). Along similar lines, Reger (2002) shows that it is possible to accommodate different positions within the same organization. Her example is the New York chapter of the National Organization for Women (NOW), which included both feminists oriented to political advocacy and those privileging practices of personal empowerment. Even the identity of a single group can therefore be seen as a meeting point for histories, personal needs, and heterogeneous representations.

Similar mechanisms are to be found in the relationship between single organizations and movements, in the broad sense. On the one hand, organizations aim to affirm their own specific formulation of their collective identity as the global identity of the movement. On the other hand, the reinforcement of an organizational identity allows, at the same time, for differentiation from the rest of the movement (Taylor 1989). Therefore, one identifies with an organization not only to feel part of a wider collective effort but also in order to be a particular, autonomous, distinctive component of such an effort. In this way it becomes possible to anchor identity to organizational forms, which are more structured and solid than those constituted by networks of informal relationships among the various components of a movement. What is cursorily termed "movement identity" is, in reality, largely a contingent product of negotiations between collective images produced by various actors and various organizations. Moreover, even small groups can experience the multiple orientations which characterize the identity of a movement in its entirety (Melucci 1984a). In Milan, for example, analysis of the experience of the Ticinese Collective facilitated the identification of two basic tensions in the way in which feminist practice was perceived (Bianchi and Mormino 1984). The first distinguished between action aimed at society beyond the movement and that which was inwardly directed, towards small groups; the second between action which was purely affective and solidaristic and action which aimed to value women's competences and professional qualities. The same dichotomies offered a useful key to reading the identity of the movement as a whole. There were, in fact, consciousness-raising groups, or lesbian groups which were virtually unconcerned with public action and concentrated on the affective-solidaristic side of action. On the other hand, writers' groups and those concerned with reflection on intellectual issues from a women's perspective associated a low level of external intervention with their goal of calling attention to women's intellectual and professional capacities. Among the groups concerned with external intervention, some placed a high value on the solidaristic element, such as feminist collectives in squatter communes; others were concerned with consolidating women's social presence, both on the economic level and on that of cultural production (Bianchi and Mormino 1984: 147).

It must be remembered that movement identities can be shared by individuals, detached from every organizational allegiance. In fact, it is possible to feel part of a movement without identifying with any specific organization and, indeed, even express an explicit dissent towards the notion of organization in general. In particularly effervescent conditions, simply to participate in meetings and demonstrations gives the sensation of being able to count on the definition of strategies and on goals, even without having passed through the filter of specific organizations. In fact, when identification mechanisms tend to shift mainly towards specific organized actors, this is an indicator of a movement demise. One of the characteristic traits of the wave of working-class protest which crossed Italy between 1968 and 1972 was the modification of the relationship between militancy in specific trade-union organizations and militancy in the workers' movement in its broad sense (Pizzorno et al. 1978). New forms of representation were introduced in factories (factory councils). They offered ample opportunities for participation even to those who were not enrolled in any of the traditional unions. The push towards trade-union unity and to overcome preexisting group allegiances was also strong in those years. Group allegiances came to dominate once more only when mobilization was in decline and movement identity was weak. Analysis of grassroots working-class action in the USA also supports this claim: phases of rising conflict tend to strengthen broader collective solidarities rather than identification with specific unions (Fantasia 1988).

In some cases, collective identities expressed by different movements or different movement organizations can be mutually incompatible. The rise of feminism has revealed the persistent subordination of women within workers' movement organizations or in many of the "new movements" themselves. In this way, they have shown the deep contradictions in actors' identities which, nevertheless, can generally be explained with reference to the same area of "progressive" movements. From another point of view, the salience of religious or ethnonationalist identities has often left actors facing dramatic dilemmas, in view of the difficulty of integrating these and other sources of identification. For example, allegiance to a radical nationalist ideology such as that of the Serbs, or to a religious movement such as Algerian fundamentalism, places considerable difficulties in the path of those women who want both to maintain and affirm their gender identity (Calhoun 1994a; see also Fantasia and Hirsch 1995). On the other hand, global justice activists have so far displayed a great tolerance towards each other's combinations of multiple identities (della Porta 2005e; Bennett 2004c).

4.3   Does Identity Facilitate Participation?

Reference to identity is essential – even if, as we shall see, controversial – in order to understand the mechanisms underlying individuals' decisions to become involved in collective action. The debate started in the 1960s with Mancur Olson's (1963) provocative thesis on the irrationality of collective action. Olson's argument is well known and can therefore be reviewed in a few sentences. The starting point for his reflection is the concept of collective action as concerned with the production of collective goods. These derive their nature from the fact that, once obtained, they may be enjoyed by any member of a social group, regardless of his/her contribution to the cause. Sometimes the "social group" consists of people living in a given territory. For example, once a local environmental coalition has had stricter controls on car emissions implemented in its community, the collective good "cleaner air" is accessible to all the residents, no matter whether they supported the campaign or not. At other times, the "social group" may consist of a collectivity defined by specific characteristics. For example, once voting rights were extended to women, any woman was entitled to them, again irrespective of her contribution to the suffrage movement. Or, if a regional business association successfully pressures the government to launch a plan of massive investment in public communications in the area, all single-business operators will profit from it, including those who are not members of the association. The properties of collective goods determine the fundamental irrationality of collective action, if valued on the basis of criteria of instrumental, individualistic rationality. It would not be at all rational for individual actors to invest resources in an undertaking – the production of a collective good – if they had to bear all the costs of failure but could enjoy all the fruits of success without having contributed directly to the production of the good.

For collective action to occur, political entrepreneurs or organizations have either to coerce prospective participants or to distribute selective incentives – thus enabling participants to receive greater benefits than those who do not participate. This problem applies above all to large groups – or in other words to those groups in which no individual contribution is so relevant as to affect the final result of a collective undertaking. Two factors increase the difficulties of mobilization for large groups: first, their great size implies high coordination costs, second, certain social incentives   prestige, respect, or friendship – which can work with small groups become more difficult to activate as the dimensions of the group increase.

Not surprisingly, reactions to Olson's model have been very different.[9] Some scholars have extended the notion of selective incentives in such a way as to include rewards of a solidaristic and normative type. These can, in their turn, be divided into at least two categories. External selective incentives consist of expectations which individuals have of the group to which they refer; these are seen, more generally, as rewards and as sanctions which this group and other social actors can make use of when facing a decision or else a refusal to become involved collectively. Internal selective incentives cover the internal mechanisms which bring individuals to attribute to collective action a certain normative value, or else to derive from this an intrinsic pleasure or to experience a cathartic transformation (Opp 1989: 58–9). According to numerous pieces of research on individual participation, among the "selective incentives" it is references to the values and the solidarity bonds shared within the group, rather than motivations of a material kind, which have emerged as the best predictors of collective action

(Marwell and Ames 1979; Walsh and Warland 1983; Oliver 1984; Opp 1988, 1989; Passy 2003).

The incorporation of normative and symbolic elements into selective incentives does not, however, resolve one of the main problems of Olson's model, namely its lack of attention to the diachronic dimension. The microeconomic rationality on which Olson's argument is based unravels itself in a short period of time. In contrast, collective action is a process which develops over time, in particular when considering the achievement of goals. It is difficult, if not impossible, to determine costs and benefits appropriately, therefore. On the one hand, there is the certainty of engagement and of the acceptance of risk in the short term; on the other, the unknown territory of results which are not only difficult to calculate from the point of view of the individual but whose achievement also seems a distant prospect. Collective identity reduces these difficulties. Olson's approach assumes a short-term timeframe for the maximization of individual utility. In contrast, as we have seen, collective identity takes a longer time perspective. Even the definition of actors' interests is a social process which requires a definition of a "we" and a "them," and thus is inextricably linked to identity construction. As a result, feeling part of a shared endeavor and identifying one's own interests not only at the individual level but also at the collective level makes costs and risks more acceptable than they would otherwise have been. Physical risks and material deprivation, hardly rational from an individualistic, short-term perspective, may be justified if looked at as the costs attached to carrying on a longer-term historical project (Pizzorno 1978, 1983, 1986).

Moreover, the intensity and, above all, the exclusiveness of collective identity in defining actors' limits can vary. A key question is therefore whether various identity traits influence decisions to move to action, and if so how. Some have hypothesized a link, in inverse proportion, between the level of inclusiveness and openness of a particular definition of identity and the capacity for mobilization: "Some groups attempt to mobilize their constituents with an all-inclusive we. . . . Such an aggregate frame turns the 'we' into a pool of individuals rather than a potential collective actor . . . Collective action frames, in contrast, are adversarial" (Gamson 1992b: 85). This does not mean that all social movements at all times develop exclusive identities: a wealth of examples, recently including environmental and global justice movements, actually suggests the opposite. However, the lack of explicit adversaries for environmentalism has long been pointed out as a source of weakness for that movement (e.g. Diani 1995a), and some have raised doubts about the global justice movement's capacity to mobilize its constituency beyond the most visible events on very similar grounds (Tarrow 2005).

The problem is therefore how to achieve a balance between reach and selectivity (Marwell and Oliver 1993: 157–79); namely, how to define identity to include as many people as possible in a movement's potential constituency, while continuing to provide strong incentives to the movement's core supporters. An inclusive and flexible identity will not associate a movement with a particular social group, a specific ideology, lifestyle, or symbolic code. In this way, it will facilitate communication among movement activists and the outside world, as well as their capacity to speak to different cultural and political contexts. An exclusive identity which defines the profile of a particular movement with some force will instead tend to stress isolation in relation to the outside world: but will probably be able to provide more notable (selective) incentives for action, making the definition of both the actor and of its adversaries more precise in the process (Friedman and McAdam 1992).

One should be aware, though, that how to combine these two contradictory demands effectively is only partially under actors' control. Collective identity is surely affected by actors' deliberate attempts to craft and manipulate identifying symbols. It is, in other words, partly a result of strategic action. But it also depends – and in all likelihood, much more heavily – on mental attitudes and collective memories, consolidated over time, and over which movement activists have little control. Not to mention the fact that other social actors may be capable of manipulating in varying degrees the image which a particular collective has of itself (for example, the media: Gitlin 1980; Gamson and Wolfsfeld 1993; van Zoonen 1996; Gamson 2004; Earl, Martin, McCarthy, and Soule 2004; Myers and Caniglia 2004).

Furthermore, it is important to distinguish in this regard between the mobilization of people and the mobilization of other resources, for example organizational or financial (Oliver and Marwell 1992). Exclusive identities appear to be more effective in motivating direct participation. Inclusive identities, however, seem more useful, in principle, to the mobilization of the second type of resource (Diani and Donati 1996). Attempts to mobilize resources on the part of movement organizations are increasingly conducted by traditional marketing techniques and strategies like direct mail (McFarland 1984; Donati 1996; Jordan and Maloney 1997). Although messages of this type are often carefully tailored to specific sectors of the public and specific market niches, still their contents tend to be far more inclusive and all-embracing than those passed by movement activists through their personal networks (Snow et al. 1980). Access to the general public is therefore globally easier for movement actors who are bearers of an inclusive identity. Conversely, organizations with a more clear-cut cultural and political identity will have easy access only to the most sympathetic sectors of public opinion.

While they recognize both the limits of a strictly economic reading of collective action, and the opportunity to take into account nonmaterial incentives, the positions we have just presented are compatible with a rationalist paradigm. Other movement scholars have, however, expressed serious reservations about the opportunity to apply to the analysis of collective action concepts which were originally developed with reference to individual action of a utilitarian type

(Fireman and Gamson 1979; Ferree 1992; Melucci 1989). Speaking of nonmaterial incentives, or looking at identity as a criterion, enabling the costs and benefits of action to be calculated over time, is inappropriate for various reasons. First and foremost, the assumption that social actors always move on the basis of rational principles is debatable. On the contrary, nonrational elements, such as emotions, affections, and feelings, are also very important (Melucci 1989; Flam 1990; Taylor and Whittier 1995; Scheff 1994a, 1994b; Jasper and Poulsen 1995; Jasper 1997; Goodwin et al. 2001). The predominance of rationalist perspectives since the 1960s is easily explainable in the light of the need to challenge those analyses which reduced movements to a show of irrationality, the mere product of gaps in socialization processes (Taylor and Whittier: 179–80). However, this does not authorize support for the notion that emotions and reason are irreconcilable (Turner and Killian 1987; Goodwin et al. 2001: 2–16; Kim 2002).

Critics also charge the rationalist approach with overlooking the fact that social actors act and make choices within a system of interdependence with other actors. The decision to participate in action is, in reality, conditioned by the actor's expectations of those to which it is linked. The actor's capacity for autonomous choice varies according to the social class to which it belongs, and is limited by asymmetries in the distribution of power and social resources (Ferree 1992). When one recognizes that even economic action is governed by networks of relationships and by actor-binding social norms (for example, White 1988; DiMaggio and Powell 1991; Granovetter 1985), recourse to the concept of a rational actor for the analysis of collective phenomena appears to critics even more debatable.

A further problem derives from the fact that the goods among which the actor has to choose would naturally be different from those to which models of economic derivation normally refer (Fireman and Gamson 1979: 23–7). The legitimacy of the analogies between individual and collective interests should not be discounted. Many of the "goods" for which movements mobilize owe their very existence to collective action. Let us think for example of the reinforcement of women's identity and the transformations in women's private and public lifestyles. This particular "good" comes into existence also because of the very fact that women's collective action takes place. This is not to deny that many "goods" for women (e.g., those originating from policy change) may be treated within the boundaries of Olsonian models. But we want to point out that the collective action dilemma may also be seen in terms not necessarily compatible with Olson's approach to public goods.

Finally, even the last presupposition of rationalist paradigms – that of the stability of the structures of preference on which individual decisions to act are based – seems very unlikely in the case of collective action. The matter would be broadly plausible if the problem of collective action were one of decisions limited to a single moment, such as those relating to whether or not to participate in a particular demonstration. However, collective action is often a process which develops over time, in which the motivations which lead to action, and the underlying concerns, are modified through relationships with other actors, and where decisions to remain involved are continually renewed. In particular, many participants in collective action do not necessarily mobilize on the basis of solid preexisting identities, but these may develop in the course of action (Hirsch 1990; Fantasia 1988). This makes it difficult to support the idea that a structure of preferences exists.

To summarize, the model of the rational actor proposes a vision of action which, according to its critics, is fairly unrealistic and fails to take account either of the dynamic nature of action or of the importance of processes of identity creation. Furthermore, the adoption of a rational-choice perspective, paradoxically, ends up by obscuring even the role of interests: actors do not mobilize on behalf or in support of specific concerns or demands. Rather, they tend to become involved in those forms of collective action for which the greatest incentives are available. Finally, extending the model to normative and solidaristic incentives would imply broadening the concept of incentive to the point of tautology (Fireman and Gamson 1979).

As this is a controversy which covers the whole gamut of the social sciences, it would be unrealistic to dream of an appropriate synthesis of the two perspectives which we have reviewed here (Cohen 1985). Suffice to recall that supporters of rational-choice approaches have attempted to confront criticism directed at them by those upholding the identity paradigm. In particular, they have tried to analyze the location of actors in complex interdependent relationships, developing a vision of action which is more realistic and further away from the original hypothesis of the independent actor (Marwell and Oliver 1993; Gould 1993b; Opp and Gern 1993; Oberschall and Kim 1996; Heckathorn 1996).

4.4 How Is Identity Generated and Reproduced?

4.4.1 Self- and hetero-definitions of identity

If identity is a social process rather than a property of social actors, then feelings of belongingness and solidarity in relation to a certain group, the recognition of elements of continuity and discontinuity in the history of individuals, and the identification of one's own adversaries, may all be subject to recurring re-elaboration. Identity emerges from the processes of self-identification and external recognition. Actors' self-representations are, in fact, continuously confronted with images which institutions, sympathetic and hostile social groups, public opinion, and the media produce of them (Melucci 1996; Drury and Dreicher 2000; Howard 2000).

The construction of identity at the same time contains an aspiration to differentiate oneself from the rest of the world and to be recognized by it (Melucci 1982; Calhoun 1994a). A collective actor cannot exist without reference to experiences, symbols, and myths which can form the basis of its individuality. At the same time, however, symbolic production cannot count solely on self-legitimacy. It is necessary for certain representations of self to find recognition in the image which other actors have of the subject. Movements do indeed struggle for the recognition of their identity. It is only in the context of mutual recognition among actors that conflict and, more generally, social relationships can exist (Simmel 1955; Touraine 1981). Without this, self-affirmed identity on the part of a group will inevitably lead to its marginalization and its reduction to a deviant phenomenon.

The story of movements is therefore also the story of their members' ability to impose certain images of themselves, and to counter attempts by dominant groups to denigrate their aspirations to be recognized as different. A major example comes from the conflicts related to the construction of the modern nation-state. The development of vast, highly centralized political units led to an emphasis on cultural homogenization, through the affirmation of one "national" language and one "national" culture. Assimilationist policies often followed from this, in view of the multicultural nature of the territories coming under the dominion of new state formations. Cultural traditions different from those of the social groups, promoting the construction of the new nation-states, were stigmatized as relics of the past. For example, the construction of the French national identity led to the marginalization of the Provençal and Breton cultures. These became mere residues of a backward, premodern society, whose survival represented an unwelcome obstacle to the spread of the positive values of progress of which the French state made itself the bearer (Beer 1977, 1980; Safran 1989; Canciani and De La Pierre 1993).

The power to impose negative and stigmatized definitions of the identity of other groups constitutes, in fact, a fundamental mechanism of social domination. Especially at the early stages of mobilization, social movement activists are routinely described by powerholders as depraved, morally weak, corrupted people, unable to adapt to society's basic values. This applies to the early nineteenth-century's reactionaries facing massive social change (Tilly 1984a: ch. 1) as well as to the establishment's attempts to delegitimize protestors following the 2001 anti-G8 mobilization in Genoa. In the period between August 2001 and November 2002, when the Florence European Social Forum took place peacefully, the Italian government and sympathetic media waged a massive campaign portraying the movement as an unruly bunch, and invoking severe restrictions on rights to demonstrate (Andretta et al. 2002; see also chapter 7 below). As the accounts of protagonists of the post-Genoa phase suggest (Agnoletto 2003: ch. 3), a great effort had to be put into counterframing activity by movement activists.

At the same time, definitions of movement identity by movement opponents are not necessarily of the dismissive type. For example, over the last few years representatives of business have repeatedly attempted to portray global justice protestors as good-faith carriers of worthy sentiments and orientations, who despite their often unacceptable means should be taken seriously (think e.g. of George Soros's quotation, reported in the case history at the beginning of chapter 3 above). It has been suggested that big business should actively engage with protestors in order to find common grounds and create a space for dialogue (Callinicos 2001: 391).

Social movements challenging forms of domination deeply embedded in cultural practices, lifestyles, mental habits, and inbred stereotypes offer a particularly fitting illustration of these dynamics. Stigmatization from the outside often ends up blocking the development of a strong autonomous identity and limiting the possibilities for collective action. This is very clear, for instance, in the case of gay and lesbian movements (Armstrong 2002; Bernstein 1997; Valocchi 1999) as well as in less controversial movements like those acting on behalf of animal rights (e.g., Einwhoner 2002). In all cases, challenging negative stereotyping is a major component of movements' cultural production. A most blatant example is the stereotyping of women as uninterested in the public and political dimensions of social life, inclined towards the private sphere, most particularly family life, and as lacking the rational abilities which are held to be essential in order to act in the public sphere (Taylor 1996; Ferree and McClurg Mueller 2004: 596). Alongside creating practical opportunities to facilitate women's participation, political feminism has long attempted to overturn such images in places as diverse as the affluent postindustrial West (e.g., Taylor and Whittier 1995; Taylor 1996; Ferree and Roth 1998) or deprived South America (Auyero 2004; Bandy and Bickham-Mendez 2003) or India (Ray 1999). "I did not accept being beaten and staying quiet . . . any more. I didn't accept him [controlling] my body. . . . If I painted my nails, he would say, 'I'm going to crush them with a hammer,' and I didn't accept that any more" (quoted in Thayer 2001: 250). This sentence comes from a community organizer from one of the extreme peripheries of the world, the Brazilian *sertão*, but it could have come from women anywhere in the world.

4.4.2 Production of identity: symbols, practices, rituals

Among contemporary movements, nationalist movements are probably those most explicitly rooted in historical experience. Even students of nationalism, however, are skeptical of essentialist views of identity. Differences run in the historical foundations of the symbols and myths used to fabricate modern national identities. Some argue that modern national identities draw upon events, institutions, myths, and narrations which precede by a long period of time the existence of the nation-state (Smith 1981, 1986). Others object that large parts of the myths on which these are based do not have any historical foundation, and that one should rather talk of "invention of tradition" (Hobsbawm and Ranger 1983; see also Anderson 1983; Hobsbawm 1991).

Even where identity appeals to the history of the group and to its territorial and cultural roots, symbolic re-elaboration is always present. Studies of collective memory have shown that actors reappropriate social experiences and history, manipulating them and transforming them creatively, forging new myths and new institutions (Swidler and Arditi 1994: 308–10; Franzosi 2004). In fact, it is not necessary to attribute "objective" foundations to identity in order to recognize its continuity over time. A national sense of belonging, for example, is not reproduced solely at times of great patriotic fervor. On the contrary, its revitalization over time also depends – perhaps most importantly of all – on preconscious practices and on the persistence of mental forms and consolidated lifestyles (Billig 1995). But if this is the case, then it becomes important to look at the forms through which identity is developed and sustained, beyond intellectual and doctrinal production.

It would be dangerous to hazard a complete classification, but it is nevertheless possible to identify some basic manifestations.[10] The identity of a movement is, first, reinforced by reference to models of behavior which define in various ways the specificity of its activists in relation to "ordinary people" or their adversaries. In adopting certain styles of behavior or certain rituals, movement militants directly express their difference. Think for example of the Black Block and the Tute Bianche (literally, "white overalls") in the global justice movement (Andretta et al. 2002, 2003). They also refer to a series of objects, associated in various ways with their experience. Among these are a series of identifiers which enable supporters of a particular cause to be instantly recognizable (such as the smiling sun of antinuclear protesters, or the Palestinian *keffiyeh*, or the tattoos and shaven heads of right-wing movements [Blee 2002]); characters who have played an important role in the action of a movement or in the development of its ideology (M. L. King and Malcom X in the 1960s black mobilizations in the US , Ronald Laing and Franco Basaglia of the radical mental health movements in the 1970s and 1980s [Crossley 1998, 1999]); artifacts, including books or visual documents which help people to reconstruct the history of the movement and its origins in time, or to identify its stakes (Carson's *Silent Spring* [1962], Klein's *No Logo* [1999], or even Lenin's *What Is To Be Done?* [1961/1902]); and events or places of a particular symbolic significance (the Seattle anti-WTO demonstrations in 1999 [Smith 2001], the killing of Carlo Giuliani during the anti-G8 demonstrations in Genoa in 2001 [Andretta et al. 2002, 2003], the Tiananmen square massacre of 1989 in Beijing [Calhoun 1994c]). These elements are merged into stories or narratives (Somers 1994) which circulate among members of a movement, reflecting their vision of the world and reinforcing solidarity.

Combining these elements often produces identities that are difficult to associate strongly with any specific social trait or historical experience. For example, it has been observed that in societies characterized by multiple cultures and traditions, as in the USA, conditions exist for the development of forms of "symbolic ethnicity" (Gans 1979). These forms of identification have no foundation in the historic and cultural heritage of a given group, but mix together symbols and references deriving from diverse social groups to form a new synthesis. For example, collective identities such as Rastafarianism are founded only partly on specific cultural models and religious allegiances. They are also the product of choices made by individuals who come from a range of backgrounds but derive feelings of belonging and incentives for action through reference to a particular culture. It is therefore possible to be a "Rasta" without having historical roots in this group (Kuumba and Ajanaku 1998).

Models of behavior, objects, and narratives are often merged in specific ritual forms. The ritual component fulfills an important role in movement practice, and above all in the production of identities. In general, rituals represent forms of symbolic expression by which communications concerning social relationships are passed on, in stylized and dramatized ways (Whutnow 1987; Kertzer 1988). These consist, in particular, of procedures which are more or less codified, through which a vision of the world is communicated, a basic historical experience is reproduced, a symbolic code overthrown (Sassoon 1984a, 1984b). They contribute to the reinforcement of identity and of collective feelings of belonging; and at the same time, they enable movement actors to give free rein to their emotions (Goodwin et al. 2001).

Recurrences of particularly significant events in the history of opposition movements or their constituency are often marked by ritual practices (Kertzer 1996). By demonstrating on May 1st or March 8th, workers' and women's movements remind themselves and society at large of their roots, thus revitalizing their identity. On a more modest scale, protest movements across the world have promoted demonstrations on the anniversaries of crucial events in their development, from the assassinations of black American leaders Martin Luther King and Malcolm X, to the Chernobyl nuclear accident, to the Milan bombings which, in 1969, marked the beginning of a particularly dramatic period in Italy's life. Rituals remain important even in those cases where movements have succeeded in gaining power. The French revolutionary government celebrated the advent of "new man" in ceremonies at the Champs de Mars; the Italian Fascist regime, for its part, stressed its continuity with Italy's glorious past by celebrating the anniversary of the foundation of Rome (Hunt 1984; Berezin 2001).

Religion, especially but not only in authoritarian regimes, offers many contexts for the production of identity (Smith 1996). Opposition to the communist regime in Poland heavily relied on religious symbols and practices to reinforce identity and commitment to the cause (Osa 2003a, 2003b). Religious celebrations provided the context for the production and spread of nationalist interpretative frames in the Baltic republics at the time of their enforced association with the Soviet Union. The Catalan and Basque churches played a similar role during Franco's dictatorship in Spain (Johnston 1991a, 1991b, 1994). The legitimization of religious rituals creates opportunities for collective gatherings, and therefore for the strengthening and the diffusion of alternative messages, in repressive regimes. The funeral of the Abbot of Montserrat monastery, a well-known Catalan nationalist and opponent of the Franco regime, in 1968, represented an opportunity for different sectors of Catalan opposition to get together and reinforce their collective solidarity (Johnston 1991b: 156–8). Likewise, religious functions in Reza Pahlevi's Iran not only supported the emergence of opposition cultures in that country, but also ensured that these cultures developed a marked theocratic character, paving the way for the advent of the ayatollahs' regime (Moaddel 1992).

Ritual practices cannot, however, be reduced simply to public demonstrations of a celebratory nature. All protest events promoted by movements have a ritual dimension, which often assumes a powerfully dramatic and spectacular quality. The forms which demonstrations take, the type of slogans shouted, the banners or placards waved, even the conduct of marshal bodies, are all elements which, potentially, render the practice of a movement distinctive. Opponents of nuclear energy have often acted out, in the course of their demonstrations, the catastrophic consequences of an atomic explosion. Similarly, women's, ethnonationalist, and youth movements have included theatrical-type performances in their repertoire of collective action, alongside political demonstrations (see also chapter 7 below). Through rituals, traditional symbolic codes are overturned and the rules which habitually determine appropriate social behavior are denied. For example, by recounting in public their experiences of sexual abuse, many American women have transformed episodes, which might otherwise have produced only feelings of shame and personal isolation, into a source of pride (Taylor and Whittier 1995).

Identities are often created and reproduced in specific social and/or communitarian settings. Over 20 years ago, Melucci (1984a) spoke of "movement areas" to identify the actors involved in various forms of identity politics in Milan, and the relationships which linked them, not only through participation in associations but also and most importantly through the involvement in cultural activities, the patronage of specific cafes, bookshops, meditation centers, etc. In doing so, he referred to a form of social organization that was far less rigid and exclusive than world-rejecting alternative communities or sects, but still provided the social context to experiment with new lifestyles. Over the last decades, the concepts of subculture and counterculture have often been used to characterize sectors of the population sharing similar cultural orientations (see also chapter 3 above), yet with varying degrees of hostility and open challenges to cultural power and dominant lifestyles (e.g. the gay and lesbian scene: Duyvendak 1995; Rupp and Taylor 2003). Some have spoken of "social movement scenes" to stress the association of these sub- and counter-cultures to specific physical space, normally city neighborhoods (Haunss and Leach 2004). Others (Kaplan and Lööw 2002) have used the concept of "cultic milieu" to characterize the collection of organized labor and environmentalist groups, anarchists and progressive Christians, gay and lesbian organizations, and Catholics involved in the recent global justice campaigns and stress analogies to the cultural underground of the 1960s.

Rituals which relate to the internal life of a group and are not in public view should not be forgotten. Procedures signaling the admission of new members into movement organizations often take on the form of genuine "rites of passage" (van Gennep 1983; Sassoon 1984a, 1984b). The fact that membership entails – to a degree, at least – the death and rebirth of one's personality, is of particular relevance in the case of neoreligious movements (Berger and Luckmann 1966). Furthermore, procedures which signal some form of transformation of the position of militants, at times when their involvement seems to have increased, are found in virtually every type of organization. In radical extra-parliamentary groups, becoming a member of marshal bodies was usually preceded by other forms of militancy which were less demanding and less risky, such as distributing leaflets. These duties also fulfilled the task of determining the trustworthiness and firmness of the political passion of the new militant (della Porta 1990). In many feminist groups, behavioral rituals support the action of consciousness-raising and personal transformation (Taylor and Whittier 1995); the same may be found in white supremacist organizations (Blee 2002).

4.4.3 Identity and the political process

For political movements, the construction of identity is often conditioned by variables of a strictly political nature. The criteria by which social groups identify themselves and are identified externally echo characteristics of the political system and of the political culture of a given country. It seems that the development of collective identity can be explained by reference to a reformulated version of the well-known argument that forms of policymaking determine forms of political action, and not vice versa (Lowi 1971). Social actors, in fact, tend to structure their action and establish alliances in different ways on different policy issues, with large interest groups dominating distributive policies and more pluralistic networks characterizing regulatory policies.

Other peculiarities of policy areas have also been singled out for their impact on the structure of contentious politics in those areas (Bartholomew and Mayer 1992; Jenson 1995). For example, the emergence in the USA of a specific identity linking Asian-Americans, and the development of "pan-ethnic collective action" (Okamoto 2003) at that level, have been put down to the fact that, in crucial areas such as those of immigration policy and the rights of minority groups, public agencies tended to treat ethnic groups as homogeneous. This despite their seeing each other as profoundly different, such as the Vietnamese or the Koreans. In this case, the adoption of a certain political/administrative criterion has produced interests and identities which enable different groups to act collectively on a number of issues (Omi and Winant 1994).

On another level, actors' identities are defined also in the context of dominant political divisions/cleavages in a given society. Movements develop in political systems which already have a structure: they try to modify it and to activate processes of political realignment (Tilly 1978; Dalton et al. 1984; Bartolini and Mair 1990). When established political identities are salient, i.e. still capable of shaping political behavior and solidarities (Kriesi et al. 1995: ch. 1), emerging social movements have to produce identities which are sufficiently specific to provide the foundations for the diversity of the movement in relation to its adversaries; but at the same time, sufficiently close to traditional collective identities in order to make it possible for movement actors to communicate with those who continue to recognize themselves in consolidated identities. Under those conditions, opportunities for genuinely "new" movements, i.e. movements cutting across established cleavages, will be relatively limited (Diani 2000a).

Interactions with authorities often represent important sources of identity. It has long been noticed how "encounters with unjust authority" (Gamson, Fireman, and Rytina 1982) may facilitate the consolidation of both motivations to act and hostility towards powerholders and their representatives (see also chapter 8 below). For example, accounts of Italian terrorists of the 1970s often mentioned mistreatment by police or by the judiciary as one of the driving forces behind their radicalization (della Porta 1990; Catanzaro and Manconi 1995). In much broader – and milder – terms, we can view interactions with state agents who do not behave according to expectations or political representatives who fail to recognize people's genuine needs as facilitators of the development of political identity. For example, Drury et al. (2003) analyzed how the identities of local residents, participating in an antiroad protest in England in 1993–4, evolved during the conflict. They found that the role of the police in supporting the bailiffs in the eviction of protestors from the area contributed to enlarge participants' feelings of identification from the boundaries of the local communities towards a global social movement. Investigating the relation between everyday life and protest in 1990s Argentina, Auyero (2004) showed that the transformation of an unemployed, divorced woman with no tradition of political interest whatsoever into a prominent community organizer depended in no small measure on the sense of outrage that she experienced at her interactions with two types of "unjust authorities": "political authority," in the form of the local governor, who portrayed hungry protestors as a mob; and "social authority," in the shape of a fellow male protestor who reproduced gender stereotypes by dismissing the role of women in the struggle.

4.5 Summary

Identity construction is an essential component of collective action. It enables actors engaged in conflict to see themselves as people linked by interests, values, common histories – or else as divided by these same factors. Although identity feelings are frequently elaborated in reference to specific social traits such as class, gender, territory, or ethnicity, the process of collective identity does not necessarily imply homogeneity of the actors sharing that identity, or their identification with a distinct social group. Nor are feelings of belonging always mutually exclusive. On the contrary, actors frequently identify with heterogeneous collectives who are not always compatible among themselves on fundamental issues. To reconstruct the tensions through the different versions of identity of a movement, and how these versions are negotiated, represents, according to some scholars, a central problem for the analysis of collective action.

Identity plays an important role in the explanation of collective action even for those who see in collective action a peculiar form of rational behavior. Those who perceive in collective identity certain criteria for evaluating, in the medium and long terms, the costs and benefits of action, are numerous. However, those who hold that this use of the concept of identity cannot be proposed are equally numerous. Because of its strongly emotive and affective components, as well as its controversial and constructed nature, it is difficult to associate identity with behavior of a strategic type. Identity develops and is renegotiated via various processes. These include conflicts between auto- and hetero-definitions of reality; various forms of symbolic production, collective practices, and rituals. It is important, furthermore, to bear in mind the characteristics of the political process, which can influence definitions of identity.

INDIVIDUALS, NETWORKS, AND PARTICIPATION

Viale Sarca is a long, fairly anonymous road on the Milanese periphery, lined with tenements that mostly used to host workers of the Pirelli factory nearby. In the late 1990s, urban renewal brought new intellectual glamour to the area, following the location, on the former Pirelli estate, of the campus of the second state university of Milan. Developers were nowhere to be seen, however, in 1985, when Mario Diani traveled there to meet Antonio, a local environmental and political activist. Mario was researching the Milanese environmental movement and Antonio's name had been passed to him as the contact person for a grassroots political ecology group operating in the area. The offspring of southern Italian farmers turned industrial workers who migrated to Milan in the 1950s, Antonio had followed a fairly common path of political socialization: exposed to trade unionism and communist party politics in his teens, he had become involved with radical left group Lotta Continua (Continuous Struggle) in the 1970s and had later developed an interest in the link between social deprivation and environmental degradation. He was also an active member of a local Green List that was forming at the time. In order to promote campaigning on environmental issues in the highly polluted northern Milanese periphery, he had drawn upon the contacts developed during his previous militancy. The core activists in his new environmental group all shared a past of activism in the same local branch of Lotta Continua. Acquaintances and contacts developed over the years had also proved useful with the promotion of specific actions: Antonio had collaborated with a range of local organizations across the broad spectrum of the New and the Old Left, including local branches of parties and unions, cultural and cooperative associations.

Antonio's story is interesting for various reasons. First of all, although it is set in the 1980s, well before antiglobalization movements developed, there are more than passing analogies to what has been going on since the late 1990s. Antonio was actually an early example of what we would now call an "environmental justice activist" (Çapek 2003), successfully integrating concern for social inequality with interest in environmental conditions in urban areas. His story also is a good illustration of the main themes of this chapter, namely the dynamic nature of the relationship between networks and participation, and the duality of the link between individuals and organizational activities. First of all, social networks affect participation in collective action, while in turn participation shapes networks, reinforcing preexisting ones or creating new ones. Social networks may increase individual chances to become involved, and strengthen activists' attempts to further the appeal of their causes: when Antonio decided to start a local environmental action group, he successfully tried and convinced his former comrades in Lotta Continua to join him in the new enterprise. That they not only quickly got involved with the environmental issues, but agreed to support the particular agenda Antonio was proposing, depended in no small measure on the mutual trust, sense of companionship, solidarity, and the shared understandings and worldviews that had been forged and developed through their long-term acquaintance in Lotta Continua. From this perspective, therefore, previous social networks facilitated the development of new forms of collective action at later stages.

At the same time, social networks are not only a facilitator but also a product of collective action: while people often become involved in a specific movement or campaign through their previous links, their very participation also forges new links, which in turn affect subsequent developments in their activist careers (and indeed in their lives at large). Let us look at Antonio's involvement with Lotta Continua from this angle: the members of his local branch had been recruited to New Left radicalism via a range of ties, developed in school and peer groups, in political organizations (e.g., youth branches of traditional left parties) as well as in other associations (e.g., church-related ones). Participation in Lotta Continua was therefore as much the product of previous networks (including previous forms of participation) as it was the source of networks which people like Antonio could draw upon at later stages.

However, there is another important dynamic which Antonio's story draws our attention to, namely the duality of individuals and organizations: our uniqueness as individuals is determined by the particular combination of our group memberships; at the same time, by being members of different groups, we create linkages between them (Simmel 1955; Breiger 1974). Looking at people's membership in associations and organizations, and at their participation in social and cultural activities close to social movement milieus, we can derive important information about their involvement in collective action. Antonio is a case in point. His identity as a "political man" was determined by the intersection of militancy in a grassroots ecology group and in a left-wing local Green List; on this ground, he differed markedly from other environmental activists, who combined environmentalism with membership in mainstream, moderate recreational, or cultural associations. At the same time, though, by being active in a local political ecology group and in a New Left party, and by participating occasionally in other local groups, Antonio somehow linked them all; he provided a channel of communication which proved useful for promoting joint initiatives, and also facilitated the growth of mutual trust and solidarity between the different groups. One might not go as far as talking about "collective identity" in this case, yet a social bond was definitely there: people do not usually join organizations which perceive each other as radically incompatible and hostile. It is also worthwhile noting that individuals also connect organizations across time: for example, Antonio's and his friends' previous involvement with Lotta Continua also linked – via their individual biographies – grassroots politics of the 1970s and the 1980s.

To sum up, the relationship between individuals and the networks in which they are embedded is crucial not only for the involvement of people in collective action, but also for the sustenance of action over time, and for the particular form that the coordination of action among a multiplicity of groups and organizations may take. In the next section, we ask whether being linked to people who already participate may facilitate individuals' decisions to devote time and energy to collective action. We map the origins of this question, as well as the criticisms that a response based on the role of networks has attracted. Behind these questions lurks a much broader debate on the relationship between structure and action. Over the past decade this discussion has attracted many contributions from scholars with a specific interest in collective action (Sewell 1992; Emirbayer and Goodwin 1994; Emirbayer 1997; Emirbayer and Mische 1998; Livesay 2002). Although we cannot address that debate here, we nevertheless have to be aware of the broader theoretical context in which our specific research interests are located.

Later in the chapter, we move to the other side of the individual–networks relationship, that is, the contribution that individuals give to the making of social movements out of the multiplicity of groups, associations, and concerned individuals involved in collective action on certain broad issues. Although some organizations require exclusive commitments, most do not. We explore these processes of network-building and mutual understanding, made possible by individuals' multiple memberships in various types of informal groups and more formal associations. In doing so we connect our discussion – once again mostly implicitly – to the broader debate on the role of social networks as a source of individual as well as collective opportunities (Coleman 1990; Putnam 1993; Putnam 2000; Edwards, Foley, and Diani 2001; Prakash and Selle 2004). From that particular angle, networks facilitating involvement in social movement activities may be regarded as one particular version of "social capital" (Diani 1997).

However, individuals do not create connections solely through organizational memberships, but also through their participation in various types of social and cultural activities (music festivals, communities of taste, reading groups, alternative cafes, cinemas, theaters, etc.). By doing so they reproduce specific subcultural or countercultural milieus that offer both opportunities for protest activities and for the maintenance and transformation of critical orientations even when protest is not vibrant (Melucci 1996). The final part of the chapter deals with this issue; it also addresses in that context the question of whether the diffusion of computer-mediated communication may alter the conditions under which alternative critical communities and cultural settings are reproduced. The literature on the role of networks and virtual and real communities in the "network society" (Castells 1996; Calhoun 1998; Wellman and Haythornwhyte 2002; Rheingold 2002; van de Donk, Loader, Nixon, and Rucht 2004) provides the broader context for this discussion.

5.1   Why Do People Get Involved in Collective Action? The Role of Networks

How frequent is recruitment through social networks *vis-à-vis* other mobilization channels, such as exposure to media messages, or spontaneous, unsolicited decisions to participate? In one of the first studies to document the importance of personal networks for recruitment processes, Snow, Zurcher, and Ekland Olson (1980) showed social networks to account for the adhesion of a large share (60 to 90 percent) of members of various religious and political organizations, with the only exception being Hare Krishna. They suggested that only sects, overtly hostile to their social environment, attracted a significant share of people with personal difficulties and lacking extended relational resources (see also Stark and Bainbridge 1980). Looking at nonreligious organizations, Diani and Lodi (1988) found a similarly strong role for networks, showing that 78 percent of environmental activists in Milan in the 1980s had been recruited through personal contacts developed either in private settings (family, personal friendship circles, colleagues) or in the context of other associational activities.

While joining religious sects that are deeply hostile to the secular world may not require strong networks, the opposite seems to hold for adhesion to radical political organizations. Available evidence suggests that the more costly and dangerous the collective action, the stronger and more numerous the ties required for individuals to participate. Studying recruitment to the civil rights project Freedom Summer, aimed at increasing blacks' participation in politics in the southern states of the US in the 1960s, McAdam (1986) suggested that joining was not correlated with individual attitudes but rather with three factors: the number of organizations individuals were members of, especially the political ones; the amount of previous experiences of collective action; the links to other people who were also involved with the campaign. In her study of a similarly risky, though very different, type of activism, della Porta (1988) found that involvement in terrorist left-wing groups in Italy was facilitated by strong inter-personal linkages, many to close friends or kin. A recent study of the role played by single members in the development of the Nazi party in 1920s Germany (i.e., members who were not associated with any local chapter: Anheier 2003) adds a further dimension to this argument. At one level, Nazi political entrepreneurs were far from isolated. On the contrary, they were strongly embedded in the broader networks connecting right-wing, nationalistic, and paramilitary organi-zations in the turbulent years that had followed defeat in the First World War. At the same time, those were strongly "concentric" (Simmel 1955) networks: i.e., networks that were dense internally, but secluded from other types of social or political organizations.

Embeddedness in social networks not only matters for recruitment; it also works as an antidote to leaving, and as a support to continued participation. For example, members of voluntary associations in America whose social ties are mostly to other organization members are more likely to remain committed to those organizations than are those who instead have a greater share of connec-tions to nonmembers (McPherson, Popielarz, and Drobnic 1992). In his study of dropouts from Swedish temperance organizations, Sandell (1999) also discovered substantial positive and negative bandwagon effects, as people tended both to join and leave in clusters, and to be affected more heavily by their closest links (see also Sandell and Stern 1998; Tindall 2004).

The relevance of these findings is not restricted to recruitment to social movements or religious organizations. Similar mechanisms seem to exist in organizations, such as charities and volunteer groups, with no explicit political goals, and/or which are reluctant to include protest and direct action among their tactical options (Wilson 2000); the same seems to apply to established interest representation groups such as unions (Dixon and Roscigno 2003). Accordingly, it is advisable to approach the issue by considering network mechanisms in refer-ence both to radical, grassroots organizations and other types of association (Knoke 1990c; Knoke and Wisely 1990; Kitts 2000; Oliver and Marwell 2001; Passy 2001, 2003; Diani 2004b).

How do social networks affect decisions to participate in collective action? Through what mechanisms do they operate? Florence Passy (2003) has drawn a distinction between the socialization, structural connection, and decision-shaping functions of networks in the mobilization process. In the first instance, networks operate to create predispositions to action. Being linked to people who are already committed to a certain cause enables individuals to feel part of a "collective we," to elaborate systems of meaning that render collective action both a meaningful and a feasible undertaking, to perceive certain issues as socially relevant and worthy of collective efforts. At the same time, social networks often create opportunities for transforming predispositions into action (what Passy calls the structural connection function). People with certain predispositions will be more likely to contact organizations and come across opportunities for participation if they are connected to people already involved. Finally, holding certain views and having opportunities to act does not guarantee that mobilization will occur. Decisions to act will also be affected by one's network ties. Individuals do not make decisions in isolation but in the context of what other people do, hence the importance of network connections (Passy 2003: 23–7). Passy also showed how these functions take different forms depending on the traits of the organization trying to recruit, and its visibility in the public space. For example, the social connection function is more important for adhesion to organizations that are not very visible in the public space, like the Third World solidarity group Bern Declaration studied by Passy, than for organizations with a strong public presence, like the Swiss branch of WWF.[1]

Recognizing the role of networks in facilitating recruitment and sustaining participation in collective action has been crucial for the development of sounder interpretations of protest behavior, because it has enabled scholars to challenge views of protest and countercultural behavior as unruly and deviant. Still in the early 1970s, established academic wisdom regarded individual involvement in social movements as the result of a "mix of personal pathology and social disorganization" (McAdam 2003: 281). At the micro level, collective action was explained by the marginal location of the individuals involved in protest activity, and the lack of integration in their social milieu; at the macro level, by the disruption of routine social arrangements, brought about by radical processes of change and modernization. Both explanations posited a fundamental opposition between protest politics and democratic politics (Kornhauser 1959; Lipset 1960; Buechler 2004).

The separation of protest and routinized politics was challenged by scholars who claimed that grassroots, contentious collective action was ultimately "politics by other means." From this perspective, social movements were merely one of the options that challengers could draw upon to pursue their policy outcomes and their quest for membership in the polity (Tilly 1978). In contrast to accounts of participation in social movements as dysfunctional behavior, social movement activists and sympathizers were portrayed as rich in both cognitive resources and entrepreneurial and political skills (Oberschall 1973; McCarthy and Zald 1977). Most important to us, they were also found to be rich in relational resources, i.e., well integrated in their communities, and strongly involved in a broad range of organizations, from political ones to voluntary associations and community groups (Snow et al. 1980; McAdam 1986; Diani and Lodi 1988). The development of cross-national surveys analyzing individual participation has largely backed this argument with reference to both institutional politics and protest politics, as participation in the two is strongly correlated (Barnes, Kaase, et al. 1978; Jennings et al. 1990; Norris 2002).

Mass society theorists posited that associations would discourage radical collective action because of their capacity to integrate elites and ordinary citizens, socialize their members to the rules of the game, give them a sense of political efficacy, and provide them with primary attachments and a more satisfactory life. Now we know that organizational participation can work in the opposite direction as well: for instance, membership in associations can also socialize people to orientations critical of the status quo rather than supportive of it; it can put people who sympathize with a certain cause in touch with fellow citizens with the necessary political skills for mobilization; it can cause individuals to experience feelings of moral pressure if they do not participate when their close acquaintances are active in a given cause (Pinard 1968: 683; Kitts 2000; Passy 2003).

Mobilization in social movements frequently occurs through mechanisms of "bloc recruitment" (Oberschall, 1973): cells, branches, or simply significant groups of members of existing organizations are recruited as a whole to a new movement, or contribute to the start of new campaigns (as in Antonio's case, where the local branch of Lotta Continua was instrumental to the foundation of a Green List in the area). Far from necessarily preventing social conflict, intermediate structures also have mobilizing effects, and can motivate and legitimate both individual and collective participation. Another argument vigorously put forward by mass society theory, namely that formal organizations are bound to become the most important reference group for their members in contemporary society, has also been proved wrong; to the contrary, primary groups and social networks within small communities often play that role for individuals (Pinard 1968: 684; see also Bolton, 1972; Pickvance, 1975; Fantasia 1988; Lichterman 1995a).

Recognizing the impact of social networks on both individual participation and overall levels of collective action among a given population also provides the foundations for a critique of structuralist theories of collective action (including deterministic versions of Marxism). They explained action as the result of the shared attributes of a given population (whether a class, a nation, or an otherwise defined group). By this token, the overall mobilization capacity of a given social group should be related to its dimensions, and so should its changes over time; for example, the diminished levels of mobilization by the working class in Western democracies are imputed to its contraction and its overall reduced centrality in the economic process.[2] In contrast, many students of social movements nowadays associate collective action with catnets, i.e., with the co-presence in a given population of cat(egorical traits) and net(works). Sharing certain class locations, gender, nationality, or religious beliefs certainly provides the elements on the basis of which recognition and identity-building may take place. But it is through the channels of communication and exchange, constituted by social networks, that the mobilization of resources and the emergence of collective actors become possible (Tilly 1978).

5.2 Do Networks Always Matter?

The role of networks in recruitment processes has been questioned from different angles. On logical grounds, the network thesis would be inconsistent with the fact that those most inclined to action are young people, biographically available because their original family ties no longer bind them as they used to, and new family and professional ties are still developing (Piven and Cloward 1992: 308–9). Most fundamentally, the network thesis would also be largely tautological, given the spread of ties across groups and individuals: "lateral integration, however fragile, is ubiquitous, thus making opportunities for protest ubiquitous" (Piven and Cloward 1992: 311). Rather than highlighting exclusively those cases in which ties are found to be predictors of involvement, analysts should also look at those cases when networks are present yet participation does not result.

It has also been suggested that focusing on networks diverts attention away from the really crucial process for mobilization, namely the transmission of cognitive cultural messages (Jasper and Poulsen 1995). Although this may happen through networks, it may also take place through other channels such as the media. Campaigners may have to resort to "moral shocks" with strong emotional impact in order to recruit strangers that they cannot access via personal networks. This may be particularly the case for movements who try to bring new issues onto the political agenda, and/or whose leaders do not have a significant political background:

> The use of condensing symbols without social networks may mean that a movement is more likely to employ extreme moralistic appeals that demonize its opponents. It may be more likely to rely on professional or highly motivated bands to do much of its work, as with animal rights activists who break into labs. In contrast . . . movement organizers [who] can tap into an active subculture of politically involved citizens . . . can rely on earlier framing activity . . . They have correspondingly less need of moral shocks administered to the public.
>
> *(Jasper and Poulsen 1993: 508)*

Sustained involvement in collective action may also be facilitated by the participation, not necessarily planned or anticipated, in events that turn out to have a powerful emotional impact – sometimes on entire collectivities, other times, on specific individuals (Turner and Killian 1987; Goodwin et al. 2001). We have already come across Javier Auyero's analysis of the mechanisms through which a woman with no interest in politics nor ties to political activists turned into a community leader in a small Argentinian town in less than a week, following her occasional involvement in a blockade, promoted by local residents to complain about joblessness and hardship in the region. Given her background, a network explanation for such developments seems implausible. That this happened was due in much larger measure to the interplay of several expressions of outrage: at a judiciary system that was failing her in her struggle to secure help for her kids' upbringing from her estranged husband; at local politicians attempting to manipulate local people's protests to pursue their own political ends; at the provincial governor's framing of hungry people's collective action as criminal behavior; not to mention dismissive attitudes by male fellow protestors (Auyero 2004).

Empirically, we can identify several instances of mobilization both occurring largely outside social networks, or not occurring despite the presence of social networks. For example, only one-fifth of participants in anti-abortion mobilizations in California had been recruited through networks (Luker 1984); and we have already seen that members of religious sects may have joined them largely independently from their previous connections (Snow et al., 1980). Conversely, Mullins (1987) showed that the wealth of interpersonal contacts in a Brisbane local community did not result in mobilizations against plans for a freeway crossing the neighborhood. Even when network effects are discovered, findings are sometimes ambiguous. For example, Oliver (1984) found people acquainted with their neighbors to be more likely to become involved in neighborhood associations, but network effects, overall, were mixed in her analysis. More recently, Nepstad and Smith (1999) duplicated McAdam's study of Freedom Summer by looking at participants and dropouts in the Nicaragua Exchange Brigade in the 1980s. In that case, ties to people directly involved were the most powerful predictor of participation, but the number of prospective participants' ties to other organizations did not matter. However, the relationship was reversed for people who joined after the organization's third year in existence, with the number of organizational links being important and ties to actual participants no longer helping.

These criticisms have prompted analysts of social networks to substantially qualify their points. It is now widely recognized that, when looking at the relationship between networks and participation, it is important to specify its terms. Questions such as "What networks actually explain what?" and "Under what conditions do specific networks become relevant?" are crucial in this regard. At the moment, however, we have no conclusive answers to such questions. At times, it is the position one occupies within a network which matters, rather than the mere fact of being involved in some kind of network. In one of their explorations of participation in Freedom Summer, Fernandez and McAdam (1989) looked at individual centrality in the network, which consisted of all the activists who had applied to take part in the campaign in Madison, Wisconsin. Joint memberships in social organizations of all sorts represented the links between individuals. Those who were more central in that network (i.e., who were either linked to a higher number of prospective participants, and/or were connected to people who were also central in that network) were more likely to go through the training process undeterred, and eventually to join the campaign. In that case, involvement in networks did not count as much as one's location within them.

The context in which mobilization attempts take place is also very important, as local conditions affect how social networks operate. Kriesi (1988b) studied recruitment to the 1985 People's Petition campaign, which collected signatures against the deployment of SS20 cruise missiles in the Netherlands. In areas where countercultural milieus were weak, people already had to be members of local political organizations in order to mobilize in the campaign; where counter-cultural milieus were strong, and the overall attitudes toward collective action were in general more favorable, there was less need for links to members of specific political organizations to encourage adhesion: more people were recruited through personal friendship networks or even in other forms not based on network links at all (e.g. self-applications: Kriesi 1988b: 58). Strong countercultural milieus seemed to have an autonomous capacity to motivate people, which in turn made specific organizational connections less necessary. Along similar lines, McAdam and Fernandez (1990) found that recruitment to the Freedom Summer campaign depended more strongly on membership in organizational networks on a campus with a weak tradition of activism like Madison, Wisconsin, than on a campus with a strong tradition of alternative politics like Berkeley.

We have already seen (section 5.1) that radical activism often needs dense supporting networks. At the other extreme, participation in organizational activities that are not very demanding might not necessarily require the backing of strong social networks. For example, adhesion to cultural associations or even religious groups that promote practices fairly close to market activities (e.g., individual meditation, alternative health practices like yoga, etc.) may easily occur even though people's decisions to get involved are not supported by specific social networks (Stark and Bainbridge 1980). Even public interest groups, like those active in the environmental movement, may rely on networks to a variable extent, depending on their levels of moderation and institutionalization. For example, Diani and Lodi (1988) found that recruitment to organizations in the more established conservation sector depended more on private networks than recruitment to more critical groups, which largely took place through ties developed in previous experiences of collective action. They explained this difference by suggesting that exclusively private ties (i.e., ties developed in contexts detached from collective action milieus) may be enough to facilitate adhesion to organizations that have widely accepted policy goals (for example, supporting a local group campaigning to create new green spaces in the neighborhood). In contrast, joining organizations with some radical stances, like political ecology ones, may require people to overcome higher barriers. Accordingly, this may be easier if people are linked to acquaintances met during specific experiences of collective action rather than in more generic settings like one's neighborhood. However, adhesion to very demanding forms of collective action may also occur without networks playing a major role. In the case of world-rejecting religious sects, who require of their members a total break with their previous lifestyles and habits, involvement may be easier for isolated individuals than for people who are well embedded in social networks. In all likelihood, network links would exert some kind of cross-pressure, thus discouraging prospective adepts from joining (Snow et al. 1980).

Increasingly, researchers have recognized that people are involved in multiple ties, and that while some may facilitate participation, others may discourage it (Kitts 2000). Taking this possibility into account, McAdam and Paulsen (1993) tried to determine what dimensions of social ties are most important, and how different types of ties shape decisions to participate. Their conclusions substantially qualified earlier arguments (including their own: McAdam 1986) on the link between participation and former organizational memberships. As such, embeddedness in organizational links did not predict activism, nor did strong ties to people who already volunteered. Instead, what mattered most was a strong commitment to a particular identity, reinforced by ties to participants, whether of an organizational or private type. Having been a member of, say, left-wing groups in the past did not represent a predictor of participation in Freedom Summer unless it was coupled with a strong, subjective identification with that milieu.

Being directly linked – mostly via organizational ties – to people who already participate may thus not be an essential precondition for recruitment. Lack of direct ties may be overcome if prospective participants are embedded in organizational networks compatible with the campaign/organization they are considering joining (Kriesi 1988b; McAdam and Fernandez 1990; McAdam and Paulsen 1993). However, we can also think of the reverse situation, with people mobilizing through contacts developed in contexts not directly associated with participation, but that nonetheless create opportunities for people with similar presuppositions to meet and eventually develop joint action. Research on adhesion to two action committees campaigning against low-flying military jets in two German villages (Ohlemacher 1996), showed that recruitment attempts were far more successful for the committee whose members were mostly part of neutral organizations in their village rather than of explicitly political ones. Membership in apparently innocuous organizations such as parent–teacher associations or sport clubs enabled members of the committee to reach, and gain the trust of, a broader range of people than they could have had they been members of organizations with a more clear-cut political identity. Similar mechanisms may also influence involvement in nonprotest actions. For example, Becker and Dhingra (2001) illustrated how membership in religious congregations, and the resulting ties to fellow members, enabled people to engage in a variety of activities in the community, but without any bearing on levels of involvement in the congregational activities. Congregations offered individuals the opportunity to form close links of friendship and support, but the resulting social capital seemed to exert its effects mainly beyond the boundaries of the congregation.

To sum up, studies of the relationship between networks and participation have gone a long way toward specifying its terms. Questions such as "what networks account for what type of participation?" have been addressed from a variety of perspectives. Although findings are not always consistent, nor necessarily comparable, it is possible to identify some recurring themes. First, the role of networks seems to vary, depending on the costs attached to the action which they are supposed to facilitate. Whether costs defined in terms of personal risks, or of the energy and commitment required to join a specific action or organization, more demanding forms of action have often (but not always: Snow et al. 1980) been backed by stronger and more specific networks. Number and intensity of ties to other participants have been found to play a role in recruitment to dangerous actions of the violent (della Porta 1988) as well as of the peaceful (McAdam 1986, 1988a) kind. A central position in the networks linking prospective participants has also been identified as an important predictor of actual participation (Fernandez and McAdam 1989).

The extent to which the mobilizing messages and the cultural orientation of a movement differ from, and are at odds with, the dominant orientations in society also seems to make certain networks more effective than others. Private networks, consisting for example of ties to friends or acquaintances without involvement in specific organizations or subcultural milieus, have been found to matter most in cases when the message of a movement was well accepted in the social milieus in which prospective participants lived and operated – whether conservation styles of environmental activism in 1980s Milan (Diani and Lodi 1988), radical civil rights action in 1960s Berkeley subcultures (McAdam and Fernandez 1990), or peace campaigns in Dutch cities in the 1980s (Kriesi 1988b). Networks more directly embedded in political and at times radical organizations and subcultures have been found to count relatively more for recruitment to organizations whose message was less mainstream, although not necessarily antagonistic, in their specific context (such as political ecologists in Milan, civil rights activism in Madison, or peace action in Dutch cities with a weak presence of alternative subcultures).

Finally, not only do different networks matter in different contexts, they also perform different functions, ranging from socialization to the creation of con-

crete opportunities to become involved, and to influencing prospective participants' decisions at crucial points in time (Kitts 2000; McAdam 2003; Passy 2001,
2003; Tindall 2004). The relevance of such functions may change, depending on
whether we are looking at recruitment rather than at the strengthening of commitment and the extension of militancy over long periods of time. The different
public exposure of different organizations may also affect the relative weight of
specific types of networks over others (Passy 2003).

5.3 Individuals and Organizations

As the story of Antonio, with which we opened this chapter, illustrated well, the
importance of social networks for collective action in movements goes beyond
their support of individual activism. On the contrary, by participating in the life
of a movement and, in particular, in that of its various organizations, activists
create new channels of communication among them and increase the scope for
promoting common campaigns. Links founded on multiple allegiances are also
important as they create channels of communication between movements and
their environment. There are, of course, exclusive allegiances in which a single
organization monopolizes the commitment and the affective investment of its
individual members; but the inclusive model is more common.

5.3.1 Exclusive affiliations

In some movements, participation implies committing to specific organizations.
Exclusive organizations demand a long novitiate, rigid discipline, and a high level
of commitment, intruding upon every aspect of their members' lives (Zald and
Ash 1966; Curtis and Zurcher 1974). In general, the greater the degree to which
an organization is founded on symbolic incentives – either ideological or solidaristic – the more exclusive it will be.

The most obvious illustrations of this pattern include self-referential communities or sects whose main characteristics are closure in the face of the outside
world, a totalitarian structure, incompatibility with other forms of collective
engagement, and the view – among themselves – that adherents are the reposi-
tories of truth (Wallis 1977). Though they are not necessarily residential communities, the lifestyle of these groups is markedly separate. Interaction with
other groups is usually limited, while the tendency to concentrate on activities
internal to the group is very strong. Organizations active in neoreligious or
neocommunitarian movements often easily fall into this category; but political fundamentalist and radical organizations are not dissimilar (Blee 2002;
Anheier 2003).

In these cases, the single adherent/activist inhabits a world in which relationships and norms are highly structured: this leads to a radical transformation
of personality (see chapter 4 above). The prevalence of sectarian organizations
within a movement sector produces networks which are highly, if not completely,
fragmented. The only significant level of interaction is among adherents to a specific organization. In some cases (for example, those sects which can count on
numerous local groups, such as the Jehovah's Witnesses, but also political organizations with a strong territorial presence) these contacts can also develop over
a wide geographical area. However, contacts rarely extend beyond the confines
of the single organization. The "movement network" consists therefore of a
series of cliques[3]; that is to say, groups of actors – members of a given organization – who are strongly linked to each other and barely or not at all with adherents to other groups.

5.3.2 Multiple affiliations

In most cases, however, participation takes place in inclusive organizations that
allow multiple memberships and have no aspiration to monopolize their
members' commitment. Already in the early 1970s, Curtis and Zurcher (1973)
regarded individual activists as interorganizational links, and thus as basic structural features of movement "organizational fields" (see also Di Maggio and
Powell 1983; Di Maggio 1986). Along similar lines, Bolton (1972) talked of "chains
of group affiliations" in relation to the structure of overlapping memberships in
voluntary organizations. Many empirical investigations have followed, adding
details to the broad picture. Diani and Lodi (1988) have documented multiple
commitments in Italian environmentalism, with 28 percent of activists being
involved in several other environmental organizations, and the same percentage
active in both environmental and other political or social groups. Looking at
Dutch environmentalism, Kriesi (1993: 186) found 43 percent of core activists to
have personal links to other movement activists (25 percent in Italy according to
Diani and Lodi), and 67 percent to be connected to other new social movement
participants. Patterns of multiple participation seem to be affected by organizational features. Investigating members of voluntary associations in the US,
McPherson (1983) found that bigger organizations not only were able to secure
their members' commitment for a longer time, but could also rely on more ties
to other groups, generated by their members' overlapping affiliations. However,
other data (e.g. Diani 1995a: 113) suggest a more ambiguous relationship
between an organization's size and its members' propensity to engage in multiple activities.

Multiple affiliations play an important role in integrating different areas of
a movement. To belong to the same movement organizations (just as, more

generally, to organizations of other types) facilitates personal contact and the development of informal networks which, in turn, encourage individual participation and the mobilization of resources. Personal contacts are also instrumental in linking organizations to each other. As happens in economic organizations (Stokman et al. 1985; Mizruchi and Schwartz 1987), political organizations are often connected by the fact that they share certain activists; or else by personal relationships and friendships among their members and leaders.

Carroll and Ratner's (1996) study of movement activism in the Greater Vancouver area exemplifies these processes well. By looking at the joint affiliations of over 200 activists in 7 social movements (labor, urban/antipoverty, gay/lesbian, feminism, environmentalism, peace, aboriginal) they have been able to document not only the extent of overlapping memberships, but their patterning. Among Vancouver activists, only 27 percent were active in a single organization, whereas 28 percent collaborated with multiple organizations within the same movement, and 45 percent with multiple organizations in several movements (Carroll and Ratner 1996: 605). Activists in peace and urban/antipoverty movements were the most inclined towards multiple memberships (67 percent and 71 percent were involved in multiple organizations in multiple movements), while gay/lesbian, feminist, environmentalist, and aboriginal activists seemed to be the least so (34, 32, 39, and 42 percent of them, respectively, were actually committed to a single organization). Overlapping memberships constituted a core bloc of labor, peace, and urban/antipoverty organizations. Feminist and environmental organizations were linked to this bloc through their connections to labor and peace movements (1996: 605–6). While the specific pattern of linkages discovered by Carroll and Ratner need not be taken as the norm, and it may well vary substantially in different periods and localities, the Vancouver study still shows the potentiality of a network approach to the study of movement sectors.

Recent data on people who demonstrated against the Iraq war on February 15, 2003, in 8 Western countries[4] likewise indicate the extent of multiple memberships. Of the demonstrators who were members of peace organizations before February 15, 53 percent were also active in other organizations mobilizing on transnational issues such as Third World development or migrants' rights; 45 percent in social, cultural, or religious organizations; 35 percent in classic interest representations organizations such as parties and unions; 32 percent in environmental or women's organizations. Among first-time peace protestors, rates of involvement fell drastically, though they remained far from negligible (11, 29, 15, and 13 percent respectively in the four categories we have just mentioned: Diani 2005b).

Overlapping memberships contribute to social movement activity in a variety of ways. In many ways, one could say that they do for movement organizations what interpersonal networks do for individual activists. First, they facilitate the circulation of information and therefore the speed of the decision-making process. This is essential, inasmuch as the speed of mobilization compensates at least in part for the lack of organizational resources over which movements have control. In the absence of formal coordination among organizations, mobilization becomes possible through informal links among activists (Killian 1984; Knoke and Wisely 1990). Persons working across organizations also facilitate the development of shared representations of conflicts. Among Vancouver activists there were different ways of framing the conflicts, one based on a political-economy perspective, another based on an identity perspective, and a third based on a liberal perspective. The distribution of these frames varied depending on activists' commitment to overlapping memberships: those who acted as linkages between different movements and organizations were disproportionately close to a political-economy frame, whereas adopters of an identity frame were more inclined to concentrate on individual organizations (Carroll and Ratner 1996: 611).

Another important function of multiple memberships lies in their contribution to the growth of mutual trust. Whether it is a question of economic activities or of political mobilization, committing resources to a joint initiative involving other actors is always, to some extent, risky. In each case, the route to mobilization requires actors to conduct some exploration of, or "investigative process" with regard to (Diani 1995a: ch. 1), their environment, in search of trustworthy allies. This process is much simpler if there are ongoing links between the central activists of the various organizations concerned. This does not mean that other alliances are not possible, or even more frequent. But the relative cost of forging these other alliances will usually be higher, inasmuch as contacts between the different groups are not "routinized" through interpersonal connections.

The hypothesis that cooperation among organizations is more likely where personal contacts exist among their leaders has been supported by a few studies, dedicated both to movements and to political organizations in the wider sense. In both cases it has become clear that the leaders of organizations who work or campaign together tend to be linked by shared experiences which precede the formation of the coalition itself (Galaskiewicz 1985: 293; Turk 1977; Diani 1990 and 2003c). The denser the relationships among the leaders and the activists of various movement organizations, the higher the chances of cooperation among them (Zald and McCarthy 1980). There is no reason to think that the impact of networks which pre-date the emergence of a particular movement is limited to individual decisions to participate; rather, they also influence opportunities for cooperation among organizations.

Finally, looking at activists' multiple affiliations can constitute a useful way of comparing the structure of particular movements in different periods, and of tracing its modifications over time. In their pioneering study of the organizational affiliations of 202 key figures in the women's movements of the state of New York between 1840 and 1914, Naomi Rosenthal and her collaborators reconstructed the structure of the interorganizational networks in three different historical phases, identifying the central organizations in each phase (Rosenthal et al. 1985; Rosenthal et al. 1997). A phase of powerful activism between 1840 and the end of the 1860s saw numerous overlaps between participation in women's organizations and in antislavery or temperance organizations. The following phase, until the end of 1880, saw a reduction in conflict, and in contrast to the previous phase was characterized by the disappearance of many organizations and by the difficulty of revitalizing organizations of national importance. Between 1880 and 1914, there was a revival of activism and a new intensification of multiple affiliations, corresponding to campaigns for universal suffrage.

The configuration of networks seems to have depended significantly on the characteristics of the environment in which the movements were operating and on the availability of resources for mobilization. In local networks, where resources were usually limited, the integration and density of relationships were higher. As it was essential to use available resources to best effect, there was little space for factionalism and core activists distributed their multiple memberships fairly evenly across the board of local women's organizations. In contrast, organizations with national structures and which were therefore able to count on greater organizational resources, could be more tempted to accentuate their rivalries and ideological distinctions. As a result, the networks created by multiple memberships were more fragmented and consisted of different subgroups (or cliques) barely connected to each other.

In another exploration of the same data, Rosenthal et al. (1997) looked at multiple memberships in women's organizations in four different milieus (three local communities, plus one network of women active at state level in New York) between 1840 and 1920. They highlighted the different roles played by national and local women's organizations (e.g., in terms of their different relationship to other radical movements); the division of labor between few multi-issue organizations and the multiplicity of groups operating on a smaller scale and in semi-isolation; the limited contacts between suffrage organizations and charitable ones.

While most studies of the duality of individuals and groups focus on rank-and-file activists, we can also apply this perspective to relationships between movement leaders, eventually extending the analysis to the ties involving members of other sectors of the elites. For example, Schmitt-Beck (1989) explored the connections between central figures in the German peace movement of the 1980s. Data about the overlapping memberships linking core activists of peace movement organizations to members of other political groups documented the strong integration of the movement leadership with churches, trade unions, university, media, and other established social and political organizations (see also Schou 1997). On the other hand, movement activists who are well connected to external actors may also increase the centrality of their own organizations in their specific movement networks. For example, looking at transnational environmental movement organizations, Caniglia (2001) found that their centrality and influence in the environmental network depended in no small measure on the extent of their members' informal ties to key officials of United Nations agencies or other international governmental organizations.

5.4 Individual Participation, Movement Subcultures, and Virtual Networks

Individual participation in a movement's life is by no means restricted to membership in specific (mainly political) organizations. By going places, being connected to several groups or associations, patronizing specific venues, cafes, or bookshops, individuals create and reproduce dense webs of informal exchanges. As a result, informal social networks constitute subcultural oppositional dynamics. These help to keep collective identities alive even when open challenges to authority may not be taking place (when, in Melucci's [1989, 1996] words, movements are going through phases of "latency"). In this sense, networks provide the structure of social movement "free spaces" (Polletta 1999), i.e., areas of social interaction in which holders of specific worldviews reinforce mutual solidarity and experiment with alternative lifestyles (see also Haunss and Leach 2004).

Taking part in the life of several organizations and coming into contact with their activists and supporters, individuals construct a series of unique social relationships. In these, the political dimension of action intersects and overlaps with the private dimension, to generate the foundations of a specific form of subculture. In a movement network, individuals pursue goals which are not only concerned with political ends but also and often more significantly with personal self-realization. Even individuals who are not members of any specific organization may come together from time to time for specific initiatives and activities organized by cultural operators, service structures, and so on. Affiliation to a particular movement area can therefore be seen as a strictly personal choice, which brings with it a low level of identification with movement organizations. Similarly, the adoption by movement activists of alternative symbolic codes does not automatically create a homogeneous identity, nor does it provide the legitimacy for rigid organizational structures. Some degree of shared identity certainly characterizes a movement understood in its entirety, but this is then articulated with extreme variability and flexibility by different actors (Melucci 1984a).

Different versions of these models can be found in the movements which have emerged since the 1960s. In the 1980s, Melucci and associates documented how in Milan the end of a Leninist model of politics, based on mass, "revolutionary" organizations with a rigid structure, had given way to a style of movement participation that was largely individualistic and saw people's involvement in several types of cultural and political activities, from consciousness-raising groups to single issue campaigns. Some sectors of the contemporary global justice movement and of the direct action sector also reflect this model (Wall 1999; McDonald 2002; J. Jordan 2002; T. Jordan 2002). These sectors express a radical indifference, if not hostility, to the role of organizations as promoters and/or coordinators of collective action. For people involved in these networks, political activism is first and foremost a matter of lifestyle, the expression of deeply felt cultural and political orientations rather than adhesion to any specific political project and the organizations that could support it.

In these cases, participation in a movement life most of the time consists of involvement in cultural and/or social activities – music concerts, dramatic performances, happenings, always with a critical edge and an element of symbolic and/or political challenge to some kind of authority – rather than of public demonstrations. The latter are far from absent, and some may be massive and with a great public impact – think of the demonstrations taking place in the context of G8 or WTO meetings (Smith 2001; della Porta et al. 2005; Pianta 2001a, 2002), but also of the anticapitalist riots that shattered the City of London on June 18, 1999. But demonstrations are not the most important activity, nor are they associated with the idea of formal organization. When pooling resources is required, this tends to take the form of "affinity groups" (McDonald 2002; Bennett 2004b) that form to pursue a specific goal (stop a new road, save a tree, mount a boycott to the local branch of a global brand) and disband within a short period of time. The street parties promoted by the Reclaim the Streets network in the late 1990s in the UK provided opportunities for radical challenges to dominant ideas of urban space which were public yet did not rely on any organizational structure, depending instead on the dense subcultural networks of the participants (J. Jordan 2002). While it is far too simplistic to conclude from these examples that a radical transformation of collective action has actually taken place (McDonald 2002), it is certainly important to recognize the presence of these forms alongside others – the vast majority – in which organizations and organizational identities still play a major role (Diani 2005a; Diani and Bison 2004; Rootes 2003).

The debate on the role of subcultural and countercultural activities within contemporary social movements has become even livelier since the 1990s, with the spread of computer-mediated communication (henceforth, CMC). Questions whether organizations still have a role in grassroots mobilization, whether dense face-to-face community networks are still necessary to support collective action, whether identity bonds still need some kind of shared direct experience and/or "real" interaction to develop, have all been made more acute by technological developments.

The extent of this impact is more debatable. Some have been particularly vocal in arguing that new technologies will generate – better, have already generated – the multiplication of personal identities and the differentiation and segmentation of the self (Rheingold 1993; Turkle 1995; Castells 1997). Many conclude from this that patterns of political action would be deeply affected too (e.g. Castells 1996, 1997; see also Washbourne 2001; Bennett 2004a, 2004b). In relation to political and social participation, we may safely expect CMC to operate as a powerful facilitator through "the maintenance of dispersed face-to-face networks," the development of cultural and "socio-spatial enclaves," and technical support to interest group activity (Calhoun 1998: 383–5). And it is certainly reasonable to expect the internet to play a decisive role in connecting all sorts of communities that are either geographically dispersed (Rheingold 1993; Pini, Brown, and Previte 2004) or forced to operate underground by the very nature of their activities (e.g. hate groups).

However, the contribution of CMC to the creation of new types of identities, and in particular collective identities, is far from clear. First of all, most instances of personal interaction in electronic discussion groups actually miss some of the requirements usually associated with the concept of social relations (Cerulo 1997; Cerulo and Ruane 1998). Participants in those lists often hide their personal identity, participate occasionally, are not tied by any sort of committed relationship, and are mostly involved in dyadic or at most triadic interactions. For skeptics, this seems unlikely to generate the levels of trust and mutual commitment that past research suggests is required of participants in costly and potentially disruptive collective action (Calhoun 1998: 380; Diani 2000b; Tilly 2004a: ch. 5). For others, however, the internet creates a specific set of interactions rather than being the mere interface of "real" social life. In that context, recourse to hidden identities, anonymity, etc. may represent in its own right a specific way to challenge power and destabilize it (Wright 2004: 84; Bennett 2004a).

Empirical evidence on the type of ties established by CMC so far is mixed. It is certainly true that there are now several illustrations of social links which imply some degree of solidarity and mutual trust, and which developed between people who got in touch through the internet (e.g. Freschi 2000, 2003; Nip 2004). On the other hand, examples of community networks suggest that virtual networks operate at their best when they are backed by real social linkages in specifically localized communities, while their capacity to create brand new ones is uncertain (Virnoche and Marx 1997; Pickerill 2000; Hampton and Wellman 2001; Tranvik 2004). As for transnational networks, again, there is strong evidence that they contribute to the efficient coordination of global campaigns (Bennett 2004a; Van Aelst and Walgraave 2004). But they seem mostly to link people (an international activist elite) who also know each other and meet in person on the occasion of meetings and other events, rather than ordinary "virtual citizens" (Keck and Sikkink 1998; Lahusen 2004). To sum up, the jury is still out on the issue of whether CMC has mostly facilitated the action of activists and organizations by reinforcing existing links, or whether it has created new types of alternative communities from scratch.

5.5 Summary

In this chapter we have illustrated some aspects of the impact on recruitment and participation processes and on the overall structure of social movements, of the networks in which social movement activists are embedded. First, we have showed that individuals often become involved in collective action through their personal connections to people already involved. Those connections help them overcome the innumerable obstacles and dilemmas that people usually face when considering whether to become active on a certain cause. Not only that: the amount and type of individual networks also affect the chances of people remaining active for a long time, or instead reducing their commitment, or cutting it altogether, after brief spells. In reaction to criticisms of the role of networks in individual mobilization, researchers have qualified their arguments by exploring what types of networks are more likely to affect what types of collective action, and how the relationship between the two may change under different social and political circumstances.

We have also paid attention to the fact that individuals not only become active in a movement through their previous connections, but also create new connections by the very fact of being involved in multiple forms of activism and associations. From this perspective, individual activists operate as bridges between different organizational milieus, linking, for example, social movement organizations to established political actors or institutions, or organizations mobilized for different causes. By doing so, they affect the overall structure of social movement "industries" (McCarthy and Zald 1987a) or "families" (della Porta and Rucht 1995). At the same time, though, ties resulting from overlapping memberships are not always restricted to organizations; individual movement activists are also frequently involved in countercultural or subcultural practices. This may take the form of "real life" experiences, through personal participation in specific activities, but also develop through involvement in virtual communities, such as those made possible by the diffusion of computer-mediated communication.

SOCIAL MOVEMENTS AND ORGANIZATIONS

Neoliberal globalization has many enemies – or at least critics – in the southwest of England at the start of the new millennium. Even in a city with a reputation for its moderate and nonconflictual political culture like Bristol, the spectrum of organizations challenging neoliberal policies, highlighting their negative impact on people's welfare as well as on the integration of local communities, advocating alternative economic options and greater respect for human rights by global companies and national governments alike, is very broad indeed (Diani 2005a). Let us take a closer look at some of them. On the one hand we have organizations like Oxfam, a big charity active nationwide, with many ramifications overseas. Oxfam promotes both advocacy on behalf of dispossessed populations and service delivery. It has a formal structure and a huge fee-paying membership which, combined with a range of marketing strategies and substantial help from unpaid volunteers, results in an impressive capacity to mobilize resources on specific projects. Also active on global justice issues is the local chapter of Greenpeace. Consistently with the strategy of this particular organization, local activities are mostly meant as a contribution to the high-profile campaigns that the organization promotes on a global scale. The running of the latter relies on voluntary work only to a very limited extent. Greenpeace indeed operates mostly as a professional protest group. Small left-wing parties, critical of New Labour, are also very active on the issue. Once again, these are organizations with a fairly defined structure, membership criteria differentiating between who is and who is not a member, and a clear organizational identity alongside the identity of the global justice movement as a whole.

At the same time, globalization in Bristol is opposed by sectors of radical activists who adopt very loose forms of organization. While the city has become known over the years for its countercultural scene and its openness towards alternative forms of participation on issues such as the environment, animal and human rights, and feminism (i.e., the classic issues associated with "new social movements"), the transformation of the potential for grassroots activism in organizational forms, even of the radical type, has proved problematic (Purdue, Diani, and Lindsay 2004). Radicals mobilizing on globalization – and indeed on a number of other issues, from road-building to live animal export to asylum-seekers to workers' rights – have mostly refrained from involvement in specific organizations. Rather, they have adopted looser, more informal methods of coordination. They rely on personal ties, helped along by the fact that the core of activists is no more than a few dozen (i.e., those who can be regarded as virtually full-time campaigners, if on a totally nonprofessional basis); they use as meeting points alternative cafes or other cultural and leisure-time venues; they coordinate through newsletters, fanzines, or email lists. In these cases, the organizational model very much overlaps with the style of individualized subcultural or countercultural participation we described at the end of the previous chapter.

In between these two poles of organizational structure fall organizations with varying degrees of internal complexity and formalization: neighborhood groups interested in better integration between white and nonwhite local residents; associations of ethnic minorities – including many women's associations – aiming at improving private and public opportunities for their group; cultural associations promoting alternative lifestyles in areas such as food or health, for instance through fair trade practices; groups of professionals – e.g. lawyers – willing to offer their services to deprived groups or people without basic rights, such as migrants.

While all the different organizational forms we have just described are functional to specific activities of interest to organization members – or, in the case of informal activist networks, to those who are involved in them – they often converge in broader campaigns and coalitions on specific issues. In the last few years, examples of such actions include campaigns on asylum seekers' rights, the cancellation of developing countries' debt, and of course opposition to the Afghan and Iraqi wars. Moreover, the density of ties between organizations with a strong interest in transnational issues such as globalization, Third World debt, migration, peace and war, is actually much higher in Bristol than the density of ties between organizations with other issue priorities (Diani and Bison 2004). On top of that, extensive links run between the various sectors of Bristolian civil society through the activities of their members, their multiple memberships, their personal acquaintances (the links we described in the previous chapter). And of course, the connections of these groups are by no means restricted to the local area: either through formal links to national head-quarters, like in the case of Oxfam, or even transnational ones, like Green-peace, or through involvement in transnational networks such as Jubilee 2000, Drop the Debt, or the Climate Action Network, or through informal exchanges with organizations based in other countries, Bristol organizations are part of much broader mobilization networks.

What we found in Bristol is certainly not new. Social movements have long been identified with loosely structured collective conflict, in which "hundreds of groups and organizations – many of them short-lived, spatially scattered, and lacking direct communication, a single organization, and a common leadership – episodically take part in many different kinds of local collective action" (Oberschall 1980: 45–6). Far from being a unique case, Bristol provides an excellent example of both the role of organizations in promoting and sustaining collective action, and of the different organizational logics that one can locate within social movements (Edwards and Foley 2003; Andrews and Edwards 2005; Davis, McAdam, Scott, and Zald 2005). Even though social movements do not equate with the organizations active in them (see chapters 1 and 5 above), organizations often play very important roles within them. Like any kind of organization, organizations active in social movements fulfill – if to varying degrees and in varying combinations – a number of functions: inducing participants to offer their services; defining organizational aims; managing and coordinating contributions; collecting resources from their environment; selecting, training, and replacing members (Scott 1981: 9). Social movement organizations must mobilize resources from the surrounding environment, whether directly in the form of money or through voluntary work by their adherents; they must neutralize opponents and increase support from both the general public and the elite (see e.g. McCarthy and Zald 1987b [1977]: 19).

Organizations are also important because they act as powerful sources of identity for a movement's own constituency, its opponents, and bystander publics. No matter how aware people may be of the complexity and hetero-geneity of any movement, its public perception is likely to be associated with its most conspicuous characters. These need not necessarily be organizations, as the role of people like Martin Luther King in the US civil rights movement of the 1960s, or of Vandana Shiva or Jose Bove in the global justice movement, reminds us. Nevertheless, it is often organized groups that are associated with a movement, for better or worse: for instance, Greenpeace or WWF with environmentalism, Amnesty International with human rights activism, Attac or the so-called "Black Block" with the global justice movement.

For people committed to a certain cause, organizations are an important source of continuity, not only in terms of identity, but also in terms of action. At times of collective effervescence, when enthusiasm is high and the will to participate is strong, it is easier to mobilize people and resources even informally as individuals. But when opportunities for action are more modest and it gets more difficult to attract people spontaneously "to the streets," then organizations can secure continuity to collective action precisely because of their tendency to self-perpetuation. Of course not all organizations survive the end of protest waves of particular intensity (Minkoff 1995), yet without organizations collective action would be subject to extreme levels of variability, and challengers' political weight would be far more limited than it actually is. The role of organizations as sources of identity and as actors securing continuity to collective action also results in them playing representation and, to some extent, leadership roles on behalf of a movement. One of the reasons why political actors have trouble dealing with social movements, and media actors struggle to represent them in their accounts, is the lack of recognized movement representatives. With variable levels of acceptance from movements' grassroots, organizations often end up playing such a role simply by virtue of their greater visibility and greater ease of access (Diani 2003b).

At the same time, organizations perform their tasks by taking up very diverse forms. Following Scott's classic treatment (1981: ch. 2), we can look at organizations as rational, natural, and open systems. The first approach sees organizations mainly as collectivities oriented to relatively specific goals, with a relatively formalized social structure; the second approach maintains that organizations are collectivities whose members/participants are little influenced by formal structures or official goals, but share an interest in the survival of the system and engage in activities, coordinated informally, to secure such survival; the third approach conceives of organizations mainly as unstable coalitions of interest groups that determine goals through a negotiation process: the structure of the coalition, its activities, and its outcomes are strongly affected by environmental factors.

It needs to be made very clear that these are analytical models and not empirical descriptions of specific types of organizations; in other words, we may also apply the three different logics to the same organization in order to identify different aspects of its way of operating and address different problems. For example, it may make eminent sense to look at Greenpeace by focusing on their explicitly stated goals and structure (adopting, in other words, a rational system perspective); by looking at the informal practices through which the people operating within Greenpeace ensure the reproduction of the organization (i.e., taking a natural system perspective); or by looking at how Greenpeace may be the result of tensions and struggles between different actors within it, and how such struggles may also be affected by the social, economic, and political environment in which the organization operates (thus following an open system model).

From our point of view, however, it is also legitimate and useful to recognize that each model best suits one of the organizational forms we have just identified. More specifically, in the Bristol global justice movement, as well as in any other movement, we can either focus on the characteristics of the groups and organizations who are mobilized within it, or on the organization of the movement as a whole, i.e., on the way that the different groups, organizations, and even individual activists interested in globalization issues relate to each other. If we take the first line of inquiry, we are likely to look first and foremost for varying combinations of rational and natural systems approaches. In general, a rational system approach makes more sense for heavily bureaucratic organizations with relatively specific goals such as firms or hospitals, than for organizations advocating broader and often vaguely defined social changes, like many of those involved in social movements. However, it can also provide useful insights in relation to the most formalized organizations active in movements (in our example, the likes of Oxfam and Greenpeace).

The more we refer to loose organizational forms, like those reflected in informal networks of radical activists, the more the natural systems perspective seems useful. The aspirations to radical change held by those activists are unlikely to be fulfilled; accordingly, for the reproduction of activism over time, internal solidarity and identity – and hence the informal links between the people involved – are of paramount importance (Wall 1999; McDonald 2002; Routledge 2003; Doherty, Plows, and Wall 2003). Finally, if our interest lies in the organizational structure of a movement taken as a whole, then the open system approach is likely to generate very useful insights. Again, it is all too obvious that negotiations about goals, instability of the coalitions, and strong exposure to environmental effects may shape any specific organization; however, these dynamics are probably most visible when we are talking about a broad range of different organizations, such as those making up social movements.

In our discussion of organizational dynamics in social movements we shall distinguish between organizations taken as individual specific actors and the organization of the movement taken as a complex system of connected, interdependent organizations. More specifically, our argument will develop as follows: first, we shall introduce a number of alternatives or organizational dilemmas that organizations face; then identify a few basic organizational models; then look at patterns of organizational change, focusing first on the relationship between organizations and the institutional structure in which they operate, and later on the impact of technological change (the internet revolution) on social movements' organizational forms. Finally, we shall analyze the factors behind the segmentation of the networks that link different organizations to each other.

6.1 Organizational Dilemmas in Social Movements

In social movement analysis, the acronym SMO (standing for "social movement organization") has proved one of the most popular (McCarthy and Zald 1977). But it has also proved very ambiguous, as it has taken very different meanings among different authors. Its original proponents defined the social movement organization as a "complex, or formal, organization which identifies its goals with the preferences of a social movement or countermovement and attempts to implement those goals" (McCarthy and Zald 1987 [1977]: 20), a conception that only fits highly structured and formal organizations. Conversely, another definition sees SMOs as "associations of persons making idealistic and moralistic claims about how human personal or group life ought be organized that, *at the time of their claims making*, are marginal to or excluded from mainstream society" (Lofland 1996: 2–3), but that hardly seems applicable to strong organizations such as Greenpeace, Amnesty International, or the like. Still others (e.g. Rucht 1994) distinguish social movements (and thus SMOs) from parties and interest groups because of their main source of power and legitimacy (protest-mobilizing capacity as opposed to votes and influence respectively), but this does not necessarily imply distinct organizational forms.

Although most researchers in the field would not go as far as suggesting getting rid of the SMO label altogether (but see Burstein 1999; Burstein, Einwohner, and Hollander 1995; Burstein and Linton 2002; Diani 2004a), it is definitely important to be aware of the heterogeneity of organizational forms adopted by social movement activists (Rao, Morrill, and Zald 2000). In a systematic analysis of such forms, drawing on the experience of the west European new social movements of the 1980s, Hanspeter Kriesi (1996) has described their internal structuration as deriving from: (1) formalization, with the introduction of formal membership criteria, written rules, fixed procedures, formal leadership, and a fixed structure of offices; (2) professionalization, understood as the presence of paid staff who pursue a career inside the organization; (3) internal differentiation, involving a functional division of labor and the creation of territorial units; and (4) integration, through mechanisms of horizontal and/or vertical coordination.[1] The degree to which specific SMOs meet those criteria reflects some basic organizational dilemmas, that are not peculiar to social movements only (see e.g. Janda [1970] on political parties), but are certainly very important to our understanding of movement dynamics. Let us focus on three of them, without claiming to provide an all-encompassing review (see instead Lofland 1996).

6.1.1 Mobilizing people or resources?

Political organizations – in our case, specifically SMOs – may try to mobilize the largest possible support from the general public, and therefore the resources which are essential to the maintenance of a semi- or quasi-professional group. Available strategies range from calling upon broadly supported sets of values to the provision of selective incentives to prospective members/subscribers in the form of services, leisure-time activities, discount packages, etc. But this is not the only option: SMOs may also try to mobilize smaller but more carefully selected groups of committed activists. These are essential for the more demanding tasks of movement participation, including persistent organizational commitment and the promotion of costly forms of collective action.

Putting it differently, there is a basic alternative between the mobilization of people's "money" or "time" (Oliver and Marwell 1992). These options are not easily compatible. Emotional messages, which provide a clear-cut definition of a movement's identity and opponents, are essential to mobilize core activists (Gamson 1992a). Yet, their sharpness may alienate sectors of sympathizers and prospective supporters with less clear-cut orientations and motivations (Friedman and McAdam 1992). It may also discourage potential supporters among established actors, not only public agencies but also "concerned" private sponsors, whose contribution will be easier to attract the larger the size of public support for a given movement.[2] The choice of whether to mobilize time or money has important implications for SMOs: the two options require different "mobilization technologies" and therefore different organizational models (Oliver and Marwell 1992).

SMOs differ in the opportunities available for their grassroots members' participation. Many of them emphasize participation and direct democracy, oppose delegation of power, and privilege consensual decision-making. This applies to contemporary Social Forums (Agnoletto 2003; Baiocchi 2001, 2002a; della Porta 2005b) as well as to virtually all social movements who have followed each other from the 1960s (Breines 1989; Rosenthal and Schwartz 1989: 46; Polletta 2002). A participatory structure also favors internal solidarity. Having only limited access to material resources, social movement organizations may substitute for this with symbolic resources. Accordingly, many SMOs give particular importance to internal relations, transforming the very costs of collective action into benefits through the intrinsic rewards of participation itself. As well as formal organizations, small groups held together by personal relations survive during periods of latency, providing important bases for the revival of movement activities (Taylor 1989; Melucci 1996). In particular, a small group of activists "uses naturally occurring social relationships and meets a variety of organizational and individual needs for emotional support, integration, sharing of sacrifice, and expression of shared identities" (Gamson 1990: 175). Within cohesive groups the conditions for the development of alternative value systems are constituted and "communal associations become free spaces, breeding grounds for democratic change" (Evans and Boyte 1986: 187). In these "free spaces," a "sense of a common good" develops alongside the construction of "direct, face-to-face, and egalitarian relationships" (Gamson 1990: 190–1). Thus, an all-embracing participation tends to permeate every aspect of activists' everyday lives. "In the climate of the late 1960s," Whalen and Flacks note with reference to the US student movement, "commitment to revolution had implications for carrying out virtually every detail of daily life: to be a revolutionary was to dress, eat, make love, and speak in certain ways and not others" (1989: 249). Where politics "marks every moment of the day," fellow militants become a "family," as it is sometimes put on the extreme left in Italy (della Porta 1990: 149–50). So much so that, in their value system and lifestyle, "those who participated in the youth revolt continue to be affected by it" (Whalen and Flacks 1989: 247).

6.1.2 Hierarchical or horizontal structures?

The distribution of power within an organization also needs to be considered. Power can be more or less centralized, as the literature on political parties in particular has revealed. National structures can have greater or less weight; there can be greater or lesser participation in decisions concerning resource allocation, goal definition, candidacies, or disciplinary procedures; and there can be greater or lesser centralization of leadership (Janda 1970: 104–12). Social movement organizations have different styles of leadership. Many organizations from religious sects to student movements, via revolutionary parties like the Bolsheviks or the Nazis, have displayed charismatic forms of leadership whose legitimacy was dependent above all on leaders' ability to manipulate ideological resources and to embody the movement as a whole, contributing to the creation of its collective identity (see, for example, Alberoni 1984). Overall, however, several different leadership styles have been noted in the literature: agitator, prophet, administrator, or statesman (Lang and Lang 1961); charismatic, administrator, or intellectual (Killian 1964); charismatic, ideological, or pragmatic (Wilson 1973); instrumental or affective (Downton 1973).

Given their participatory nature and – frequently – democratic orientation, social movement organizations have always faced the dilemma of how to reconcile leadership roles with the requirements of grassroots democracy. They often reject authority and hierarchy on principle (Pearce 1980; Diani and Donati

1984; Brown 1989; Lichterman 1995a: 196), but this does not necessarily eliminate the need for leadership functions, such as coordination and public representation (Melucci 1996: 344–7). If we think of social movement leadership in relational terms (Melucci 1996: 335–8; see also Downton 1973), then "leadership roles need not entail control over a unified organization, or explicit recognition of charisma from followers. They may also, far less obtrusively, result from certain actors' location at the center of exchanges of practical and symbolic resources among movement organizations. This will not generate domination, if by that we mean actors' capacity to impose sanctions over others in order to control their behavior, but rather varying degrees of influence" (Diani 2003b: 106).

From this perspective, rather than with charisma or authority, "leadership" may be associated with actors' ability to promote coalition work among movement organizations, or to establish connections to the media and political institutions, which in turn lead to operating de facto as movement "representatives" (see e.g. Diani and Donati 1984; Rosenthal et al. 1985, 1997; Staggenborg 1988; Mushaben 1989; Schmitt-Beck 1989; Diani 1995a, 2003b; Schou 1997). The plurality of functions important for social movement mobilization also means that playing influential, "leadership" roles depends on possession of constantly changing resources. Recently, for example, experts have often replaced ideologues as social movement leaders (Moore 1995). Involved as they are in technological issues, contemporary movements assign a very important role to natural scientists and engineers: "challenging sophisticated technologies . . . such organized protests are dependent on recognized experts to interpret the issues and achieve public credibility" (Walsh 1988: 182). As a result of these multiple roles and requirements, leadership in social movements is often ad hoc, short lived, relates to specific objectives, and is concentrated in a limited area of the movements themselves (Diani and Donati 1984; Barker, Johnson and Lavalette 2001; Morris and Staggenborg 2004).

6.1.3 Challengers or "service providers"?

Not all social movement organizations are directly concerned with external challenges, oriented on political powerholders. Organizations may also act mainly with reference to the needs of social movement constituencies, and/or to support cultural and symbolic challenges or the practice of new lifestyles. Kriesi (1996) called these organizations movement associations, but other terms have also become popular (e.g. halfway houses [Morris 1984] or abeyance structures [Taylor 1989]). Communes, therapy groups, and rape crisis centers were formed through the feminist movement, for example (Ryan 1992: 135–44; Minkoff 1995; Kaplan 1995; Daniels and Brooks 1997). Within student movements, used-book

stalls and advice centers of various kinds offered logistical support to sympathizers, allowing protest action in favor of the right to education to be combined
with concrete activity aimed at "putting the goal into practice," while at the same
time they helped widen support. Movement associations, too, are diverse in
terms of levels of organization, internal power distribution, and degree of participation. Self-help groups, for example, tend to be informal, decentralized, and
are frequently totalizing, while associations offering services to a wider public
may adopt a more formal structure, and a hierarchical distribution of power, and
fuse symbolic and instrumental incentives (see e.g. Taylor 1996; Taylor and van
Willige 1996).

Besides groups involved in political mobilization and movement associations,
both predominantly inward-looking, supportive organizations (Kriesi 1996) are
also part of the social movement organizational structure. These consist of
service organizations such as newspapers, recreation centers, educational institutions, or publishing presses, which contribute to a movement's aims but at the
same time work on the open market. The film clubs, theaters, publishing houses
created within several movements in order to further collective mobilization
increasingly became market-oriented commercial enterprises with audited
accounts, salaried staff, and a competitive market ethos. The same applied to
natural food and health shops, originally set up by sympathizers if not activists
of environmental movements.

The spread of this kind of structure contributes to the creation of movement
countercultures in which political engagement permeates the whole of life.[3] The
Italian social centers (centri sociali) that originated from the autonomist and anarchist movement sectors of the late 1970s, have over time evolved from inward-
looking countercultural communities towards an organizational model which is
closest to that of supportive organizations (although this has not happened
without conflicts and dissension between different orientations within the sector:
Dines 1999; Ruggiero 2000; Mudu 2004). The fair-trade businesses and ethical
banks that have developed in parallel with the global justice movement also fall
under this heading (Micheletti 2003; Micheletti, Follesdal, and Stolle 2003; Diani
2005a; Aguiton 2001). So does a network of alternative media operators linked
together through various websites, like Indymedia (see also section 7.4.). Several
neoreligious organizations over the last decades have also adopted organizational
models combining elements from the movement associations and the supportive organizations types. For example, Hank Johnston (1980) characterized the
Transcendental Meditation group as a "marketed social movement." While referring to a "marketed social movement organization" might have been more accurate, Johnston's analysis nonetheless captured important aspects of the role
played by organizations providing specific services to "clients" longing for personal and social change.

6.2 Types of Social Movement Organizations

Different responses to the dilemmas illustrated above generate different organizational models. Here we introduce some of them, without any aspiration to generate systematic typologies (for examples, see Kriesi 1996; Diani and Donati 1999; Rao et al. 2000).

6.2.1 Professional movement organizations

A professional social movement organization is characterized by "(1) a leadership that devotes full time to the movement, with a large proportion of resources originating outside the aggrieved group that the movement claims to represent; (2) a very small or non-existent membership base or a paper membership (membership implies little more than allowing a name to be used upon membership rolls); (3) attempts to impart the image of 'speaking for a constituency,' and (4) attempts to influence policy toward that same constituency" (McCarthy and Zald 1987a [1973]: 375).[4] Ordinary members have little power and "have no serious role in organizational policymaking short of withholding membership dues. The professional staff largely determines the positions the organization takes upon issues" (McCarthy and Zald 1987a [1973]: 378).

However, professional SMOs do not necessarily address themselves to their "natural" constituents, i.e., those groups (whether dispossessed like the unemployed or the homeless, or fairly well-off like in many new middle-class mobilizations) whose interests they promote, the way a normal pressure group would. Rather, they have a "conscience constituency" composed of those who believe in the cause they support. Their leaders are entrepreneurs whose "impact results from their skills at manipulating images of relevance and support through the communication media" (McCarthy and Zald 1987a [1973]: 374). They rely more on their reputation for technical expertise on specific matters than on mass mobilization (McCarthy and Zald 1987a [1973]: 379; 1987b [1977]: 29).[5]

There are recognizable advantages associated with professional organizations. Back in the 1970s, in his comparative analysis of American social movements, Gamson (1990 [1975]) found that challengers are more likely to win when they possess a well-structured organization. Formal organizations would appear better placed to mobilize "because they facilitate mass participation, tactical innovations, and rapid decision-making" (Morris 1984: 285). Structured organizations are also more likely to survive beyond a wave of protest to favor mobilization in succeeding waves (McCarthy and Zald 1987b [1977]). Professional organizers often spread mass defiance rather than dampening it, and "professionalization of leadership and the formalization of movement organizations are not necessarily incompatible with grass-roots protest" (Staggenborg 1991: 154–5; also Jenkins 1985). Moreover, long-term survival is favored by the presence of motives for and methods of action which are already legitimated (Minkoff 1993, 1995; Clemens and Minkoff 2004).

However, there are also problems. While professional organizations can generate a constant flow of funding they are bound by the wishes of their benefactors. "The growth and maintenance of organizations whose formal goals are aimed at helping one population but who depend on a different population for funding are ultimately more dependent upon the latter than the former" (McCarthy and Zald 1987b [1973]: 371). Patrons provide important resources, but they are usually available only for groups with low-level claims and consensual legitimacy – the disabled rather than the unemployed, for example (Walker 1991).

Similar consequences may result from growing collaboration with authorities: "The establishment of a working relation with the authorities also has ambivalent implications for the development of the SMO: On the one hand, public recognition, access to decision-making procedures and public subsidies may provide crucial resources and represent important successes for the SMO; on the other hand, the integration into the established system of interest intermediation may impose limits on the mobilization capacity of the SMO and alienate important parts of its constituency, with the consequence of weakening it in the long run" (Kriesi 1996: 155–6; see also Lahusen 2004)

Echoing Robert Michels' analysis of the bureaucratization of socialist parties, Piven and Cloward (1977) have been most explicit in considering the development of formal organizations as hampering goal attainment in protest movements of the poor. Investment in building a permanent mass organization was seen as a waste of scarce resources. Moreover, such organizations tended to reduce the only resource available to the poor: mass defiance. It is certainly true that even professional bureaucratic organizations may promote radical challenges and defiance, and engage in various forms of vicarious activism on behalf of a fee-paying passive membership (see e.g. Greenpeace, Diani and Donati 1999). But organizations focused entirely on fund-raising and the attraction of financial resources are likely sooner or later to face problems with their capacity to mobilize people (Donati 1996; Diani and Donati 1999). All in all, according to critics, professionalization might lead to defeat by taming protest (Piven and Cloward 1977; see also section 9.1 and, for a broader argument, Skocpol 2003).

The same dilemmas characterize an organizational type that has recently gained increasing attention, the "transnational social movement organization" (TSMOs). Jackie Smith defines TSMOs as "international nongovernmental organizations engaged in explicit attempts to [change] some elements of the social structure and/or reward distribution of society" (1999: 591), and shows how they grew from 110 in 1953 to 631 in 1993 (see also chapter 9 below). Their growth has exceeded that of international nongovernmental organizations at large (Anheier and Themudo 2002). TSMOs comprise a small number (sometimes referred to as "the Big Ten") of organizations with numerous national chapters, membership in the millions, and strong levels of bureaucratization. These include the likes of Amnesty International (over a million members, formal chapters in 56 countries, 7,500 action groups in nearly 100 countries: Anheier and Themudo 2002: 193), Greenpeace (between 2 and 3 million), Friends of the Earth (a federation of 61 national associations that coordinates about 5,000 local groups and a million members [Anheier and Themudo 2002: 203]), WWF (5 million), or Oxfam (a confederation of 12 organizations). These organizations display many traits of the professional organization, even though participation is encouraged – if largely in the form of voluntary work and contributions to specific projects, rather than in decision-making processes, and with low levels of investment in the building of internal solidarity. However, TSMOs also include organizations with a distinctive profile but much smaller in terms of resources, and less neatly fitting the professional model. Well-known examples include ATTAC, an organization that campaigns against the deregulation of financial markets, founded in 1997 in France though it has made significant inroads in other Western countries (Ancelovici 2002; Kolb 2004); ACT UP, active since the 1980s in challenging the consequences of AIDS (Gould 2002); or conservation organizations such as Conservation International or the Environmental Defense Fund (Lewis 2000).

6.2.2 Participatory movement organizations

We use the plural deliberately, to refer to different organizational types that can be grouped under this broader model. In particular we differentiate between mass protest organizations and grassroots groups.

Mass protest organizations

This model combines attention to participatory democracy with certain levels of formalization of the organizational structure. In the social movements of the 1970s, many political organizations like the communist K-Gruppen in Germany, the New Left parties in Italy, the Trotskysts in France, had adopted fairly rigid and hierarchical organizational structures, close to the model of the Leninist party (della Porta 1995: ch. 4; Lumley 1990). Gradually, however, this model fell out of favor for its excessive emphasis on the professional revolutionary role, and its indifference to grassroots democracy. With the crisis of the 1970s protest movements, alternative forms of organization developed, as exemplified by the emergence of green parties. These were formed for the most part during the 1980s campaigns on environmental issues, and nuclear energy in particular, although they have never been the official political representatives of the environmental movement (Rootes 1994). In seeking to defend nature, these parties also sought to apply the "think globally, act locally" principle to their organizations. The greens rejected, initially at least, any structured organizational power, just as they rejected centralizing technologies. They developed a ritual of direct democracy by introducing consensual decision-making, rotation of chair roles, and so on.

The model of open assemblies and always revocable delegates did not survive long, however. Participatory democracy may often reduce the decision-making efficiency of assemblies and lead to very long periods of confusion and incertitude. Particularly after they entered first regional and then national parliaments, the greens began to develop stable organizational structures, with membership cards, representative rather than direct democracy within the party, and a stable leadership. Public funding of the parties created a constant and generous flow of finance which was used to develop a professional political class, set up newspapers and supportive associations. The green parties' structure thus became formal and centralized. Participation moved towards excluding membership of other organizations, and ideological incentives began to predominate. Recently, however, grassroots democratic practices have been revitalized in the context of the growth of global justice mobilizations, and also extended to nontraditional unions such as the Cobas in Italy or Sud in France (see chapters 2 and 9 in the present volume).

It is not difficult to identify the processes behind these recurrent switches. They not only have to do with the oligarchic tendencies to be found in any sort of organization, but also with problems associated with the model of participatory organizational democracy. In fairness, the concrete realization of the organizational principles of grassroots democracy has never been a simple matter. Many activists have complained of the *de facto* oligarchies which tend to form and impose their will when collective decision-making becomes difficult. An organized minority can win out in an assembly by wearing down the majority, and forcing them to give up and leave after hours of strenuous discussion. In a few extreme cases physical force has been used by some groups to occupy important decision-making positions such as the chair of meetings. Even without reaching those excesses, the risks of a "tyranny of emotions," whereby the most committed activists profit from the lack of formal procedures and secure control of decision-making processes, have been pointed out in reference to several movements of the recent and not-so-recent past (Breines 1989: 49; Polletta 2002). They have also been restated in reference to the global justice movement (Epstein 2001; see also section 9.4 below).

Grassroots organizations

In contrast to the mass protest model, the grassroots model combines strong participatory orientations with low levels of formal structuration. The existence of organizations of this kind depends on their members' willingness to participate in their activities. Such participation may be encouraged through different combinations of ideological and solidaristic incentives. Oftentimes this is related to locality. For example, the local groups that opposed road building in many corners of Britain in the 1990s (Doherty 1999; Wall 1999; Drury et al. 2003) could not rely on a strong ideological profile given the heterogeneity of their participants, and instead emphasized shared concerns in specific issues; so do the single-issue citizens' committees that characterize so much political activity in contemporary democracies (della Porta 2004c) or the residents' associations promoting environmental justice collective action in deprived urban areas (Taylor 1995; Lichterman 1995a). Other times, shared critical attitudes play a stronger and more explicit role in motivating participation, as in the semiformal direct action groups that have developed in the context of growing opposition to neoliberal globalization (Doherty, Plows, and Wall 2003), or in the local independent women's groups that marked the spread of feminist movements in the 1970s and 1980s (Rupp and Taylor 1987; Whittier 1995).

Despite their lack of resources, there are innumerable examples of grassroots organizations that have been successful in the pursuit of their goals, both in countries lacking a vibrant civil society (Desai 1996; Broadbent 1998; Ray 1999) and in Western countries. For example, grassroots environmental mobilizations have proved a constant feature of Western democracies, stopping threatening projects on innumerable occasions (Rootes 2003; della Porta and Rucht 2002). At the same time, depending so heavily on their members' voluntary participation, grassroots organizations' capacity to act with continuity over time is obviously limited. Many of them actually see an alternation of phases of activism and latency, comparable to those identified by Melucci and his associates (Melucci 1984a) for social movements as a whole. They operate as "intermittent structures," i.e., "organizations or organizational units which are deployed and then "folded up" until their period of activity arrives again" (Etzioni 1975: 444, quoted in Lindgren 1987). "Intermittent social movement organizations" (Lindgren 1987), that resurface each time their issues of concern become salient political topics again, remind us that permanent stable structures are not necessarily a requirement for success.

Grassroots organizations may also face problems if they rely too heavily on ideology to secure their members' cohesion and commitment. Ideological incentives are an important surrogate for the lack of material resources, but their use increases the rigidity of the organizational model because transformations have to be incorporated into the normative order of the group (Zald 1970). Moreover, organizations employing symbolic incentives will run a greater risk of internal conflict (McCarthy and Zald 1987b [1977]: 33). Especially for grassroots groups with very critical views of mainstream society, closure to the external world helps the formation of identity but also reduces the capacity to handle reality and identify reasons for failure.[6]

6.3　How Do Social Movement Organizations Change?

6.3.1　Patterns of change

Just as the organizational characteristics of social movements vary, there is no single model accounting for organizational changes. A Weberian approach, focusing primarily on bureaucratization, initially dominated in the sociology of social movements as in other areas. Michels' "iron law of oligarchy," which states that in order to survive as an organization a political party increasingly pays attention to adapting to its environment rather than to its original goals of social change,[7] was also held valid for social movements. Institutionalization used to be considered a natural evolution for social movement organizations. Recurrent lifecycles were identified in the histories of a number of movements. Herbert Blumer (1951: 203), for example, distinguished four stages in the typical social movement lifecycle. The first, or "social ferment," stage would be characterized by unorganized, unfocused agitation during which great attention is paid to the propaganda of "agitators." In the second phase, of "popular excitement," the underlying causes of discontent and the objectives of action are more clearly defined. In the third phase, of "formalization," disciplined participation and coordination of strategies for achieving the movement's aims are arrived at by creating a formal organization. Finally, in the "institutionalization" stage the movement becomes an organic part of society and crystallizes into a professional structure.

Others have questioned the "necessity" of such an evolution, however. Even organizational sociologists point out that adaptation is only one evolutionary possibility among many. In fact, an organization need not react by moderating its aims when conflict with the surrounding environment arises. It can also become more radical, hoping that a small but powerful nucleus of dissent will form in this way (Jackson and Morgan 1978). Moreover, rather than adapt to external demands it may simply reduce contacts with the outside world (Meyer and Rowan 1983). Although he referred to the Michelsian hypothesis (and emphasized that "there are organizational characteristics that dictate organization maintenance over every other possible goal"), Ted Lowi (1971: 31) noted that "the phenomenon has little to do with goal displacement. Rather, the goals of an organization have become outwon with the need of maintaining the organization."

In fact, SMOs rarely get institutionalized. In the first place, few of them actually survive for a significant time spell (Minkoff 1995: ch. 3). Some dissolve because their aims have been achieved. Organizations formed to coordinate specific campaigns, for example, tend to disappear as soon as that campaign is over (Zurcher and Curtis 1973).[8] Leadership splits during downturns in mobilization, and the resultant processes of disintegration and realignment cause others to disappear. In the case of SMOs, whose life expectancy is short and whose aims are limited, an interest in the organization's continuing existence may not even develop. In other words, their members' first loyalty continues to be to the movement and the organization is simply seen as a temporary instrument for intervention.

Moderation of an organization's aims is not, of course, the only possible development even for those organizations that actually do survive in the long term. Other social movement organizations become more radical. Their aims become more ambitious, the forms of action adopted less conventional, and they become increasingly isolated from the outside world. One outcome of 1968, although certainly not the only one, nor the most important, was the formation of clandestine organizations which grew out of the student movement in Italy and Germany and adopted increasingly radical forms of action, including in some cases murdering political opponents. They are a tragic and extreme example of how reacting to a hostile environment can bring about an increasing closure of channels of communication with the outside world (della Porta 1995). In less extreme cases, spontaneous groups such as the German Spontis and the Indiani Metropolitani (literally, "metropolitan indians") in Italy, illegitimate offspring of the student movement in decline, increased rather than diminished their use of symbolic incentives, primarily in order to reinforce internal solidarity (Lumley 1990; della Porta 1996a).

The direction taken by a social movement, therefore, may be that of moderation, but equally that of radicalization; of greater formalization, but also of progressive destructuration; of greater contact with the surrounding environment, or of sectarian "implosion." One must not forget that changes in specific organizations do not necessarily all take the same direction: the institutionalization of one organization can go along with the radicalization of another, and the overall profile of a social movement sector may remain relatively stable over time as a result. For example, in their analysis of changes in environmental organizations in the 1990s, Diani and Donati (1999) showed that trends towards institutionalization and professionalization went along with the emergence of new grassroots radical actors, and that established organizations had played a key role in environmental movements since the rise of environmental mobilization in the late 1980s.

Mapping all the possible factors behind changes in social movements' organizational forms exceeds the scope of this volume (see e.g. Scott 1981). Here we shall focus on three determinants of change that have attracted a lot of attention recently. Let us look first at the role of institutional factors (Edwards and McCarthy 2004).

6.3.2   Institutional factors and organizational change

The availability of public or semipublic resources may facilitate the creation of powerful lobbies with links to social movements. Research on the civil rights movement in the United States, for example, has shown that funds from federal and local government agencies and programs such as the Community Action Programs or Volunteers in Service to America stimulated the creation of movement organizations at the same time as the Peace Corps and alternative military service provided paid positions for activists. The conditions governing access to public and private funding, tax exemptions, or advantageous postage rates influence the organizational structure of groups who wish to benefit from these possibilities. Thus the terms "funded" (McCarthy and Zald 1987a: 358 ff.) or "registered social movement organizations" (McCarthy, Britt, and Wolfson 1991: 68) have been used.

In many countries, organizations wishing access to a series of material resources must respect a long list of laws and regulations, first and foremost in their organizational structure. In the US these include "federal tax laws and policies and their enforcement by the Internal Revenue Service, the actions of formal coalitions of fundraising groups, United States Postal Service Regulations and their consequences for access to the mails, the rules and actions of private organizations monitoring groups, the dynamics of combined charity appeals, and state and local level fundraising regulations and their enforcement" (McCarthy et al. 1991: 46; Andrews and Edwards 2004). In particular, "not-for-profit" or "nonpartisan" organization status, usually necessary for access to the above-mentioned resources, involves adherence to models considered legitimate for such organizations, such as the presence of a governing body and an annual audit (McCarthy et al. 1991: 61). From this point of view certainly, increased availability of institutional resources accentuates the presence of formal, centralized organizations, as American public interest groups (such as Common Cause), with thousands of contributors and hundreds of local branches, demonstrate (McFarland 1984: 61–92; Andrews and Edwards 2004; for a comparative perspective, Salamon and Anheier 1997).

The openness of other institutional structures may also favor the development of formal organizations (Rucht 1994). In Europe, in contrast to the US, parties originating from social movements have often obtained remarkable results thanks partly to the rules regulating challengers' access to decision-making procedures. Proportional representation, for example, can promote the formation of movement parties, as happened when the various organizations of the new left in Italy fielded candidates at administrative and political elections in the 1970s,[9] or when green parties enjoyed success in countries like Belgium, Germany, or Italy in the 1980s (Richardson and Rootes 1994).

At the same time, however, formal organizations with a clear structure are not necessarily the outcome of an open, inclusive political environment. Often, formal, hierarchical structures have been established to better fight a hostile state apparatus. A repressive, centralized state may well produce well-organized movements (Rootes 1997), with solid alliances between different organizations and movements (McCarthy and Zald 1987b), sometimes with radical repertoires of action (della Porta 1995). For example, the Italian student movement of the 1970s found itself involved in an extremely polarized political conflict. The political system's closure and frequent physical clashes with neofascists and police favored the development of the centralized and bureaucratic organizations of the new left. However, 30 years later, the events in Genoa 2001, and the violent behavior of police even towards peaceful demonstrators, did not result in a growing militarization of the global justice movement and in the adoption of organizational forms suited to conducting violent clashes with police (della Porta et al. 2005).

Conversely, an open, decentralized political system may also facilitate similar trends towards decentralization and informality among movement organizations. In Germany, again in the 1970s, and in contrast to Italy, institutional openness (particularly when Social Democrat Willy Brandt was chancellor) apparently favored the proliferation of decentralized movement organizations, such as the Bürgerinitiativen (della Porta 1995: ch. 4). Similar considerations have also been suggested in relation to the American social movement sector (Rucht 1996), in contrast to the hypothesis that the American institutional system should be conducive only to formal, bureaucratic organizations. To sum up, rather than positing a rigid relationship between the form that social movement activists give to their organizations, and the traits of the institutional system in which they operate, it is wiser to recognize that multiple organizational forms may be accommodated within the same system.

6.3.3 Organizational cultures and organizational change

Although social movement actors have margins of choice when they are trying to adapt creatively to their environment, such margins are subject to limitations.

Just as we may speak of repertoires of forms of protest (chapter 7), we may do so for organizational forms (Clemens 1996). In any given country and at any given time, the repertoire of organizational forms is restricted. It can be expanded by borrowing from other countries or domains, but such transformations are slow. A particular organizational model is more likely to be adopted, "to the extent that the proposed model of organization is believed to work, involves practices and organizational relations that are already familiar, and is consonant with the organization of the rest of those individuals' social worlds" (Clemens 1996: 211).

Thus, the organizational resources already present within the social movement sector tend to influence the evolution of single organizations and, more generally, the forms of protest adopted. The dominant organizations in any given phase tend to contribute organizational resources to later mobilizations, thus contributing also to the definition of their strategies. Adopting the terminology of the resource mobilization approach, the SMOs created during a particular phase of mobilization "manufacture" resources for succeeding phases, influencing, or at least attempting to influence, their character (see also chapter 9 below).

Organizational choices, therefore, are influenced by the preexisting structures within which movements form, inheriting ideas, constraints, and facilities as well as allies and opponents. Thus earlier historical movements or "early riser" movements help produce their "spin-offs." During periods of mobilization new insurgents assimilate inputs from existing movements. The student movement provided the organizational resources for the formation of groups with objectives as diverse as defending the rights of the poor (Delgado 1986) and those of animals (Jasper and Nelkin 1992). Similarly, the women's movement, formed within its student predecessor, would later transmit ideological frameworks, tactical innovations, organizational structures, and leadership to the peace movement (Meyer and Whittier 1994). Today, global justice movement organizations also draw, if often critically, on the experiences of the organizations that in the recent and not-so-recent past have mobilized transnationally on issues such as the environment, human rights, or Third World development (Anheier and Themudo 2002). Over time, then, a sort of collective memory on organizational possibilities is passed down from one generation of militants to the next or from one movement to another: "one movement can influence subsequent movements both from outside and from within: by altering political and cultural conditions it confronts in the external environments, and by changing the individuals, groups and norms within the movement itself" (Meyer and Whittier 1994: 282; Isaac and Christiansen 2002). For this reason, it can be very difficult to change certain initial organizational traits, as they come to form a kind of genetic patrimony for movement organizations (see, among others, Panebianco 1988).

6.3.4 Modernization, technological innovation, and organizational change

One should also consider the relationship between modernization and organizational change. In general terms, economic progress may have a beneficial effect on the organizing capacity of social movements, since "as the amount of discretionary resources of mass and elite publics increases, the absolute and relative amount of resources available to the SMS [Social Movement Sector] increases" (McCarthy and Zald 1987b [1977]: 25). These resources include time and money, but also political freedom, means of communication, transportation, etc. As they grow, the amount of resources available for new organizations and movements is also likely to increase. Economic development, and the economic and time resources it creates, should lead to a growth in professionalized, formal groupings: "The larger the income flow to an SMO, the more likely that cadre and staff are professional and the larger these groups are" (McCarthy and Zald 1987b [1977]: 35).

However, technological change has attracted most attention of late, as it has influenced the organizational structure of social movements as well as their tactics. The expansion of both printed and electronic means of communication has permitted an "externalization" of certain costs (Tarrow 1994: 143–5). If organizations were previously required to be highly structured to get a message across, today a lightweight one may be adequate, provided it can gain media attention. The impact of the internet on social movement organizing is beautifully illustrated by a authoritative, nonacademic source like the Canadian Security Intelligence Service: "The internet will continue a large role in the success or failure of antiglobalization protests and demonstrations. Groups will use the internet to identify and publicize targets, solicit and encourage support, organize and communicate information and instructions, recruit, raise funds, and as a means of promoting their various individual and collective aims" (quoted in Van Aelst and Walgrave 2004: 121).

Websites operate with information, mobilization, or community-oriented functions (Rosenkrands 2004: 72–3). In the case of antiglobalization sites, they provide an easy way for information to circulate not only through email lists but through links between websites (van Aelst and Walgrave 2004). It seems reasonable to suggest that the major no-global initiatives of the late 1990s and early 2000s have been made possible by the internet (Bennett 2004a: 133), even though, as Seattle demonstrates, it is combination of local grassroots organizing and web-based information diffusion that has done the trick (Bennett 2004a: 145; Van Aelst and Walgrave 2004: 101; see also Seattle activists' accounts on www.wtohistory.org).

In some cases, computer-mediated communication simply expands the capacity to act of already solid organizations such as Greenpeace or Oxfam; in other cases, however, it brings together networks of activists with very informal organizational structures, if any. Two examples are the Cokespotlight or McSpotlight websites, which expose Coca Cola's environmental record or McDonald's indifference to workers' rights and food quality; another example is the independent information network Indymedia, the first site of which was born during the 1999 Seattle campaign, and then spread to form other networks, including the European Counter Network that connects anarchists and autonomists and *centri sociali* (Wright 2004). In still other cases, specific organizations are created that would not exist without the internet: e.g., Subversive Enterprises International, which is actually little more than a website that connects likeminded people interested in mobilizing support for the anticapitalist movement, with no hierarchical structure of any kind (Anheier and Themudo 2002: 210).

It has been suggested that changes in both technology and conceptions of political activity will result in the disappearance of traditional organizational forms. Some have stressed the role of media as independent sources of organizational resources. For example, Walgrave and Massens (2000) showed how the media played a major autonomous role in the success of the White march that took place in Brussels in 1996 to voice people's anger at the authorities' handling of the Dutroux pedophilia case. The opportunities for the formation of affinity groups, consisting of people who share a broad vision of political and social engagement, and come together on specific issues of interest and short-term campaigns, have also been greatly enhanced by new communication technologies. For example, mobile phone communications between private citizens have been credited with the success of the demonstrations that in January 2001 forced Philippine president Joseph Estrada to resign (Tilly 2004a: ch. 5). For some radical critics of the role of traditional political organizations, "affinity groups" (i.e., self-organized and self-governing groups based on a commonality of values and interests) represent a major organizing principle behind the global justice movement, which denies any space to organizational identity and to organizations themselves (McDonald 2002; see also Finnegan 2003). Skeptics would counter, however, that affinity groups' attempts to solve the problem of maintaining members' loyalty in a nonbureaucratic way lead to difficult decision-making and ultimately ineffective performance (Gamson 1990; for an insider's account, see also Klein 2002).

6.4 From Movement Organizations to Social Movement Networks

The network nature of social movements has long been highlighted. In a few seminal contributions, Luther Gerlach pointed out that social movements are:

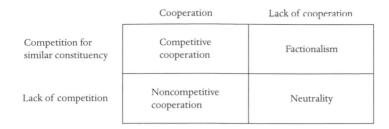

Figure 6.1 Patterns of interorganizational relations among movement organizations

(1) segmented, with numerous different groups or cells in continual rise and decline; (2) polycephalous, having many leaders each commanding only a limited following; and (3) reticular, with multiple links between autonomous cells forming an indistinctly bounded network (Gerlach 1971; Gerlach and Hine 1970). Recently he qualified his argument by stressing the undirected, acephalous, rather than polycephalous, nature of such networks (Gerlach 2001).

Movements so frequently take network forms because political organizations rarely manage to monopolize the representation of a certain complex of interests and values. When this happens, that usually spells the end of a social movement process and its replacement with organizational processes. Normally, a multiplicity of organizations operates on the same issues and on behalf of similar, if not identical, political and ethical projects. Exploring the nature of the relationships between them is crucial for our understanding of social movements.

Even though alliance-building seems a generally sensible and desirable option, in practice, however, interorganizational relationships can vary markedly in both content and intensity. One way to capture those differences is by asking whether organizations are in competition for the acknowledgment and support of the same social base; whether, that is, they are trying to acquire essential resources for action by tapping the same (limited) mobilization potential. By combining the presence or absence of cooperation and presence or absence of competition we can elaborate a typology of forms of interorganizational relationships (figure 6.1).

We have first of all to recognize that many citizens' organizations, despite broadly dealing with similar problems, are basically involved in a relation of neutrality (or indifference) to each other, whereby an absence of cooperation corresponds to lack of competition. Such situations occur when organizations' definitions of issues make cooperation difficult, but at the same time they do not have to compete for members and support, because they appeal to diverse sectors of public opinion. The environmental movement of the 1970s in Italy was close to this model. Its conservation and political ecology components were ideologically far enough apart to make it difficult for them to cooperate with each other. This did not lead to conflict, however, as both sectors were somewhat eccentric in relation to the principal, class-based conflicts in that period (Diani 1995a). Similar remarks may apply to environmentalism in a country with a far lower salience of the left–right divide like Britain. There, a political-ecology sector hardly developed at all in the 1970s, as new left groups were focusing strictly on traditional class issues while paying little attention to environmental problems (Lowe and Goyder 1983).

High levels of competition and low levels of cooperation among movement organizations are instead likely to produce factional relationships. In such cases, the struggle to represent the same constituency leads to fragmentation and sectarian divisions. Cooperation among movement organizations is thus hindered, despite the proximity of their cultural models and styles of action. Donatella della Porta (1990) and Sidney Tarrow (1989a) have shown how the competitive dynamics within Italian movements eventually produced outcomes of this type at the end of the 1970s. The Italian situation was characterized at that time by transition from models which were predominantly cooperative, although also competitive, to models where cooperation was absent. The reduction of the potential to mobilize played a crucial role in this context, as it brought various organizations into open competition with each other, emphasizing their ideological differences. As a result, the potential for conflict within movement areas grew (for other instances of factional dynamics, see e.g. Lichterman 1995b; Balser 1997).

Intense exchanges between organizations with different natural constituencies produce noncompetitive cooperation. Movement organizations are not appealing to the same political market but have, at the same time, sufficient interests and motives for convergence to activate joint mobilizations. Cooperation is, moreover, limited, to the extent that it neither presupposes nor requires the development of a homogeneous perspective or of a "strong" and (semi)exclusive notion of collective identity. Relationships between central organizations with diverse concerns in the Italian environmentalist field in the 1980s were close to this model: political ecology groups such as Legambiente cooperated with conservationist groups such as Italia Nostra without coming into competition, inasmuch as their potential sources of support differed substantially (Diani 1995a: ch. 5).

Where collaboration develops between organizations competing for the same base of support, situations which we will define as competitive cooperation occur. In such cases, two (or more) movement organizations concerned with the same issues are keen to develop joint initiatives, based on compatible definitions of the issues and some degree of identity; but at the same time they find themselves facing stiff mutual competition for the same support base, and for similar sectors of public opinion whose interests they wish to represent. The resulting model of interaction may be characterized by a degree of interorganizational polemic, but that does not lead to a breakdown of resource exchanges and communication. The new left groups which in the 1970s competed for control of radical youth movements in Italy adequately illustrate this model (Tarrow 1989a; della Porta 1995); so do the relationships between women's organizations supporting abortion rights in the USA (Staggenborg 1991). When collaboration between organizations takes place, ties may be largely instrumental, restricted to the exchange of resources for practical purposes, or may involve mutual obligation and a shared identity. This provides the foundation for the distinction between coalitional and social movement processes that we introduced in chapter 1 (see also Diani and Bison 2004). Both coalitional and social movement processes generate extended networks of interaction between distinct social actors.

Social movement action on a large scale has always been organized in network forms. Examples may be found throughout the history of modern contention, from nineteenth-century working class (Thompson 1963; Ansell 1997, 2001) and women's organizations (Rosenthal et al. 1985, 1997), to antiwar or antipoverty coalitions (Bagguley 1991; Hathaway and Meyer 1993–4; Barkan, Cohn, and Whitbaker 1995; Rochon and Meyer 1997; Lavalette and Mooney 2000), to environmental or women's movements (Philips 1991; Sawer and Groves 1994; Diani 1995a; Ansell 2003), to mention just a few. Recently, however, the spread of global justice mobilizations has made the role of networks particularly visible. Increasingly, we see examples of coalitions that involve both transnational actors and networks and local actors on issues such as environmental protection, deprivation, or human rights, thus expanding the range of forms of transnational contention (Bennett 2004b; Rothman and Oliver 1999; Reimann 2001; Subramaniam, Gupte, and Mitre 2003; Rohrschneider and Dalton 2002).

In many cases, network dynamics remain purely informal. Often, however, a hybrid model of "network organization" develops, combining elements of formality with those proper to a loose network structure. In contrast to classic formal organizations, which are based on the vertical integration of multiple units, the "network organization" model in organization theory points at another way of coordinating activities, based on the independence of the single components, horizontal integration, flexibility in goals and strategies, and multiple levels of interaction with the possibility of communitarian elements (Powell 1990; Podolny and Page 1998; Gulati and Gargiulo 1999). Most frequently associated with the novel forms of production introduced by firms like Benetton or IBM (Castells 1996: ch. 3), the "network organization" model, when it is applied to a social movement as a whole, also allows a greater degree of specificity and a more specific definition of goals than the network metaphor does (Diani 2003a).

Network organizational models are useful to coordinate efforts around specific campaigns or policy issues, in which many different activists and organizations have a stake. They do so while being neither dependent on the organizations that originally set them up, nor able to exert a leadership role beyond the boundaries of their specific domain. Many network organizations are inherently temporary – they do not survive the specific mobilization or campaign they are supposed to coordinate; however, some of them may convert into full-fledged organizations, increasingly independent from their original founders, and with a distinct identity. For example, in the environmental justice movement of the 1990s, many grassroots groups preferred to coordinate through an informal networking strategy, rather than relying on the intermediation of the rigid environmental bureaucracies who had so far secured "ownership" of those issues (Taylor 1995; Schlosberg 2002: ch. 5). Many organizations mobilizing on a transnational scale also have a network form. Recent examples include the Rainforest Action Network, that campaigns to protect the rainforest and targets financial actors backing destructive projects; the People's Global Action network, that connects hundreds of grassroots organizations worldwide; or the Alliance for Sustainable Jobs and the Environment, that played a visible public role in the 1999 Seattle anti-WTO demonstrations in bringing together environmentalists, working-class activists, and local community organizers (Bircham and Charlton 2001: 271–89; see also Rose 2000 on cross-class coalitions). The most visible example of network organization, however, is probably the Social Forum model. Inspired by the experience of the World Social Forum in Porto Alegre, this model has then been extended to coordinate in a flexible and negotiated way the multiplicity of actors involved in global justice campaigns at the continental, national, and local levels (see chapter 9 below for a thorough discussion).

Just to make the difference clear: we speak of "network organizations" in reference to relatively bounded organizational forms such as the European Counter Network or the Climate Action Network (Waddell 2003), defined by the interest in specific issues or by a distinct cultural perspective; but we also speak of networks in reference to whole movements, like the global justice movement or the environmental movement. Either way, many have long regarded flexible and decentralized network forms of organizing as particularly effective in achieving the aims of protestors. The ability to coordinate action and promote joint campaigns facilitates the diffusion of protest, and increases the relevance of certain themes on the political agenda and the opportunities to disseminate new interpretations of political and social conflict. The existence of a significant number of allies increases the chances of success for groups promoting protest (Laumann and Knoke 1987: 387; Knoke 1990a: 208). Network links also make movement organizations better equipped to deal with emergencies and threats coming from their environment. In particular, such structures should avert the danger of suppression by opponents (so much easier when the leadership is concentrated in a few people), maximize adaptability, allow the escalation of action by distributing the effects of one group's activities to all of them, promote innovation, and reduce the negative effect of failures (Gerlach 1971). A network organization also allows some kind of mediation between the participatory ethos behind grassroots organizing and the coordination guaranteed by formal structures.

On the other hand, the problems associated with this model – as well as with various coalition forms – have also been highlighted. For example, loose networks increase the resources available to social movement organizations but also the danger of internal conflict, both between different organizational units and different ideological factions (Kleidman 1993: 39–40). In general, the life of many network organizations is shorter and less stable – if often very effective in the short term – than that of organizations adopting more bureaucratic forms. For instance, Jubilee 2000, a network which originated in the UK in 1996 and then spread worldwide, and which campaigns for debt cancellation, collected about 24 million signatures on one petition, but failed to secure the cohesion of the different components of the network. In the early 2000s it fell apart and was replaced by Drop the Debt and other organizations acting on similar issues, yet with an altogether more limited impact (Anheier and Themudo 2002: 192–3).

6.5 Summary

The organizations engaged in social movements have often been described as loosely structured, decentralized, and prone to engage in contentious political challenges or countercultural practices. However, research has shown that, in reality, a plurality of organizational models co-exist within any social movement. Organizations differ, sometimes to a very high degree, in their response to dilemmas such as whether focusing on the mobilization of people or other types of resources, adopting some kind of formal hierarchy or a totally informal structure, targeting their efforts at opponents or also providing services and life opportunities to their own constituents. In this chapter we presented a minimum number of basic models, out of many more that could be identified: the professional social movement organization and the participatory movement organization (more specifically, two versions of it, the mass organization and the grassroots organization, that differ in levels of bureaucratization).

Later, we showed that not even the evolution of social movement organizations is unidirectional: some organizations become institutionalized, turning themselves into political parties or interest groups; others become more radical and turn to violent forms of action; some turn commercial and involve themselves in the market; yet others turn inward, becoming similar to religious sects. Again, rather than searching for general laws or all encompassing accounts, we identify some factors likely to affect organizational change: in particular, the impact of the opportunities offered by the configurations of the political system; the weight of organizational cultures; and the role of technological change, most notably, the spread of information and communication technology.

In the final part of the chapter, we discussed the nature of network forms of organization as a useful corrective to the deficiencies of both formal and loose organizational models. Although always present in contemporary history, those forms have proved particularly adequate to coordinate and support mobilization in the global justice and other transnational movements.

ACTION FORMS, REPERTOIRES, AND CYCLES OF PROTEST

November 30, 1999. Seattle, a city which, thanks to Microsoft, has become emblematic of the New Economy, saw some 50,000 demonstrators protest against the third WTO conference assembled to launch the Millennium Round, a new series of negotiations aimed at increasing market liberalization, in particular of investment and public services. The protest had been called for a few months before in Geneva by a committee of organizations from various backgrounds that had already (successfully) mobilized to prevent the signing of the Multilateral Agreement on Investment (MAI). As with the MAI, the WTO negotiations were criticized for restricting individual states' power to intervene on social and environmental issues in the name of free trade. No fewer than 1,387 groups (including NGOs, trade unions, environmentalists, and a number of religious organizations of various affiliations) signed the call to demonstrate against the Millennium Round. Thousands of meetings in many countries and a global information campaign were organized to prepare for the protests. The demonstrators marched to slogans such as "the world is not for sale"; "No Globalization Without Participation"; "We Are Citizens, Not Only Consumers"; "WTO = Capitalism without Conscience"; "Trade: Clean, Green and Fair."

From the morning of the very first day, a series of sit-ins, coordinated by the Direct Action Network (DAN), stopped most of the 3,000 delegates from 135 countries from reaching the inaugural ceremony. Organized into "affinity groups" only loosely linked with each other, some 10,000 demonstrators sat tied together in chains on the ground, using so-called "lock down" and "tripod" techniques that made the work of the police in removing the blockages more difficult (Smith 2000). When the police arrived to clear the streets leading to the summit, the demonstrators made no move to resist but applied the tactics they had learned during courses in nonviolence. In the streets of Seattle, thronged with musical bands and theater groups, Greenpeace activists appeared with gigantic condoms bearing the legend "Practice Safe Trade," while French farmers gave away some 250 kilos of roquefort cheese, subject to customs duties in the United States, in a tit-for-tat measure against the EU's restrictive legislation against "hormone beef." Activists of Jubilee 2000, a coalition of groups (including many religious-based ones) whose aim was to cancel third-world foreign debt, linked up in a human chain. A massive march was called by the AFL-CIO (American Federation of Labor–Congress of Industrial Organizations) mobilizing over 20,000 workers, in particular dockers and public-service workers, demanding worldwide application of workers' rights. Farm-worker organizations banded together with consumer activists and environmentalists to demand that food products be kept out of liberalization agreements in the name of precaution.

More than 200 demonstrators dressed as sea turtles – an endangered species – wandered through the crowd with the task of troubleshooting any violence. As Ben White, designer of the colorful costumes and an activist with the Sea Turtle Restoration Project, explains: "Since the dawn of time, turtles have always been a symbol of wisdom. They never fight, they don't use violence. We represent them and we must be their voice . . . anyone who acts aggressively, even if it's only vocal, has to take his costume off . . . we're not only nonviolent ourselves, we're also against the use of violence by others. Wherever the turtles come across violence they try to make peace" (in Reimon 2002: 73). On the fringes of the demonstrations, however, small groups did turn violent, smashing the windows of shops dealing in multinational products such as Nike, Levi's, and McDonald's, accused of using child labor or unhealthy products. Before the anarchists started to damage property, the police stepped in *en masse* against the nonviolent blockages, deploying tear gas and pepper spray (Smith 2000: 13; also Morse 2001). After local authorities declared a curfew, blockades and police charges continued for three days and nights until the intergovernmental summit broke up without any agreement having been reached. Among the 600 people arrested were activists from Global Exchange who had used their passes to get into the inaugural ceremony and spoke from the podium to the few delegates who had managed to get in, criticizing the WTO. A petition being circulated over the internet in protest against the lack of transparency of the talks managed to gather in just 24 hours the signatures of 1,700 groups of various kinds, many from the world's South (Kaldor 2000: 112).

Seattle has been defined as a turning point but also the high point of an aggregation process involving groups and organizations active in countries all over the world: blue-collar workers and farm workers, consumers and environmentalists, churches and feminists, pacifists and human-rights associations. In fact even before Seattle, heterogeneous and initially loosely connected groups had mobilized together, mainly against international organizations, using different strategies: from lobbying to marches, from boycotts to petitions, from strikes to netstrikes. In Seattle and afterwards, demonstrators from many countries challenged the legitimacy of the decisions of some international governmental organizations and sought to hinder their plans. They did not do so through normal diplomatic channels or through elections. Rather, they sought to influence public opinion in various ways.

In fact, as we shall see in section 7.1, a characteristic of protest is its capacity to mobilize public opinion through unorthodox forms of action and so put pressure on decision-makers. The brief outline given above of the protest in Seattle describes a series of different actions which, taken together, form what we will define in section 7.2 as a repertoire of collective action. In section 7.3 the global justice movement will be referred to in order to illustrate that tactics very different in terms of their radicalism and the "logic" driving them co-exist within contemporary repertoire of protest. For social movement actors, choices concerning the forms of action to adopt are important but difficult decisions, involving strategic calculations but also considerations of values and culture. In fact, as we shall see in section 7.4, the necessity to simultaneously address different types of public creates a number of tactical dilemmas. In addition, such choices are influenced both by internal variables and by interactions with other actors (section 7.5), inside as well as outside national borders (7.6). The mutable character of these decisions leads, in section 7.7, to an analysis of the cyclical dynamics of protest and the nature of changes over time.

7.1   Protest: A Definition

In the protest in Seattle and afterwards, activists marched and arranged blockades; there were concerts and vigils. People went around masked as nearly extinct turtles; others wore black masks. They occupied real and virtual spaces. What, then, do all these actions have in common? In the first place, they are forms of protest: i.e. nonroutinized ways of affecting political, social, and cultural processes. In fact, "social movements employ methods of persuasion and coercion which are, more often than not, novel, unorthodox, dramatic, and of questionable legitimacy" (Wilson 1973: 227). Protests are "sites of contestation in which bodies, symbols, identities, practices, and discourses are used to pursue or prevent changes in institutionalized power relations" (Taylor and van Dyke 2004: 268).

According to the principles of representative democracy, the decisions of a government can be challenged immediately by the parliamentary opposition or punished subsequently by the voting choices of citizens in elections. Aside from military intervention, the channels for exerting pressure on a foreign government include bilateral diplomacy or negotiations in one of the many international government organizations (IGOs). However, particularly since the 1970s, increasing numbers of citizens have come to affirm the legitimacy of other forms of pressure on governments. When faced with laws or decisions considered to be unjust these citizens adopt forms of action that challenge established norms. Especially from the 1960s on, a "new set of political activities has been added to the citizens' political repertoire" (Barnes et al. 1979: 149).[1] In fact, researchers added a long list of new and unconventional forms of political participation – including signing petitions, lawful demonstration, boycotts, withholding of rent or tax, occupations, sit-ins, blocking traffic, and wildcat strikes – to the more traditional ones, such as following politics in the newspapers, discussing politics with others, working for political parties or their candidates, attending political meetings, contacting public officials, or persuading friends and acquaintances to vote in particular ways. These newer forms have become increasingly legitimized: "In advanced industrial societies direct political action techniques do not in fact bear the stigma of deviancy. Nor are they seen as antisystem-directed orientation" (1979: 157).

This expansion of the repertoire of political participation appeared to be a "lasting characteristic of democratic mass publics" (1979: 524). Indeed, more than two decades later, Pippa Norris (2002: 221) observed, on the bases of World Value Surveys polls, that "There are many reasons to believe that the shift from traditional interest groups to new social movements has influenced the agencies, repertoires, and targets of political participation . . . The analysis of protest politics shows that many of these forms of activity, such as petitions, demonstrations, and consumer boycott, are fairly pervasive and have become increasingly popular during recent decades. Protest politics is on the rise as a channel of political expression and mobilization." According to Norris's data (2002: 197), in "older democracies" 60.7 percent of the population have signed a petition, 19.1 percent have attended a demonstration, and 17.1 percent have joined in boycotts. In eight postindustrial societies (Britain, West Germany, the Netherlands, Austria, the United States, Italy, Switzerland, and Finland), the percentage of those who have signed petitions rose from 32 in the mid-seventies to 60 in the mid-nineties; of those who had demonstrated, from 9 to 17; of those who took part in boycotts from 6 to 15, of those who occupied buildings from 1 to 2, those who took part in unofficial strikes from 2 to 4 (ibid.: 198).

An important characteristic of protest is the use of indirect channels to influence decision-makers. As Michael Lipsky noted (1965), protest is a political resource of the powerless. The events that shook the United States in the 1960s

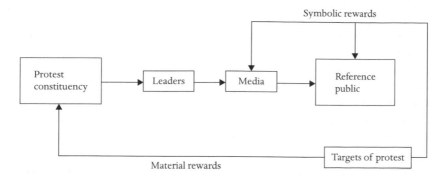

Figure 7.1 The communication process of protest
Source: Adapted from Lipsky 1965: 163–82.

– from the "Freedom Summer" campaign to register black voters in the South-ern states, launched by civil rights activists in 1964, to the "March on Washing-ton" in support of ethnic minority civil rights – all had something in common: "They were engaged in by relatively powerless groups; and they depended for success not upon direct utilization of power, but upon activating other groups to enter the political arena. Because protest is successful to the extent that other parties are activated to political involvement, it is one of the few strategies in which even politically impoverished groups can aspire to engage" (Lipsky 1965: 1). Indeed, in Seattle the people that took part in the demonstrations felt them-selves to be the "losers" of economic neoliberal policies. Even if not exactly "powerless," the unions, NGOs and grassroots groupings that launched the protest were outsiders (or, in Tilly's words, challengers) in a world politics where representatives of IGOs, powerful nations, and big corporations are insiders.

Protest, then, sets in motion a process of indirect persuasion mediated by mass media and powerful actors. As figure 7.1 suggests, powerless actors must mobilize the support of more powerful groups. In fact, protest mobilizes a variety of actors. Those directly interested in political decisions comprise a protest constituency. From this constituency a leadership emerges to lead action and maintain external relations. The mass media spreads their message, a message directed in the first instance at the reference public of the decision-makers. The latter are the true targets of protest. In order to succeed, protest must produce positive stimuli, winning the sympathies of those who have more resources to invest in the arenas where decisions are taken. While collective action by groups who already possess power can be aimed directly at decision-makers, the powerless must seek to involve those who have the possibility of influencing them. In addition, the influence exerted by social movements can be either positive, creating sympathy for their cause, or negative, threatening (for example) to create disorder. This is why the characteristics of the mass media, and of channels of communication in general, are particularly relevant for social movements: their capacity to address public opinion is indeed a crucial component of their action.

Social movements certainly do not use protest alone and do not have a monopoly on protest. Other actors, such as political parties or pressure groups, also make use of protest action and occasionally make alliances with social movements for particular campaigns. However, protest (particularly at its most innovative and radical) has been considered a form of action typical of social movements because, unlike political parties and pressure groups, they have fewer channels through which to access decision-makers. Forms of action are particularly important for them since social movements are "often remembered more for the methods of persuasion adopted by them than for their objectives" (Wilson 1973: 226).

7.2   Repertoires of Action

The marches, boycotts, occupations, and other forms of action used in the campaigns for global justice have something else in common. They are all part of a modern repertoire of collective action, defined as the "whole set of means [a group] has for making claims of different types on different individuals" (Tilly 1986: 2). Charles Tilly has made an important contribution to the study of collective action by identifying the differences in types of contentious action[2] in particular historical periods. Protest was certainly not unheard of prior to the formation of the nation-state: peasants burnt down mills in protest against increases in the price of bread; subjects dressed up in order to mock their superiors; funerals could be turned into the occasion for denunciations of injustice.[3] The tactics adopted by protestors varied from the utilization of irreverent symbols and music (as in charivari) to field invasions and grain seizures. However, they all had two characteristics in common: "Broadly speaking, the repertoire of the mid-seventeenth to the mid-nineteenth century had a parochial scope: it addressed local actors or the local representatives of national actors. It also relied heavily on patronage – appealing to immediately available power holders to convey grievances or settle disputes, temporarily acting in the place of unworthy or inactive power holders only to abandon power after the action" (Tilly 1986: 391–2).

The forms taken by collective action began to change in the nineteenth century when the old parochial and patronage-dependent repertoire was replaced by one which was national ("though available for local issues and enemies, it lends itself easily to coordination among many localities") and autonomous ("instead of staying in the shadow of existing power holders and adapting routines sanctioned by them, people using the new repertoire tend to initiate their own statements of grievances and demands" – Tilly 1986: 391–2), involving actions such as strikes, electoral rallies, public meetings, petitions, marches, insurrection, and the invasion of legislative bodies. In the past, assemblies converged on the private residences of the crowd's enemies, whereas today the preferred targets are the seats and symbols of national public power (Tilly 1986: 392–3). The older repertoire tended to use the same type of action as the authorities, either in the form of caricature or temporary substitution; the new one invented autonomous forms. People used to participate in the traditional repertoire of collective action as members of preconstituted communities, whereas they do so as representatives of particular interests in the modern repertoire. The old repertoire took advantage of official celebrations or occasions; the new involves the deliberate organization of assemblies and occasions for action. This transformation in the form of protest followed from the creation of the nation-state, the development of capitalism, and the emergence of modern means of communication. As Tilly (1986: 395–6) puts it:

> As capitalism advanced, national states became more powerful and centralized local affairs and nearby patrons mattered less to the fates of ordinary people. Increasingly, holders of large capitals and national power made the decisions that affected them. As a result, seizure of grain, collective invasions of fields and the like became ineffective, irrelevant, obsolete. In response to the shifts of power and capital, ordinary people invented and adopted new forms of action, creating the electoral campaign, the public meeting, the social movement, and the other elements of the newer repertoire.

The new repertoire responded therefore to a new situation in which politics was increasingly national in character, the role of communities diminished and organized association spread, particularly among the laboring classes (Tilly 1984b: 309). There is another characteristic typical of the modern repertoire besides its national scale and autonomous character: its modular quality, i.e. the possibility of being used by a variety of actors to achieve a variety of objectives. In traditional societies the repertoire was specific, direct, and rigid: "In a society divided into orders, isolated by poor communication and lack of literacy and organized into corporate and communal groups, it was rare to find forms of collective action distinct from the conflicts that gave rise to them" (Tarrow 1994: 35). The consolidation of the nation-state, the expansion of the means of communication (whether roads or newspapers), and the growth of private associations favored instead the development of a new, general, flexible, and indirect repertoire. This in its turn facilitated the diffusion of protest and the mobilization of new and diverse groups within the population.

According to Tilly and Tarrow, the modern repertoire which emerged with the French Revolution has changed little since. Boycotts, barricades, petitions, and demonstrations are all still present (and indeed probably dominant) in the panorama of protest. However, if we look back at the example that opened this chapter, a number of new elements can be identified – elements that can be explained by transformations in the very characteristics held to be essential for the emergence of the modern repertoire. First, capitalism developed from nation-state-based industries to multinational corporations. Second, while the nation-state has certainly not disappeared, it is now flanked by sub- and supra-national entities possessing increasing powers (see chapters 2 and 9 in the present volume). Mobilizations such as the one in Seattle are transnational in nature. Third, new media such as television, but especially more recently fax, mobile phones, and the internet, have transformed the ambitions and communication capacity of social movements. In particular, the internet is exploited for online mobilization and acts of dissent: the term "electronic advocacy" refers to "the use of high technology to influence the decision-making process, or to the use of technology in an effort to support policy-change efforts" (Hick and McNutt 2002: 8). Also, in part thanks to the internet, transnational campaigns have grown longer, less centrally controlled, more difficult to turn on and off, and forever mutable in terms of networks and goals (Bennett 2003).

7.3   The Logics and Forms of Protest

The citizens and organizations opposing neoliberal globalization did so in a variety of ways. First, the forms of action presented at the beginning of the chapter were more or less radical in nature, ranging from more conventional petitioning to more conflictual blockades, and including a number of episodes of violence. Opinion poll research has ordered forms of participation on a single continuum from least to most extreme, singling out various thresholds: "The first threshold indicates the transition from conventional to unconventional politics. Signing petitions and participating in lawful demonstrations are unorthodox political activities but still within the bounds of accepted democratic norms. The second threshold represents the shift to direct action techniques, such as boycotts. A third level of political activities involves illegal, but nonviolent, acts. Unofficial strikes or a peaceful occupation of a building typify this step. Finally, a fourth threshold includes violent activities such as personal injury or physical damage" (Dalton 1988: 65).

Second, although the forms of action adopted concentrated to a large extent on the political system, it should be noted that movements also made use (to differing degrees) of cultural strategies aimed at changing value systems. While political strategies seek, above all, to change external realities, cultural strategies seek an interior transformation. As already noted, some social movements are directed primarily to value systems, while others concentrate on the political system (for example, Rucht 1994). Moreover, movements themselves alternate between phases of greater "politicization" and retreat into countercultural activity (Melucci 1984a; on Italy, della Porta 1996a). In addition, both cultural and political strategies are also characterized by varying degrees of extremeness, ranging from moderate subcultural evolution to radical countercultural challenge in the first case and from negotiation to confrontation in the second (Rucht 1990a).

However, as we shall seek to demonstrate more fully in what follows, forms of action can also be distinguished according to the "logic," or *modus operandi*, which the activists assign them.

7.3.1 The logic of numbers

The logic of numbers, to which James DeNardo referred in *Power in Numbers* (1985), underlies numerous forms of protest. Since "there always seems to be power in numbers" (1985: 35), a movement's destiny depends to a great extent on the number of its supporters. As DeNardo notes, the "size of the dissidents' demonstrations affects the regime both directly and indirectly. Naturally the disruption of daily routines increases with numbers, and the regime's ability to control crowds inevitably suffers as they grow larger. In addition to the immediate disruption they cause, demonstrations by their size also give the regime an indication of how much support the dissidents enjoy" (1985: 36). Just as political parties attempt to increase the number of electors who support them and pressure groups seek to maximize the number of their adherents, social movements should seek to mobilize the greatest number of demonstrators possible.

From this point of view, protest stands in for elections. The logic behind it is the same as that behind representative democracy: implementation of the majority's decisions. Protest serves to draw the attention of elected representatives to the fact that, at least on certain issues, the majority in the country is not the same as the majority in parliament. Thus, the fear of losing electoral support should push the people's representatives into changing their position, realigning themselves with the country "at large."

Marches are one of the main tactics designed to demonstrate the numerical strength behind protest. The Seattle demonstration started a new wave of "politics on the street" with large marches that had seemed just a memory of the past. Large demonstrations are organized during countersummits, defined as arenas of "international-level initiatives during official summits and on the same issues but from a critical standpoint, heightening awareness through protest and information with or without contacts with the official version" (Pianta 2002: 35). After some preliminary experiences in the 1980s, countersummits multiplied over the succeeding decade, simultaneously with large-scale UN conferences, supported by the frenetic activism of NGOs that claimed to represent not only their hundreds of thousands of members, but more generally the interests of billions of citizens without a public voice. Millions of people joined the international day of protest against the Iraq war on February 15, 2003 (della Porta and Diani 2005; Waalgrave and Rucht forthcoming).

Petitions (as well as referendums) are also used to demonstrate the numerical strength of support for movements. In the eighties, petitions and demands for referendums were presented in all of the countries affected by the deployment of cruise and pershing missiles. Millions of signatures were collected in Italy, the Netherlands, Germany, and the United States. In 1984 and 1985, pacifist groups in a number of European countries suggested that voters demand guarantees on peace issues from the electoral candidates of all parties. In the nineties, the campaign led by Jubilee 2000 collected 24 million signatures under a petition asking to drop the debt of the poorest countries (Anheier and Themundo 2002). The use of petitions has been facilitated by the internet: transnational campaigns against multinational corporations such as De Beers, Microsoft, Monsanto, Nike, etc., run especially via online petitions, with the collection of signatures via mailing lists and websites.[4]

Netstriking also follows a "logic of numbers," and is another form of online protest that has proliferated in recent years among radical organizations as a "virtual practice for real conflicts" (according to the association StranoNetwork: see Freschi 2000: 104; della Porta and Mosca 2005). A netstrike is "comparable to a physical procession that occupies a road to make it inaccessible" (www.netstrike.it). Netstriking consists of a large number of people connecting simultaneously to the same domain at a prearranged time, in order to "jam" a site considered a symbolic target, and to make it impossible for other users to reach it. The mobilization and its motivation are normally communicated in advance to the owner of the site targeted by the protestors. When a netstrike is in progress online protestors activate a channel of communication (generally a chat-line or a mailing-list) in order to coordinate their protest action. Netstriking can accompany nonvirtual protest that ideally links offline and online environments – for instance, a netstrike was promoted against the WTO website during the protests in Seattle (T. Jordan 2002). Similar to the netstriking, but less used, is mail-bombing, which consists of sending emails to a website or a server until it overloads and gets jammed.

The logic of numbers is coherent with the principles of representative democracy: an attempt is made to influence public opinion, the final repository of political power. Given that demonstrators are also voters, it is assumed that their representatives will change their position rather than risk not being reelected. However, the bombing of Iraq by the international war coalition led by the American administration, in defiance of massive protest, demonstrated that the logic of numbers does not always work. Despite opinion polls in most of the countries involved demonstrating that a majority opposed the war, the governments of European countries (such as Italy and Spain) offered their troops in support of the American occupation.

Indeed it would be naive to assume that the opinions of elected representatives simply follow those of the general public on every occasion (McAdam and Su 2002). First, voting is structured by a whole series of questions and depends on a balance between different motivations. It is far from certain that an individual will abandon their traditional electoral choice on the basis of a preference on a particular issue, even when the individual agrees with the movement on that issue. Movement activists have, therefore, not only to increase support, but also to produce "strong preferences" in favor of their claims. Second, protest campaigns have a limited duration and, as a result, their political influence is less direct. Indeed, "the problem with all movement alliances, but especially those with the parties, is how to keep commitment firm once the persuasive sounds of the marching thousands have become a distant echo" (Rochon 1988: 174). Third, even mass events – such as online petitions, campaigns, and netstrikes – are often ignored by those they target (Rucht 2003a), their impact on observers depending on how much they capture the attention of the mass media (Gurak and Logie 2003: 26). Moreover, as the Seattle events again signaled, power is shifting towards decision-makers that are less and less accountable to public opinion and citizens–electors (see chapter 8 below). As the numerous defeats in social movement-inspired referendums demonstrate, a further and perhaps more decisive factor counts against the logic of numbers: protestors (sometimes referred to as "active minorities") do not always reflect the opinions of a majority of the public (Wisler and Kriesi 1998). Thus, it would be extremely dangerous for social movements to depend solely on such a logic; a logic which does not in any case fully reflect their own concept of democracy, which emphasizes participation, not majority vote (see chapter 9 below). We can add, however, that beyond externally oriented strategic considerations, the logic of numbers also plays an important symbolic function for the movement activists themselves. Large demonstrations empower participants by spreading the feelings of belonging to a large community of equals.

7.3.2 The logic of damage

The logic of inflicting material damage, in a *modus operandi* analogous to war, must be considered alongside the logic of numbers. This logic is reflected, in its most extreme form, by political violence. The Black Block in Seattle and elsewhere has used targeted, small-scale violence. Long before Seattle, urban bread riots in Latin America as well as in Africa had dramatically contested free-trade policies, and the austerity measures connected with them, demanded by the

International Monetary Fund, and asked for "Work, bread, justice and liberty" (Walton and Seddon 1994; see also Eckstein 2001 on Latin America and Bennani-Chaibri and Fillieule 2003 on Islamic countries). In violence against property the costs are still largely economic, but the logic becomes increasingly "military" in violence against persons. In all these events, however, violence has both symbolic and instrumental aims. Violence is justified often as a symbolic refusal of an oppressive system, but it is also used, as in the anti-austerity riots, to win specific battles, or to obtain media attention. In the words of a Black Blocker, "As a protest tactic, the usefulness of destroying property is limited but significant. It gets newspaper reporters running to where it's taking place and sends out the message that certain apparently unassailable companies aren't really so unassailable after all. Those who take part in the protest and the others sitting at home in front of the TV can see how one small brick in the hands of a really determined person can break down a symbolic wall. Breaking a Nike window doesn't place anybody's life in jeopardy" (cited in Notarbartolo 2001: 81). Urban riots staged by excluded ethnic minorities as well as exclusionary riots against ethnic minorities have usually aimed at specific concessions, and rioters usually practiced much more self-restraint than is often admitted (Hobsbawm 1952; Bergmann 2002).

Using violence also has many limitations and constraints. In the first place, violent action may cause an escalation in repression and alienate sympathizers. Violence polarizes the conflict, transforming "relations between challengers and authorities from a confused, many-sided game into a bipolar one in which people are forced to choose sides, allies defect, bystanders retreat and the state's repressive apparatus swings into action" (Tarrow 1994: 104). Although it is true that a lack of resources may encourage the use of more extreme tactics, "this impulse is constrained . . . by the erosion of support occasioned by repression and moral backlash. The crucial question, therefore, is whether the government's additional responsiveness to violent protest will provide sufficient compensation for the movement's smaller size" (DeNardo 1985: 219). While direct action has on occasion been associated with substantive successes, it has also been noted that violent action often leads to an escalation in conflict.[5] In a democratic regime the state holds a monopoly on the legitimate use of force and most challenges to that monopoly are doomed to fail, transforming political conflict into a military confrontation in which the state has by far the greater firepower (della Porta 1995). This is why, in the global justice movement in the northern hemisphere, nonviolence dominates as both an option of value and a strategic choice. References to Gandhi and Martin Luther King are frequently made by the groups especially concerned with the development of nonviolent techniques, which often requires specific training.

Leaving aside violence, however, a certain amount of material disruption is present in many forms of protest. The action taken by social movements is often inherently disruptive in the sense that it obstructs the normal course of events by threatening disorder (Tarrow 1994: 103). Their challenge to the elites accentuates uncertainty and by so doing produces tangible, and on occasion material, losses. Some protest strategies stress economic damage. Typical is the labor strike, oriented to suspend production, and therefore reduce the profits of the factory owners. By striking, workers halt production and inflict damage on their employer; this economic cost should lead a rational employer to reach agreement with the workforce. More extreme forms of action such as wildcat or rolling strikes and industrial sabotage are sometimes used to increase pressure on the employer by exacerbating the economic cost.

The logic which underlies the industrial strike is difficult to translate into non-industrial contention. In these cases the opposing party is less easily identified, and disruption tends to work through the trouble it causes to third parties not directly responsible for public decisions and who may turn against the protestors as a result. Strikes in public services are, indeed, particular delicate as their immediate victims are the citizen-users. Thus, one of the principal dilemmas of protest lies in the often contradictory requirements of threatening disorder on the one hand, while on the other seeking to avoid stigmatization by public opinion. Indeed, unions in the service industries are themselves becoming more cautious about using the strike weapon, knowing that they risk losing public support rather than undermining the legitimacy of government decisions.

Boycotts (a tactic that became very popular in the global justice movement) also aim at reducing the sales, and therefore the profits, of targeted firms. The underlying logic of many movement campaigns is "naming and shaming" which, especially when conducted against multinationals, aims at making public opinion aware of especially glaring cases of ignoring human rights by spreading detailed information about them, and often asking people to punish the companies involved by boycotting their products. For instance, the Clean Clothes Campaign – launched in 1993 by a coalition of student associations, religious groups, human rights organizations, and trade unions – boycotted department stores like C&A, Peek&Cloppenburg, and M&S Mode, whom, it was alleged, were selling products manufactured using extreme worker exploitation, with low salaries and unsafe conditions, in countries like South Korea, Bangladesh, Hong Kong, Mexico, Guatemala, and Honduras (Mies 2002). Other later examples of boycotts aimed at multinationals were to involve Shell, criticized for polluting the North Sea and the Niger river (and indirectly for the brutal repression of protests staged by the Ogoni people); Nike, accused of subcontracting production to small enterprises in Indonesia and Vietnam that use child labor as well as highly polluting products; Nestlé, which by promoting the use of powdered milk in developing countries, was accused of abetting the spread of children's diseases by lowering their immune response; Monsanto, for producing sterile seeds; Unilever, of introducing genetically modified soy beans into the market; Del Monte, after the broadcasting of a videotape showing the slaughter of dolphins during tuna fishing; McDonald's, for allegedly using the meat of animals raised extensively on antibiotics (which produces an addiction effect on consumers); Bridgestone/Firestone, who were obliged to rehire workers they had fired; and the Pfitzer pharmaceutical company to relinquish patent rights on life-saving anti-AIDS drugs in poor countries in Africa and Brazil. The boycott, producing direct damage to the targeted economic enterprises, adapt to a situation in which multinational companies have growing power (according to the activists, even more power than many nation-states). The boycott of specific multinational companies follows this logic, also exploiting the need for, that rely more on their logo than on the quality of their products, to have a clean image. A similar tactic is used by online activists who mock international organizations by building fake websites in order to attract users looking for the official websites or create websites with similar names.

These forms of protest, although not as stigmatized as the violent ones are, have some shortcomings. For instance, the boycott is very much dependent on mass-media coverage in order to be effective in producing a "loss of face" (Vegh 2003; Gamson 2004: 258). Moreover, they have to be managed carefully in order to limit the risk of negative effects on the workers of boycotted firms or countries. In fact, even potential allies can become the unplanned victims of a boycott: the boycott against French roquefort cheese threatened during a wave of protest against French nuclear testing in the nineties risked hitting the French peasants, who were to protest against the WTO in Seattle. Moreover, when practiced by individual citizens, unconnected to each other, boycotting may become solipsistic, and "a poor way to sustain a sense of injustice and indignation" (Jasper 1997: 265).

7.3.3 The logic of bearing witness

Forms of protest which might be defined as based on a logic of bearing witness have developed alongside those based on the logic of numbers or the logic of inflicting damage, particularly since the 1970s. Such action is not designed to convince the public or decision-makers that the protestors constitute a majority or a threat. Rather, it seeks to demonstrate a strong commitment to an objective deemed vital for humanity's future. This logic is perhaps most in accord with the concept of participatory democracy that is widespread among social movement activists (see chapter 9 below). The right to influence decision-making processes comes from neither formal investiture nor intrinsic power but from force of commitment. In actions of this kind, activists are willing to run personal risks to demonstrate their convictions and reinforce the moral message being conveyed by their protest.

Bearing witness is expressed, in the first instance, through participation in actions which involve serious personal risks or cost. Civil disobedience, knowingly breaking what are considered to be unjust laws, rests on this logic. Typical actions of this type of repertoire have been the destruction of fields of genetically modified maize by the Confédération Paysanne, Greenpeace raids against whaling boats, the blockages of nuclear sites, but also episodes of passive resistance to police intervention. While attempting to penetrate "red zones" during countersummits, demonstrators in Prague, Gothenburg, and Genoa were perfecting what in Great Britain is called "pushing and shoving," namely the shoulder-to-shoulder pressing that police and strikers do in picket lines. Symbolic provocation is also crucial in the revival of civil disobedience in demonstrations against globalization. In the words of the prominent activist Naomi Klein, "Confrontations are staged at the fence – but not only the ones involving sticks and bricks: tear-gas canisters have been flicked back with hockey sticks, water cannon have been irreverently challenged with toy water pistols and buzzing helicopters, mocked with swarms of paper airplanes" (Klein 2002: xxv). Part of the global justice movement, the Disobedients stage conflicts by covering their bodies with protective materials and using plastic shields to protect themselves against police batons, but they proceed with their hands up in the air as a sign of nonaggression. In many such actions, the risk of arrest testifies to the conviction that something had to be done about a decision considered profoundly unjust, even if this involved running very serious costs indeed.

A further characteristic of action based on the logic of bearing witness is its sensitivity to alternative values and culture. Conferences, journals, concerts, and documentaries have the task of educating the public to a different understanding of the world. Although in the majority of cases contemporary social movements seek to bring about political transformations they share the conviction that reform cannot come from above. Changes in individual consciousness must accompany the transformation of political structures. Thus cultural as well as political strategies must be adopted. This logic is especially visible in the consumer activism that indeed "challenges our sense that money and morality cannot be mixed" (Micheletti 2003: 3). Presenting consumption as a potentially political act, ethical consumerism stresses the central role of individuals in taking responsibility for the common goods in their everyday life. Boycotts of bad products, but also buycotts of fair ones (environmentally friendly and solidaristic) as well as socially responsible investments are ways not only of resocializing wrongdoers and changing business activities, but also of practicing certain values (Follesdal 2004). As Micheletti (2003: 150) stresses, political consumerism defends a normative stance; "virtues should be embedded in market transactions. Democratic political consumerism is a virtue practicing activity." Moreover, it is a form of action that resonates with an individualized culture (Stolle and Hooghe 2004: 273), as "cosmopolitan citizens in global societies process their political choices increasingly in terms of how those choices affect their own lifestyles" (Bennett 2004a: 102).

The capacity of directly transmitting their message is a characteristic of forms of action which rely most heavily on the logic of bearing witness. Because they oppose the idea that the ends justify the means, contemporary social movements have sought forms of action that reflect the objective to be obtained as closely as possible. The attention paid to the immediate impact of symbols seeks to facilitate the diffusion of the social movement message in a situation where the media tends to report superficially: "If the message is embedded in the activity, then a report of the activity makes people think about the issue as well" (Rochon 1988: 120). "Guerrilla theater" and other uses of drama "embody preferred frames in the symbolism they used – in effect performing the frame through costume, props, puppets, and other visual images" (Gamson 2004: 253).

The logic of bearing witness also leads to an accentuation of the emotional intensity of participation. The peace movement has often borrowed from and adapted the old repertoire of public demonstration in this direction. Inspired by religious tradition (and, in particular, the model of pilgrimage), pacifists organized numerous long-distance marches, as well as masses, vigils, torchlight processions, communal prayers, and the Stations of the Cross on Good Friday. Human chains connected places of symbolic importance, meetings of the world's leaders were symbolically besieged, and street demonstrations were turned into theatrical "happenings," acting out the consequences of nuclear war. Later on, the global justice movement "uses some of the tropes of earlier repertories – giant puppets, satirical masks . . . – but it slants these in innovative ways, often as a result of broad coalition participation in protests" (Whittier 2004: 539). Direct action was, for instance, inherited by the women's movement, but with the attempt of "developing complex means of assuring equal participation by all group members in consensus decision-making, and emphasizing both logistical and emotional connections among participants" (ibid.).

7.4 Strategic Options and Protest

Forms of protest, then, are extreme to different degrees and, most importantly, follow different types of logic. How and why is one form of protest chosen rather than another? A first answer can be sought in the complexity and multiplicity of the objectives protest is meant to achieve. If we look again at figure 7.1, Lipsky notes that "protest leaders must nurture and sustain an organization comprised of people with whom they may or may not share common values. They must articulate goals and choose strategies so as to maximize their public exposure through communications media. They must maximize the impact of third parties in the political conflict. Finally, they must try to maximize chances of success among those capable of granting goals" (Lipsky 1965: 163, emphasis in the original). As Rochon (1988: 109, emphasis added) observes in connection with the peace movement, "the ideal movement strategy is one that is convincing with respect to political authorities, legitimate with respect to potential supporters, rewarding with respect to those already active in the movement, and novel in the eyes of the mass media. These are not entirely compatible demands."

First, given that every action has an attached cost but can also be a benefit in and of itself (Hirschman 1982), it is important for social movements to find tactics which are also suitable for realizing internal aims. Many forms of protest "have profound effects on the group spirit of their participants," since "in the end, there is nothing as productive of solidarity as the experience of merging group purposes with the activities of everyday life" (Rochon 1998: 115). Protest action has an important internal function: creating that sense of collective identity which is a condition for action towards a common goal (Pizzorno 1993). In fact, "movement strategists are fully aware that at least some of their tactics must widen the pool of activists and develop 'solidarities,' rather than 'merely' having an impact on politicians" (Rochon 1998: 159). For the labor movement strikes had more than a simply instrumental function (Fantasia 1988), and this is also true of occupations for the student movement (Ortoleva 1988), both reinforcing a sense of identity. Solidarity is born out of shared risks on the barricades: "As they faced off against hostile troops or national guardsmen, the defenders of a barricade came to know each other as comrades, developed a division of labor of fighters, builders and suppliers, and formed social networks that would bring their survivors together in future confrontations" (Tarrow 1994: 44). The peace camps, which spread throughout Europe in the wake of the First European Convention on Peace and Disarmament in Brussels in 1981, similarly played an important role in the elaboration of a pacifist identity. According to participants, one of the main benefits of the many transnational countersummits has been increasing mutual knowledge and understanding (Pianta 2001a). In particular, the United Nations-sponsored intergovernmental summits on women's issues, environment, and poverty served as arenas for networking, frame-bridging, and protest training (for a review, Smith 2004b: 322). Nonviolent direct action strengthens the feeling of belonging; "a community that is formed in the process of struggle is a very precious thing, and fulfills a lot of needs that are not met in daily life" (Epstein 1991: 8).

However, actions that strengthen internal solidarity not always serve to create support outside the movement. Looking at figure 7.1 it can be remarked that, if leaders of protest often must favor more radical action in order to maintain rank-and-file support, these are precisely the kinds of action that risk alienating potential allies. Protest leaders must avoid action that is too extreme if they are to win over their target groups within the public, but in doing so they run the risk of losing the confidence of their protest constituency.[6] Opinion polls have shown that the more peaceful and institutional a course of unconventional political action is (petitioning, for example) the greater the level of public approval. Approval falls where the action taken is direct but nonviolent, and is minimal where violent action is concerned (Barnes et al. 1979).[7] If the protest on global justice sensitized the public opinion to the goals of the activists, their forms of protest were often criticized as too radical (della Porta, Andretta, Mosca, and Reiter 2005). Especially in relation to sympathetic governments, radical tactics risk being counterproductive (Cress and Snow 2000: 1097–8).

Similar problems develop in the relations between activists and the media, as the latter play an important role in determining the resonance given to, and therefore the effectiveness of, protest. Even though it is debatable to what extent protest events are first of all "newspaper demonstrations," i.e. oriented mainly on media coverage (Neveu 1999: 28 ff.), media are indeed the most obvious shaper of public sensitivity (Jasper 1997: 286). The success of protest action is undoubtedly related to the amount of media attention it receives, and this also affects the character of social movement organizations (Gitlin 1980).

As careful research on protest coverage has demonstrated (McCarthy, McPhail, and Smith 1996), in order to obtain media coverage, action must involve a great many people, utilize radical tactics, or be particularly innovative. It should be remembered that it is the content of the message transmitted as well as the quantity of publicity received which is important for a social movement. Journalists can be particularly demanding as concerns protest: on the one hand they demand "news," and therefore novelty; on the other, they tend to conform to accepted standards of "good taste" (see also chapter 8 below). Though their obligation to the wider community may lead many journalists to sympathize with certain demands, they will, nonetheless, condemn extreme forms of action. On the other hand, more moderate action, although it might garner greater support, is rarely "newsworthy."[8] Thus, "Conformity to standards of news worthiness in political style, and knowledge of the prejudices and desires of the individuals who determine media coverage in political skills, represent crucial determinants of leadership effectiveness" (Lipsky 1965: 170). Successful movements are often those that are able to develop controversies in such a way that they are more newsworthy by using symbols and images that capture attention – "the secret of movement access to the media is to engage in colorful protest" (Rochon 1998: 180).

Beyond visibility, social movements have the problem of having their messages spread by media often more interested in scandals than information:

> One difficulty for political movements is that the media generally present images of their protest without any elaboration of the substantive issues involved. Demonstrations are described as large or small, well-behaved or unruly, a cross section of the populace or composed of fringe elements. But the issues that brought the pro-

testors together are presented in terms of one-line slogans, if at all. The problem is not so much one of political bias as it is a matter of the exacting criteria used by the media to determine what is newsworthy. Size, novelty, and militancy are newsworthy. Critical policy perspectives are not.

(Rochon 1988: 102)

In conclusion, for the most part social movements use forms of action which can be described as disruptive, seeking to influence elites through a demonstration of both force of numbers and activists' determination to succeed. At the same time, however, protest is concerned with building support. It must be innovative or newsworthy enough to echo in the mass media and, consequently, reach the wider public which social movements (as "active minorities") are seeking to convince of the justice and urgency of their cause. Forms of protest must therefore adapt as occasion requires to the needs of potentially conflicting objectives such as threatening elites and winning over the public (through the intervention of a third actor, the media, which has an agenda of its own).

In order to overcome these limitations, social movement organizations indeed try to hone their communicative skills and pay careful attention to communication campaigns, press conferences, and, especially, carefully written dossiers (for instance, on ecological associations, see della Porta and Diani 2004). Moreover, movements develop their own media: labor movements had dailies and publishers; more recent movements have developed their own radio stations as well as websites (see chapter 8 below).

7.5   Factors Influencing Repertoire Choice

The leaders of social movement organizations find themselves faced with a series of strategic dilemmas in choosing the form that protest should take. Any form of action needs to cover a plurality of sometimes contradictory objectives. In addition, strategic options are limited by a series of factors internal as well as external to protest itself. Material resources constrain strategic choices, but repertoires are not just instruments: they belong to, and represent, a movement culture, and are therefore linked to the activists' values. The aims, in this sense, do not fully justify the means, and much of the debate inside social movements about issues of repertoires does not only address their efficacy but also their meaning and symbolic value. Indeed, stressing the euphoria and pleasure involved in protest, James Jasper (1997: 237) observes that "tactics represent important routines, emotionally and morally salient in these people's lives'."

The repertoire of action is finite, constrained in both time and space. The "technology" of protest evolves slowly, limited by the traditions handed down from one generation of activists to the next, and crystallized in institutions. The public march is a good example: although, as we saw, there have been changes in the rituals, it is still one of the principal forms of protest in the campaign against neoliberal globalization. Having developed out of the practice of electoral banqueting, the technique was slowly perfected and institutionalized by the elaboration of rituals and structures such as the closing rally and the stewarding of marches (Favre 1990).

Repertoires are the byproduct of everyday experiences: for instance, the barricades derived from the tradition of using chains in order to block access to neighborhoods at night or in moments of turmoil. As Traugott (1995: 47) writes of the "Day of the Barricades," a people's revolt against the French king Henri III, "The great innovation of 12 May 1588 was to fortify the line of demarcation represented by the chains and to use the barriers thus created to impede the movements of King Henri III's Royal Guards." The success of those first barricades contributed to keep that form of action alive for more than four centuries.

Thus, repertoires are handed down, reproduced over time, because they are what people know how to do when they want to protest. The forms of action used in one protest campaign tend to be recycled in subsequent ones. The anti-Vietnam War movement in the United States adopted tactics that had earlier been used by civil rights campaigners. The youth movement in mid-1970s Italy inherited (in a radicalized form) the modes of protest used by the student movement of the late 1960s (della Porta 1995). The global justice movement mixed forms of nonviolent direct action developed by the peace movements with the large marches and petitions strategies coming from the nineteenth-century repertoire: "In fact, demonstrations that include violent and nonviolent factions and a range of constituencies and cultural styles addressing shared opposition to globalization constitute an innovative combination of tactics drawn from previously-separated movements" (Whittier 2004: 539).

In addition, the choice of tactics symbolically expresses proximity to previous movements. The adaptation of older forms of action legitimizes protest by referring to myths and heroes of the past, since "the use of standard protest forms also evokes past political movements whose struggles have long since been vindicated as just" (Rochon 1988: 110). For instance, protestors against the World Bank meeting in Washington in 2001 wore gas masks in order to refer to a history of police repression (Whittier 2004: 540).

Such references to the past are a constraint on social movements as well as a resource. In any given period, knowledge concerning "what is to be done" to protest against a decision by those holding power is limited, and this limits collective action: "The existing repertoire constrains collective action; far from the image we sometimes hold of mindless crowds, people tend to act within known limits, to innovate at the margins of the existing forms, and to miss many opportunities available to them in principle" (Tilly 1986: 390). Rooted in the shared subculture activism, repertoires contain the options considered practicable, while excluding others: "These varieties of action constitute a repertoire in something like the theatrical or musical sense of the word; but the repertoire in question resembles that of commedia dell'arte or jazz more than that of a strictly classical ensemble: people know the general rules of performance more or less well and vary the performance to meet the purpose at hand" (Tilly 1986: 390).

These limitations on the range of protest forms are only part of the story: although some forms of action can be adapted to more than one situation, many others cannot. They divide, among other, along social-group lines: prisoners climb onto the roofs of jails; soldiers refuse rations; students organize "alternative" courses; the unemployed occupy a factory and start working. One of the most common forms of collective action taken today, the strike, was until recently considered a tactic adapted almost exclusively to the working class. In fact, repertoires depend to a great extent on the cultural and material resources available to particular groups. The most militant styles of action will be most widespread among those groups which face particular difficulty in obtaining material rewards and for whom symbolic gratification acts as a substitute. Moreover, the particular subcultures to which movements refer contribute to the creation of distinctive repertoires. Religious organizations, for example, employ and modify rituals typical of their faith. The peace movement is nonviolent because the use of violence is too close a reminder of the militarism they wish to condemn. Hackers look for forms of online protest that express their specific concerns about having free access to information (in particular, free software) and rights to privacy (Castells 2001: ch. 2; Freschi 2003; T. Jordan 2002). Finally, repertoires change from state to state. It is more common to build barricades in France than in Switzerland; on the other hand, direct democracy is resorted to more frequently in Switzerland than in France (Kriesi et al. 1995).

While the weight of tradition must be acknowledged, there is also innovation in protest as in other forms of action: "contenders experiment constantly with new forms in the search for tactical advantage, but do so in small ways, at the edge of well-established actions. Few innovations endure beyond a single cluster of events; they endure chiefly when associated with a substantial new advantage for one or more actors" (Tilly 1986: 7). Forms of action initially restricted to particular actors (and condemned by others) become generalized: white-collar workers go on strike, shopkeepers block the streets. New tactics are constantly being created in order to meet media criteria of "newsworthiness." Particularly in phases when collective action is on the rise, given forms of action spread from one social group to another, and often from one country to another. Nonviolent direct action was imported to Martin Luther King's America from Gandhi's India (Chabot 2002). The student movement brought sit-ins across the ocean to Europe. In the wake of a massive wave of labor mobilization in Italy in the late 1960s, the use of striking quickly became widespread among many different sections of the population. In the peace movement dozens of camps sprang up around nuclear missile bases after the initial example of Greenham Common. The global justice movement also adopted a series of protest forms which had originated in other traditions: vigils from religious groups, civil disobedience from the women's movement, and so on.

It should be added that socialization in protest tactics is not a matter of blind reflex but a critical learning process. Thus, not all forms of action carry over from one period to the next, one social group to another, or from one country to another. It is, above all, those considered successful or particularly well adapted to a movement's context or culture which are most easily transferred from one movement to the next (Koopmans 2004: 26; Soule 2004: 302). During the campaign against neoliberal globalization, the rapid spread of boycott tactics (Micheletti 2003: 83) can be explained by its previous use against international corporations such as Shell or Nike. Protest forms that have proved unsuccessful have far less probability of surviving. In Italy, for example, the movement against cruise missiles marked a major change in tactics by left-libertarian movements. While the late 1970s had been characterized by violent escalation, the peace movement emphasized nonviolence with the specific objective of marking its discontinuity with the past and contributing to dissociate the 1980s protest from the bloody memory of the preceding decade in the collective imagination (della Porta 1996a).

Beside success, however, different generations can develop different tastes for specific forms of action (Jasper 1997: 250). Interestingly enough, the ritual of marches has changed to adapt to modern (or "postmodern") times: from those intended to show unity and organization to more theatrical forms, emphasizing a colorful expression of diversity and subjectivity (see, for instance, Rucht [2003b] for an analysis of the Labor Day marches in Germany). In recent demonstrations of the global justice movements, the younger cohorts of activists have transformed the images of marches with their more playful and spontaneous outlook.

Repertoires also emerge, and are transformed, in the course of physical and symbolic interactions. Changes take place in encounters with the authorities, in a series of reciprocal adjustments. Political violence, for example, is rarely adopted overnight or consciously. Rather, repeated clashes with police and political adversaries gradually, and almost imperceptibly, heighten extremism, leading to a justification for ever more violent forms of action. In Italy during the 1970s extremist tactics emerged in the course of an escalation of the use of force during marches and demonstrations (della Porta 1995). The interventions of the police and *carabinieri* became increasingly determined, while extreme left and right groups clashed with ever more lethal weapons: stones, molotov cocktails, tools, and eventually guns. Radicalization develops in a spiral of negative and unforeseen feedback. Those involved (particularly the police and demonstrators) interact, causing escalation through a series of vicious circles.[9] In these situations participants react according to their own worldview, gambling that the outcome will be as they expected. Their choices, however, are often based on erroneous calculations. This circle of action and reaction becomes a routine until a more or less casual event (such as an accidental killing of a demonstrator or a police officer during low-intensity clashes) produces a qualitative leap in the level of violence (Neidhardt 1981). Violence does indeed have a relational component – deriving from interchanges between people – as interpersonal processes "promote, inhibit or channel collective violence and connect it with nonviolent politics" (Tilly 2003: 20).

Protest does not always develop towards violence, however: waves of contention might follow different paths (Koopmans 2004: 29). A learning process on the part of both movement activists and the police defused the forms of conflict that had characterized the 1970s. In the 1980s, despite moments of (sometimes severe) tension, particularly during direct action such as the blocking of gates at military bases, peace activists and police were experienced enough to avoid escalation into violence: "Demonstrations are carefully choreographed in advance. Similarly, activists who expect to participate in actions of civil disobedience, such as blockades, are usually required to undergo training in passive resistance and nonviolence. The police they face have been trained in crowd control and in dealing with nonviolent protest. The image so frequently broadcast of police carrying a demonstrator off to jail looks like an image of conflict. It is. But it is also an instance of two sets of professionals carrying out their jobs with precision" (Rochon 1988: 186–7).

True, violence escalated in Seattle, and then in Prague, Gothenburg, and Genoa. But there were also attempts by the large majority of nonviolent activists to keep violence under control through tactical innovation: they went from the definition of "violence-free zone," to the division of marches into blocks, according to the adopted tactics; and the separation, on the same bases, of different movement areas in different localities. After the violent escalation in Gothenburg and Genoa, a learning process developed within the global justice movement bringing about the invention of new forms of marshal bodies ("armed" only with video cameras) and a stricter implementation of nonviolent tactics (della Porta and Reiter 2004a and 2004b).

There is a further variable (to be dealt with at greater length in the next chapter) that affects the strategic choices made by social movements. Lipsky noted that protest must be in a position to mobilize potential allies and influences elites. It is normal that the greater the possibility of widening their range of alliances, the greater the attention social movements will pay to the preferences of potential supporters. For the global justice movement, the support of many well-known and respected NGOs as well as prominent individuals both attracted media attention and often discouraged coercive intervention on the part of the police (Andretta, della Porta, Mosca, and Reiter 2002 and 2003).

7.6 The Cross-National Diffusion of Protest

Particularly relevant in the process of strategic adaptation are processes of cross-national diffusion. More and more, ideas about forms of action (as well as ideology and organizational repertoires) travel cross-nationally. Like scientific or technological innovations, social movement ideas set in motion processes of diffusion:[10] "Protest makers do not have to reinvent the wheel at each place and in each conflict . . . They often find inspiration elsewhere in the ideas and tactics espoused and practiced by other activists" (McAdam and Rucht 1993: 58). Ideas concerning organizational structure, strategies of action, or definitions of the world "travel" from movement to movement, sector to sector, city to city, center to periphery, and, on occasion, periphery to center. Diffusion can be either direct or indirect depending on whether it comes about through unmediated contacts between movement members or is mediated by the mass media (Kriesi et al. 1995: 185). In addition, diffusion can come about through either unconscious or conscious imitation. In the past it has been claimed that collective behavior spread through "circular reactions," the responses of each individual reproducing the stimuli coming from his neighbor (Blumer 1951: 170), without much attempt by individual participants to evaluate the situation and rationally respond to it. However, since the 1970s it has been recognized that the "interpretative interactions," based upon a conscious evaluation of the situations, underlying more institutional forms of political participation are also present in protest. More "interpretative" processes such as identification and imitation are also present alongside mechanisms such as suggestibility and circular reaction (Turner and Killian 1987). The greater awareness of the actors involved should favor, although it cannot automatically ensure, the success of mobilization.

Cross-national diffusion is not new. The student movement in the 1960s, the feminist movement in the 1970s, and the peace movement and the ecological movement in the 1980s are all examples of what have been called "global" movements, developing contemporaneously throughout the world and displaying significant similarities in different countries. Going further back in time, the revolutions of 1848 and the antislavery movement were collective phenomena which grew to cover more than one continent. However, it is also true that the process of diffusion does not involve all movements equally, nor is the exchange always symmetrical.

First, it is more likely that diffusion will take place between countries that are close together geographically. In fact, interaction will tend to be strongest between neighboring countries. There are more links between the Scandinavian countries than between Denmark and Italy, for example. Geographical proximity is not always important, however. The past must also be taken into account. It is more likely that diffusion will take place between movements from countries with a history of past interaction; between movements in Italy and France, for example, rather than between movements in Italy and Ireland. Besides direct interaction itself, the "cultural understanding that social entities belong to a common social category [also] constructs a tie between them" (Strand and Meyer 1993: 490). Similarities in social and political structure must also be taken into account. Thus, diffusion is more likely between Great Britain and the United States than it is between Great Britain and India, say, even if the latter is a part of the British Commonwealth. Finally, the status of the "transmitting" country also has a certain importance. In fact, although there are exceptions, in the social movement sector as in others, moving from center to periphery, from the "first" to the developing world, brings a reduction in influence.

All of the characteristics just mentioned influence both the direct diffusion through personal interaction emphasized by the traditional literature, and the indirect diffusion by way of the media noted in more recent studies (Strand and Meyer 1993). As far as direct interaction is concerned, geographical proximity, historical interaction, and structural similarities all tend to produce language and norms which facilitate direct contacts between the activists of parallel movements. Unmediated exchanges are rendered more probable by the existence of cross-border associations, cultural exchange programs, linguistic knowledge, or even a common language.

The various levels of proximity discussed above also favor the development of more formal contacts and organized channels of communication. More particularly, relations will become more formal after personal contacts have permitted initial exchanges to take place and as the movements become increasingly structured. Diffusion of ideas can then take place through the translation of movement documents, the organization of international conferences, the creation of computer-mediated networks, and so on. Mediated forms of diffusion therefore take on increasing importance. It has been noted that in the 1960s the process of diffusion between student movements was initiated through personal contacts, but that "once established, this identification enabled diffusion to take place via a variety of nonrelational channels. These channels included television, newspapers, and writings of both a scholarly and a radical nature" (McAdam and Rucht 1993: 71). Countersummits and supranational social forums are indeed praised by activists, especially as occasions for exchanging ideas and networking (Pianta 2002).

Geographical and cultural proximity is also important in producing functional equivalence, similarity in the situation of the "transmitting" and "adopting" movements being a factor in facilitating this process of diffusion. Furthermore, the same elements facilitate the social construction of that similarity, the definition of their situation as similar to that of the transmitter on the part of adopters (Strand and Meyer 1993). Regardless of actual similarities, the subjective perception of common circumstances leads to an idea being considered relevant and adopted. The passage of ideas from the American student movement (the transmitter) to its German counterpart (the adopter) was facilitated by the similarities in the definition of the collective identities of the two groups (McAdam and Rucht 1993). Similarly, appeal to global identities facilitates cross-national campaigns against neoliberal globalization (della Porta, Andretta, Mosca, and Reiter 2005).

The traditions of particular movements also help to explain a greater or lesser propensity to exchange information and to "copy" each other at the international level. Despite appeals to internationalism, for example, the conviction that their destinies were more closely linked to those of capitalists in their own country than they were to workers in other countries appears to have prevailed in national labor movements for a long time. Environmentalist groups, on the other hand, have always been conscious of the difficulties in providing national solutions to environmental problems, which spread from country to country by way of polluted rivers and air. The rich and various repertoire of action of the global justice movement is indeed the product of enhanced occasions for transnational encounters.

7.7 Cycles of Protest, Protest Waves, and Protest Campaigns

The strategic choices made by social movements evolve over time and are the result of interaction between a number of different actors. In fact, a final concept, particularly useful for analyzing evolution over time, must be introduced to conclude the analysis of forms of collective action: the protest cycle. Though varying in dimension and duration, protest cycles have had a number of common characteristics in recent history: they coincide with "a phase of heightened conflict and contention across the social system that includes: a rapid diffusion of collective action from more mobilized to less mobilized sectors; a quickened pace of innovation in the forms of contention; new or transformed collective action frames; a combination of organized and unorganized participation; and sequences of intensified interactions between challengers and authorities which can end in reform, repression and sometimes revolution" (Tarrow 1994: 153). If some scholars criticize the use of the concept of a cycle as seeming to imply a regular, "periodically recurrent sequence of phenomena" (Koopmans 2004: 21), they nevertheless confirm the unequal distribution of contention over time: "periods of relative quiet alternate with waves of intense mobilization that encompass large sections of societies, and quite often affect many societies simultaneously" (ibid.: 21). Waves of protest are often composed of interrelated campaigns – i.e. a series of interactions connected to each other from the thematic point of view and oriented towards a common aim (Della Porta and Rucht

2002a and 2002b). Examples of campaigns are protests on abortion rights in the women's movements, or against the deployment of cruise and pershing II missiles in the peace movement, or for "dropping the dept" of less-developed countries in the global justice movement. The global justice movement has indeed adopted the campaign as a formula which is particularly effective in linking heterogeneous social movements and movement organizations.

The concepts of cycles, waves, or campaigns all attempt to describe and explain periods of intensified protest. As in cultures and the economies,[11] there is indeed a recurrent dynamic of ebb and flow in collective mobilization. In particular, by demonstrating the vulnerability of the authorities, the first movements to emerge lower the cost of collective action for other actors. In addition, the victories they obtain undermine the previous order of things, provoking countermobilization. Repeatedly, spin-off movements contributed to the mobilization of other groups, inventing new forms of action, enlarging the protest claims, and winning some concessions, but also pushing elites and countermovements to form law-and-order coalitions (della Porta 1998b). Mobilization proceeds in waves,

> from institutional conflict to enthusiastic peak to ultimate collapse. After gaining national attention and state response, they reached peaks of conflict that were marked by the presence of movement organizers who tried to diffuse the insurgencies to a broader public. As participation was channeled into organizations, the movements, or part of them, took a more political logic – engaging in implicit bargaining with authorities. In each case, as the cycle wound down, the initiative shifted to elites and parties.
>
> *(Tarrow 1994: 168)*

This pattern has consequences for the repertoires of collective action. In the initial stages of protest the most disruptive tactics are often to the fore. New actors invent new tactics as emerging collective identities require radical action (Pizzorno 1978). As the cycle of protest continues, the reaction of the authorities produces simultaneous processes of radicalization and institutionalization. Evolution in protest tactics, therefore, accompanies changes in the external environment:

> When disruptive forms are first employed, they frighten antagonists with their potential cost, shock onlookers, and worry elites concerned with public order. But newspapers gradually begin to give less and less space to protests that would have merited banner headlines when they first appeared on the streets. Repeating the same form of collective action over and over reduces uncertainty and is greeted with a smile or a yawn. Participants, at first enthused and invigorated by their solidarity and ability to challenge authorities, become jaded or disillusioned. The authorities, instead of calling out the troops or allowing the police to wade into a

crowd, infiltrate dissenting groups and separate leaders from followers. Routinization follows hard upon disruption.

(Tarrow 1994: 112)

The analysis of protest cycles is particularly useful for an understanding of
the development of political violence, frequently one (though not the only nor
the most important) of protest's outcomes. In fact, the forms of violence used
tend to vary according to the stage of the cycle. At the outset of protest, violent
action is usually limited in its presence, small in scope, and unplanned. Typically
violence in these phases is an unforeseen result of direct action such as sit-ins or
occupations. As protest develops, violent forms of action initially spread more
slowly than nonviolent ones. They frequently take the form of clashes between
demonstrators and police or counter-demonstrators. Starting out as occasional,
such episodes, nonetheless, tend to be repeated and take on a ritual quality.
During this process small groups begin to specialize in increasingly extreme
tactics, build up an armory for such action, and occasionally go underground.
The very presence of these groups accelerates the exodus of moderates from the
movement, contributing to a demobilization which only the most violent groups
escape (at least temporarily). The final stages of the cycle thus see both a process
of institutionalization and a growing number of violent actions.

A glance at the development of the global justice movement would confirm
at least some of these dynamics. The incubatory stages of mobilization were
characterized by activity which concentrated prevalently on information campaigns and lobbying, with only a handful of symbolic demonstrations carried out
by small activist networks. The movement extended beyond its initial base during
this phase, mobilizing groups involved in earlier movements (the women's movement and the environmental movement, but also the labor movement) or in
political parties and religious associations. Each of these actors contributed particular forms of action to a common repertoire: the feminist groups brought the
practices of civil disobedience they had honed in the campaign to legalize abortion; the religious associations brought with them the gospels; the environmentalists the practice of nonviolent occupation they had previously used against
nuclear power-station sites; the parties of the left mobilized a mass following and
offered channels of communication with public institutions. Although the heterogeneity of the various constituencies involved inevitably led to disagreements
over what forms of action should be adopted, this diversity enriched rather than
hindered the movement's capacity for mobilization during its expansionary
phase. After their initial indecision, governments reacted by ordering police intervention, particularly to suppress the attempts at blocking the sites of international summits. While remaining on the whole peaceful, nonviolent civil
disobedience escalated on some occasions, above all when police reacted in a
muscular fashion to attacks by fringe anarchist groups.

At least two tendencies must be added to the cyclical evolution described so far. First, each cycle broadens the repertoire of collective action. This was as true of the Warsaw Pact countries in the years around 1989 as it had been of the waves of protest which swept Europe and the United States in the 1930s and the 1960s. It is indeed especially at the peak of a wave of mobilization that citizens develop new forms of collective action: "The factory occupations that marked the French 1936 strikes were similar to the sit-down strikes of Flint and Akron; while the university occupations of Berlin, Turin and Paris in 1968 linked students to their American homologues. As for Solidarity, its most striking feature would prove to be the roundtable discussions between Solidarity leaders and the government that foreshadowed the forms of negotiations that swept Eastern Europe in 1989" (Tarrow 1994: 167–8).

Second, the most radical forms of action declined, at least among left-wing activists. In the 1970s there had been a tendency to maintain media attention and "threat potential" through an accentuation of extreme forms of action. Since the 1980s, various forms of protest have spread to institutional as well as noninstitutional actors, and most types of new social movements testify to a growing moderation in the repertoires of collective action (della Porta 1996a, 1996b, and 1996c; also Raschke 1988: 322–32). Indeed, in this area the logic is more dynamic, with a growth in the first instance in actions which involve serious personal risks or cost. Civil disobedience, knowingly breaking what are considered to be unjust laws, rests on this logic.

This does not mean, however, that the use of violence as a political means declined. As Charles Tilly (2003: 58) sadly summarized, since 1945 "the world as a whole has taken decisive, frightening steps away from its painfully achieved segregations between armies and civilian populations, between war and peace, between international and civil war, between lethal and nonlethal applications of force. It has moved toward armed struggle within existing states and towards state-sponsored killing, deprivation, or expulsion of whole population categories."

7.8 Summary

The present chapter has been dedicated to the analysis of the principal forms of action adopted by social movements; in other words, to forms of protest. Protest has been defined as nonroutinized action in which indirect channels of influence are opened through the activity of a series of collective actors. Although protest forms are so widespread that it would be difficult to define them as unconventional, it is still true that protest goes beyond the routinized forms of participation in representative democracy. It has been said that the tactics used by social movements form repertoires with specific characteristics. In particular, a repertoire of national, autonomous, and modular forms of protest has developed since the nineteenth century. More recent transformations in both the distribution of power at national and international level and in the structure of mass communications are reflected in the development of new forms of protest such as countersummits and transnational boycotts, as well as in internet protest actions. In distinguishing in this chapter between the various forms of protest, the fact that different logics of action were simultaneously present in each repertoire was stressed: the logic of numbers, which seeks to display the strength of support for a movement; the logic of material damage, based on the capacity to interrupt everyday routine; and the logic of bearing witness, which seeks to demonstrate the emotional commitment of protestors.

Social movement leaders face a series of strategic dilemmas in choosing one or another form of action, because each sends messages to different publics with different demands: the movement activists who seek to reinforce internal solidarity; the media, in search of "news"; potential allies, who prefer more moderate forms of action; and, finally, decision-makers, who seek partners whom they can trust. However, repertoires of actions are not just instruments of protest, but also reflect the activists' values. Historical traditions fostered through institutions and socialization limit the range of options that can be considered, but forms of protest travel from one movement to the other and from one country to the other, with frequent innovation and learning processes. Additionally, repertoires are produced via relational mechanisms, during interactions between various (movement and nonmovement) actors. Series of cyclical dynamics create a succession of waves and troughs in protest, and radicalization and institutionalization in the forms of action adopted. Alongside these cyclical fluctuations, however, two more stable tendencies appear to apply, at least as far as Western democracies are concerned, with a broadening of the repertoire of protest action and simultaneously a growing rejection of political violence.

THE POLICING OF PROTEST AND POLITICAL OPPORTUNITIES FOR SOCIAL MOVEMENTS

The 2001 G8 summit was held in Genoa between July 19 and 22. A year earlier, at the international meeting in Port Alegre of what came to be known as the global justice movement, it had been decided to mobilize on an international scale against the neoliberal version of globalization. About 800 organizations combined into the Genoa Social Forum (GSF), which organized the protest together with other groups.[1]

Given that international summits over the previous two years had sometimes been met with violent protests, the government's preparations for the G8 concentrated on keeping demonstrators out of the area, and the most radical away from the city itself. In addition to installing high barriers to protect the so-called "red zone" around the summit meetings, the airport, railway stations, and freeway exits were closed, and both confirmed and suspected activists were returned to the city limits. In his testimony to a Joint Parliamentary Commission, Chief De Gennaro of the Italian Police spoke of 140,000 checks made and more than 2,000 people turned back. Expulsion orders were used to keep some militants from entering Genoa. With the city center closed and access to the city tightly controlled, Genoa emptied: two days before the start of the summit, electrical consumption and waste disposal had dropped by 40 percent.

Despite the imposing show of force and the tension caused by some attacks before the start of the summit, as well as somewhat alarmist information from the Secret Service (in the Joint Parliamentary Commission [minutes of August 28, 2001: 66], former head of the political police, the UCIGOS, La Barbera, spoke of "a flood of information mostly failing to provide any result"), the peaceful march on July 19 included 50,000 people. However, this situation changed radically the following day due to what newspapers described as the provocations of the radical Black Block, followed by indiscriminate police responses. According to press estimations, between 400 and 1,000 Black Block members were involved; the police spoke of 500 Italians and 2,000 foreigners. On the morning of July 20 they were unchallenged in attacking banks, shops, the prison, and public buildings. For the entire day, events followed a similar pattern: after the Black Block attacks, the police responded by setting upon those in or near peaceful protests, including doctors, nurses, paramedics, photographers, and journalists.

The fight with the so-called "civil disobedience protestors," encircled and repeatedly charged, started in this fashion. After the police charge, some groups of demonstrators reacted by throwing stones, provoking the police to use armored cars. During one incursion, a *carabinieri* jeep became stuck and its occupants were attacked by demonstrators. One of the *carabinieri* inside opened fire, killing 23-year-old Genovese activist Carlo Giuliani. Within the red zone, the police used water cannon loaded with chemicals against demonstrators from the transnational ATTAC and the Italian trade unions, who were banging on the fences and throwing cloves of garlic. The Democrats of the Left (DS) mayor Pericù, who had tried to negotiate with the organizers, complained about the absence of negotiators from police headquarters. In the evening, the movement's spokespersons were careful to distance themselves from the Black Block, but also criticized the police actions. According to the government, the responsibility for the disorder was the GSF's. The largest center-left party, the DS, withdrew its support for the following day's demonstration, instructing its members not to go to Genoa.

At the July 21 demonstration, between 200,000 and 300,000 demonstrators gathered. (Organizers claimed that 100,000 people were expected, while the police chief claimed that no more than 40,000 attended.) Again, there were attacks by the Black Block, which the demonstrators tried to prevent. The police this time used armored cars and tear gas fired from helicopters and kept themselves at a distance from the demonstrators. The first charge, at 2:25 p.m., took place as the march was about to set off; similar charges took place at 2:50 and 5:35 p.m. The daily papers – and not just those supporting the demonstrations – reported numerous attempts by the movement, which had formed its own rudimentary security force, to push back violent protestors and to rescue demonstrators and lawyers being beaten by police. The day's totals came to 228 injured (including 78 police officers) and 60 arrests.

On the evening of July 21, the police burst into the Diaz School, where the GSF, its legal advice team, the Indymedia press group, and a dormitory for protestors were based, searching for weapons. The press described the behavior of the police as particularly brutal – a description supported by some members of parliament who were present. According to the report by Interior Ministry Inspector Pippo Micalizio: "Of the 93 persons detained and arrested in the building, 62 (around 66 percent) [had been injured and] were referred with varying medical prognoses: 24 percent up to 5 days recovery; 36 percent between 6 and 10 days; 11 percent between 11 and 20 days; 18 percent from 21 to 40 days; 6 percent were given the all-clear. However, prognoses were uncertain for the remaining 5 percent." The charge was conspiracy to commit acts of plunder; but magistrates immediately released 92 of the 93 detainees. The police confiscated the hard disk from the lawyers' computer, while the Indymedia computers were destroyed.

In the days that followed, various testimonies were published recounting civilians' mistreatment in the Bolzaneto barracks, where a center for identifying detainees had been set up, operated by a group of penitentiary officers from the GOM (Mobile Operations Unit). Witness statements, many of them from foreigners, described physical and psychological assaults. Using tear gas and truncheons, and forcing detainees to stay on their feet for hours, police compelled those being held to repeat fascist and racist slogans. The police handling of the demonstrations raised protests in Italy and abroad. In December 2004, 28 Italian policemen, including senior riot and antiterrorist officers, were tried on charges of abuse of authority, slander, and involvement in severe damage for their role in the assault on the school. The announcement of the trial came at the conclusion of preliminary hearings, where it was alleged that police had planted two molotov cocktails they claimed to have found at the school. The claim by one senior police officer that an activist had tried to stab him was also discredited. All the activists arrested during the raid at the school were released without charges.

The Genoa demonstrations represented a major break (albeit a predictable one) with the image of social movements in the 1980s and 1990s, which had portrayed them as integrated and "civilized," more at ease at the bargaining table than in the streets. After decades of predominantly peaceful activities, emphasis has now been put on the dangers of the radicalization of political and social conflict. In recent countersummits there have been frequent clashes between police and demonstrators, including at the demonstrations against the WTO in Seattle in 1999; in Davos at the World Economic Forum; in Prague and in Washington at the meeting of the international committee of the World Bank and the IMF in

2000; in Quebec City at the NAFTA meetings; and in Gothenburg at the EU summit in June 2001.

What accounts for this evolution in the characteristics of mobilization and the responses to it? Naturally, the particular strategies of social movements can have an impact on the size and form of mobilization. As noted in earlier chapters, ideology, repertoires, and structures constitute material and cultural resources for action, which vary from country to country. Moreover, social structure, the degree of civic culture, and economic development, have helped in explaining protest (Moore 1966; Skocpol 1979; see also chapter 2 above). In attempting to select the most influential of the many determinants of collective action, quite a number of comparative analyses of social movements have concentrated on political variables. It has already been noted that the activities of social movements are in part expressive; in part instrumental; in part directed at their own members; in part designed to transform the external environment. In their protest activities social movements are eminently political: as such they are influenced by and influence first and foremost the political system. As was noted in the introductory chapter, the concept of political opportunity structure has become central to interpretations of interaction between institutional and non-institutional actors.

By taking illustrations principally from countersummits against neoliberal globalization, what follows will seek to identify the main variables of the political system and suggest some hypotheses on the way they influence particular characteristics of social movements. A problem in the research on political opportunities is a lack of clarity concerning the explanandum (recently also discussed in Meyer 2004). The political dimension has been investigated in order to explain a growing number of dependent variables. Political opportunities have been used to explain social movement mobilization (Eisinger 1973), the emergence of the protest cycle (Tarrow 1983), the relationship between allies' attitudes and movement behavior (della Porta and Rucht 1995), and the predominance of either confrontational or assimilative protest strategies (Kitschelt 1986: 67–8). And, indeed, from what has been said here it is clear that the character of institutions, prevailing strategies, varieties of repression, and alliance structures are all useful for explaining one or other of the characteristics of social movements. Few attempts have been made until now, however, to address the question of which variables in the complex set of political opportunities, explain which (of the numerous) characteristics of social movements. In what follows, we shall try to single out the specific effects of specific opportunities on emergence of movements, levels of mobilization, protest repertoires, and chances of success. Beginning with an analysis of the policing of protest (8.1), we shall then identify some characteristics of the institutional opportunities (8.2) as well as prevailing strategies (8.3). The role of political parties as potential allies will be discussed in depth (8.4). As we shall stress, however, political opportunities are far from structural, in the sense of both immutable and "given": not only are their effects filtered through the activists' perceptions, but moreover they interact with "discursive oppor-tunity" (8.5).

8.1 The Policing of Protest

As the Genoa example illustrates, an important aspect of the state's response to protest is the policing of protest, or police handling of protest events – more neutral terms for what protestors usually refer to as "repression" and the state as "law and order" (della Porta 1995, 1996c; Earl, Soule, and McCarthy 2003). Protest policing is a particularly relevant issue for understanding the relationship between social movements and the state. According to Lipsky (1970: 1) the

> study of the ways police interact with other citizens is of primary importance for anyone concerned with public policy and the just resolution of contemporary urban conflict. Police may be conceived as 'street-level bureaucrats' who 'represent' government to people. And at the same time as they implement government policies, police forces also help define the terms of urban conflict by their actions. The influence of police on political attitudes and developments is fundamental because of the unique role of law enforcement agencies in enforcing and reinforcing the norms of the system.

One can add that, in their turn, protest waves have had important effects on police organizations (see, for example, Morgan 1987; Reiner 1998).

In fact, the various styles of police intervention have received some attention in the sociological literature. Gary T. Marx (1979), working from a phenomeno-logical perspective, distinguished acts of repression according to their purpose: creating an unfavorable image of opponents; gathering information; restricting the flow of resources for movements; discouraging activists; fuelling internal conflicts within the leadership and between groups; sabotaging specific actions. Charles Tilly (1978: 106–15) classified political regimes according to the degree of repression or "facilitation" they manifest towards different collective actors and actions.

Research has picked out three main strategic areas for protest control, favored differently by the police in various historical periods (della Porta and Reiter 1998a): coercive strategies, i.e. use of weapons and physical force to control or disperse demonstrations; persuasive strategies, meaning all attempts to control protest through prior contacts with activists and organizers; informative strategies, consisting in widespread information-gathering as a preventive feature in protest control; and the targeted collection of information, including use of modern audiovisual technologies, to identify law-breakers without having to intervene directly.

Police actions can vary in terms of force used (brutal or soft), extent of conduct regarded as illegitimate (ranging between repression and tolerance), strategies for controlling various actors (generalized or selective), police respect for the law (illegal or legal), moment when police act (preemptive or reactive), degree of communication with demonstrators (confrontation or consensus), capacity to adjust to emerging situations (rigid or flexible), degree of formalization of rules of the game (formal or informal), degree of training (professional or improvised) (della Porta and Reiter 1998b: 4).

It has been noted that the combination of these dimensions tends to define two different, internally consistent models for controlling public order. The escalated-force model gives low priority to the right to demonstrate, innovative forms of protest are poorly tolerated, communication between police and demonstrators is reduced to essentials, there is frequent use of coercive means or even illegal methods (such as *agents provocateurs*). The negotiated control model, by contrast, sees the right to demonstrate peacefully as a priority; even disruptive forms of protest are tolerated, communication between demonstrators and police is considered basic to peaceful conduct of protest, and coercive means are avoided as far as possible, emphasizing selectivity of operations (McPhail, Schweingruber, and McCarthy 1998, 51–4; della Porta and Fillieule 2004). To these dimensions one might add the type of information strategy police forces employ in controlling protest, with a distinction between generalized control on all demonstrators and control focusing on those possibly guilty of an offense.

In Western democracies, a radical transformation in strategies for controlling public order and associated operational practices and techniques, from the escalated-force model to negotiated control, can be noted, particularly following the great protest wave that culminated in the late 1960s. While the widespread conception of rights to demonstrate one's dissent has tended to become more inclusive, intervention strategies have moved away from the coercive model until then predominant. During the 1970s and 1980s, though with pauses and temporary reversals, we may note a trend towards growing tolerance and breaches of the law being regarded as minor. Among changes apparent in strategies for controlling public order is a reduction in the use of force, greater emphasis on "dialogue," and the investment of large resources in gathering information (della Porta and Reiter 1998a). These strategies, officially called de-escalation (or also, in the Italian case, prevention), are based on a number of specific pathways and assumptions. Before protest events, demonstrator representatives and the police have to meet and negotiate in detail on routes and conduct to be observed during demonstrations (including the more or less symbolic violations permitted to demonstrators), charges are never to be made against peaceful groups, agreements reached with demonstration leaders are never to be broken, and lines of communication between them and the police must be kept open throughout the demonstration. The police must first and foremost guarantee the right to demonstrate peacefully; violent groups must be separated from the rest of the march and stopped without endangering the security of the peaceful demonstrators (Fillieule 1993a; Fillieule and Jobard 1998, McPhail et al. 1998, Waddington 1994, Winter 1998, della Porta 1998a).

What was seen by many as the consolidated "post-68" standard, no longer subject to debate, proved fragile when faced with the new challenge of a transnational protest movement. The Genoa G8 reignited an almost forgotten debate on the fundamental rights of citizens and the question of how much power the state is allowed in protecting the rule of law (Andretta, della Porta, Mosca, and Reiter 2003, ch. 4). What produced the escalation in Genoa and previously in Seattle, Washington, Quebec City, Prague, and Gothenburg, as well as the many accusations of police brutality against the demonstrators? Various explanations could be suggested. First, even "policing by consent" (Waddington 1998) is a police strategy to control protest, albeit while respecting demonstrators' rights and freedoms as much as possible. There are frequent conflicts between demonstrators and police: Situations may be particularly tense when the territory in a protest has a particular symbolic and strategic value – as is the case, for instance, with the "red zones" closed to the demonstrators around international summits. Moreover, even if coercive control is rarely used, its use easily leads to escalation due to the psychological dynamics connected with physical fights in conditions of relative anonymity (ibid.). The events of the 1990s led to the militarization (in terms of type of equipment, training, and deployment) of some police units specializing in counterterrorism or fighting violent organized crime; these tools were then often deployed in everyday policing.

We have to add that the development of negotiating strategy has always been selective. Even in established democracies, escalated force survived at the margins, in particular in the control of young squatters or hooligans. In fact, research has pointed to the survival, in police knowledge about protest, of a distinctions between "good" demonstrators (peaceful, pragmatic, with a direct interest in the conflict and a clear aim, etc.) and "bad" demonstrators (predominantly young, misinformed, destructive, professional troublemakers with no direct interest in the conflict, etc.) (della Porta 1998a; della Porta and Reiter 1998b). Participants in emerging movements, such as the global justice movement that became visible in Seattle and Genoa, tend indeed to carry the stigma of "bad," and often "dangerous," demonstrators.

But what are the effects of protest policing? Changes in the repressive capabilities of regimes are an important factor in explaining the emergence of social movements. In France, Russia, and China, social revolution broke out when political crisis weakened state control and repressive power (Skocpol 1979). Likewise, an inability to maintain social control facilitated the rise of the civil rights movement in the United States (McAdam 1982).[2] And in Italy, the protest cycle of the late 1960s first emerged as a more tolerant style of policing was developing (della Porta 1995).

As far as levels of mobilization are concerned, the harshest styles of protest policing ought to increase the risk of collective action and diminish the disposition of actors to take part. However, it should be added that many forms of repression, particularly when they are considered illegitimate, could create a sense of injustice that increases the perceived risk of inaction (e.g. Khawaja 1994). It is not surprising therefore that these two divergent pressures produce contradictory results, and empirical research indicates a radicalization of those groups most exposed to police violence in some cases and renunciation of unconventional forms of action in others (Wilson 1976). In fact, the relationship between the degree of violence in protest and coercive intervention by the authorities would appear to be curvilinear (Neidhardt 1989).

Institutional control strategies influence protest strategies especially. First, they affect the organizational models adopted within movements. This was the case with French republicanism in the nineteenth century, where "intensified repression typically reinforced the role of secret societies and informal centers of sociability like cafés, vintners, and cabarets" (Aminzade 1995: 42); on the other hand, "the extension of universal male suffrage and civil liberties as well as a new geography of representation fostered the development of more formal organization" (1995: 59). In more recent times, too, repression has led to a process of "encapsulation" of social movement organization, in some cases to the point of going underground (della Porta 1990, 1995; Neidhardt 1981). In the global justice movement, groups such as the Black Block that choose to use violent strategies, adopt a very fluid and semiclandestine form of organization that is resistant to police investigation. Strong repression is more likely to be successful when a cycle of protest has not yet been initiated, and solidarities around movement identities are therefore not yet strong enough; "indiscriminate repression is likely to provoke further popular mobilization only during the ascendant phase of the protest cycle" (Brokett 1995: 131–2).

Strategies of repression also influence repertoires of action. A comparative study of Germany and Italy (della Porta 1995), for instance, indicated that tough policing techniques tend to discourage peaceful mass protest and at the same time encourage the more radical fringes of protest. Radicalization among social movements in Italy in the 1970s coincided with a period of harsher repression during which the police killed a number of demonstrators at public marches. Moreover, the belief that the state was conducting a "dirty war" poisoned relationships between elected politicians and movement activists. In Germany, on the other hand, the reformist attitudes of the social democrat and liberal government and a tolerant, selective, and "soft" style of protest policing were reflected in a comparatively lower level of radicalization in the social movement sector. In both countries the high point of repression coincided with a shrinking of the movements' more moderate wing, a decline that indirectly helped the most extreme elements to prevail, particularly in Italy during the 1970s. The lower levels of violence in the 1980s corresponded instead to an increasing tolerance of protest. In the global justice movement, escalation developed again in the course of physical interactions with the police forces deployed in order to block demonstrators from entering the part of the cities where IGO meetings were taking place.

Police intervention influences the very aims of protestors, whose focus shifts from single issues and policy demands to the "meta-issue" of protest itself. In his study of the Chicano movement in Los Angeles, Edward Escobar has stated that in "a dialectical relationship, while the Los Angeles Police Department's tactics partially achieved the goal of undermining the Chicano movement, the police and their tactics became an issue around which Chicano activists organized the community and increased grass-roots participation in movement activity" (Escobar 1993: 1485). In conclusion, more tolerant and selective styles of protest policing have facilitated the integration of social movements within a complex structure of political bargaining. This has legitimated certain forms of protest and led to the stigmatization of violence, increasingly viewed as a form of deviancy (della Porta and Reiter 1998b).

Finally, as far as movement success is concerned, Tilly (1978) has suggested an inverse relationship between the opportunities for access to the system and coercion. This relation does not always seem to hold true, however. Comparative openness to access from below does not necessarily correspond to minor repression: on the contrary, the availability of instruments of direct democracy might delegitimize protest in the eyes of the government and the public opinion, producing calls for law and order (as has been the case, for instance, in the German-speaking part of Switzerland; see Wisler and Kriesi 1998).

8.2 Political Institutions and Social Movements

The police are of course not autonomous: in varying degrees and forms, they depend on political institutions that might (and often do) react to protest not only via police deployment, but also with policy reforms. Public-order responses are therefore linked to the political response given to the movement in question. Here we move to another level of analysis, addressing the political institutions.

Alexis de Tocqueville's famous contrast between "weak" American government and "strong" French government is usually an implicit or explicit starting point for analyses which link institutional factors and social movement development (Kriesi 2004: 71). Postulating an opposition between state and civil society, Tocqueville considered that a system in which the state was weak and civil society strong (the United States) would face a constant but peaceful flux of protest from below. Where the state was strong and civil society weak (France), on the other hand, episodic and violent revolt would result. Sidney Tarrow (1994: 62–5) has convincingly criticized this hypothesis, claiming that Tocqueville's analysis was partial even in respect of the historical situation to which the author referred. Not only does the American Civil War raise doubts about the capacity of a "weak" state to integrate conflicting interests, but also recent studies of the French Revolution have demonstrated the existence of a very robust civil society in that country. As Tarrow remarks, in both countries the state and the rights of its citizens grew in steps: conscription mobilized citizens as soldiers, stimulating new demands; the unified fiscal system created a single target for protest; conflict within the elites pushed the various parties involved to appeal to public opinion, extending the franchise; the means of communication built by the state were also used by challengers; new forms of aggregation and expression were legitimized by elections; the creation of new administrative units led to the creation of new collective identities.

If Tocqueville appears to have "exaggerated" the characteristics of both France and the United States in order to construct a dichotomy between the "good" and the "bad" state, the idea that the strength or weakness of states influence social movement strategies remains central to the literature on collective action in general and on revolutions in particular. This approach, "à la Tocqueville," has frequently been linked to a pluralist conception that a large number of points of access to the political system are an indication of "openness."

Many case studies which use categories that refer to the "power of the state" are really referring to the power of the central executive. In general, a system has been considered more open (and less repressive) the more political decisions are dispersed. The prevalent belief is that the greater the number of actors who share political power (the greater the checks and balances), the greater the chance that social movements gain access to the system. However, while a weak executive may ease access to the decision-making process, it will have little hope of implementing policies to meet social movement demands.[3] The hypotheses concerning the effects of institutional variables on the evolution of social movements cover three main areas: territorial decentralization of power, functional dispersal of power, and the extent of power in the hands of the state (Kitschelt 1986: 61–4; Rucht 1994: 303–12; Kriesi 1995).

A first set of hypotheses concerns territorial decentralization. The basic suggestion is that the more power is distributed to the periphery (local or regional government, states within a federal structure), the greater the possibility individual movements have of accessing the decision-making process. The "nearer" an administrative unit is to ordinary citizens (in a conception of democracy very common in American social science, but also within social movements themselves), the easier it will be to gain access. Thus, all else being equal, the greater the degree of power passed from the national government to the regions, from the regions to the cities, from the cities to local neighborhoods, the greater the openness of the political system to pressure from below. Following the same logic, federal states are considered more open than centralist ones (see, for example, Kitschelt 1986; Kriesi 1995; Giugni 1996). In fact, decentralization of power to regional and local bodies often increases the opportunities for social movements mobilizing at the local level. As research in, for instance, Italy and France (see, respectively, della Porta and Andretta 2002; della Porta 2004c) indicates, citizens' committees protesting against the construction of infrastructure for high-speed trains or hazardous waste significantly increase their chances of victory when they can ally themselves with influential local administrators.

As far as the functional separation of powers is concerned, the system can broadly be considered more open the greater the division of tasks between legislature, executive, and judiciary. Moreover, looking at each of these powers separately, the greater the autonomy of individual actors the more numerous will be the channels of access to the system. In the first place, the parliamentary arena has been considered more open the greater the number of seats assigned by proportional representation, so increasing the possibilities for access by a variety of actors (see, for example, Amenta and Young 1999). From the general proposition that "a higher number of autonomous actors equals greater openness of the system," it follows that, as far as the characteristics of the executive are concerned, the possibilities for access will be fewer in a presidential system than in a parliamentary one because there are fewer decision-makers. In the arena of government, it can generally be expected that elite attitudes to challengers will depend on whether the government is homogeneous or a coalition. The more fragmented the government or the greater the differences between the parties that compose it, the easier it will be to find allies, although the chances of actually implementing policies will be fewer. Cultural variables such as traditions of loyalty to the leadership or personalistic divisions within parties and the prevalence of individualistic or collective mediation of consensus also influence government stability and compactness. The openness of the system to pressure from below should also increase in proportion to the power of elected organs.[4]

The characteristics of the public bureaucracy also influence social movements. Kriesi et al. (1995: 31) note that "the greater the amount of resources at its disposal, and the greater the degree of its coherence, internal coordination and professionalization, the stronger it will be. Lack of resources, structural fragmentation, lack of internal coordination and of professionalization, multiply the points of access and make the administration dependent on its private interlocutors in the system of interest-intermediation." A further element of relevance for the functional distribution of power is the autonomy and powers of the judiciary. A strong judicial power can intervene in both legislative and executive functions, as when the Constitutional Court or the magistracy become involved in legal controversies between social movements and countermovements or state institutions. The greater the independence of the judiciary, the greater the possibility of access for social movements.

The last matter to be dealt with concerns the overall amount of power in the hands of the state, as compared with other actors such as pressure groups, political parties, the media, and ordinary citizens. For example, returning to public administration, the possibility of outside intervention varies a great deal from state to state. In general, where public administration is rooted in Roman law, which rejects external contacts, there tends to be greater resistance to pressure from noninstitutional actors (not simply social movements but political parties also). The Anglo-Saxon model of public administration, on the other hand, with more numerous channels of access for noninstitutional actors, tends to be more open. In this respect the institutional structure of political opportunity will be more open (and the state weaker) where citizens maintain the possibility of intervening with the legislature and executive independently of mediation through political parties, interest groups, or bureaucrats. The greater the degree of citizens' participation through referendums for the proposition or abrogation of particular measures and the procedures for appealing against the decisions of the public administration, the more open the system.

In the 1990s, the general trends in the evolution of political institutions, where they can be said to exist, were somehow contradictory in terms of the openness/closedness of political opportunities. Devolution at the subnational levels and a growing autonomy of the judiciary has certainly increased the points of access to public decision-making. However, the shift of power from legislative assemblies to administrations has made decision-making processes less transparent and decision-makers less accountable to the electorate. The neoliberal shift of the 1990s significantly reduced the space for political intervention (see chapter 9 below). The privatization of public services and the deregulation of the labor market have in fact limited the possibilities for citizens and workers to exert pressure via political channels.

More importantly, movements face a shift in the locus of power from the national to the supranational (see chapter 2 above), with increased power wielded by a number of international organizations – especially economic ones (WB, IMF, WTO) – as well as a number of macroregional organizations (first and foremost the EU) (Haas 1964; Sharpf 1997). International governmental organizations have been both tools for economic globalization, through policies liberalizing trade and the movement of capital, and the result of an attempt to govern processes that can no longer be handled at national level. In this sense, globalization has not just weakened the power of politics over economics, but has generated transnational conflicts on the policies of international institutions, producing different results depending on the organization and field of intervention involved. In particular, opposition has arisen to the neoliberalist policies of the so-called international financial institutions that wield strong coercive power through the threat of economic sanctions and conditionalities on international credit. More generally, parallel to the acquisition of power by these largely non-representative, nontransparent bodies, criticism has centered on their manifest "deficit of democracy."

But what are the effects of all these institutional properties on the characteristics of social movements? In the first place, since they tend to be stable over the long term while protest evolves cyclically, it is improbable that, beyond a certain level of democratic development, institutional assets do much to explain the emergence of movements. Similarly, institutional arrangements do not appear to have much weight in relation to levels of mobilization either, since this appears as more sensitive to contingent circumstances than to structural variables. Opinion polls as well as cross-national comparative analyses of specific movements (for instance, the antiwar movement in 2003) indicate that the existence of protests cannot be easily explained by institutional variables such as the degree of functional or territorial distribution of power (Waalgrave and Rucht forthcoming; della Porta 2004d and 2005a).

Second, depending on whether or not a movement has allies within the central executive power, the openness of the institutional system would appear to have ambivalent effects on the possibilities of success for social movements. To begin with, it has frequently been observed that in decentralized states challengers can rely on a variety of actors to penetrate the system. Concerning the antinuclear movement, Nelkin and Pollack (1981: 179) stated that the "German decentralised decision-making context has provided ecologists with greater political opportunity, because they can play one administration against the other." Unlike their counterparts in other countries, the German environmentalists were successful in using the judicial system. While the centralized system in France, for example, favored political control by the government, in Germany the wide distribution of power "allowed some courts to take a very powerful and independent role in nuclear disputes" (Nelkin and Pollack 1981: 159).

However, decentralization of power does not always work in social movements' favor: "multiple points of access is a two-edged sword . . . , as multiple points of access also means multiple points of veto" (Amenta and Caren 2004: 472). Dispersal of power increases the chances of access not just for social movements but also for all political actors, including countermovements.[5] It can happen that a movement's allies find themselves in government at national level and take decisions favorable to that movement, only to find these decisions blocked by either decentralized bodies governed by other political forces or by other arms of the state such as the courts. Both of these things happened in Germany in the 1970s on the issues of abortion and nuclear power. Even the use of referendums can favor the opponents of social movements as well as the movements themselves.[6] Similarly, the public bureaucracy can be influenced by political parties and pressure groups as well as by social movements; the mirror image of this is that a strong and independent bureaucracy increases the autonomous points of access to the decision-making process for social movements but also for other collective actors (Amenta and Young 1999). Thus, the early accommodating responses by institutionally open states to the antinuclear movement did not always have much effect on later developments in the conflict. In fact, it was precisely in more open states that powerful pro-nuclear interest groups could regroup and regain lost ground (Flam 1994b: 317, 321; see also Flam 1994a).

In a more interactive perspective, the institutional context influences which strategies are more effective, but not if and when a movement will be successful: "as political circumstances become more difficult, more assertive or bolder collective action is required to produce collective benefits" (Amenta and Caren 2004: 473).

Institutional variables may have a stronger influence on the strategies adopted by social movements, however. Social movements, in fact, tend to use the channels of access made available to them by "weak" states. In Switzerland, where there is a strong tradition of referendums, 195 per 1,000 inhabitants were mobilized in forms of action involving the use of direct democracy, compared with only 4 per 1,000 in Germany and none in France and the Netherlands (Kriesi et al. 1995: 45).

As will become clear in what follows, as far as the relative moderation of repertoires is concerned, institutional openness must be combined with traditional political culture (itself naturally codified, at least partly, in legislation).

8.3 Prevailing Strategies and Social Movements

Social movements are permeated by the political culture of the systems in which they develop. The strategies adopted by collective actors are influenced by the mutable and flexible spirit of the times – the Zeitgeist – which echoes developments within the economic cycle (Brand 1985), and also by certain relatively stable characteristics of national political cultures (Kitschelt 1985: 302–3). The more egalitarian, liberal, inclusive, and individualistic the political culture, the less the opposition should be antagonistic and confrontational. Taking further the analysis of those aspects of political culture relevant to interaction between social movements and institutions, Hanspeter Kriesi has emphasized the importance of prevailing strategies, which he defines, following Scharpf (1984: 260), as "an overall understanding, among those who exercise effective power, of a set of precise premises integrating world-views, goals and means." Referring in particular to the procedures used by members of a system when dealing with "challengers," he claims that "national strategies set the informal and formal rules of the game for the conflict between new social movements and their adversaries" (1989a: 295). According to this hypothesis, countries with a strategy of exclusion (that is, repression of conflict) will tend to have an ideologically homogeneous governing coalition and polarization of conflict with opponents. Where there is a strategy of inclusion (co-optation of emergent demands), on the other hand, governments will be ideologically heterogeneous and open towards external actors.

A country's democratic history also influences its prevailing strategies. Past authoritarianism often reemerges in times of turmoil. Young democracies tend to fear political protest, and also have police forces which remain steeped in the authoritarian values of the preceding regime (Flam 1994c: 348; on Italy, see Reiter 1998; della Porta and Reiter 2004a and 2004b). In fact, it has been argued that in each country new social movements have "inherited" consequences from the reactions reserved originally for the labor movement. In Mediterranean Europe, France, and Germany, absolutism and the late introduction of universal suffrage led to a divided and radicalized labor movement. In the smaller, open-market countries, in Great Britain and in Scandinavia, on the other hand, where there was no experience of absolutism and universal suffrage was introduced early, inclusive strategies produced a united and moderate labor movement. As a comparative study of American, British, and German unions show:

> State repression of the rights of workers to combine in the labor market appears to have had three related consequences for unions. First and most obviously, repression politicized unions because it compelled them to try to change the rules of the game . . . A second consequence of repression is that, if sufficiently severe, it could reduce differences among workers originating in their contrasting capacity to form effective unions . . . Finally, . . . repression politicized unions in an additional and more subtle way, by giving the initiative within the labor movement to political parties.
>
> *(Marks 1989: 14–15, passim)*

These (self-reproducing) prevailing strategies influenced the way in which the conflict between labor and capital was played out, leading to exclusion in certain cases and integration in others (Kriesi 1989a). Initially elaborated in response to trade unionism, these strategies developed their own self-perpetuating logic through political socialization and interaction: "Once the relationship between the union and party-political wings of the labor movement had been molded, it was difficult to break" (Marks 1989: 175). The tendency of national strategies to live on beyond the conditions that gave rise to them helps to explain reaction to new social movements. Political systems characterized by inclusion are more open to these new challengers, just as they had been to the old; systems with exclusionary strategies, in contrast, continue to be hostile to newly emerging claims. In fact, the difference in elite attitudes to challengers would appear to be linked to prevailing conceptions of relations with interest groups. The following has been said concerning the antinuclear movement: "The speedy and substantial responses came in the nation-states whose political and bureaucratic state elites have either long ago (Sweden, Norway) or immediately after the Second World War, if not earlier (Austria, the Netherlands, West Germany) learnt to recognize as legitimate and even formalized interest group representation and the influence that trade unions and employers exert over governmental decision making" (Flam 1994b: 309). The elites in these countries tend to recognize the legitimacy of interests lying outside the party system, knowing that the movement of today may be the interest group of tomorrow. In other countries, France for example, an exclusionary attitude has prevailed.

What, then, can be explained by this set of variables? First, it should be reiterated that an aspect that tends to remain constant cannot help explain the (cyclical) emergence of protest. In terms of its success, what was said concerning institutional openness also applies here, at least in part. While strategies of accommodation and inclusion may favor social movement access to the system, they will do the same for its opponents too. In an inclusive system, governments hostile to social movement claims can be forced to compromise; on the other hand, a government inclined to be friendly might also be constrained to follow a more moderate policy than they would otherwise.

The relative predominance of either a strategy of inclusion or a strategy of exclusion may also have contradictory effects on levels of mobilization. On the one hand, the anticipated costs of mobilization will be lower in traditionally inclusive countries; on the other hand, the advantage expected from protest would be smaller, since inclusive countries tend to value consensus. Cross-national comparisons do not offer strong support here either. In the 1970s and 1980s, the overall levels of mobilization in Switzerland and the Netherlands, both traditionally inclusive countries,[7] are similar to those in France and Germany, countries with long traditions of repression (Kriesi et al. 1995). Added to that, according to opinion poll evidence, the number of citizens who have taken part in direct action is particularly high in France; higher than in Great Britain, a traditionally inclusive country.[8] Moreover, the so-called "old" movements, and the labor movement in particular, have been more active in France and Germany than in the Netherlands and Switzerland. This would seem to confirm that neither the degree of exclusion nor the prospects for accommodation have an unequivocal effect on mobilization levels. Although exclusionary strategy heightens the costs of collective action, it also renders it in a certain way more necessary. The other side of the coin is that accommodatory strategies lessen the costs of action but also the costs of inaction.

The link between prevailing strategies and repertoires of action seems stronger: repertoires of protest are more conventional in traditionally inclusive countries. In a comparison of political repression in nineteenth-century Europe, for example, it has been noted that "those countries that were

consistently the most repressive, brutal, and obstinate in dealing with the consequences of modernization and developing working-class dissidence reaped the
harvest by producing opposition that was just as rigid, brutal, and obstinate"
(Goldstein 1983: 340). In general, the most radical ideologies and strategies developed in countries characterized by low parliamentarization and the political
isolation of the labor movement (Bartolini 2000: 565–6). On the other hand,
institutionalization of collective bargaining contributed to depoliticize conflicts
on social inequality by constraining them within industrial relations (Gallie
1989). In fact, "repression stimulated working-class radicalism; whilst political
relaxation and a structure of free collective bargaining encourages reformism"
(Geary 1981: 179). However, individual participation in protest action, including
the most extreme forms, on occasions turns out to be relatively high in
traditionally inclusive countries and, vice versa, low in countries with a tradition
of exclusion. For example, in a comparison of eight democracies, the Dutch
had the highest propensity to participate in direct action. They also had a greater
disposition than citizens in many countries with exclusionary traditions, such
as Germany, to participate in radical protest: wildcat strikes, writing graffiti,
refusal to pay rent or taxes, damage to property, and violence against the
person.

While acknowledging a certain influence of past experiences on social movement strategies, it should be remembered that a country's "traditions" are hardly
set in stone. The nineteenth-century French elites, for example, were considered
open to change, while their German counterparts were hostile to any and every
reform:

> Where a national bourgeoisie is weak or tied to an existing and authoritarian state,
> as in Russia before the First World War, or countries in which the middle class
> increasingly abandons liberal values and comes to support a semi-authoritarian
> political system, as was to some extent the case in Imperial Germany and prewar
> Spain, there the prospect of working-class liberalism appears to be weaker, while
> political radicalism on the part of labor becomes more marked. Conversely, the
> Republican traditions of at least some sections of the French bourgeoisie and
> the buoyant liberalism of the British middle class enabled a fair proportion of the
> workers to remain in the liberal camp.
>
> *(Geary 1989: 2–3)*

The picture changes in the second half of the twentieth century, however. In
fact, after the Second World War, the collapse of Nazism and the Allied Occupation led to a rethinking of past repressive traditions in Germany and the adoption of inclusive strategies towards the labor movement. In France, on the other
hand, the absence of such a historical rupture allowed strategies of exclusion to
be maintained until at least the 1960s. Similarly, it has also been noted that past

elite behavior is not enough to explain recourse to repressive strategies in relation to the antinuclear movement (Flam 1994c: 345).

In conclusion, while national strategies do have a certain influence on the
repertoires of action adopted by social movements, they are not sufficient to
explain the strategic choices they make. In the first place, they are not equally
long-lived in every country. Second, they do not have the same effects on all movements. Third, they appear to affect some movement strategies and not others.

8.4 Allies, Opponents, and Social Movements

So far, we considered relatively constant political opportunities: both institutions
and political cultures change slowly. For social movement activists these are
mainly givens. However, another more dynamic set of variables – susceptible to
change in the short term and the object of pressure from social movements – is
also considered part of the political opportunity structure. Indeed, as already
noted, among the first definitions of the political opportunity structure were
those looking at changes that could cause sudden ruptures in the system. Attention has therefore concentrated on aspects such as electoral instability or elite
divisions (see, for example, Piven and Cloward 1977; Jenkins 1985; Tarrow 1983,
1989a).

8.4.1 Social movements in a multi-organizational field

Social movements move in a multi-organizational field, interacting with a variety
of other actors. They find both allies and opponents within the public administration, the party system, interest groups, and civil society. During a cycle of
protest, social movement organizations, political parties, interest groups, and voluntary associations frequently enter into relations of conflict or cooperation both
on specific issues and the more general one of the right to protest. Many actors,
including institutional actors, become involved in protest campaigns on particular demands such as peace or abortion, but coalitions also form on the issue of
"law and order" on the one side, and "civil rights" on the other (della Porta 1998b).

In fact, institutional factors are mediated by two intervening sets of variables:
the alliance structure and the opposition structure. Considering the field of
action within which social movements move, the alliance structure can be
defined as composed by those political actors who support them; the opposition
structure as composed by those political actors who are against them (Kriesi
1989a and 1991; Klandermans 1989b and 1990; della Porta and Rucht 1995).
Alliances provide resources and political opportunities for challengers; opposi-

tion erodes them. Institutional actors (such as political parties and interest groups) and other social movements can be found on both sides. The configuration of power – that is, the distribution of power among the various actors operating within the party or interest group system – will influence the result of the conflicts (Kriesi 1989a). While it is elections that determine whether the party allies or opponents of a social movement will be in power, the attitudes of the various actors mentioned above are influenced by other factors.

When looking at the opponents of social movements, we can start observing that they can be either institutional or noninstitutional actors. In fact, the term countermovements has been coined in relation to these latter actors. Countermovements arise in reaction to the successes obtained by social movements, and the two then develop in symbiotic dependence during the course of mobilization. In general, the relationship between movements and countermovements has been defined as one of loosely coupled conflicts, in which the two sides rarely come to together face to face (Zald and Useem 1987; cf. also Lo 1982). To use Rapoport's typology (1960), conflicts between social movements and countermovements resemble debate to the extent that they are based on an attempt to persuade opponents and the authorities, and games to the extent they are based on rational calculations of costs and benefits. Sometimes, however, as was the case in Italy in the 1970s, their interaction resembles far more a battle in which the objective is to annihilate the enemy. Interactions between movement and countermovement lead to a strong sense of conflict and the prevalence of a manichean view of politics (Klandermans 1989b; della Porta 1995). Moreover, the two tend to imitate each other, reciprocally adapting particular tactics and the choice of arenas in which to act (see, for example, Rucht 1991c; Meyer and Staggenborg 1996; Bernstein 1997). The presence of nonviolent countermovements chiefly affects the chances of success for social movements; the presence of violent countermovements, on the other hand, leads to radicalization of their repertoires of action.

As for the institutional opponents, it must be stated at the outset that the state cannot be identified merely as an enemy of social movements. Rather, the state is "simultaneously target, sponsor, and antagonist for social movements as well as the organizer of the political system and the arbiter of victory" (Jenkins and Klandermans 1995: 3). State agencies may be either allies or opponents: Government agencies can support or oppose movement claims, since some of the agencies might believe in movement goals and others hold opposing beliefs (Gale 1986: 205). Both can offer important resources to their respective sides. Not all public agencies are aligned, however, and, as the chapter that follows makes clear, many of them become arenas for transactions between different collective actors, social movements among them.

The greater the closure of institutional opportunity, the more important is the presence of allies for movements gaining access to the decision-making process. Such allies come in a variety of forms. First, as noted in chapter 6, the resource-mobilization approach has emphasized the role of "reform professionals" (bureaucrats from certain public agencies, charities, religious organizations, and so on) in helping some social movements. In the United States, for example, the churches, certain foundations, and the agencies involved in federal antipoverty programs supported the civil rights movement (Morris 1984; McAdam 1982). Religious associations and third-sector groups were among the organizers of the Genoa Social Forum, and shortly before the G8 meeting many more established Catholic church institutions met to pray for a "more just" globalization.

In addition, the trade unions have often been an important ally for emerging actors, such as the student movement or the women's movement, particularly in Europe. With a wide social base and very often privileged channels of access to institutional decision-makers (both directly through the public administration and indirectly through the political parties), the trade unions can increase the mobilization capacities and chances of success for social movements. It is probable that the weaker the institutional recognition of workers' representatives in the workplace and the decision-making process, the greater will be their propensity to assume a political role, allying themselves with social movements and taking part in public protest. The more influential interest groups are, the smaller will be the space for relatively unorganized movements because "a well-resourced, coherently structured, and professionalized system of interest groups may also be able to prevent outside challengers from having access to the state. Moreover, highly institutionalized, encompassing arrangements of policy negotiations between the public administration and private interest associations will be both quite inaccessible to challengers and able to act" (Kriesi et al. 1995: 31). According to this point of view, neocorporatism – that is, a model of interest representation with monopolistic, centralized interest organizations (Schmitter 1974) that participate in public decision-making (Lehmbruch 1977) – should reduce the incidence of protest. Access to the institutional system of public decision-making would facilitate agreement between different social groups and the state without the need for noninstitutional forms of collective action. Both control over the formation of social demand (Schmitter 1981) and the capacity to satisfy that demand (Nollert 1995) would have the effect of discouraging protest. However, if a neocorporatist structure undoubtedly reduces strikes in industry,[9] its effect on protest in other sectors is far from clear. In fact, guaranteeing privileges to powerful interests could lead to rebellion by their weaker rivals and thus to the rise of powerful new movements (Brand 1985).[10] On the other hand, neocorporatism could as easily create a tendency to incorporate emerging groups within the structure of concerted policymaking. A comparison between the American and German antinuclear movements revealed that the American system, with its multiple points of access and traditionally weak executive, favored legal strategies and pragmatic movements. The initial closure of the German state (traditionally assertive of its supremacy over civil society) towards interests that cut across its corporatist outlook, on the other hand, favored strategies of direct action (Joppke 1993). However, "once new issues and interests pass the high hurdles of party and parliament, the German polity firmly institutionalizes them" (Joppke 1993: 201).

In Seattle, as in Genoa, various unions joined the demonstrations, asking for protection for labor standards and social policies. Recent mobilizations on labor issues, in the South and the North, have indeed initiated a trend of research on "social movement unions" (see chapter 2 above). As Beverly Silver (2003) has brilliantly synthesized, in the last decades research on unions has stressed their growing weakness, attributing it either to capital hypermobility and the resulting decline in national sovereignty (e.g. Castells 1997), or to post-Fordist fragmentation of workers (e.g., Jenkins and Leicht 1997: 378–9). On the other hand, some more optimistic approaches stress the persisting role of unions, capable of taking advantage of globalization and imposing a strengthening of workers' rights in countries where capital was invested. In particular, unions appear quite active in developing countries – as Silver (2003: 164) observes, "the deep crisis into which core labor movements fell in the 1980s was not immediately replicated elsewhere. On the contrary, in the late 1980s and 1990s, major waves of labor militancy hit 'showcases' of rapid industrialization in the Second and third Worlds." As with Fordism, initially considered a source of unavoidable defeat for the working class, post-Fordism would also present both challenges and opportunities for the workers' organization. In fact, the WTO protest in Seattle has been seen as a sign of the remobilization of labor.

8.4.2 Social movements and parties

Where social movement allies are concerned, however, it is on the political parties that, especially in Europe, attention has mainly focused. Social movements' relationship with parties evolved in time: from articulating party positions to permeating parties in order to try to influence them; from co-optation to independence (Hanagan 1998a). Movements have often developed special links with a political party or party family: the labor movements rise from, or gave birth to, socialist parties; ethnic movements often refer to regionalist parties for support; ecologists tend to vote for the Greens; the pro-choice movement in the US tends to support the Democrats, while the pro-life is oriented towards the Republicans. So strict have been their reciprocal relations that "indeed in the United States and Europe, political parties and social movements have become overlapping, mutually dependent actors in shaping politics" (Goldstone 2003: 4). Past research has especially focused on new social movements, which have had, although with tensions, the left as an ally. For example, a survey of environmental groups revealed that while only 11 percent claimed to have frequent contacts with political parties, both the greens and the old and new left were mentioned (by 21, 38, and 29 percent respectively of those interviewed) as tending to represent the movement's interests (only 2 percent mentioned conservative parties in this context) (Dalton 1995: 308). In fact, the configuration of power on the left is particularly important for social movements (Kriesi 1989a: 296). More particularly, a whole series of potential exchanges develop between social movements and left-wing parties. As mediators between civil society and the state, the parties of the left need to mobilize public opinion and voters. For this reason they are far from indifferent to social movement pressure. Indeed, the programs and membership of the institutional left, be it British Labor, German Social Democrats, French Socialists, or Italian Communists, have all been altered by interaction with social movements (see Maguire 1995; Duyvendak 1995; Koopmans 1995; Koelble 1991).

The strategy adopted by the left towards social movements has, however, not been unchanging over time and space. Hostility has sometimes prevailed, sometimes negotiation and sometimes co-optation. Recently, some left-wing parties (among them prominently British New Labor) have supported the Iraq war; others (such as the German Social Democrats) have firmly opposed it. Up to the Genoa marches, most of the European institutional left considered free-market globalization as the main and only way to fight unemployment; after Genoa some doubts emerged, for instance between the Italian Left Democrats and the French Socialists (Andretta, della Porta, Mosca, and Reiter 2002: ch. 5). What explains the strategic choices made by the parties on the left? And second, what are the consequences of their attitudes for the emergence, mobilization capacity, repertoires, and chances for success of social movements?

In attempting to answer the first question, attention has been directed to political cleavages. While some have suggested that a rigid left–right division retards the development of new social movements (Brand 1985: 319), others have highlighted the stimulus provided by strong communist parties. Among the latter, Tarrow has argued that the parties of the left, in particular the Italian Communist Party (PCI), acted as "offstage but creative prompters in the origins, the dynamics, and the ultimate institutionalization of the new movements" (1990: 254). In general the old left appears more disposed to support social movements where exclusionary strategies have impeded the narrowing of the left–right divide. In southern Europe, for instance, left-wing governments made several concessions to a left-leaning feminist movement (della Porta 2003a; Valiente 2003).

Second, the existence of party divisions within the traditional left influences attitudes to social movements. Where the left is divided between a social-democratic (or socialist) and a communist party, this increases the relevance of the working-class vote, discouraging the addressing postmaterial issues (Kriesi 1991:

18). On the contrary, the global justice movement, stressing the traditional demands of social rights and justice, seems to have been more able to influence the institutional left in countries such as Italy, France, or Spain, where the moderate left feared the competition of more radical communist or Trotskyite parties.

In fact, electoral competition is an important variable in explaining the reaction of potential allies towards social movements. The propensity to support protest has been connected with electoral instability, which renders the winning of new votes particularly important. In fact, member–challenger coalitions are most probable in closely divided and competitive political situations (Tilly 1978: 213–14). Political instability favors protest movements: "the political impact of institutional disruptions depends upon the electoral conditions. Even serious disruptions, such as industrial strikes, will force concessions only when the calculus of electoral instability favors the protestors" (Piven and Cloward 1977: 31–2). The success of the United Farm Workers in the United States, for example, has been explained by the electoral realignment which brought to power the liberal wing of the Democratic Party, particularly well disposed towards social movements (Jenkins 1985). From the 1950s on, the white, Protestant, upper middle classes and the black electorate of the big cities began to abandon the Republicans and became increasingly volatile. As patronage politics became less and less effective, the traditional constituencies of New Deal politics (blue-collar workers, white ethnics, the Jewish community, and Southerners) were also moving towards the center (Jenkins 1985: 224). It was above all electoral uncertainty that pushed the Democratic Party to work with social movements. Later on, also in Italy, as well as in Spain and France, the hope of winning the large slice of the electorate that supported the peace movements, as well as some of the many activists that had participated in the demonstration for global justice, pushed the institutional left towards more critical position on issues such as privatization of public services, deregulation of the labor market, or sending troops to Iraq.

Fourth, the position of the left towards social movements can be influenced by whether or not they are in government. Kriesi (1991: 19; see also Kriesi 1989b: 296–7) has suggested that when in opposition social democrats take advantage of the push provided by social movements; in power, on the other hand, they are forced by budgetary and other constraints to limit their openness to emerging demands. To maximize their reelection chances they must privilege those economic questions that interest their hardcore vote. Out of power, the willingness of the left to support social movements grows with its needs to mobilize people around left-wing demands. However, there is not always a perfect correspondence between participation in government and hostility towards social movements. In both Italy and Germany, for example, left-wing parties have been relatively sympathetic towards protest regardless of their "proximity" to government (della Porta and Rucht 1995). Neither does the empirical research conducted by Kriesi and his colleagues provide unequivocal answers concerning the degree to which the left supported protest in or out of government. In fact, although in both Germany and the Netherlands the left facilitated protest action more frequently when in opposition than when in government (strongly and visibly in the first case, more weakly in the second), the exact opposite was true of France (Kriesi et al. 1995: 79). This ambiguity in the relationship between allies in power and protest is particularly true as far as movements close to the traditional left, the pacifist movement, or the movement against racism, are concerned.[11] In the United States, the frequency of student protest decreased when the president or state governors belonged to the Democratic Party, but increased with Democratic control over legislatures (van Dyke 2003).

Beyond being in government or not, the attitudes of the parties of the left towards social movements are related to a fifth variable: their openness to reform politics. According to a comparative analysis of social movements in Italy and Germany, when both the PCI and the SPD were moving towards the center between the 1970s and the 1990s, they became less available to channel new social movements' demands into the decision-making process (della Porta and Rucht 1995). Although the SPD–FDP coalition presided over by Willy Brandt in the early 1970s in Germany, which had a broad program of reforms, was open to dialogue with social movements, later on the same coalition, now led by Helmut Schmidt, was driven to moderate its program of reforms by an economic downturn, and at the same time became "cool" towards noninstitutional actors. More generally, whether in the opposition or in government, the European center-left parties since the early 1990s have tended to trust market-driven economic policies and rejected traditional Keynesian interventions. When the global justice movement emerged with its demands of more public investments, it was greeted by skepticism and open criticism by its potential allies.

It should be added that the actions of left-wing parties in government depend on their weight within the governing coalition. They are obviously freer to take decisions when governing alone. When in coalition with more moderate parties they will be forced to adopt policies less favorable towards the left-wing social movements. When governing with other parties of the left, on the other hand, they will tend to adopt attitudes closer to some new collective actors. In France, for example, the early governments under François Mitterrand's presidency (coalitions with the Communist Party and with a majority in parliament) were more open to reform than later governments involved in "cohabitation" with a right-wing parliamentary majority. Many examples can also be found from the German Länder, where Red–Green coalitions have showed more willingness to accept social movement demands than coalitions of the SPD and FDP or, even worse in this respect, coalitions of the SPD and CDU.

Some recent major changes in political parties, especially in Europe, have significantly affected their interactions with social movements. In the past, participation often developed within mass political parties, where common values permitted the formation of collective identities. Social movements, therefore, developed in strong connection with parties: the labor movement had symbiotic relationships with the socialist parties, ethnic movements with ethnic minority parties. However, especially since the 1980s, even left-wing political parties have moved from an organizational model based upon a large membership and an important role for activists, who had a widespread presence through the party ranks, to be "electoral" parties that address voters through mass media, activate sympathizers only during electoral periods, and moderate their ideology toward the center (Pizzorno 1978, 1981; Manin 1993; della Porta 2001). The weakening of the identity-building functions of political parties has instead increased the autonomous role of social movements as arenas of public debate on political issues and construction of collective identities (see also chapter 9 below).

Turning to the second question, what consequences do the attitudes of potential allies have for social movements? It is widely held that the parties of the left play an important role, easing access to the decision-making process and increasing social movements' capacity for mobilization and chances of success. When the traditional left is hostile, on the other hand, social movements are politically marginalized.

The alliance with the traditional left has, first and foremost, reinforced social movements' capacity for mobilization. It has been noted that placing oneself on the left generally correlates positively with a willingness to use protest, particularly civil disobedience (Wallace and Jenkins 1995: 126). Because "Leftism is consistently associated with left-party support" (ibid.), the position taken by left-wing parties tends to influence the levels of mobilization of their electorate, which is in general more ready to use protest than the right-wing electorate. Indeed, left-wing activists are frequently involved in social movements as well as their own political party (see, for example, Kriesi and van Praag 1987). Conversely, leaving aside the question of their openness to influence by social movements, participation by left-wing parties in government would appear to have a negative effect on collective mobilization because it seems to discourage from actual protest those who are potentially more protest-prone. In analyzing data on Germany, France, Great Britain, and the Netherlands between 1975 and 1989, and on Germany between 1950 and 1991, Koopmans and Rucht noted that right-wing protest increases under left-wing governments and vice versa. Since the right is generally less given to using protest, mobilization tends to be greater when there is a right-wing government than when there is a left-wing government (two times greater under Christian Democrat Chancellor Helmut Kohl than was the case under the Social Democrat Helmut Schmidt) (Koopmans and Rucht 1995). If the social movement literature has considered mobilization chiefly as a response to growing hopes for change (see, for example, Tarrow 1989a), these results suggest the importance of the potential risks of inaction. When faced with a government to which they feel closer, social movements (no longer "powerless") tend to increase their use of direct pressure and reduce the use of protest. On the other hand, the risk posed by a politically opposed government leads them to consider mobilization inevitable. Not by chance, the largest peace marches on February 15, 2003, happened in those countries (such as the UK, Italy, and Spain) whose governments supported the war in Iraq. The antiwar stances of the French and German governments reduced the number of protestors in those two countries.

The attitudes of potential allies also affect the strategies of social movements themselves. First, the presence of powerful allies tends to have a moderating influence on social movement tactics. It is no accident that in the second half of the 1970s the moments of greatest political violence in Italy and Germany coincided with hostility on the part of the SPD and the PCI towards social movements (della Porta 1995; della Porta and Rucht 1995). Indeed, isolation and radicalization tend to be mutually reinforcing. The more isolated a social movement is, the greater the doubts that change can be realized in the short term, and the greater the need for ideological substitutes for missing material incentives. Thus, social movement strategies become more extreme. The more radical a movement, the greater will be the propensity of traditional left parties, scared by the risk of alienating their moderate voters, to assume a hostile attitude. The wider the base of support, on the other hand, the more the risk of losing support acts as a restraint on the use of violence.[12] It should be added that attempts at co-optation tend to transform the whole organizational and ideological structure of social movement families. In Italy, for example, between the late 1960s and the early 1980s, a tendency towards co-optation on the part of a powerful Communist Party caused an ideology and an organizational structure heavily influenced by the traditional left to prevail within the social movement sector (della Porta 1996a).

If, then, support from the parties of the left appears to influence levels of mobilization and the strategies adopted, the question relating to chances of success remains open. Despite the difficulties involved in evaluating the results obtained by social movements (to be dealt with in the next chapter), from everything said so far it is more than probable that a left-wing government would be more favorably disposed towards many of the demands put forward by the left-wing social movements than a government of the right. In particular, memories of repression experienced in the past tend to make the left more liberal in matters of public order (della Porta 1998b). The left in power, however, tends to support demands which are moderate, and on issues which are compatible with those of their traditional voters (Kriesi et al. 1995: 59).

In conclusion, the presence of powerful allies is generally a factor facilitating social movement success. In many cases alliances with the left considerably enhance the mobilizing power of protest. However, the price of this is a kind of tutelage on the part of the left that can lead, particularly when the left is in power, to a diminution in protest.

8.5 Discursive Opportunity and the Media System

The studies already cited demonstrated the explanatory power of the concept of political opportunity, but also raised some problems (see also chapter 1 above). Among them is the (unacknowledged) role of cultural variables in the perception of political opportunities and constraints, as well as in the choice of organizational models and repertoires of action. First, political opportunity approaches are criticized for failing to recognize that "cultural and strategic processes define and create the factors usually presented as 'structural'" (Goodwin and Jaspers 2004a: 27). Cultural factors filter the external reality, so that the appearance of opportunities might pass unperceived; or alternatively, activists might perceive closed opportunities as being open (Kurzman 2004). Even former proponents of the concept of political opportunity structures have recently written that "Opportunities and threats are not objective categories, but depend on the kind of collective attribution that the classical agenda limited to framing of movement goals" (McAdam, Tarrow, and Tilly 2001: 45).

8.5.1 Discursive opportunities

The debate, however, goes beyond the role of perceptions to address the restrictive effect that the focus on political opportunities has had on social movement studies (Goodwin and Jasper 2004b). The emphasis on the political has in particular obscured the role of discursive opportunities, such as the capacity of movements' themes to resonate with cultural values. The political opportunity structure has indeed been defined as "the playing field in which framing context occurs" (Gamson 2004: 249).

While they are also structural (in the sense that they are beyond the movement's sphere of immediate influence), discursive opportunities are distinct from political institutions (Koopmans 2004; Polletta 2004). Cultural environments define the resonance of movements' demands (Williams and Kubal 1999), with changes possible only in transitional times (Schudson 1989). The deeply embedded conception of citizenship as inclusive (that is, citizenship based on territorial criteria – "soil") or exclusive (citizenship based on the conception of *Volk*, or "blood") explains much of the mobilization of the racist as well as the antiracist movements (Koopmans and Statham 1999): the abolitionist movement succeeded when it could link its moral claims to dominant values (d'Anjou and van Male 1998); the way in which the abortion issue was discussed in Germany and the United States resonated with general themes in their national political cultures (Ferree, Gamson, Gerhards, and Rucht 2002); the return of public opinion toward a general support of the public sphere (versus the private sphere) helped the development of the global justice movement (della Porta, Andretta, Mosca, and Reiter 2005).

8.5.2 Media and movements

The issue of discursive opportunities is linked to the role played by mass media as the main arena for the public expression of opinions and opinion formation. It has already been noted that social movements depend on the media to get their message across (see chapter 7 above). As Gamson (2004: 243) observes, "the mass media arena is the major site of context over meaning because all of the players in the policy process assume its pervasive influence – either it is justified or not." Control of the media and symbolic production therefore becomes both an essential premise for any attempt at political mobilization, and an autonomous source of conflict. Increasingly, control of intellectual resources, traditionally indispensable to the success of collective action, risks becoming an unattainable goal if it is not supported by access to the means of mass communication (Gamson and Modigliani 1989; Wasko and Mosko 1992; Gamson and Wolfsfeld 1993; Eyerman 1994). The more autonomous and pluralistic the media structure, the greater the possibility of access for challengers.

However, social movements have been described as "weak" players in the mass-media sphere, and the relationships between activists and journalists have been seen as competitive (Neveu 1999). The media demands of visible leaders may distort movement democracy (Gitlin 1980). General tendencies (journalistic preference for the visible and dramatic, for example, or reliance on authoritative sources of information) and specific characteristics of the media system (a greater or lesser degree of neutrality on the part of journalists, the amount of competition between the different media) both influence social movements (see, for example, Kielbowicz and Scherer 1986). Recent trends towards journalistic depoliticization and increasing commercialization (Neveu 1999) further reduce activists' access.

However, the media also offer space for the spread of movements' ideas. Movement organizations have become more skilled in influencing the media, developing a specific savoir-faire as well as a reputation as reliable sources (Schlesinger 1992). Moreover, activists also represent a target market for the media (Neveu 1999: 59): the more widespread the support for the movements, the more marketing strategies create mediatic space for their discourse, with the effect of further widening the support for the movements. This sort of virtuous circle operated, for instance, in Germany in the opposition to the Iraq war. Media can also act as mobilizers of protest, especially on "highly emotional and symbolic issues that create an atmosphere of consensus, emotion, and togetherness" (Walgraave and Manssens 2000: 235) – such as the 1996 White March in

Brussels, which mobilized 300,000 Belgians to protest against institutional misconduct in the investigation of a serial murderer who had killed several children. We can add that, although the debate on the effectiveness of media manipulation has not been conclusive (Katz and Lazarsfeld 1955; Noelle-Neumann 1984; Gamson 1992b; Lenart 1993), research has repeatedly indicated that the public is not a passive receiver of news: "reading media imagery is an active process in which context, social location, and prior experience can lead to quite different decoding" (Gamson, Croteau, Hoynes, and Sasson 1992: 375). Activists challenge the symbolic power of the media, transgressing the borders between "media world" and "ordinary world" (Couldry 1999; chs. 7 and 8). Radical media have developed as alternative (counter-) public spheres (Downing 2001).

If attention to "counterinformation" is a constant concern for movements, recent technological developments have facilitated the development of autonomous media via the internet. The best-known alternative media is Indymedia (www.indymedia.org), defined on its homepage as "a collective of independent media organizations and hundreds of journalists offering grassroots, noncorporate coverage. Indymedia is a democratic media outlet for the creation of radical, accurate, and impassioned truth telling." The *raison d'être* of the network is the critique of the established media (Rucht 2003b) and promotion of the "democratization of information" and "citizens' media" (Cardon and Granjou 2003). Open publishing is an essential element of the Indymedia project: since there is no editorial board filtering information, everybody from independent journalists to unknown activists can instantaneously publish the news they gather on a globally accessible website (Cristante 2003, Freschi 2003). Anyone who respects a few ground rules can create a local node of Indymedia. During the Seattle protest, the Independent media center claimed to have received 1.5 million hits. Meso-level media, which circulate information among activists, have the uneasy task of reaching the mass media if they want their message to be heard outside of audiences sympathetic to the movement (Bennett 2004b; Peretti 2004).

8.6 Summary

The policing of protest, the styles of which have changed historically and spatially, influences social movement trajectories and characteristics. Coercive strategies have often produced escalation. While democratic countries move towards negotiated forms of control, recent global protests, although largely peaceful, have been met by tough policing. Forms of policing derive in part from police organizations and cultures; however, they are also sensitive to political opportunities. Under this label, diachronic, cross-national comparative research has discussed the characteristics and effects of four groups of variables relating to:

(1) political institutions; (2) political cultures; (3) the behavior of opponents of social movements; and (4) the behavior of their allies.

The institutional variables most frequently discussed have related to the formal openness of the decision-making process. Starting from the hypothesis that the greater the number of points of access the more open the system, the relevance of the distribution of power and the availability of direct democracy have been discussed. Informal characteristics and, in particular, traditional strategies of interaction with challengers were considered as well as structural characteristics. In the last decades, devolution at the subnational level and more autonomous competences of the public bureaucracies (and, in particular, the judiciary) have increased the points of access, while the growing power of multinational corporations and IGOs has made access to decision-makers more difficult. Neither of these (tendentially stable) dimensions, however, is well adapted to explaining conjunctural events such as the rise and decline of protest or the mobilizing capacity of social movements. As far as the consequences of collective action are concerned, the formal or informal openness of the decision-making system does not automatically privilege emergent demands because institutions are also potentially open to social movements' opponents. Although the effects of the stable political opportunity structure in terms of social movement success thus appear ambiguous, the effects on the strategies adopted by movements seem less equivocal. The greater the opportunities of access to the decision-making system, the more social movements tend to adopt moderate strategies and institutional channels.

The conjunctural characteristics of conflict and alliances would appear to have a significant influence on the emergence of protest and on mobilization potential. The strength of institutional opponents together with movement/countermovement interaction, influence the rise of protest and movement strategies. Alliances with the parties of the left and the trade unions have provided important resources for social movements and increased their chance of success in the past. The decline of mass parties, and with them of party activism, challenge the potential alliances between parties and social movements.

If the concept of political opportunity has assumed a central role in social movement research, little attention has been paid to subjective perceptions of reality. Recent research has begun to address the way in which cultural variables filter political opportunities, and discursive opportunities influence movements' strategies and chances of success. Pluralism of the mass media and the richness of meso-level media emerge as important conditions for the spread of movement messages.

SOCIAL MOVEMENTS AND DEMOCRACY

In 1988 the city government of Porto Alegre, a Brazilian metropolis with 1,360,000 inhabitants, initiated a project of participatory decision-making on the city budget, with the aim of strengthening participation through the creation of a public space for the expression of citizens' demands (Gret and Sintomer 2002: 26). Participatory budgeting has been defined as the most significant Latin American innovation for increasing citizen participation and local government accountability: an experiment in which citizen assemblies in each city district determine priorities for the use of a part of the city's revenues (Souza 2000). It is a system of governance where "regular citizens" make binding decisions on several areas of governmental action, most notably those affecting the city's new capital investments (Baiocchi 2002a). Every year, between March and June, there are widespread interactions between citizens and the administration. Large city assemblies as well as decentralized neighborhood ones discuss and vote on spending priorities, electing delegates to the Council of the Participatory Budgeting as well as to thematic committees. Each thematic committee then elects representatives to the Council of the Participatory Budgeting, in which representatives of unions, neighborhood associations, and the government also take part. In July and August, city experts, together with the assemblies' delegates, help in translating the demands into projects. Between September and December, the delegates meet and prepare a General Proposal on the Budget and a draft of the Investment Plan that will be discussed with the City Council and then approved (Allegretti 2003: 116–17). The decision procedures involve both direct and delegate democracy, with mandatory delegation in neighborhood forums. The election of the delegates stimulates participation, being proportional to the number of people taking part in the assemblies (one delegate to 10 participants). There is also a delegation of power to representative institutions, both the city council and the thematic participatory budgeting committees (on transport, health and social security, culture, education and leisure, economic development, and urban development).

In a trial-and-error process, participatory budgeting acquired a complex structure in order to achieve two different but complementary aims: more social justice, but also more participation. The enterprise is focused on the goal of reducing social inequalities, and allocation takes into account both the priority established by the citizens, and the relative levels of deprivation in the various neighborhoods. The precise timing of the process aims at reducing the acknowledged limitations of assemblyism, especially in terms of decision blocks, without giving up the advantages of direct democracy, especially in terms of citizens' empowerment.

Although far from involving the whole population, the experiments had some success in terms of participation. Involvement in the participatory budgeting process in fact increased from less than 1,000 people in 1990 to more than 30,000 in 2002 (Allegretti 2004: 204). Moreover, it allowed formerly excluded groups to decide on investment priorities in their communities and to monitor government responses (Souza 2000). Although education and social class are relevant in acquiring leading positions as delegates, the poorest groups are overrepresented in the rank-and-file assemblies. But participation is especially facilitated by previous involvement in associations and social movement organizations. Districts' participation is in fact proportional to the richness of associational life (Baiocchi 2001); individual participation increases with associational membership (although the number of participants with no associational affiliation grew from one-quarter of the participants in 1995 to less than one-third in 2002) (Allegretti 2003: 206). To minimize inequalities resulting from differences in speaking ability, the discursive setting (for instance, by allowing for very short intervention) discourages formal speech-making, which privileges the better educated (Baiocchi 2001). Authority within meetings does not come from education or class, but involves other sorts of social status such as respect within the community, often linked with membership (or even leadership) in various local groups (Baiocchi 2002). In terms of the concrete effects of the experiments, it might be worth noting that Porto Alegre seems to have gained in terms of standards of social justice, as it now ranks sixth of 5,507 towns in Brazil ranged on a scale of social exclusion (a rank of one being the least exclusive) and seventh in terms of quality of life (Allegretti 2003: 74–5). The UN has recognized participatory budgeting as one of the world's 40 "best practices" (Allegretti 2003: 173).

Various conditions facilitate the Porto Alegre experiment. First, the new Brazilian constitution of 1988 decentralized tax collection to the city level, providing resources for the financing of the participatory budget. The new city statutes, following the new constitution, also opened a window of opportunity for participation at the local level (Allegretti 2003: 110). Moreover, Porto Alegre has long been governed by the Workers' Party, a socialist party in search of a support base to address the country's democratization process and its extreme poverty. Even more important, Porto Alegre has a long tradition of associationism, especially at the community level. The neighborhood associations, which survived the country's authoritarian periods, represent an example of participatory democracy in the world's South which has deeper roots than Western representative models of democracy (Sen 2003). Although some of these associations were part of clientelistic networks of power, negotiating votes with powerful patrons, a protest tradition nevertheless survived alongside the clientelistic one. At the end of the 1980s, a wave of occupations of public buildings strengthened the associative networks (Allegretti 2003: 107). According to several observers, in contrast to a previous period of "tutelage" in which neighborhood associations vacillated between acquiescence and conflict with municipal government, the participatory reforms have fostered new institutions in civil society, a greater interconnectedness between local organizations, and a "scaling up" of activism away from solely neighborhood to citywide concerns (Baiocchi 2002).

Participatory budgeting therefore represents an empowerment of individual participation, but also an arena for the development of social movements. Not by chance, Porto Alegre has also played a central role in the global justice movement, hosting its first transnational assemblies. The World Social Forums (WSF) (Schönleitner 2003) which took place there also represent an experiment with "another democracy" – this time internal to the movement actors. Here, too, participation grew from the 16,400 participants at the first meeting in January 2001 to 52,000 in 2002 and about 100,000 in 2003. In thousands of seminars and meetings, more or less realistic and original proposals were hammered out for a bottom-up globalization; alternative politics and policies were debated and some of them tested (including the "participatory budget" that was actively sponsored by the Chart of the New Municipalities, formed during the second WSF). Since 2002, in particular, the experience of the Social Forums as a place to meet and engage in debate has been extended to the local and macro-regional levels. In particular, in the autumn of that year, Florence hosted the first European Social Forum, with three days of seminars attended by

> 60,000 participants. During the same period, debates on alternative devel-
> opment models – building "sustainable societies" – were held in Bamako
> at the African Social Forum, in Beirut at the Middle East Social Forum, in
> Belem at the pan-Amazon version, and in Hyderabad, India, at the Asian
> Social Forum. In November 2003, a second European Social Forum was
> held in Paris; the third was held in London in October 2004.

In what follows we will use the democratic experiments in Porto Alegre to illustrate the potential and limitations of research on the outcomes produced by
social movements. An analysis of their effects is an integral part of the study of
social movements as agents of social change. Different movements have achieved
different degrees of success, and discussion concerning what determines the
outcomes they achieve has been central to the debate on social movements.
A number of social movement characteristics have been frequently cited as
particularly influential in this respect. In general, research has concentrated on
such questions as: are movements that propose radical change more successful
than those that propose moderate change or vice versa? Does violence work?
Is a centralized and bureaucratic organization a help or a hindrance for social
movements?

First, we consider the difficulties movements (and analysts) face in identifying
victorious strategies (9.1). Changes in policies (9.2) and in politics (9.3) will then
be discussed. Section 9.4 will then address the specific attempts of (some) social
movements to change the conception of democracy, discussing the interactions
between normative theory of democracy and protest, while the actual interactions between broad processes of democratization and social movements are
discussed in section 9.5.

9.1 Social Movement Strategies and Their Effects

In one of the first and most influential studies on the effects produced by the
strategies social movements adopt, William Gamson (1990) identified the factors
contributing to success as a minimalist strategy ("thinking small"), the adoption
of direct action, and a centralized and bureaucratic organization. Other scholars
of collective action have not unanimously accepted this, however. As already
noted in relation to forms of action, violence has appeared a promising strategic choice at certain historical moments. Gamson himself has admitted (1990)
that wider objectives reinforce internal solidarity and favor the creation of

alliances. Finally, it has been pointed out that when organizations, including social movement organizations, become bureaucratized, the desire for organizational survival comes to prevail over declared collective objectives. According to Francis Fox Piven and Richard Cloward (1977: xxi–xxii), the effort to build organizations is not only futile but also damaging: "by endeavoring to do what they cannot do, organizers fail to do what they can do. During those brief periods in which people are roused to indignation, when they are prepared to defy the authorities to whom they ordinarily defer . . . those who call themselves leaders do not usually escalate the momentum of the people's protest." The search for material resources to ensure organizational survival leads inexorably towards the elites, who are happy to offer such resources precisely because they know it will serve to reduce the potential threat to the social order represented by its weaker members. However, it has been remarked that no particular strategic element can be evaluated in isolation and without taking into account the conditions within which social movements must operate (Burstein et al. 1995) and the presence of alliances or opponents in power (Cress and Snow 2000).

Indeed, the identification of a "strategy for success" is an arduous task for both activists and scholars. The World Social Forum in Porto Alegre provides several examples of debates about the articulation of general demands for "another possible world" in specific proposals for reforms, and the degree of acceptable compromise. The range of organizational models chosen (and defended) varies from highly structured associations (such as ATTAC) to informal affinity groups, including several examples of transnational alliances (such as, for instance, Via Campesina, networking peasant protest groups from 50 countries). Although the movement is characterized by nonviolent strategies, the use of specific forms of direct action such as the dismantling of McDonald's restaurants, the management of the land occupation by the Sem Terra, and the local democracy practiced by the Zapatistas in the Sierra Lacandona are much-debated issues. The very decision-making procedures of the WSF have been the target of criticism, which has accused it of privileging effectiveness over equality and transparency.

The attribution of credit for obtaining substantive successes also faces a series of obstacles (Tarrow 1994; Rucht 1992; Giugni 2004; Diani 1997; McVeigh, Welch, and Bjarnason 2003). A principal problem is one well known to social scientists: the existence of such close relationships between a set of variables that it becomes impossible to identify cause and effect. Urbanization and industrialization, for example, have facilitated organization by intensifying physical contacts. They have weakened certain sources of socialization and solidarity and favored the development of others (for an overview, see Sztompka 1993; also chapter 2 above). Better educational provision has increased awareness of grievances and made defending one's own interests appear legitimate. An increasingly effective communications system spreads information on mass mobilizations throughout the world. Movements are born in the course of these transformations and contribute to them. Socioeconomic, cultural, and political instances of globalization are the product of at the same time reactions to previous movements and adaptation to movement pressures, settling new resources and constraints for protest.

Third, the presence of a plurality of actors makes it more difficult to attribute success or failure to one particular strategy (Diani 1997). Social movements are themselves complex actors, composed of many organizations pursuing profoundly different strategies. In particular, recent movements proceed via campaigns in which various organizations contribute with the repertories they are most skilled in using: environmental NGOs lobby IGOs; trade unions call strikes against free-trade agreements; Sem Terra Brazilian peasants occupy unused lands; hackers jam big corporations' websites. It is difficult to single out each group's specific contribution to the final outcome.

Most importantly, movements are never the sole actors to intervene on an issue. Rather, they do so in alliance with political parties and, not infrequently, with public agencies. The policy choices of other social and political actors, for instance, are important in explaining the development of the participatory experience in Porto Alegre, where the socialist party in government invested symbolic and material resources in the project. Thus, "the outcome of bargaining is not the result of the characteristics of either party, but rather is the function of their resources relative to each other, their relationships with third parties, and other factors in the environment" (Burstein, Einwohner, and Hollander 1995: 280). As we have mentioned (see chapter 8), the results obtained by social movements (or their failure to obtain them) have often been explained by environmental conditions, particularly the openness of political opportunities and the availability of allies. It is difficult nonetheless to identify which of the many actors involved in a given policy area are responsible for one reaction or another. If, as suggested earlier, a large number of interactions characterizes a protest cycle, the results obtained will be the effect of that large number of interactions. Thus, it is always difficult to establish whether a given policy would have been enacted through other institutional actors anyway.

Fourth, the difficulties created by a plurality of actors are added to by the difficulty of reconstructing the causal dynamics underlying particular public decisions. On the one hand, events are so intertwined that it is difficult to say which came first, particularly in moments of high mobilization. On the other, social movements demand long-term changes, but the protest cycle stimulates immediate "incremental" reforms. When social movements successfully place particular issues on the public agenda this "does not happen directly or even in a linear fashion. In fact, as their ideas are vulgarized and domesticated, the early risers in a protest cycle often disappear from the scene. But a portion of their message is distilled into common frameworks of public or private culture while the rest is ignored" (Tarrow 1994: 185). This evolution is characterized by steps forward and steps back, moments in which public policy approaches the demands made by social movements and others in which the situation deteriorates.

Whether the results of protest should be judged in the short or in the long term represents a further problem. Social movements frequently obtain successes in the early phases of mobilization, but this triggers opposing interests and often a backlash in public opinion. Thus, while it is true that there is a broad consensus on many of the issues raised by social movements (peace, the defense of nature, improvements in the education system, equality), mobilization can nevertheless result in the polarization of public opinion. This normally produces a growth in movement support, but very often also a growth in opposition. Furthermore, as noted in the preceding chapter, movement success on specific demands frequently leads to the creation of countermovements: the development of neoliberalism as an ideology of the capitalist class has been explained as a reaction to the labor movement victories in terms of social rights (Sklair 1995).

Particularly when one is comparing different movements or countries, the problems outlined above hinder an evaluation of the relative effectiveness of particular movement strategies. There is also a problem, naturally, with the attribution of particular results to more institutionalized actors such as political parties and pressure groups.[1] Factors particular to social movements such as their distance from the levers of power, heterogeneous definition of their objectives, and organizational instability further complicate matters. In what follows, therefore, we will not attempt to identify winning strategies but rather to consider some of the consequences of interaction between social movements and their environment.

9.2 Changes in Public Policy

A first area for measuring the effects produced by social movements is that of actual policy, as the example with which the chapter opens showed. Generally, social movements are formed to express dissatisfaction with existing policy in a given area. Environmentalist groups have demanded intervention to protect the environment; pacifists have opposed the culture of war; students have criticized selection and authoritarianism in education; the feminist movement has fought discrimination against women; the world social forums criticized neoliberal globalization. Although it is usual to make a distinction between political and cultural movements, the first following a more instrumental logic, the second more symbolic, all movements tend to make demands on the political system.

A particular demand frequently becomes nonnegotiable, being the basis for a movement's identity. For example, in many countries the feminist movement has been constructed around the nonnegotiable right of women to "choose" concerning childbirth; the halting of the installation of NATO nuclear missiles fulfilled a similar role for the peace movement. In the first case mobilization was pro-active, seeking to gain something new, the right to free abortion; in the second it was reactive, seeking to block a decision (to install cruise missiles) which had already been taken. One of the founding organizations of the World Social Forum in Porto Alegre, ATTAC, emerged around the demands of a tax on transnational transactions; also present in Porto Alegre, the debt relief campaign asked for the foreign debt of poor countries to be totally written off. In all cases, considerable changes in public policy were being demanded. Characteristic of these nonnegotiable objectives is their role in the social movements' definitions of themselves and of the external world (Pizzorno 1978). Demands whose symbolic value is very high, such as the Equal Rights Amendment in the case of the American feminist movement, remain central for a movement even when their potential effectiveness is questionable (Mansbridge 1986). The importance of such nonnegotiable objectives is confirmed by the fact that although activists may be willing to negotiate on other demands, even partial victories on these issues, such as a woman's right to voluntarily interrupt pregnancy, are considered as defeats. Although the campaign Jubilee 2000 has been defined as "strategically challenging, politically complex, relatively successful," having "effectively pressured creditor governments to make significant moves to write off unplayable third world debt," and having "focused unprecedented public scrutiny on official macroeconomic policies" (Collins, Gariyo, and Burdon 2001: 135), many activists have been unsatisfied with the institutional responses to their claims.

While nonnegotiable demands are particularly important in the construction of collective identities, social movements rarely limit themselves to just these. In the case of the global justice movement, the general aim of "building another possible world" has been articulated in specific requests, from the opposition to privatization of public services and public good (i.e., the campaign for free access to water) to the rights of national governments to organize the low-cost production of medicines in emergency cases; from the opposition to specific projects of dam construction to a democratic reform of the United Nations. Cooperating in global protest campaigns, the ecological associations stressed the environmental unsustainability of neoliberal capitalism, trade unions the negative consequences of free trade on labor rights and levels of employment, feminist groups the suffering of women under cuts to the welfare state.

From the public-policy point of view, the changes brought about by social movements may be evaluated by looking at the various phases of the decision-making process: the emergence of new issues; writing and applying new legislation; and analysis of the effects of public policies in alleviating the conditions of those mobilized by collective action. Five levels of responsiveness to collective demands within the political system can be distinguished:

The notion of "access responsiveness" indicates the extent to which authorities are willing to hear the concerns of such a group . . . If the demand . . . is made into an issue and placed on the agenda of the political system, there has occurred a second type of responsiveness which can here be labeled "agenda responsiveness" . . . As the proposal . . . is passed into law, a third type of responsiveness is attained; the notion of "policy responsiveness" indicates the degree to which those in the political system adopt legislation or policy congruent with the manifest demands of protest groups . . . If measures are taken to ensure that the legislation is fully enforced, then a fourth type of responsiveness is attained: "output responsiveness" . . . Only if the underlying grievance is alleviated would a fifth type of responsiveness be attained: "impact responsiveness.

(Schumaker 1975: 494–5)

Research on social movements has concentrated on the production of legislation. As a recent review of the literature noted, most "studies focus on policy responsiveness, fewer on access responsiveness, and very few on the political agenda, outputs, policy impact, or structural change" (Burstein et al. 1995: 285). Having identified a series of areas in which movements intervene, quantitative and qualitative analyses attempt to measure the response of parliaments and governments. Returning to the example of the human rights movement, transnational norms emerged for the protection of indigenous people against torture and advocating their democratic freedoms (Risse and Sikkink 1999). These norms helped democratization by giving resonance in supranational forums to national movements from authoritarian countries (Keck and Sikkink 1998).

An analysis of the concrete effects of social movements can begin, therefore, from the production of legislation. This is not enough, however. As noted in discussion of social movements and political opportunities, different states have different capacities for implementing legislation, and it is precisely from the implementation of legislation that concrete gains are achieved. Even more relevant, transnational norms set in international agreements require laws to be enacted at the national level. As the cases of agreements on arms proliferation and land mines, or the Kyoto Agreement to control climate changes, indicate, very often superpowers (first of all, the United States) refuse to sign or implement international agreements. In order to evaluate the results produced by a social movement, therefore, it is also necessary to analyze how the laws or agreements they helped bring about are actually applied.

Real change, the effects produced by legislation however implemented, is even more difficult to judge. Laws which seek to meet certain of the demands of social movements may be limited in effect or even counterproductive, no matter how well implemented. The Porto Alegre experiment, with its premium for more participatory districts, risked producing imbalances in spending. During the participatory budgeting, the initial investment in road construction, oriented to improving the condition of the poorest and most marginal areas, had negative side-effects in terms of environmental sustainability (Allegretti 2003: 226). Only later did an urbanization program based on the creation of open spaces that could facilitate sociability fully develop (ibid.: 281).

Talking about norms already implies considering that, alongside structural changes in the condition of those categories or social groups mobilized by collective action, cultural transformation is a further important element in achieving and consolidating new gains. Although it is true that all movements tend to want legislative change, this is neither their only, nor even perhaps their primary, objective. Movements are in fact carriers of symbolic messages (Gamson 2004: 247): they aim to influence bystanders, spreading their own conception of the world, and they struggle to have new identities recognized. The effects of social movements are also connected with diffuse cultural change, the elaboration of "new codes" (Melucci 1982, 1984a). Typically, new ideas emerge within critical communities, and are then spread via social movements – as Rochon (1998: 179) observes, "The task of translating the chronic problem as described by the critical community into an acute problem that will attract media attention is the province of social and political movements."

While the capacity of social movements for the realization of their general aims has been considered low, they are seen as more effective in the importation of new issues into public debate, or thematization. For instance, after Seattle, the global justice movement seems to have been successful in placing on the public agenda the topics of social inequalities and the opacity of transnational decision-making. In June 2001, a short time before the G8 summit at Genoa, a national poll (run by CIRM) revealed that as many as 45 percent of Italians sympathized with the movement's arguments, 28 percent did not, and 27 percent had no opinion (La Repubblica 17/6/01). A later survey by Simulation Intelligence Research showed a large majority of the Italian citizens in favor of movements' goals, such as canceling third world debt (81 percent), establishing "equality of economic and working conditions for workers worldwide" (80 percent), unconditional opposition to the war (74 percent), doing away with tax havens (70 percent), prohibiting genetically modified foods (70 percent), introducing a Tobin Tax (64 percent), and freedom of movement for emigrants (55 percent). Overall, 19 percent of those surveyed replied that the "no-global" movement was "very positive" and 50.9 percent "quite positive." Only 16.1 percent felt it was quite or very negative (for more details, see della Porta, Andretta, Mosca, and Reiter 2005, ch. 7).

It is useful, therefore, to look at a movement's sensitizing impact, i.e. the "possibility that a movement will provoke a sensitizing of some social actor in the political arena or the public arena, which goes in the direction of the goals of the movement" (Kriesi et al. 1995: 211). Furthermore, social movements are more aware than some better-resourced actors of their need for public support. Since protest mobilization is short lived, social movements cannot content themselves with legislative reforms that can always be reversed later. They must ensure that support for their cause is so widely disseminated as to discourage any attempt to roll reforms back.

It should be added that social movements do not aim only to change public opinion. They also seek to win support among those responsible for implementing public policy, and change the values of political elites as well as those of the public. Although mass mobilization may temporarily convince political parties to pass a law, that law must also be implemented. In this case, too, social movements do not always have sufficient means of access to the less visible areas of policy implementation, and their chances of success therefore depend on influencing the public agencies responsible for implementing the laws which concern them. For instance, via direct contacts or brokers, experts within or near movements have been able to infiltrate the international advocacy community, and help spread dissent concerning neoliberal strategies within the political and nonpolitical elite. In the mid-1990s, leaders of many Western states were moving away from the pure liberalism of the Thatcher and Reagan years. In the international arena, opinions, sometimes from unexpected quarters, are making themselves heard, calling attention to the issues of social services and market reregulation (O' Brian, Goetz, Scholte, and Williams 2000: 9).

9.3 Social Movements and Procedural Changes

Social movements do not limit their interventions to single policies. They frequently influence the way in which the political system as a whole functions: its institutional and formal procedures, elite recruitment, the informal configuration of power (Kitschelt 1986; Rucht 1992). Movements demand, and often obtain, decentralization of political power, consultation of interested citizens on particular decisions or appeals procedures against decisions of the public administration. They increasingly interact with the public administration, presenting themselves as institutions of "democracy from below" (Roth 1994): they ask to be allowed to testify before representative institutions and the judiciary, to be listened to as counterexperts, to receive legal recognition and material incentives.

Protest, only a small part of overall social movement activity, is undoubtedly considered important, but also ineffectual unless accompanied by more traditional lobbying activities. Although contacts with government ministries and the public bureaucracy may not be seen on their own as particularly effective in influencing policy, they are considered useful for information-gathering and for countering the influence of pressure groups: for instance, the environmental movement has been able to counter anti-environmentalists by building alliances within the European Commission bureaucracy (Ruzza 2004). As we shall see in what follows, social movements increase the possibilities of access to the political system, both through *ad hoc* channels relating to certain issues and through institutions that are open to all noninstitutional actors.

In the late twentieth century, social movements were indeed been able to introduce changes that tend towards greater grassroots control over public institutions. In many European countries, administrative decentralization has taken place since the 1970s, with the creation of new channels of access to decision-makers. Various forms of participation in decision-making have been tried within social movement organizations. If the rise of mass political parties has been defined as a "contagion from the left" and the democracy of the mass media as a "contagion from the right," the new social movements have been acclaimed as a "contagion from below" (Rohrschneider 1993a). Social movements have brought about a pluralization of the ways in which political decisions are taken, pushed by cyclical dissatisfaction with centralized and bureaucratic representative democracy (see below). In this sense, social movements have produced a change in political culture, in the whole set of norms and reference schemes which define the issues and means of action that are politically legitimate. Repertoires of collective action, which were once condemned and dealt with simply as public order problems, have slowly become acceptable (della Porta 1998b).

In many countries direct democracy acts as a supplementary channel of access to those opened within representative democracy. On issues such as divorce, abortion, or gender discrimination, for example, the women's movement was in many cases able to appeal directly to the people using either popularly initiated legislation or referenda for the abrogation of existing laws or the implementation of transnational treaties. Referenda have become an increasingly important instrument of direct expression for ordinary citizens, particularly on issues that are not directly related to the social cleavages around which political parties have formed. Referendum campaigns present social movements with an opportunity to publicize the issues that concern them, as well as the hope of being able to bypass the obstacle represented by governments hostile to their demands.

Social movements also contribute to the creation of new arenas for the development of public policy. These new loci of decision-making vary in terms of their openness, duration, and extent of power. They have two things in common, however: their legitimation is not based on the principles of representative democracy and they have greater visibility than institutional spheres of decision-making. Several new arenas of decision-making can be identified.

Expert commissions are frequently formed on issues raised by protest, and social movement representatives may be allowed to take part, possibly as observers. The "President's Commission on Campus Unrest" which William Scranton presided over in the United States (in 1970) is one example. Others are the commission led by Lord Scarman into rioting in the United Kingdom in the 1980s and the commission of inquiry set up on "Youth Protest in the Democratic State" in Germany (Willelms et al. 1993). After Seattle, commissions of independent experts have been set to investigate the social effects of globalization (such as the Parliamentary Commission in Germany) as well as the police behavior during transnational protest events (see the Seattle City Council Commission on the Seattle events). Common to them all is the recognition that the problems they address are in some way extraordinary, and require extraordinary solutions. Although such expert commissions usually have a limited mandate and consultative power only, they enter a dialogue with public opinion through press contact and the publication of reports.

Besides commissions of enquiry, other channels of access are opened by the creation of consultative institutions on issues related to social movement demands. State ministries, local government bureaus, and other similar bodies now exist on women's or ecological issues in many countries, but also in IGOs. Such institutions, which are frequently set up on a permanent basis, have their own budgets and power to implement policies. Some regulatory administrative bodies have been established under the pressure of movement mobilizations, and see movement activists as potential allies (Amenta 1998); movement activists have been co-opted by specific public bodies as member of their staff (or vice versa). New opportunities for a "conflictual cooperation" develop within regulatory agencies that are set to implement goals that are also supported by movement activists (Giugni and Passy 1998: 85). The public administrators working in these institutions mediate particular social movement demands through both formal and informal channels and frequently ally themselves with movement representatives in order to increase the amount of public resources available in the policy areas over which they have authority. They tend to have frequent contacts with representatives of the social movements involved in their areas, the movement organizations taking on a consultancy role in many instances, and they sometimes develop common interests. Collaboration can take various forms: from consultation, to incorporation in committees, to delegation of power (ibid.: 86).

Informal negotiation has enabled some international governmental organizations to co-opt social movement associations that agree to work through discreet channels. Nongovernmental organizations have thus been accorded the status of actors, and on occasion important ones, in world governance, acknowledged as participants in the development of international norms (such as those on human rights) and on their implementation (Pagnucco 1996: 14). "International public institutions are modifying in response to pressure from social movements, NGOs and business actors, but this varies across institutions depending upon institutional culture, structure, role of the executive head and vulnerability to civil society pressure" (O' Brien, Goetz, Scholte, and Williams 2000: 6). As early as 1948, the nongovernmental Conference of NGOs with consultative status (CONGOS) was set up in the United Nations, and by the 1990s it had reached as many as 1,500 members (Rucht 1996: 33). In the European Union, the parliament in particular but other bodies as well have held informal exchanges of information with various types of associations (e.g. Marks and McAdam 1999; Mazey and Richardson 1993; della Porta 2004b; Ruzza 2004; Lahusen 2004). Social movements have been recognized with regard to processual input on the World Bank, with more emphasis on participation and the recruitment of some progressive staff (Chiriboga 2001: 81). Besides a certain degree of institutional recognition, NGOs specializing in development assistance have received funding for the development programs they have presented, or for joining in projects already presented by national or international governments (O'Brien, Goetz, Scholte, and Williams 2000: 120). Many are also involved in managing funds earmarked for emergencies and humanitarian aid, which now make up more than half the projects of the World Bank (Brecher, Costello, and Smith 2000: 114). What is more, social movements have participated in institution-building at the international level (in particular, on human rights as well as environmental protection), using their "soft power" in the form of knowledge and information (Purdue 2000; Smith 2004b: 317).

In particular, social movement activists maintain direct contacts with decision-makers, participating in epistemic communities made up of representatives of governments, parties, and interest groups of various types and persuasions. In particular, NGOs critical of neoliberalist globalization have resorted to pressure both at the national and international levels, cultivating specific expertise. From human rights groups to environmentalists, epistemic communities – composed of activists and bureaucrats belonging to international organizations, as well as politicians from many countries – have won significant gains in a number of areas: for example, decontamination of radioactive waste, the establishment of an international tribunal on human rights violations, and a ban on antipersonnel mines (Khagram, Riker, and Sikkink 2002; Klotz 1995; Risse and Sikkink 1999; Thomas 2001). Some NGOs have not only increased in size, but also strengthened their influence on various stages of international policymaking (Sikkink and Smith 2002; Boli 1999). Their assets include an increasing credibility in public opinion and the consequent availability of private funding,[2] as well their rootedness at the local level. Their specific knowledge, combined with useful contacts in the press, make many NGOs seem particularly reliable sources. With a professional staff on hand, they are also able to maintain a fair level of activity even when protest mobilization is low. Independence from governments, combined with a reputation built upon solid work at the local level, enables some NGOs to perform an important role in mediating interethnic conflict (Friberg and Hettne 1998). Finally, they enhance pluralism within international institutions by representing groups who would otherwise be excluded (Riddel-Dixon 1995) and by turning the spotlight on transnational processes, making governance more transparent (Schmidt and Take 1997).

Most important, so-called deliberative arenas have developed in the last two decades, especially at the local level. These are based on the principle of participation of "normal citizens" in public arenas for debate, empowered by information and rules for high-quality communication. There are several examples throughout Europe: Citizens' Juries in Great Britain and Spain, Planungzelle in Germany, the Consensus Conference in Denmark, Conférences de Citoyens in France, as well as Agenda 21 and various experiments in strategic urban planning. At the supranational level, nongovernmental organizations have received recognition as informal partners in consultation on policy decisions and participation in policy implementation. Among others, the White Paper on European Governance (2001) advocates the principle of participation by means of open consultation with citizens and their associations as one of the fundamental pillars of governance in the European Union. Actors associated with social movements have intervened in the development of some of these experiments, sometimes as critical participants, sometimes as external opponents.

In addition to participatory budgeting, diverse experiments are presented as part of an empowered participatory democracy model centered on participation, quality of discourse, and citizens' empowerment (Fung and Wright 2001). Examples include the inner-city Chicago neighborhood governance councils for policing and public schools, joint labor–management efforts to manage industrial labor markets, stakeholder development of ecosystem governance arrangements under the US Endangered Species Act, and village governance in West Bengal, India. The focus of these experiments is the solving of specific problems through the involvement of ordinary, affected people. It implies the creation of new institutions and devolution of decision-making power, but also includes coordination with representative institutions. The objectives of these institutions include effective problem-solving and equitable solutions as well as broad, deep, and sustained participation. In particular, the participatory budget has been credited with creating a positive context for association, fostering greater activism, networking associations, and working from a citywide orientation (Baiocchi 2002a).

But what exactly do these new arenas offer social movements? According to some authors, the presence of such channels of access presents more risks than advantages. In the first place, movements are induced to accept the shifting of conflict from the streets to less congenial arenas, where resources in which they are lacking, such as technical or scientific expertise, are particularly important. The organization of a commission may be nothing more than a symbolic, elite gesture to constituencies and a means of delaying a decision until quieter times prevail (Lipsky 1965). Indeed, the creation of new procedures and institutional arenas can be seen as a means of co-opting movement elites and demobilizing the grassroots (if they are naive enough not to notice the deception) (Piven and Cloward 1977: 53). Mistrust in the real independence of NGOs is indicated by the proliferation of such acronyms as GONGOs (Government-Organized NGOs), BONGOs (Business-Organized NGOs), and GRINGOs (Government-Run/Initiated NGOs). NGOs are predominantly based in the North of the world (two-thirds of UN-registered NGOs have their headquarters in Europe and North America) (Sikkink 2002); and major associations, in particular, are organized hierarchically with limited transparency in the way they work (Schmidt and Take 1997; Sikkink 2002). Intergovernmental organizations have, furthermore, preferred dealing with larger, more top-heavy NGOs, that are less monitored by their base of support (Chandhoke 2002; Guiraudon 2002). While some NGOs were the first to mobilize against international financial institutions (in particular the World Bank, IMF, and WTO), protests developed due to skepticism regarding the efficacy of lobbying, coupled with a perception that large NGOs' reformist approach had failed (Brand and Wissen 2002). In a time of cutbacks in public spending, NGOs run the risk of being exploited to supplant an increasingly failing public service (Chandhoke 2002: 43). Moreover, adroitly manipulated experts can be used to legitimate as most "scientifically appropriate" those solutions which suit governments. Referenda address limited questions and mobilize public opinion only for very short periods; they also carry the risk that decisions will be made by the "silent majority," uninterested in (and uninformed about) the issues and problems raised by social movements, and therefore easily influenced by those with the most resources to devote to manipulating consensus. Some studies conclude that citizen participation in policymaking increases efficiency, but others express doubts about its capacity to solve free-rider problems and produce optimal decisions or facilitate the achievement of the public good (Renn et al. 1996; Petts 1997; Hajer and Kesselring 1999; Grant, Perl, and Knoepfel 1999).

In addition, alternative participatory models of democracy are difficult to implement. The levels of effective participation, plurality, and efficacy of new arenas of decision-making are varied and far from satisfactory. As for the pluralism of the new participatory arenas, since resources for collective mobilization are unequally distributed among social groups, poorer areas and groups risk being excluded by the new institutions of policymaking. Their effective capacity for decision-making is often minimal: for various reasons, new channels of participation have usually been limited to "consultation" of citizens. If increasing participation allows for more visibility – and accountability – of policymaking, parallel (and more effective) decision-making seems to bypass public arenas.

On the other hand, social movements have frequently been able to profit (partly through alliances with experts and policymakers) from the switching of decision-making to *ad hoc* commissions, certainly more open to public scrutiny than the normal arenas of policy implementation. New issues have been brought onto the public agenda through the work of such commissions: "Commissions were themselves part of the process during which the problems were defined and the agenda set . . . Their very creation indicated that the normal praxis of the political system to make decisions was insufficient, and that it was therefore necessary to appeal to the experts belonging to the scientific institutions"

(Willelms et al. 1993). Although social movements have not always been on the winning side in referenda, the latter have nonetheless contributed to putting new issues on the public agenda and to creating public sympathy for emergent actors. The ability to transform the rules of the political game, then, is a precondition for influencing public policy. In other words, procedural victories come (at least in part) before, and are indispensable for, successes on a more substantive level (Rochon and Mazmanian 1993). Enlarging policymaking to encompass citizen participation – in the forms of auditing, people's juries, etc. – has often helped in solving problems created by local opposition to locally unwanted land use (LULU) (Bobbio and Zeppetella 1999; Sintomer 2005). As we have mentioned, the participatory emphasis on good governance, as well as its confidence in popular education (Baiocchi 2001), seems to have produced positive results in terms of empowerment of citizens as well as improvement of their quality of life.

9.4 Social Movements and Democratic Theory

Leaving aside the results obtained on particular demands, it must be added that the spread of new policy arenas has contributed to the realization of what has been considered one of the principal aims, if not the principal aim, of many (if not all: see below) social movements: the development of a new conception of democracy. In fact, it has been claimed that social movements do not limit themselves to developing special channels of access for themselves but that, more or less explicitly, they expound a fundamental critique of conventional politics, thus shifting their endeavors from politics itself to metapolitics (Offe 1985). From this point of view, social movements affirm the legitimacy (if not the primacy) of alternatives to parliamentary democracy, criticizing both liberal democracy and the "organized democracy" of the political parties: "The stakes and the struggle of the left and libertarian social movements thus invoke an ancient element of democratic theory that calls for an organization of collective decision making referred to in varying ways as classical, populist, communitarian, strong, grassroots, or direct democracy against a democratic practice in contemporary democracies labeled as realist, liberal, elite, republican, or representative democracy" (Kitschelt 1993: 15).

According to this interpretation, social movements assert that a system of direct democracy is closer to the interests of the people than liberal democracy, which is based on delegation to representatives who can be controlled only at the moment of election and who have total authority to decide between one election and another. Moreover, as bearers of a neocommunitarian conception of democracy, social movements criticize the "organized" democratic model, based on the mediation by mass political parties and the structuring of "strong" interests, and seek to switch decision-making to more transparent and controllable sites. In the social movement conception of democracy the people themselves (who are naturally interested in politics) must assume direct responsibility for intervening in the political decision-making process.

It is certainly the case that the idea of democracy developed by social movements since the 1960s is founded on bases at least partly different to representative democracy. According to the representative democracy model, citizens elect their representatives and exercise control through the threat of their not being reelected at subsequent elections. The direct democracy favored by social movements rejects the principle of delegation, viewed as an instrument of oligarchic power, and asserts that representatives should be subject to recall at all times. Moreover, delegation is comprehensive in a representative democracy, where representatives decide on a whole range matters for citizens. In comparison, in a system of direct democracy, authority is delegated on an issue-by-issue basis. Whereas representative democracy envisages the creation of a specialized body of representatives, direct democracy opts for continual turnover. Representative democracy is based on formal equality (one person, one vote); direct democracy is participatory, the right to decide being recognized only in the case of those who demonstrate their commitment to the public cause. While representative democracy is often bureaucratic, with decision-making concentrated at the top, direct democracy is decentralized and emphasizes that decisions should be taken as near as possible to ordinary people's lives.

The global justice movement criticizes the functioning of advanced democracies. It addresses in particular the oligarchic functioning of political parties, the exclusionary implications of majority rule, the monopolization of public spheres of communication, and the exclusion of marginal groups and issues from their practice of democracy. Public decision-making processes have a low degree of transparency; the extreme simplification of the political messages induced by mass media formats is also criticized. However, movement organizations do not usually aim at abolishing the existing political parties, nor do they seek to found new ones; they demand the democratization of the old politics and institutions, parties, and trade unions, and they propose the constitution of alternative, open public spheres where different positions can be developed, analyzed, and compared on an openly-stated ethical basis (such as social justice, in the case of the participatory budget in Porto Alegre). An effective, pluralist media contest would be a minimum requirement for the development of this type of public sphere. In this sense, social movements are also a response to problems which have emerged in the system of interest representation, "compensating" for the tendency of political parties to favor interests which pay off in electoral terms, and of interest groups to favor those social strata better endowed with resources while marginalizing the rest (see chapter 8 above).

The principle of an empowered participatory democracy, mentioned above, links the traditional conception of participatory and direct democracy with political theorists' emerging interest in deliberative democracy – in particular, the quality of communication.[3] Deliberative theories have developed from concerns with the functioning of representative institutions; however, scholars of deliberative democracy disagree on the locus of deliberative discussion, some being concerned with the development of liberal institutions, others with alternative public spheres free from state intervention (della Porta 2005b). The analysis of the communicative quality of democracy is central to the work of Jürgen Habermas (1996), who postulates a double-track process, with "informal" deliberation taking place outside institutions and then, as it becomes public opinion, affecting institutional deliberation. According to other authors, however, deliberations take place in voluntary groups especially (Cohen 1989). A strong supporter of the latter position and an expert in movement politics, John Dryzek (2000), has argued that social movements are best placed to build deliberative spaces that can keep a critical eye upon public institutions. Jane Mansbridge (1996) has also argued that deliberation should take place in a number of enclaves, free from institutional power – including that of social movements themselves. If social movements nurture committed, critical attitudes towards public institutions, deliberative democracy requires citizens "embedded" in associative networks able to build democratic skills among their adherents (Offe 1997: 102–3). As the experiment of Porto Alegre indicates, in the movements for globalization from below, deliberative practices have indeed attracted a more or less explicit interest.

Trying to summarize various and not always coherent definitions, we suggest that participatory democracy is empowered when, under conditions of equality, inclusiveness, and transparency, a communicative process based on reason (the strength of a good argument) is able to transform individual preferences and reach decisions oriented to the public good (della Porta 2005d). Some of the dimensions of this definition (such as inclusiveness, equality, and visibility) echo those included in the participatory models we have described as typical of new social movements, while others (above all, the attention to the quality of communication) emerge as new concerns.

First, as in the movement tradition, empowered participatory democracy is inclusive: it requires that all citizens with a stake in the decisions to be taken be included in the process and able to express their voice. This means that the deliberative process takes place under conditions of a plurality of values, where people have different perspectives on their common problems. Taking the participatory budget as an example, assemblies are held in all districts and are open to all citizens; the choice of the time and place aim at facilitating participation of all interested people (even kindergartens are organized in order to help mothers and fathers to participate).

Additionally, all participants are equals: deliberation takes place among free and equal citizens (as "free deliberation among equals," Cohen 1989: 20). In fact, "all citizens must be able to develop those capacities that give them effective access to the public sphere," and "once in public, they must be given sufficient respect and recognition so as to be able to influence decisions that affect them in a favourable direction" (Bohman 1997: 523–4). Deliberation must exclude power deriving from coercion, but also from an unequal weighting of participants as representatives of organizations of different size or influence. In this sense, deliberative democracy opposes hierarchies and stresses direct rank-and-file participation. In the participatory budget, rules such as the limited time for each intervention or the presence of facilitators are designed to allow equal opportunities for all citizens to participate.

Moreover, the concept of transparency resonates with direct, participatory democracy. In Joshua Cohen's definition, a deliberative democracy is "an association whose affairs are governed by the *public* deliberation of its members" (1989: 17, emphasis added). In deliberative democratic theory, public debate strives to "replace the language of interest with the language of reason" (Elster 1998: 111): having to justify a position before a public forces one to look for justifications linked to common values and principles.

What is new in the conception of deliberative democracy, and in some of the contemporary movements' practices, is the emphasis on preference (trans)formation, with an orientation to the definition of the public good. In fact, "deliberative democracy requires the transformation of preferences in interaction" (Dryzek 2000: 79). It is "a process through which initial preferences are transformed in order to take into account the points of view of the others" (Miller 1993: 75). In this sense, deliberative democracy differs from conceptions of democracy as an aggregation of (exogenously generated) preferences. Some reflections on participatory democracy have also included practices of consensus: decisions must be approvable by all participants (unanimous) – in contrast with majoritarian democracy, where decisions are legitimated by votes. Deliberation (or even communication) is based on the belief that, while not giving up my perspective, I might learn if I listen to another (Young 1996).

Consensus is, however, possible only in the presence of shared values and a common commitment to the construction of a public good (such as the common value of social justice in the participatory schema). In a deliberative model of democracy, "the political debate is organized around alternative conceptions of the public good," and above all, it "draws on identities and citizens' interests in ways that contribute to public building of public good" (Cohen 1989: 18–19). A deliberative setting facilitates the search for a common end or good (Elster 1998).

Above all, deliberative democracy stresses reason: people are convinced by the force of the better argument. In particular, deliberation is based on horizontal flows of communication, multiple producers of content, wide opportunities for interactivity, confrontation on the basis of rational argumentation, and attitude to reciprocal listening (Habermas 1981, 1996). In this sense, deliberative democracy is discursive. According to Young, however, discourse does not exclude protest: "processes of engaged and responsible democratic participation include street demonstrations and sit-ins, musical works and cartoons, as much as parliamentary speeches and letters to the editor" (2003: 119).

Empowered participatory democracy has in fact been discussed as an alternative to top-down imposition of public decisions, which is increasingly seen as lacking legitimacy and becoming more difficult to manage, given both the increasing complexity of problems and the increasing ability of uninstitutionalized actors to make their voices heard. Deliberative processes should in fact allow the acquisition of better information and produce more efficient decisions, as well as fostering the participation and trust in institutions that representative models are less and less able to provide. Indeed, scholars highlight a "moralizing effect of the public discussion" (Miller 1993: 83) that "encourages people not to merely express political opinions (through surveys or referendums) but to form those opinions through a public debate" (ibid.: 89). Deliberation as a "dispassionate, reasoned, logical" type of communication promises to increase citizens' trust in political institutions (Dryzek 2000: 64).

As the Porto Alegre examples of both World Social Forums and participatory budgeting illustrate, movements experiment with participatory, discursive models of democracy both in their internal decision-making and in their interactions with political institutions. Internally, social movements have – with varying degrees of success – attempted to develop an organizational structure based on participation (rather than delegation), consensus-building (rather than majority vote), and horizontal networks (rather than centralized hierarchies). The search for a participatory model of internal democracy assumes an even more central role for the "global movement" that has mobilized transnationally, with regard to the governance of the process of market liberalization, with demands for a "globalization from below."

Internal democracy also represents a challenge for social movements, posing the always vivid dilemma of balancing participation and representation, strengthening the commitments of activists and including new members, identity-building and efficacy. Social movement organizations, traditionally poor in material resources, have to rely upon the voluntary work of their members – thus developing a "membership logic." Participatory models are adopted in order to enhance the distribution of identity incentives; in particular, the assembly represents the ideal opportunity for an open and (in principle) egalitarian space, while the small "affinity" groups stimulate the development of solidarity among equals. As with other forms of "applied" democracy, however, the practical functioning of these organizational structures is much less than perfect. Unstructured assemblies tend to be dominated by small minorities that often strategically exploit the weaknesses of direct democracy with open manipulation; "speech" resources are far from equally distributed; the most committed, or better organized, control the floor; solidarity links tend to exclude newcomers. Consensual models developed to contrast the "tyranny" of organized minorities have their own problems, mainly bound up with extremely long (and sometimes "blocked") decision processes.

When protest declines (and with it, resources of militancy), movement organizations tend to survive by institutionalizing their structure: they look for money, either by building a mass paper membership, selling products to a sympathetic public, or looking for public monies, in particular in the third-sector economy. Movement organizations – as recent research has indicated – tend therefore to become more and more similar to lobbying groups, with a paid, professional staff; commercial enterprise, with a focus on efficacy on the market; and voluntary associations, providing services, often contracted out by public institutions (della Porta 2003b). These changes have usually been interpreted as institutionalization of movement organizations, with ideological moderation, specialized identities, and the fading away of disruptive protest. This evolution produces critical effects: bureaucratization, while increasing efficiency, discourages participation from below; interactions with the state and public institutions raise the question of the "representativity" of these new lobbyists.

As far as the social movement critique of existing democracy is concerned, their search for an alternative cannot be considered to have concluded. Not all students of social movement organizations agree that they have overcome the risks of producing oligarchies and charismatic leaderships, the very problems at the center of their critique of traditional politics. Although it maximizes responsiveness, the direct democracy model has weaknesses as far as representation and efficiency are concerned (Kitschelt 1993). Problems of efficiency affect the success of movement organizations themselves; problems of representation concern the legitimation of new forms of democracy. The refusal by social movements to accept the principles of representative democracy can undermine their image as democratic actors, particularly when they begin to take on official and semi-official functions within representative institutions, assuming the form of parties or public interest groups. Social forums, bringing together heterogeneous actors, pay great attention to the quality of internal communication, but with unequal results.

These limitations notwithstanding, it should be recognized that social movements have helped to open new channels of access to the political system, contributing to the identification, if not the solution, of a number of representative democracy's problems. More generally, recent research has stressed the role social movements can play in helping to address two related challenges to democratic governance. On the input side, contemporary democracy faces a problem of declining political participation, at least in its conventional forms. The reduced capacity of political parties to bridge society and the state adds to this problem, while the commercialization of the mass media reduces their capacity to act as an arena for debating public decisions. On the other hand, the effectiveness of democracies in producing a just and efficient output is jeopardized, in part by the increasing risks in complex (and global) societies. The two problems are related, since the weakening in the ability of institutional actors to intervene in the formation of collective identities reduces their capacity to satisfy (more and more fragmented) demands. As Fung and Wright (2001) have stressed, "transformative democratic strategies" are needed to combat the increasing inadequacy of liberal democracy to realize its goals of political involvement of the people, consensus through dialogue, and public policies aimed at providing a society in which all citizens benefit from the nation's wealth.

9.5 Social Movements and Democratization

Can it be said, then, that social movements have contributed to the evolution of democracy? Charles Tilly (2004a: 125) stresses the existence of

> a broad correspondence between democratization and social movements. Social movements originated in the partial democratization that set British subjects and North-American colonists against their rulers during the eighteenth century. Across the nineteenth century, social movements generally flourished and spread where further democratization was occurring and receded when authoritarian regimes curtailed democracy. The pattern continued during the first and twenty-first century: the maps of full-fledged institutions and social movements overlap greatly.

If democratization promotes democracy via the broadening of citizens' rights and the public accountability of ruling elites, most, but not all, social movements support democracy. In fact, in pushing for suffrage enlargement or the recognition of associational rights, social movements contribute to democratization – "Gains in the democratization of state processes are perhaps the most important that social movements can influence and have the greatest systemic impacts" (Amenta and Caren 2004: 265). This was not always the case: some movements – e.g., fascist and neofascist ones – denied democracy altogether, while others – e.g., some New Left movements in Latin America – had the unwanted effect of producing a backlash in democratic rights (Tilly 2004b). Identity politics, such as those driving ethnic conflicts, often ended up in religious war and racial violence (Eder 2003).

Two different conceptions of the role played by social movements in the process of democratization have been singled out (Tilly 1993–4: 1). According to a "populist approach to democracy," emphasizing participation from below, "social movements contribute to the creation of a public space – social settings, separate both from governing institutions and from organizations devoted to production or reproduction, in which consequential deliberation over public affairs takes place – as well as sometimes contributing to transfers of power over states. Public space and transfers of power then supposedly promote democracy, at least under some conditions. To the "populist" approach is counterposed an "elitist" approach according to which democratization must be a top-down process, while an excess of mobilization leads to new forms of authoritarianism, since the elites feel afraid of too many and too rapid changes.

We can agree that social movements contribute to democratization only under certain conditions. In particular, only those movements that explicitly demand increased equality and protection for minorities promote democratic development. In fact, looking at the process of democratization it can be observed that collective mobilization has frequently created the conditions for a destabilization of authoritarian regimes, but it can also lead to an intensification of repression or the collapse of weak democratic regimes, particularly when social movements do not stick to democratic conceptions. While labor, student, and ethnic movements brought about a crisis in the Franco regime in Spain in the 1960s and 1970s, the worker and peasant movements and the fascist countermovements contributed to the failure of the process of democratization in Italy in the 1920s and 1930s (Tarrow 1995).

However, social movements often openly mobilized for democracy. They formed transnational alliances in order to overthrow authoritarian regimes. In Latin America as well as in Eastern Europe, although in different forms, social movements asked for democratization, producing a final breakdown of neofascism as well as socialist authoritarian governments. Research in various regions has stressed that the first steps of democratization include a demobilization of civil society and the developments of more institutionalized political actors, following the opening up of institutional opportunities. In recent democratization processes, the availability of public and private funds in the third sector contributed to an early institutionalization of movement organizations (Flam 2001). However, this does not necessarily seem to be the fate of movements in phases of democratic consolidation (Hipsher 1998). Presence of a tradition of mobilization, as well as movements that are independent from political parties, can facilitate the maintenance of a high level of protest – as illustrated by the shantytown dwellers' movement in Chile (Hipsher 1998); the urban movement in Brazil (Sandoval 1998); or the environmental movements in Eastern Europe (Flam 2001).

Although with breaks and irregularities, democracy has brought about decreasing inequalities and protection from arbitrary government interventions

(Tilly 2004a: 127). Can we say that, in struggling for democracy, social movements have succeeded in radically changing the power distribution in society? Many signs discourage one from excessive optimism. Protest goes in cycles, and what is won during peaks of mobilization is once again jeopardized during moments of latency. The labor movement contributed to creating many social and political rights, but the neoliberal turn at the end of the twentieth century called into question the welfare state that had appeared to be an institutionalized achievement from the 1970s. Social inequalities are again on the rise. If protest is more and more accepted as "normal politics," some forms of contentious politics are more and more stigmatized as uncivilized in public opinion and are repressed by the police.

On a more optimistic note, we want to stress that a condition that is considered to limit social movement potential, at least as far as instrumental action is concerned, is in the process of changing: weak organizational structures. In fact, mobilization would appear to be a resource replenished by use. Analyses of the evolution of left-libertarian movements has concluded that different movements have developed in a similar direction, from the formation of a collective identity to its utilization in the political system (see, for example, della Porta 1996a). New movement organizations have emerged during this process and have, on occasions, survived the decline in mobilization. While public interest groups exploit the opportunity offered by the creation of new channels of access, small counterculture nuclei keep alive and reelaborate movement values within a structure of networks. This process has important effects on social movements.

Most social movements survive the decline of mobilization, oscillating between visibility and latency (Melucci 1989: 70–3), continuing within a larger family of movements, the organizational infrastructures and mobilization potential of which they help to increase. The "force" of collective identities can vary, some stronger (the women's movement), others weaker (the youth movement); some relatively visible (the environmentalist movement), others less so (the peace movement); some have a stronger presence at the national level (the antinuclear movement), others at local level (the urban movements); some are more political (federalist movements), others cultural (punks and skinheads). It rarely happens that a movement disappears leaving no cultural or organizational trace whatsoever. Instead, movements tend to reproduce themselves in sorts of virtuous (or vicious) circles. As mentioned, during cycles of protest early-riser movements set the examples for activating other movements either in support, imitation, or opposition to themselves. Some movements depart from others, in order to pursue more specific or otherwise related aims, with a spillover effect; other rise from internal splits, as spin-offs (Whittier 2004: 534).

Social movement resources increase over time, therefore, and movements become institutionalized, construct subcultural networks, create channels of access to policymakers, and form alliances. This organizational continuity means that the experiences of "early-riser" movements are both resources and constraints for those that follow (Tarrow 1994; McAdam 1995). Processes of imitation and differentiation, enforced repetition and learning, take place contemporaneously. Movement activists inherit structures and models from their predecessors. At the same time, however, they learn from the errors of movements that have preceded them and seek to go beyond them. The greater the success achieved by early-riser movements and the greater the participation of ex-activists in subsequent mobilizations, the greater will be the continuity with the past.

The tendency towards the institutionalization of social movements and their diffusion as a form of organizing and mediating interests can be explained by the diffusion, with each wave of mobilization, of the capacities required for collective action. In fact, mobilization is facilitated by the presence of networks of activists willing to mobilize around new issues – where these are "compatible" with their original identities, naturally. Moreover, the substantive gains made by one movement can have beneficial consequences for the demands of other movements, and their success encourages further mobilizations. It can be concluded, therefore, that the importance of social movements tends to grow inasmuch as there is an ever-increasing amount of resources (both technical and structural) available for collective action. This surely contributed to the spread of participatory conceptions of democracy.

9.6 Summary

Social movement mobilization has been followed by change in a variety of areas. As far as public policy is concerned, a great deal of legislation has been produced on issues raised during protest campaigns. Any evaluation of the significance of the changes introduced by these laws requires analysis of their implementation as well as of transformations in the value system and in the behavior of both ordinary citizens and elites. Changes in public policy and public opinion have been accompanied by procedural changes, with the creation of new decision-making arenas no longer legitimated by the model of representative democracy. *Ad hoc* commissions, new government ministries, and local government committees constitute channels of access to the decision-making process frequently used by social movement organizations. Empowered participatory experiments have developed from the participatory agenda in Porto Alegre, characterized by attention to participation, good communication, and decisional power. Emphasis on participation over representation thus enriches the concept of democracy. In fact, with various degrees of success, social movements have recently paid attention to inclusive and equal participation, as well as consensus-building and good communication.

Although the variety of objectives, strategies, and actors involved in this process renders it difficult to identify winning strategies for new collective actors, it can, nevertheless, be said that in recent decades the structure of power in liberal democracies appears to have been transformed in the direction of greater recognition for new actors. Social movements have helped democratization in authoritarian regimes, but also contributed to more participatory approaches in representative democracies.

NOTES

Chapter 1: The Study of Social Movements

1 Theories of frustration and deprivation – to which we will make only fleeting reference in the course of this book – have decreased in importance from the 1970s onwards, and have become largely marginal in the analysis of social movements in democratic societies. They have, however, maintained some relevance in comparative, large-scale analyses of social conflict (Gurr and Harff 1994), and in the analysis of adhesion to undemocratic movements (Anheier 2003). For recent accounts, see Crossley (2002); Buechler (2004).

2 See Scott (1990: particularly ch. 3) for an excellent synthesis of the main positions developed by this approach during its most creative phase.

3 For several applications of this perspective in empirical researches on contemporary movements, see, for example, Touraine, Dubet, Hegedus, and Wieviorka (1981, 1983); Touraine, Hegedus, Wieviorka, and Strzelecki (1983).

4 In the most recent edition of this book, Turner and Killian (1987) integrated some contributions of the resource mobilization school into their model.

5 Attention to the link between collective behavior and various indicators of social change (for example, the tendency towards large-scale organizations, population mobility, technological innovation, the growing relevance of the mass media, the fall of traditional cultural forms) connects this view to functionalist perspectives, but the interpretation provided is different. The processes of change reviewed are considered to be emerging conditions which encourage individuals to mobilize, not in order to reestablish an equilibrium which has been disturbed, but rather to develop new ways of life and new types of social relationship.

6 Blumer comments: "Sociology in general is interested in studying the social order and its constituents (customs, rules, institutions, etc.) as they are. Collective behavior is concerned in studying the way in which the social order comes to existence in the sense of the emergence and solidification of new forms of collective behavior" (Blumer 1951: 169).

7 See, for example, Gusfield's research (1963) into the prohibitionist movement, considered as an area of conflict between social systems, cultures, and groups of different status.

8 "Community" is here defined as a "relatively small community of critical thinkers who have developed a sensitivity to some problem, an analysis of the source of the problem, and a prescription for what should be done about the problem" (Rochon 1998: 22).

9 Charles Tilly (1978: 53) has spoken, in this context, of movements as "challengers," contrasting them to established members of a given polity.

10 In our notion, the idea of "collective goods" comprises both public goods à la Olson and club goods. For Samuelson (1954) the key characteristics of public goods are: (1) non-excludability and (2) nonrivalrous consumption, i.e., no scarcity once the good is produced. A club good is: (1) non-excludable for club members but excludable for outsiders, (2) possibly (but not necessarily) nonrivalrous for those with access (Buchanan 1965).

11 We see consensus movements as forms of collective action that "are distinguished from conflict movements in terms of the degree to which each recognizes and acts on oppositions of objective social interests and seeks in direct and detailed fashion to change social policy" (Lofland 1989: 163). We prefer this analytical definition to others, simply taking the proportion of people supporting a given cause as the defining element (McCarthy and Wolfson 1992: 274).

12 See Hinckley (1981: 4–6), Lemieux (1997, 1998), Pakulski (1988), Jones, Hutchinson, van Dyke, and Gates (2001). Of course nothing prevents a coalitional dynamic from evolving into a social movement one, but it is still important to recognize the analytical difference between the two processes (see e.g. Warren 2001).

13 This makes it necessary to treat with some caution the results of surveys which claim to measure the extent of movement membership (Kriesi 1992).

14 It goes without saying that the real influence of individual participants will depend largely on their personal resources (competence, prestige etc.).

15 This logic of investigation may also be conveniently applied to the formation of many contemporary parties, definitely those which emerged from the aggregation of previously autonomous organizations (Panebianco 1988; Hedström, Sandell, and Stern 2000).

16 They include, first, analyses dedicated to various types of collective behavior: from religious movements (Wilson 1982; Robbins 1988) and counterculture (Yinger 1982) to voluntary action (Pearce 1993; Wilson 2000); from political violence and terrorism (della Porta 1990) to right-wing movements (Lo 1990; Ignazi 1994); not to mention analyses of working-class action itself (for example, Pizzorno et al. 1978; Touraine 1985; Kimeldorf and Stepan-Norris 1992; Franzosi 1995; Stepan-Norris and Zeitlin 2003; Fantasia and Voss 2004). To these we must add research, conducted from a historical perspective, into phenomena ranging from nationalism (Smith 1981; Breuilly 1993; Hobsbawm 1991) to revolutions (Skocpol 1979; Tilly 1993, 2004b); from social conflict in the premodern age (Goldstone 1991; Somers 1993) to "nonclass" movements of the modern period (D'Anieri et al. 1990; Amenta and Zylan 1991; Calhoun 1993; D'Anjou 1996). See also the increasing body of work devoted to contemporary movements outside Western democracies (Eckstein 2001; Escobar and Alvarez 1992; Shah 1990; Omvedt 1993; Joppke 1994; Foweraker 1995; Zirakzadeh 1997; Ray 1999; Osa 2003a; Ferree and McClurg Mueller 2004; Reifer 2004).

Chapter 2: Social Changes and Social Movements

1 See Markoff (1996) for a broad historical account of the development of social movements in contemporary society.

2 The experience of so-called "industrial districts" – small areas characterized by specific industrial activities, which are based on densely interwoven networks of social relationships (Piore and Sabel 1984; Streeck 1992; Trigilia 1984) – seems to contradict the claim regarding the delocalization of economy. However, the conditions for working-class action do not appear to be favorable in those contexts, given the density of ties between different social groups and the resulting increased opportunities for social control (Oberschall 1973).

3 On the new middle class – or service class, as some refer to it – see among many others Bell (1973); Gouldner (1979); Goldthorpe (1982); Lash and Urry (1987); Esping-Andersen (1993); Brint (1994).

4 See Giddens (1990) for a concise treatment of this point.

5 See, for example, the critique of psychiatric hospitals which developed in the course of the 1960s; see Crossley (1998, 1999).

6 Historically the affirmation of the welfare state marks the passage from a notion of (civil and political) rights understood, first, as "against" the state, to a notion of rights which presuppose cooperation "with" the state (Barbalet 1988). With the rise of multiculturalism, however, and more generally with the critique of the colonialization of the private sphere, the relationship with welfare and in general with state intervention becomes at the same time one of cooperation (inasmuch as one can identify positive elements in the expansion of welfare action) and of antagonism (in the need to limit the effects of standardization and control).

7 The most systematic treatment of the relationship between social movements and transformations in the private sphere is still that of Alberto Melucci, to which we refer readers (1989, 1996).

8 See, among others, Garofalo (1992); Redhead (1993); Jordan (1994); McKay (1996). Reference to recent countercultural or subcultural phenomena such as rap or rave should not hide the broader relationship which can be found between musical genres and different types of political protest (Eyerman and Jamison 1994, 1997).

9 Among students of social movements, even those who recognize the persistent importance of structural processes differ in their use of the concept of class. Some (for example Eder 1995) still regard it as a useful heuristic device, provided one refrains from filling it with references to the historical experience of industrial society; others (for example Melucci 1995) reject it precisely on the ground that historical experience has infused it with meanings which prevent its useful application to a modified context.

10 In the course of his long intellectual career, Touraine has proposed a number of versions of his approach (1977, 1981, 1984, 1985, 1992). Here we are referring principally to the formulation put forward during the 1970s, which inspired the research program "Intervention Sociologique" (Touraine et al. 1983a; Touraine et al. 1983b).

For a synthesizing but systematic presentation of Touraine's contribution see Rucht (1991b), as well as Touraine's response (1991).

11 Similar themes are found in the work of Habermas (1976); Melucci (1989); Giddens (1990); among others. For a critical synthesis see Scott (1990).

12 See, in particular, Melucci (1989, 1994, 1996). For a critical but sympathetic discussion, see Bartholomew and Mayer (1992). It has to be said that later developments in Melucci's work seem to focus much more on the structural processes – in particular, the individualization process – which prevent the reproduction of traditional collective action, rather than on the structural preconditions for the development of new forms of collective action. The latter is, rather, explained in the light of the presence of interpersonal networks acting as facilitators, the relationship of which to structural dynamics is, however, somewhat underdeveloped.

13 While the rise of the new middle class has been a central theme of sociological debate since the 1970s, the empirical investigation of its relationship with political action has been a major, albeit not exclusive (e.g. Bechofer and Elliott 1985), interest of political scientists. See, among many others, Dalton (1988, 1994); Kitschelt (1989), Kitschelt and Hellemans (1990); Jennings et al. (1990), Poguntke (1993), Nas (1993), Rohrschneider (1988, 1993b), Inglehart (1990a), and Wallace and Jenkins (1995).

14 Individuals who fulfill a supervisory function, rather than managers in a narrow sense, and semi-professionals and highly qualified craft workers are included in the new middle class (Kriesi 1989b, 1993).

15 This definition includes human service professionals with other sociocultural specialist figures who were previously treated in a different way (Brint 1984). See also Cotgrove and Duff (1980).

16 See Crompton (1993) for a summary of this traditional dilemma in class analysis, opposing notions of classes as aggregates to notions of classes as collective actors.

17 This uncertainty could also depend on the various operationalizations of the concept of new middle class adopted by the studies quoted here, not to mention the dependent variable selected. While Kriesi analyzed the potential for mobilization in various types of new social movements, studies such as that of Wallace and Jenkins concentrate on a form of action – political protest – which, though particularly widespread among movements, is certainly not limited to them. Extreme caution in the comparison of results obtained in different studies is required. See Kriesi (1992) for a discussion of how different criteria for the operationalization of the potential for mobilization of the various social movements can influence the results of the analysis.

18 See, for example, Pizzorno (1981) and Tarrow (1994). From a different perspective, see also Calhoun (1993) and D'Anieri et al. (1990).

Chapter 3: The Symbolic Dimension of Collective Action

1 We use the term "generation" here in the sense originally proposed by Karl Mannheim (1946), not as a specific age group but as a cohort of the population which

has experienced and remains influenced by particular historical events. See also on this theme Braungart and Braungart (1992), Turner (1994), Pakulski (1995), Whittier (1995, 1997), Johnston and Aareleid-Tart (2000).

2 This aspect of Inglehart's analysis has also been criticized, for neglecting analogies between the development of cultural change in the period following the Second World War and other periods over the last two centuries in which expressive orientations have led to change (Brand 1990; Inglehart 1990b).

3 Data on value change from 1970 onwards are available for six European countries (France, Great Britain, Italy, West Germany, Belgium, and the Netherlands; Inglehart 1990b). Surveys have gradually been extended to an ever-increasing number of countries, within and outside the Western world (Inglehart 1997; Inglehart and Norris 2003, 2005).

4 According to some critics: "Because [Inglehart's] index assumes that one cannot simultaneously embrace both postmaterialist and materialist values, the fundamental question of whether postmaterialist and materialist values necessarily exclude one another . . . is simply assumed" (Brooks and Manza 1994: 546).

5 The inevitable reference here is to *Utopia*, used by Karl Mannheim (1946) to denote the complex of symbolic challenges presented in various historical periods to ideology as constituted at the time. Analogous themes have also been touched upon by Ralph Turner (1969, 1994), referring explicitly to *Ideology and Utopia*; and Karl-Werner Brand (1990), who has associated cycles of insurgency in collective action with the *Zeitgeist* which characterizes the general climate of the time.

6 Derloshon and Potter (1982); Plumb (1993). This is not to forget the strong element of economic, redistributive, and class conflict present in North American movements – especially in the African American movements (Morris 1984) and generally in movements of the poor (Piven and Cloward 1977).

7 This is, incidentally, a reason why the reception of mobilization messages from virtual actors – e.g. through websites – is problematic unless their sources also have a "tangible" identity (Diani 2000b; van de Donk, Loader, Nixon, and Rucht 2004).

8 See Tarrow (1998) for a broad analysis of the processes of production of interpretative schemata on the part of various movements in the nineteenth and twentieth centuries.

Chapter 4: Collective Action and Identity

1 We have reported the sources of the various quotations as published in the original texts. This explains the discrepancy in the style of referencing.

2 Roseneil (1995); see also Johnston (1991b: ch. 7) on the relationship between nationalist and working-class identity in Catalonia.

3 See Seligman (1992) on the role of trust in the emergence of civil society and Tilly (2002: ch. 14; 2004b) on trust networks in democratization processes.

4 But there are interpretations suggesting identity need not necessarily be associated with the time dimensions, e.g. Somers' (1993) analysis of the building of citizenship in modern England.

5   This is not always true, however: the research project directed by Alberto Melucci in Milan in the early 1980s showed how adherents to local neo-oriental groups had often been converted in less drastic ways (Diani 1984, 1986).

6   Calhoun (1994a: 26) has spoken, on this point, of "in-group essentialism."

7   For a now classic critique of this view: Touraine (1981); Melucci (1982, 1989, 1996).

8   See Stoecker (1995) for an interesting discussion of the relationship between different levels of identity: individual, community, movement, and organizational.

9   See DeNardo (1985) and Chong (1991) for discussions of the rationality of collective action. See also Hargreaves Heap et al. (1992) for an introduction to rational-choice theories.

10 This section is partially inspired by John Lofland's (1995: 192 ff.) analysis of the cultural forms of movements.

Chapter 5: Individuals, Networks, and Participation

1   Along similar lines, Kitts (2000) has differentiated between *information*, *identity*, and *exchange* mechanisms. "Information" refers to the capacity of networks to create opportunities for participation; "identity," to the fact that social ties to significant others create and reproduce solidarity; "exchange," to the informal circulation of social approval, rewards, and sanctions through networks. McAdam (2003) has identified four crucial mechanisms: recruitment attempts, identity–movement linkages, positive and negative influence attempts (see also Klandermans 1984; Opp, 1989; Opp and Gern 1993; Passy 2001; della Porta 1988).

2   For diverging views on the persistent role of class in politics see among others Esping-Andersen (1993); Pakulski and Waters (1996); Devine (1997); Evans (1999).

3   Network analysts define cliques as groups of actors characterized by a particularly high intensity of internal relationships: in the most extreme case, by the presence of direct contact among all the components of the group in question (Knoke and Kuklinski 1982: 56).

4   The project was coordinated by Stefaan Walgrave at the University of Antwerp and covered Belgium, England, Germany, Holland, Italy, Scotland, Spain, Switzerland, and the USA (Walgrave and Rucht forthcoming; della Porta and Diani 2005).

Chapter 6: Social Movements and Organizations

1   Sources of funding and membership size are also related here.

2   While rather frequent for established interest groups, the mobilization of resources from small groups of wealthy – individual or corporate – sponsors has traditionally been rare in the case of social movements. However, in recent years cooperation between movement organizations and, for example, the business world has gradually, albeit slowly, increased in areas like environmental or consumer protection (Donati 1996).

3   Roth (1994) has analyzed the role of such countercultures in the German *Alterna-tivenbewegung*. It should be noted, however, that the phenomenon is not peculiar to new social movements. In the labor movement, for example, "the party, unions and cultural and service associations provided the physical and social space in which an alternative community could develop" (Nolan 1981: 301).

4   McCarthy and Zald (1987b [1977]) distinguish between potential beneficiaries, who directly gain from the movement accomplishing its aims, and conscience adherents, who are part of a social movement but would not directly benefit from its success. On this basis they then differentiate between "classical SMOs," which focus upon ben-eficiary adherents for resources, and "professional SMOs," which appeal primarily to a conscience constituency and involve very few of their members in organiza-tional work.

5   Similarly, James Q. Wilson (1973) distinguishes between primary organizations, where there is a high degree of member participation, and caucus organizations, in which a large but inactive base finances a small number of active leaders.

6   This has been noted of the evolution of extremist organizations (della Porta 1995), but also of other social movement organizations, particularly the most identity ori-ented. On the United States women's movement, for example, see Mansbridge (1986: 191) and Krasniewicz (1992).

7   The institutionalization of political parties implies a passage from a system of ration-ality in which ideology dictates organizational goals, collective incentives predomi-nate, and control is exercised over the environment, to one of interests, in which the main goal is survival, incentives are selective, and the environment is adapted to (Panebianco 1988).

8   On organizational dynamics during protest campaigns see Gerhards (1991, 1993), Gerhards and Rucht (1992).

9   The suggestion that proportional representation electoral systems favor the emer-gence of political parties linked to social movements (e.g. Brand 1985: 324) has been confirmed by comparative research on European green parties. As Chris Rootes notes: "In general, in countries with federal constitutions and proportional repre-sentation electoral systems, the institutional matrix is much more favorable for the development and success of Green parties . . . than it is in centralized unitary states with majoritarian electoral systems" (Rootes 1994: 6).

Chapter 7: Action Forms, Repertoires, and Cycles of Protest

1   Barnes et al. (1979), had already noticed that in Great Britain, the United States, and West Germany the percentage of those who responded "unconventional political action, like demonstration" to the question "What can a citizen do about a local reg-ulation considered unjust or harmful?" had been increasing. In Great Britain the per-centage thus responding had grown from 0.2 percent in 1959–60 to 7.1 percent in 1974 (6.9); in the United States the figure had risen from 0.5 percent to 6.9 (6.4); and in West Germany it had increased from 0.7 percent to 7.8 (7.1) (Barnes et al. 1979:

143). A similar trend existed in responses concerning unjust national legislation, with the percentage of those willing to consider unconventional action rising from 0 to 4.3 percent in Great Britain, 0.3 to 3.6 percent in the United States, and 1.9 to 9.5 percent in West Germany (1979: 144).

2 Tilly defines contention as common action bearing directly on the interests of another acting group (Tilly 1986: 382).

3 Examples of the parochial and patronage-based repertoire include food riots, collective invasions of property, destruction of toll gates and other barriers, machine breaking, charivaris and serenades; physical expulsion of tax officers, foreign workers, or other outsiders; tendentious holiday parades; battles between villages; the pulling down or sacking of private houses; mock or popular trials and turnouts (Tilly 1986: 392–3).

4 Among others, Carty 2002 on the antisweatshop movement and Nike boycott; Rosenkrands 2004 on anticorporate online activities.

5 In research on the political integration of ethnic minorities, "positive radical flank effects" have been mentioned: "radical groups may bring about a greater level of responsiveness to the claims of moderates, either by making the latter appear more 'reasonable' or by creating a crisis which can be solved by the lesser concessions required by the moderates" (Haines 1988: 167; see also Button 1978). These positive effects are associated with direct action rather than rioting (Haines 1988: 171). Gamson (1990) similarly noted that it was willingness to use noninstitutional rather than violent means which favored social movement victories.

6 In considering the widespread debate on the civil rights movement of the time, Lipsky observed that the leaders of protest often face a choice between two equally risky paths: radicalism, which alienates external support, and moderation, which undermines the solidarity of their base. A radical leadership style, the aim of which is to win status through "acting tough," will be effective in enhancing internal cohesion. A moderate leadership style, which aims to broaden the welfare state through peaceful action, will take greater account of external objectives.

7 While more moderate action has become increasingly legitimate, this is not true of more radical forms. From 1974 to 1981 support for petitioning had grown from 22 percent to 63 percent in Great Britain and support for legal demonstrations from 6 percent to 10 percent. The equivalent figures were 30 percent to 46 percent and 9 percent to 14 percent in Germany. Support for direct action such as occupations remained rooted at around 1 to 2 percent (Dalton 1988: 65). See also Norris 2002, quoted above.

8 A further observation can be made. Until now, in discussions about the strategic choices open to social movements, their leaders have generally been treated as a unitary group. In reality, social movements are composite actors: their organizations and networks interact, choosing at least partially different directions. As already noted, Greenpeace specializes in direct action while the Green grouping in the European parliament follows the logic of parliamentary democracy; some organizations called for a boycott of French goods while others considered such action counterproductive. This diversity of strategy may be positive since different organizations will be able to speak to different sectors of public opinion. However, it needs to be

remembered that the single organizations within a movement compete with each other as well as cooperating. A particular organization's choice of strategy is also motivated, therefore, by the need to carve out a niche in the wider "market" of the movement (McCarthy and Zald 1987b [1977]). These choices are not always beneficial to the movement as a whole, as the damaging effects of terrorist organizations on the less radical groups from which they sprang tragically testifies (della Porta 1995).

9   For an example of such escalation see the very detailed description of student protest at Berkeley in 1964 by Max Heirich (1971).

10   The concept of "diffusion" has been imported into social science from physics, more exactly from studies of the diffusion of certain kinds of waves from one system to another. In the social sciences it has been used to explain the transfer across time and space of particular cultural traits, information, or ideas.

11   Cyclical patterns have been observed in strike activity, for example; and their relationship with Kondratieff's economic cycles studied. Similarly, cycles of revolution have been linked to population growth and decline (Frank and Fuentes 1994).

Chapter 8: The Policing of Protest

1   The reconstruction of events is based upon Andretta, della Porta, Mosca, and Reiter 2002: ch. 1.

2   McAdam (1982) identified three important factors in the emergence and development of the movement: its alignment within the larger political context (political opportunity structure); the level of organization of the aggrieved population (organization potential); and its assessment of the chances of success (insurgent consciousness).

3   In his comparison of the French, German, Swedish and American antinuclear movements, Herbert Kitschelt (1986: 61–4) distinguished between the conditions which influence demands entering the political system and those influencing its output in terms of public policy. On the input side, a large number of political parties, the capacity of the legislature to develop and control policy independently of the executive, pluralist patterns of mediation between interest groups and the executive branch, and the possibility of building policy coalitions (i.e., mechanisms for demand aggregation) are indicators of openness. On the output side, the capacity of the political system to implement policies is indicated by a centralized state apparatus, government control over the market, and a low level of judicial independence from the other arms of the state.

4   In fact, in the United States Eisinger (1973) found a greater degree of openness in local government regimes where electors had more control over administrators.

5   Kriesi notes that while on the input side the degree of formal access to the state increases with territorial decentralization; the separation of executive, legislature, and judiciary; low levels of coherence, internal coordination, and professionalization in the public administration; and the presence of direct democratic procedures, the same factors produce the opposite effects on the output side: "Federal, fragmented

and incoherent states with direct democratic institutions find it particularly difficult to arrive at decisions and to impose them on society" (Kriesi 1995: 172).

6 During the occupation of a community center in Zurich, for example, the local authorities' decision to leave management of the facilities with the young people in occupation was twice overturned by a popular referendum (Kriesi 1984).

7 Both small countries open to international markets, the Netherlands and Switzerland adopted a system of consensual democracy, characterized by special protection for minority rights, which has avoided the fragmentation of the state under the pressures of ethnic differences (religious in the Netherlands, linguistic in Switzerland). On consensual democracy, see Lijphart (1984); on the "small" democracies, Katzenstein (1985).

8 According to a poll taken in 1981 comparing France and Great Britain, 26 percent in the former and 10 percent in the latter had taken part in legal demonstrations. There was also greater tolerance in France for nonviolent illegal action such as unofficial strikes (10 and 7 percent) and occupations (7 and 2 percent) (Dalton 1988: 65).

9 The number of days per 1,000 workers lost through strikes between 1965 and 1974 was a great deal higher in countries with a pluralist system (1,660 in Italy, 1,330 in the United States, 740 in Great Britain, and 810 in Finland) than it was in countries with a neocorporatist one (270 in the German Federal Republic, 70 in the Netherlands, 40 in Switzerland, and 20 in Austria) (Wallace and Jenkins 1995: 106).

10 According to Frank L. Wilson (1990), however, the level of neocorporatism has no influence on indicators of mobilization such as public attitudes towards a social movement, inclination to support a cause, or willingness to use nonconventional protest tactics.

11 Moreover, changes in the attitudes of social democratic parties do not always coincide with entering or leaving office. They can be anticipated where a perception of electoral instability or conflict within elites open a "window of opportunity" for social movements. On the other hand, a change in attitude may be delayed after leaving government, particularly where too much openness towards new movements is held responsible for electoral misfortune.

12 According to DeNardo, the effectiveness of violence is influenced by regime responsiveness and the distribution of preferences concerning dissidents' demands: "When the bulk of the movement's potential support lies near its demands, however, the constraints on escalations are relaxed considerably" (DeNardo 1985: 223).

Chapter 9: Social Movements and Democracy

1 Although one speaks of the "successes" obtained by a socialist party in government or by a trade union, the same problems identified concerning social movements are also likely to be met in such cases.

2 Just to give one example, Amnesty International – which has often adhered to antiglobalization protests – could in 2000 count on the support, including funding, of

over one million members organized in formal national branches in 56 countries (Schneider 2000; Anheier and Themudo 2002: 193).

3 Similarly, concepts such as associative democracy (Hirst 1994) or radical democracy (Mouffe 1996) also stress the need for complementing representative democracy with alternative models of democracy.

REFERENCES

Abramson, Paul R. and Inglehart, Ronald 1992: Generational Replacement and Value Change in Eight West European Societies. *British Journal of Political Science*, 22, 183–228.

Agger, Ben 1991: Critical Theory, Poststructuralism, Postmodernism: Their Sociological Relevance. *Annual Review of Sociology*, 17, 105–31.

Agnoletto, Vittorio 2003: *Prima persone. Le nostre ragioni contro questa globalizzazione.* Roma: Laterza.

Aguiton, Christophe 2001: *Le monde nous appartient.* Paris: Plon.

Alberoni, Francesco 1984: *Movement and Institution.* New York: Columbia University Press.

Allegretti, Giovanni 2003: *L'insegnamento di Porto Alegre. Autoprogettualità come paradigma urbano.* Firenze: Alinea.

Amenta, Edwin and Neal, Caren 2004: The Legislative, Organizational, and Beneficiary Consequencesof State Oriented Challengers. In Davis A. Snow, Sarah H. Soule, and Hanspeter Kriesi (eds.), *The Blackwell Companion to Social Movements*, Oxford, Blackwell, 461–88.

Amenta, Edwin and Zylan, Yvonne 1991: It Happened Here: Political Opportunity, the New Institutionalism, and the Townsend Movement. *American Sociological Review*, 56, 250–65.

Amenta, Edwin, and Young, Michael P. 1999: Democratic States and Social Movements. Theoretical Arguments and Hypotheses. *Social Problems*, 46, 153–72.

Amin, Ash (ed.) 1994: *Post-Fordism.* Oxford: Blackwell.

Aminzade, Ronald 1995: Between Movements and Party: The Transformation of Mid-nineteenth-century French Republicanism. In J. C. Jenkins and B. Klandermans (eds.), *The Politics of Social Protest. Comparative Perspectives on States and Social Movements.* Minneapolis: University of Minnesota Press, 39–62.

Ancelovici, Marcos 2002: Organizing against Globalization: The Case of ATTAC in France. *Politics and Society*, 30, 427–63.

Anderson, Benedict 1983: *Imagined Communities.* London: Verso.

Andretta, Massimiliano 2003: Making transnational social movements work. Master, sectorial and individual frames and identitification. Paper for the Seminar *Social Movements and Contentious Politics in a Democratizing World*, Villa Serbelloni, Bellagio, July (forthcoming as ch. 3 in della Porta, Andretta, Mosca, and Reiter, *Global, Noglobal, New Global.* Minneapolis: University of Minnesota Press, 2005).

Andretta, Massimiliano, della Porta, Donatella, Mosca, Lorenzo, and Reiter, Herbert 2002: *Global, Noglobal, New Global. La protesta contro il G8 a Genova.* Roma: Laterza.

Andretta, Massimiliano, della Porta, Donatella, Mosca, Lorenzo, and Reiter, Herbert 2003: *Global – new global. Identität und Strategien der Antiglobalisierungsbewegung.* Frankfurt am Main: Campus Verlag.

Andrews, Kenneth and Edwards, Bob 2004: Advocacy Organizations in the US Political Process. *Annual Review of Sociology*, 30, 479–506.

Andrews, Kenneth and Edwards, Bob 2005: The Structure of Local Environmentalism. Unpublished paper.

Anheier, Helmut 2003: Movement Development and Organizational Networks: The Role of "Single Members" in the German Nazi Party, 1925–1930. In M. Diani and D. McAdam (eds.), *Social Movements and Networks*. Oxford/New York: Oxford University Press.

Anheier, Helmut and Themudo, Nuno 2002: Organizational Forms of Global Civil Society: Implications of Going Global. In Marlies Glasius, Mary Kaldor and Helmut Ahheier (eds.), *Global Civil Society 2002*. Oxford: Oxford University Press, 191–216.

Anheier, Helmut, Glasius, Marlies, and Kaldor, Mary 2001: Introducing Global Civil Society. In Helmut Ahheier, Marlies Glasius, and Mary Kaldor (eds.), *Global Civil Society 2001*. Oxford: Oxford University Press, 3–22.

Ansell, Christopher 1997: Symbolic Networks: The Realignment of the French Working Class, 1887–1894. *American Journal of Sociology*, 103, 359–90.

Ansell, Christopher 2001: *Schism and Solidarity in Social Movements. The Politics of Labor in the French Third Republic.* Cambridge: Cambridge University Press.

Ansell, Christopher 2003: Community Embeddedness and Collaborative Governance in the San Francisco Bay Area Environmental Movement. In M. Diani and D. McAdam (eds.), *Social Movements and Networks*. Oxford/New York: Oxford University Press.

Armstrong, Elizabeth 2002: *Forging Gay Identities: Organizing Sexuality in San Francisco, 1950–1994.* Chicago: University of Chicago Press.

Arrighi, Giovanni and Silver, Beverly 1999: *Chaos and Governance in the Modern World System.* Minneapolis: University of Minnesota Press.

Arrighi, Giovanni, Hopkins, Therence K., and Wallerstein, Immanuel 1989: *Antisystemic Movements.* London: Verso.

Auyero, Javier 2001: Glocal Riots. *International Sociology*, 16, 33–53.

Auyero, Javier 2004: When Everyday Life, Routine Politics, and Protest Meet. *Theory and Society*, 33, 417–41.

Ayres, Jeffrey M. 1998: *Defying Conventional Wisdom: Political Movements and Popular Contention against North American Free Trade.* Toronto: University of Toronto Press.

Ayres, Jeffrey 2004: Framing Collective Action Against Neoliberalism: The Case of the Anti-Globalization Movement. *Journal of World Systems Research*, 10, 11–34.

Bachrach, Peter and Baratz, Morton S. 1970: *Power and Poverty: Theory and Action.* New York: Oxford University Press.

Bagguley, Paul 1991: *From Protest to Acquiescence: Political Movements of the Unemployed.* London: Macmillan.

Bagguley, Paul 1992: Social Change, the Middle Class and the Emergence of "New Social Movements": A Critical Analysis. *Sociological Review*, 40, 26–48.

Bagguley, Paul 1994: Prisoners of the Beveridge Dream? The Political Mobilization of the Poor against Contemporary Welfare Regimes. In R. Burrows and B. Loader (eds.), *Towards a Post-Fordist State?* London: Macmillan.

Bagguley, Paul 1995a: Middle Class Radicalism Revisited. In T. Butler and M. Savage (eds.), *Social Change and the Middle Classes*. London: UCL Press.

Bagguley, Paul 1995b: Protest, Poverty and Power: A Case Study of the Anti-Poll Tax Movement. *Sociological Review*, 43, 693–719.

Baiocchi, Gianpaolo 2001: Participation, Activism, and Politics: The Porto Alegre Experiment and Deliberative Democratic Theory. *Politics and Society*, 29, 43–72.

Baiocchi, Gianpaolo 2002a: Synergizing Civil Society: State–Civil Society Regimes in Porto Alegre, Brazil. *Political Power and Social Theory*, 15, 3–52.

Baiocchi, Gianpaolo 2002b: *From Militance to Citizenship: The Workers' Party, Civil Society, and the Politics of Participatory Governance in Porto Alegre, Brazil*. Dissertation Abstracts International, A: The Humanities and Social Sciences; Available from UMI, Ann Arbor, MI. Order No. DA3020749.

Balme, Richard, Chabanet, Didier, and Wright, Vincent (eds.) 2002: *L'action collective en Europe*. Paris, Presses de Sciences Po.

Balser, Deborah B. 1997: The Impact of Environmental Factors on Factionalism and Schism in Social Movement Organizations. *Social Forces*, 76, 199–228.

Banaszac, Lee A. and Plutzer, Eric 1993: The Social Bases of Feminism in the European Community. *Public Opinion Quarterly*, 57, 29–53.

Banaszak, Lee Ann, Beckwith, Karen, and Rucht, Dieter 2003: *When Power Relocates: Interactive Changes in Women's Movements and the State*. In Lee Ann Banaszak, Karen Beckwith, and Dieter Rucht (eds.), *Women's Movements Facing the Reconfigured State*. Cambridge: Cambridge University Press, 1–29.

Bandy, Joe and Bickham-Mendez, Jennifer 2003: A Place of Their Own? Women Organizers in the Maquilas of Nicaragua and Mexico. *Mobilization*, 8, 173–88.

Bandy, Joe and Smith, Jackie (eds.) 2004: *Coalitions Across Borders: Negotiating Difference and Unity in Transnational Struggles Against Neoliberalism*. Lanham, MD: Rowman and Littlefield.

Barbalet, Jack M. 1988: *Citizenship*. Milton Keynes: Open University Press.

Barcena, Inaki, Ibarra, Pedro and Zubiaga, Mario 1995: *Nacionalismo y ecologia. Conflicto e institucionalizacion en el movimiento ecologista vasco*. Madrid: Libros de la Catarata.

Barkan, Steven E., Cohn, Steven F., and Whitbaker, William H. 1995: Beyond Recruitment: Predictors of Differential Participation in a National Antihunger Organization. *Sociological Forum*, 10, 113–33.

Barker, Colin 2001: Fear, Laughter, and Collective Power: The Making of Solidarity at the Lenin Shipyard in Gdansk, Poland, August 1980. In J. Goodwin, J. M. Jasper, and F. Polletta (eds.), *Passionate Politics*. Chicago: University of Chicago Press, 175–94.

Barker, Colin and Dale, Gareth 1999: Protest Waves in Western Europe: A Critique of New Social Movement Theory. *Critical Sociology*, 24, 65–104.

Barker, Colin, Johnson, Alan, and Lavalette, Michael (eds.) 2001: *Leadership in Social Movements*. Manchester: Manchester University Press.

Barnes, Barry and Edge, David (eds.) 1982: *Science in Context*. Milton Keynes: Open University Press.

Barnes, Samuel H., Kaase, Max, Allerbeck, Klaus, Farah, Barbara, Heunks, Felix, Ingle-hart, Ronald, Jennings, M. Kent, Klingemann, Hans D., Marsh Alan, and Rosenmayr, Leopold 1979: *Political Action*. London / Newbury Park, CA: Sage.

Bartholomew, Amy and Mayer, Margit 1992: Nomads of the Present: Melucci's Contri-bution to "New Social Movement" Theory. *Theory, Culture and Society*, 9, 141–59.

Bartolini, Stefano 2000: *The Political Mobilization of the European Left*. Cambridge, Cam-bridge University Press.

Bartolini, Stefano 2004: Trasformazione e trascendenza dei confini. Integrazione europea e stato-nazione. *Rivista italiana di scienza politica*, 34, 167–95.

Bartolini, Stefano and Mair, Peter 1990: *Identity, Competition and Electoral Availability. The Stabilization of European Electorates*. Cambridge: Cambridge University Press.

Battistelli, Fabrizio (ed.) 1990: *Rapporto di ricerca su: I movimenti pacifisti in Italia*. Gaeta: Rivista Militare.

Bauss, Gerhard 1977: *Die Studentenbewegung der sechziger Jahre*. Köln: Pahl-Rugenstein Verlag.

Bearman, Peter S. and Everett, Kevin D. 1993: The Structure of Social Protest, 1961–1983. *Social Networks*, 15, 171–200.

Bechofer, Frank and Elliott, Brian 1985: The Petite Bourgeoisie in Late Capitalism. *Annual Review of Sociology*, 11, 181–207.

Beck, John 1999: Makeover or Takeover? The Strange Death of Educational Autonomy in Neo-liberal England, *British Journal of Sociology of Education*, 20, 223–38.

Beck, Ulrich 1999: *Che cos'è la globalizzazione: Rischi e prospettive della società planetaria*. Roma: Carocci.

Becker, Penny E. and Dhingra, Pawan 2001: Religious Involvement and Volunteering: Implications for Civil Society. *Sociology of Religion*, 62, 315–35.

Beer, William R. 1977: The Social Class of Ethnic Activists in Contemporary France. In M. J. Esman (ed.), *Ethnic Conflict in the Western World*. Ithaca / London: Cornell Univer-sity Press, 143–58.

Beer, William R. 1980: *The Unexpected Rebellion: Ethnic Activism in Contemporary France*. New York: Columbia University Press.

Beissinger, Mark R. 2002: *Nationalist Mobilization and the Collapse of the Soviet Union*. Cam-bridge: Cambridge University Press.

Bell, Daniel 1973: *The Coming of Post-Industrial Society*. New York: Basic Books.

Benford, Robert D. 1993: Frame Disputes within the Nuclear Disarmament Movement. *Social Forces*, 71, 677–701.

Benford, Robert D. 1997: An Insider's Critique of the Social Movement Framing Per-spective. *Sociological Inquiry*, 67, 409–30.

Benford, Robert D. and Hunt, Scott A. 1992: Dramaturgy and Social Movements: The Social Construction and Communication of Power. *Sociological Inquiry*, 62, 36–55.

Benford, Robert D. and Snow, David 2000: Framing Processes and Social Movements. *Annual Review of Sociology*, 26, 611–39.

Bennani-Chraïbi, Mounia and Fillieule, Olivier 2003: *Résistances et protestations dans les sociétés musulmanes*. Paris: Presses de Sciences Po.

Bennett, W. Lance 2003: Communicating Global Activism: Strengths and Vulnerabilities of Networked Politics. *Information, Communication & Society*, 6 (2), 143–68.

Bennett, W. Lance 2004a: Communicating Global Activism: Strength and Vulnerabilities of Networked Politics. In W. van de Donk, B. Loader, P. Nixon, and D. Rucht (eds.), *Cyberprotest*. London: Routledge.

Bennett, W. Lance 2004b: Social Movements beyond Borders: Understanding Two Eras of Transnational Activism. In D. della Porta and S. Tarrow (eds.), *Transnational Protest and Global Activism*. Lanham, MD: Rowman & Littlefield, 203–26.

Bennett, W. Lance, Givens, Terry E., and Willnat, Larse 2004: Crossing Political Divide: Internet Use and Political Identification in Transnational Anti-War and Social Justice Activists in Eight Nations. Paper presented at the ECPR Joint Sessions, Uppsala.

Berezin, Mabel 2001: Emotions and Political Identity. In J. Goodwin, J. M. Jasper, and F. Polletta (eds.), *Passionate Politics*. Chicago: University of Chicago Press, 83–91.

Berger, Peter and Luckmann, Thomas 1966: *The Social Construction of Reality. A Treatise in the Sociology of Knowledge*. Garden City, NY: Anchor Books.

Bergmann, Werner 2002: Exclusionary Riots: Some Theoretical Considerations. In C. Hoffmann et al. (eds.), *Exclusionary Violence. Antisemitic Riots in Modern German History*. Ann Arbor: University of Michigan Press, 161–83.

Berkowitz, Steve D. 1982: *An Introduction to Structural Analysis: The Network Approach to Social Research*. Toronto: Butterworths.

Bernstein, Mary 1997: Celebrations and Suppression: The Strategic Use of Identity by the Lesbian and Gay Movement. *American Journal of Sociology*, 103, 531–65.

Béroud, Sophie, Mouriaux, René, and Vakaloulis, Michel 1998: *Le movement social en France. Essai de sociologie politique*. Paris: La Dispute.

Best, Joel (ed.) 1989: *Images of Issues: Typifying Contemporary Social Problems*. New York: de Gruyter.

Betz, Hans-Georg 1993: The New Politics of Resentment. Radical Right-wing Populist Parties in Western Europe. *Comparative Politics*, 25, 413–27.

Betz, Hans Georg 1994: *Radical Right-wing Populism in Western Europe*. Basingstoke: Macmillan.

Bew, Paul, Gibbon, Peter, and Patterson, Henry 1979: *The State in Northern Ireland, 1921–72: Political Forces and Social Classes*. Manchester: Manchester University Press.

Bianchi, Marina and Mormino, Maria 1984: Militanti di se stesse. Il movimento delle donne a Milano. In A. Melucci (ed.), *Altri codici*. Bologna: il Mulino, 127–74.

Billig, Michael 1995: Rhetorical Psychology, Ideological Thinking, and Imagining Nationhood. In H. Johnston and B. Klandermans (eds.), *Social Movements and Culture*. Minneapolis/London: University of Minnesota Press/UCL Press, 64–81.

Biorcio, Roberto 1991: La lega come attore politico: Dal federalismo al populismo regionalista. In R. Mannheimer et al. *la Lega Lombarda*, Milan: Feltrinelli, 34–82.

Biorcio, Roberto 1992: The Rebirth of Populism in Italy and France. *Telos*, 90, 43–56.

Bircham, Emma and Charlton, John (eds.) 2001: *Anti-Capitalism. A Guide to the Movement*. London/Sydney: Bookmarks Publications.

Blee, Kathleen M. 2002: *Inside Organized Racism: Women in the Hate Movement*. Berkeley: University of California Press.

Blumer, Herbert 1951: Social Movements. In A. McClung Lee (ed.), *Principles of Sociology*. New York: Barnes & Nobles, 199–220.

Blumer, Herbert 1971: Social Problems as Collective Behavior. *Social Problems*, 18, 298–306.

Bobbio, L., and Zeppetella, A. (eds.) 1999: *Perché proprio qui? Grandi opere e opposizioni locali*. Milano, Franco Angeli.

Bock, Hans-Manfred 1976: *Geschichte des linken Radikalismus in Deutschland. Ein Versuch*. Frankfurt/M.: Suhrkamp Verlag.

Bohman, James 1997: Deliberative Democracy and Effective Social Freedom: Capabilities, Resources, and Opportunities. In James Bohman and William Rehg (eds.), *Deliberative Democracy: Essays on Reason and Politics*. Cambridge, MA: MIT Press, 321–48.

Boles, Janet K. 1991: Form Follows Function: The Evolution of Feminist Strategies. *The Annals of the American Academy of Political and Social Science*, 515, 38–49.

Boli, John 1999: Conclusion: World Authority Structures and Legitimations. In John Boli and George Thomas (eds.), *Constructing World Culture. International Nongovernmental Organizations since 1875*. Stanford: Stanford University Press, 267–300.

Boli, John and Thomas, George (eds.) 1999: *Constructing World Culture: International Nongovernmental Organizations Since 1875*. Stanford: Stanford University Press.

Boltken, Ferdinand and Jagodzinski, Wolfgang 1985: In an Environment of Insecurity. *Comparative Political Studies*, 17, 453–84.

Bolton, Charles D. 1972: Alienation and Action: A Study of Peace Group Members. *American Journal of Sociology*, 78, 537–61.

Bonazzi, Tiziano and Dunne, Michael (eds.) 1994: *Cittadinanza e diritti nelle società multiculturali*. Bologna: il Mulino.

Bontadini, Paolo 1978: *Manuale di Organizzazione*. Milan: Isedi.

Booth, Alan and Babchuk, Nicholas 1969: Personal Influence Networks and Voluntary Association Affiliation. *Sociological Inquiry*, 39, 179–88.

Bosi, Lorenzo 2003: The New Social Movement Approach: The Case of the Civil Rights Movement in Northern Ireland. Paper for the Social Movements Stream, European Sociological Association Conference, Murcia, September.

Bourdieau, Pierre 1992: *The Practice of Reflexive Sociology*. In Pierre Bourdieu and Loïc J. D. Wacquant, *An Invitation to Reflexive Sociology*. Chicago: University of Chicago Press, 218–60.

Bourdieu, Pierre 1977: *Outline of a Theory of Practice*. Cambridge/New York: Cambridge University Press.

Bourdieu, Pierre 1980: *Le sens pratique*. Paris: Minuit.

Bourdieu, Pierre 1984: *Distinction*. Cambridge, MA: Harvard University Press.

Bourdieu, Pierre 1990: *The Logic of Practice*. Stanford: Stanford University Press.

Bourneau, François, and Martin, Virginie 1993: *Organiser les sans emploi? L'expérience de l'Apeis dans le Val-de-Marne*. In O. Fillieule (ed.), *Sociologie de la protestation*. Paris: L'Harmattan, pp. 157–80.

Brand, Karl-Werner 1985: Vergleichendes Resümee. In Karl-Werner Brand (ed.), *Neue soziale Bewegungen in Westeuropa und den USA. Ein internationaler Vergleich*. Frankfurt am Main: Campus, 306–34.

Brand, Karl-Werner 1990: Cyclical Aspects of New Social Movements: Waves of Cultural Criticism and Mobilization Cycles of New Middle-class Radicalism. In R. Dalton and M. Kuechler (eds.), *Challenging the Political Order*. Cambridge: Polity Press, 23–42.

Brand, Ulrich, and Wissen, Markus 2002: Ambivalenzen praktischer Globalisierungskritik: Das Bispiel Attac. *Kurswechsel*, 3, 102–13.

Braungart, Richard G. and Braungart, Margaret M. 1986: Life-course and Generational Politics. *Annual Review of Sociology*, 12, 205–31.

Braungart, Richard G. and Braungart, Margaret M. 1992: Historical Generations and Citizenship: 200 Years of Youth Movements. In P. C. Wasburn (ed.), *Research in Political Sociology*, vol. 6. Greenwich, CT: JAI Press, 139–74.

Brecher, Jeremy and Costello, Tim (eds.) 1990: *Building Bridges: The Emerging Grassroots Coalition of Labor and Community*. New York: Monthly Review Press.

Brecher, Jeremy, Costello, Tim, and Smith, Brendan 2000: *Globalization from Below: The Power of Solidarity*. Boston: South End Press.

Breiger, Ronald L. 1974. The Duality of Persons and Groups. *Social Forces*, 53, 181–90.

Breiger, Ronald L. 1988: The Duality of Persons and Groups. In B. Wellman and S. D. Berkowitz (eds.), *Social Structures: A Network Approach*. Cambridge: Cambridge University Press, 83–98.

Breines, Wini 1989: *Community and Organization in the New Left. 1962–1968: The Great Refusal*. New Brunswick, NJ: Rutgers University Press.

Breuilly, John 1993: *Nationalism and the State*. Chicago: University of Chicago Press.

Brint, Steven 1984: New Class and Cumulative Trend Explanations of the Liberal Political Attitudes of Professionals. *American Journal of Sociology*, 90, 30–71.

Brint, Steven 1994: *In an Age of Experts: The Changing Role of Professionals in Politics and Public Life*. Princeton: Princeton University Press.

Brissette, Martha B. 1988: Tax Protest and Tax Reform: A Chapter in The History of The American Political Process. *Journal of Law and Politics*, 5, 187–208.

Broadbent, Jeffrey 1998: *Environmental Politics in Japan: Networks of Power and Protest*. Cambridge: Cambridge University Press.

Brokett, Charles D., 1995: A Protest-Cycle Resolution of the Repression/Popular-Protest Paradox. In Mark Traugott (ed.), *Repertoires and Cycles of Collective Action*. Durham, NC: Duke University Press, 117–44.

Brooks, Clem and Manza, Jeff 1994: Do Changing Values Explain the New Politics? A Critical Assessment of the Postmaterialist Thesis. *Sociological Quarterly*, 35, 541–70.

Brown, Cliff and Boswell, Terry 1995: Strikebreaking or Solidarity in the Great Steel Strike of 1919: A Split Labor Market, Game-theoretic, and QCA Analysis. *American Journal of Sociology*, 100, 1479–1519.

Brown, Helen M. 1989. Organizing Activity in the Women's Movement. In B. Klandermans (ed.), *Organizing for Change*. Greenwich, CT: JAI Press.

Bruce, Steve 1988: *The Rise and Fall of the New Christian Right*. Oxford/New York: Oxford University Press.

Brysk, Alison 2000: *From Tribal Village to Global Village: Indian Rights and International Relations in Latin America*. Stanford: Stanford University Press.

Buchanan, James 1965: An Economic Theory of Clubs. *Economica*, 32 (125), 1–14.

Buechler, Steven M., 2004: The Strange Career of Strain and Breakdown Theories of Collective Action. In Davis A. Snow, Sarah H. Soule, and Hanspeter Kriesi (eds.), *The Blackwell Companion to Social Movements*. Oxford: Blackwell, 47–66.

Bukowski, Jeannie, Piattoni, Simona, and Smyrl, Marc (eds.) 2003: *Between Europeanization and Local Societies: The Space for Territorial Governance*. Boulder, CO: Rowman & Littlefield.

Burstein, Paul 1999: Social Movements and Public Policy. In M. Giugni, D. McAdam, and C. Tilly (eds.), *How Social Movements Matter*. Minneapolis: University of Minnesota Press.

Burstein, Paul and Linton, April 2002: The Impact of Political parties, Interest Groups, and Social Movement Organizations on Public Policy. *Social Forces*, 75, 135–69.

Burstein, Paul, Einwohner, Rachel L. and Hollander, Jocelyn A. 1995: The Success of Political Movements: A Bargaining Perspective. In J. C. Jenkins and B. Klandermans (eds.), *The Politics of Social Protest*. Minneapolis: University of Minnesota Press, 275–95.

Burt, Ronald S. 1980: Models of Network Structure. *Annual Review of Sociology*, 6, 79–141.

Burt, Ronald S. and Minor, Michael J. (eds.) 1983: *Applied Network Analysis: A Methodological Introduction*. Beverly Hills/London: Sage.

Button, James W. 1978: *Black Violence: Political Impacts of the 1960s Riots*. Princeton: Princeton University Press

Bystydzienski, Jill M. and Schacht, Steven (eds.) 2001: *Forging Radical Alliances Across Difference: Coalition Politics for the New Millennium*. New York: Rowman and Littlefield.

Cadena-Roa, Jorge 2002: Strategic Framing, Emotions, and Superbarrio – Mexico City's Masked Crusader. *Mobilization*, 7, 201–16.

Calhoun, Craig 1982: *The Question of Class Struggle: Social Foundations of Popular Radicalism during the Industrial Revolution*. Oxford: Blackwell.

Calhoun, Craig 1991: The Problem of Identity in Collective Action. In J. Huber (ed.), *Macro–Micro Linkages in Sociology*. London/Beverly Hills, CA: Sage, 51–75.

Calhoun Craig (ed.) 1992: *Habermas and the Public Sphere*. Cambridge, MA: MIT Press.

Calhoun, Craig 1993: New Social Movements of the Early 19th Century. *Social Science Journal*, 17, 385–427.

Calhoun, Craig (ed.) 1994a: *Social Theory and the Politics of Identity*. Oxford/Cambridge, MA: Blackwell.

Calhoun, Craig 1994b: Nationalism and Civil Society: Democracy, Diversity, and Self-Determination. In C. Calhoun (ed.), *Social Theory and the Politics of Identity*. Oxford/Cambridge, MA: Blackwell, 304–35.

Calhoun, Craig 1994c: *Neither Gods Nor Emperors: Students and the Struggle for Democracy in China*. Berkeley: University of California Press.

Callinicos, Alex 2001: Where now? In E. Bircham and J. Charlton (eds.), *Anti-Capitalism: A Guide to the Movement*. London/Sydney: Bookmarks Publications, 387–99.

Canciani, Domenico and De La Pierre, Sergio 1993: *Le ragioni di Babele. Le etnie tra vecchi nazionalismi e nuove identità*. Milano: Angeli.

Caniglia, Elisabeth Schafer 2001: Informal Alliances vs Institutional Ties: The Effects of Elite Alliances on Environmental TSMO Networks. *Mobilization*, 6, 37–54.

Capek, Stella 2003: The "Environmental Justice" Frame: A Conceptual Discussion and Application. *Social Problems*, 40, 5–24.

Cardon, Domenique, and Granjou, Fabien 2003: Peut-on se liberer des formats mediatiques? Le mouvement alter-mondialisation et l'Internet. *Mouvements*, 25, 67–73.

Carroll, William K. and Ratner, R. S. 1996: Master Framing and Cross-Movement Networking in Contemporary Social Movements. *Sociological Quarterly*, 37, 601–25.

Carson, Rachel 1962: *Silent Spring*. Boston: Houghton Mifflin.

Cartuyvels, Yves et al. 1997: *L'Affaire Dutroux*. Brussels: Editions Complexe.

Carty, Victoria, 2002: Technology and Counter-hegemonic Movements: The Case of Nike Corporation. *Social Movement Studies*, 1, 129–46.

Castells 2001: *The Internet Galaxy: Reflections on the Internet, Business and Society*. Oxford: Oxford University Press.

Castells, Manuel 1977: *La Question Urbaine*. Paris: Maspero.

Castells, Manuel 1983: *The City and the Grass-Roots*. London: E. Arnold.

Castells, Manuel 1996: *The Information Age. Vol. I: The Rise of the Network Society*. Oxford/Cambridge, MA: Blackwell.

Castells, Manuel 1997: *The Information Age. Vol. II: The Power of Identity*. Oxford/Cambridge, MA: Blackwell.

Catanzaro, Raimondo and Manconi, Luigi (eds.) 1995: *Storie di lotta armata*. Bologna: il Mulino.

Cerulo, Karen and Ruane, Janet M. 1998: Coming Together: New Taxonomies for the Analysis of Social Relations. *Sociological Inquiry*, 68, 398–425.

Cerulo, Karen. 1997. Reframing Sociological Concepts for a Brave New (Virtual?) World. *Sociological Inquiry*, 67, 48–58.

Cesarani, David and Fulbrick, Mary (eds.) 1996: *Citizenship, Nationality and Migration in Europe*. London: Routledge.

Chabanet, Didier 2002: Les marches européennes contre le chômage, la précarité et les exclusions. In Richard Balme, Didier Chabanet, and Vincent Wright (eds.), *L'action collective en Europe*. Paris: Presses de Sciences Po.

Chabot, Sean 2002: Transnational Diffusion and the African-American Reinvention of the Gandhian Repertoire. In Doug Imig and Sidny Tarrow (eds.), *Contentious Europeans: Protest and Politics in an Emerging Polity*. Lanham, MD: Rowman & Littlefield.

Chandhoke, Neera 2002: The Limits of Global Civil Society. In Marlies Glasius, Mary Kaldor, and Helmut Ahheier (eds.), *Global Civil Society 2002*. Oxford: Oxford University Press, 35–53.

Chatfield, Charles, Pagnucco, Ron, and Smith, Jackie (eds.) 1996: *Solidarity Beyond the State: The Dynamics of Transnational Social Movements*. Syracuse, NY: Syracuse University Press.

Chesler, Mark 1991: Mobilizing Consumer Activism in Health Care: The Role of Self-help Groups. *Research in Social Movements, Conflicts and Change*, 13, 275–305.

Chiriboga, Manuel 2001: Constructing Southern Constituency for Global Advocacy: The Experience of Latin American NGOs and the World Bank. In Michael Edwards and John Gaventa, eds., *Global Citizen Action*. Boulder, CO: Lynne Rienne, 73–86.

Chong, Dennis 1991: *Collective Action and the Civil Rights Movement*. Chicago: University of Chicago Press.

Cinalli, Manlio 2002: Environmental Campaigns and Socio-Political Cleavages in Divided Societies. *Environmental Politics*, 11, 163–71.

Clark, Martin 1984: *Modern Italy, 1871–1982*. London: Longman.

Clark, Robert 1989: Spanish Democracy and Regional Autonomy. In J. Rudolph and R. J. Thompson (eds.), *Ethnoterritorial Politics, Policy, and the Western World*. Boulder, CO/London: Lynne Rienner, 15–44.

Clark, Terry N. and Inglehart, Ronald 1998: The New Political Culture: Changing Dynamics of Support for the Welfare State and other Policies in Postindustrial Societies. In Terry N. Clark and Vincent Hoffmann-Martinot (eds.), *The New Political Culture*. Boulder, CO: Westview Press, 9–72.

Clark, Terry N. and Lipset, Seymour M. 1991: Are Social Classes Dying? *International Sociology*, 4, 397–410.

Clark, Terry N. and Rempel, Michael (eds.) 1997: *Citizen Politics in Post-Industrial Societies*. Boulder, CO: Westview Press.

Clemens, Elisabeth S. 1996: Organizational Form as Frame: Collective Identity and Political Strategy in the American Labor Movement. In Doug McAdam, John McCarthy, and Mayer N. Zald (eds.), *Comparative Perspectives on Social Movements: Political Opportunities, Mobilizing Structures, and Cultural Framing*. Cambridge/New York: Cambridge University Press, 205–25.

Clemens, Elisabeth S. and Minkoff, Debra 2004: Beyond the Iron Law: Rethinking the Place of Organizations in Social Movement Research. In David A. Snow, Sarah H. Soule, and Hanspeter Kriesi (eds.), *The Blackwell Companion to Social Movements*. Oxford: Blackwell, 155–70.

Cleveland, John W. 2003: Does the New Middle Class Lead Today's Social Movements? *Critical Sociology*, 29, 163–88.

Cohen, J. 1989: *Deliberation and Democratic Legitimacy*. In A. Hamlin and P. Pettit (eds.), *The Good Polity*. Oxford: Blackwell, 17–34.

Cohen, Jean L. 1985: Strategy and Identity: New Theoretical Paradigms and Contemporary Social Movements. *Social Research*, 52, 663–716.

Coleman, James 1990: *Foundations of Social Theory*. Cambridge, MA: Belknap.

Collins, Carole J. L., Gariyo, Zie, and Burdon, Tony 2001: Jubilee 2000: Citizen Action Across the North–South Divide. In Michael Edards and John Gaventa (eds.), *Global Citizen Action*. Boulder, CO: Lynne Riener, 135–48.

Connolly, Linda 2002: *The Irish Women's Movement From Revolution to Devolution*. Basingstoke: Palgrave.

Connor, Walker 1994: *Ethnonationalism: The Quest for Understanding*. Princeton, NJ: Princeton University Press.

Cook, Karen S. and Whitmeyer, J. M. 1992: Two Approaches to Social Structure: Exchange Theory and Network Analysis. *Annual Review of Sociology*, 18, 109–27.

Cortright, David 1991: Assessing Peace Movement Effectiveness in the 1980s. *Peace and Change*, 16, 46–63.

Cortright, David 1993: *Peace Works: The Citizen's Role in Ending the Cold War*. Boulder, CO: Westview Press.

Cotgrove, Stephen and Duff, Andrew 1980: Environmentalism, Middle-class Radicalism and Politics. *Sociological Review*, 28, 333–51.

Couldry, Nick 1999: *The Place of Media Power: Pilgrims and Witnesses in the Media Age*. London: Routledge.

Crenshaw, Martha 1997: *Encyclopedia of World Terrorism*. Armonk, NY: Sharpe Reference.

Cress, Daniel and Snow, David 1996: Mobilization at the Margins: Resources, Benefactors, and the Viability of Homeless Social Movement Organizations. *American Sociological Review*, 61, 1089–1109.

Cress, Daniel M. and David A. Snow 2000: The Outcomes of Homeless Mobilization: The Influence of Organization, Disruption, Political Mediation, and Framing. *American Journal of Sociology*, 105, 1065–1104.

Cristante, Stefano (ed.) 2003: *Violenza mediata. Il ruolo dell'informazione nel G8 di Genova*. Roma: Editori Riuniti.

Crompton, Rosemary 1993: *Class and Stratification: An Introduction to Current Debates*. Cambridge: Polity Press.

Crook, Stephen, Pakulski, Jan, and Waters, Malcolm 1992: *Postmodernization: Change in Advanced Society*. London/Thousand Oaks: Sage.

Crossley, Nick 1998: R. D. Laing and the British Anti-Psychiatric Movement: A Socio-Historical Analysis. *Social Science and Medicine*, 47, 877–89.

Crossley, Nick 1999: Working Utopias and Social Movements: An Investigation Using Case Study Materials from Radical Mental Health Movements in Britain. *Sociology*, 33, 809–30.

Crossley, Nick 2002: *Making Sense of Social Movements*. Buckingham: Open University Press.

Croteau, David 1995: *Politics and the Class Divide: Working People and the Middle Class Left*. Philadelphia: Temple University Press.

Crouch, Colin 1999: *Social Change in Western Europe*. Oxford: Oxford University Press.

Crouch, Colin 2004: *Post Democracy*. London: Polity.

Cuminetti, Mario 1983: *Il dissenso cattolico in Italia*. Milan: Rizzoli.

Curtis, Russel L. and Zurcher, Louis A. 1974: Social Movements: An Analytical Exploration of Organizational Forms. *Social Problems*, 11, 356–70.

Curtis, Russell L. and Zurcher, Louis A., Jr. 1973: Stable Resources of Protest Movements: The Multi-organizational Field. *Social Forces*, 52, 53–61.

D'Anieri, Paul, Ernst, Claire, and Kier, Elizabeth 1990: New Social Movements in Historical Perspective. *Comparative Politics*, 22, 445–58.

D'Anjou, Leo 1996: *Social Movements and Cultural Change: The First Abolition Campaign Revisited*. New York: Aldine de Gruyter.

D'Anjou, Leo and van Male, John 1998: Between Old and New: Social Movement and Cultural Change. *Mobilization*, 3, 297–26.

Dahl, Robert 1961: *Who Governs? Democracy and Power in an American City*. New Haven: Yale University Press.

Dahl, Robert 1967: *Pluralist Democracy in the United States: Conflict and Consent*. Chicago: Rand McNally.

Dahrendorf, Ralf 1988: *The Modern Social Conflicts*. London: Weidenfeld & Nicolson.

Dahrendorf, Ralf 1995: *Quadrare il cerchio. Benessere economico, coesione sociale e libertà politica*. Roma, Bari: Laterza.

dalla Chiesa, Nando 1987: *Il Giano bifronte. Società corta e colletti bianchi*. Milano: Etas Libri.

Dalton, Russell (ed.) 1993: Citizens, Protest and Democracy. Special issue of *The Annals of the American Academy of Political and Social Sciences*, 528.

Dalton, Russell 1988: *Citizen Politics in Western Democracies*. Chatham, NJ: Chatham House.

Dalton, Russell 1994: *The Green Rainbow: Environmental Groups in Western Europe*. New Haven: Yale University Press.

Dalton, Russell 1995: Strategies of Partisan Influence: West European Environmental Movements. In J. C. Jenkins and B. Klandermans (eds.), *The Politics of Social Protest: Comparative Perspectives on States and Social Movements*. Minneapolis: University of Minnesota Press, 296–323.

Dalton, Russell 1996: *Citizen Politics in Western Democracies*. Chatham, NJ: Chatham House.

Dalton, Russell J. and Kuechler, Manfred (eds.) 1990: *Challenging the Political Order: New Social and Political Movements in Western Democracies*. Cambridge: Polity Press.

Dalton, Russell J., Flanagan, Scott C., and Beck, Paul A. (eds.) 1984: *Electoral Change in Advanced Industrial Democracies: Dealignment or Realignment?* Princeton: Princeton University Press.

Daniels, Cynthia and Brooks, Rachelle (eds.) 1997: *Feminists Negotiate the State: The Politics of Domestic Violence.* Lanham, MD: University Press of America.

Davies, James 1969: The J-Curve of Rising and Declining Satisfactions as Cause of Some Great Revolutions and a Contained Rebellion. In H. D. Graham and T. Gurr (eds.), *Violence in America.* New York: Praeger, 690–730.

Davis, Gerald, McAdam, Doug, Scott, Richard, and Zald, Mayor N. (eds.) 2005: *Social Movements and Organization Theory.* New York: Cambridge University Press.

Dawson, Jane 1996: *Eco-nationalism. Anti-nuclear Activism and National Identity in Russia, Lithuania, and Ukraine.* Durham/London: Duke University Press.

de Graaf, Nan Dirk and Evans, Geoffrey 1996: Why are the Young More Postmaterialist? A Cross-National Analysis of Individual and Contextual Influences on Postmaterial Values. *Comparative Political Studies,* 28, 608–35.

Delgado, Gary 1986: *Organizing the Movement: The Roots and Growth of ACORN.* Philadelphia: Temple University Press.

della Porta, Donatella 1988: Recruitment Processes in Clandestine Political Organizations: Italian Left-wing Terrorism. In B. Klandermans, H. Kriesi and S. Tarrow (eds.), *International Social Movement Research,* Vol. 1, *From Structure to Action.* Greenwich, CT: JAI Press, 155–72.

della Porta, Donatella 1990: *Il terrorismo di sinistra.* Bologna: il Mulino.

della Porta, Donatella 1992: Lige Histories in the Analysis of Social Movement Activists. In M. Diani and R. Eyerman (eds.), *Studying Collective Action,* London: Sage, 168–93.

della Porta, Donatella 1995: *Social Movements, Political Violence and the State.* Cambridge/New York: Cambridge University Press.

della Porta, Donatella 1996a: *Movimenti collettivi e sistema politico in Italia, 1960–1995.* Bari: Laterza.

della Porta, Donatella 1996b: Il terrorismo. In *Enciclopedia Treccani.* Rome: Treccani.

della Porta, Donatella 1996c: Social Movements and the State: Thoughts on the Policing of Protest. In D. McAdam, J. McCarthy, and M. N. Zald (eds.), *Comparative Perspectives on Social Movements. Political Opportunities, Mobilizing Structures, and Cultural Framing.* Cambridge/New York: Cambridge University Press, 62–92.

della Porta, Donatella 1996d: Movimenti sociali. *Rassegna Italiana di Sociologia,* 37, 313–31.

della Porta, Donatella 1998a: Police Knowledge and the Public Order in Italy. In D. della Porta and H. Reiter (eds.), *Policing Protest: The Control of Mass Demonstrations in Western Democracies.* Minneapolis: University of Minnesota Press, 1–32.

della Porta, Donatella 1998b: The Political Discourse on Protest Policing. In M. Giugni, D. McAdam, and C. Tilly (eds.), *How Movements Matter.* Minneapolis: University of Minnesota Press.

della Porta, Donatella 2001: *I partiti politici.* Bologna: Il Mulino.

della Porta, Donatella 2003a: *The Women's Movement, the Left and the State: Continuities and Changes in the Italian Case.* In L. A. Banaszak, K. Beckwith, and D. Rucht (eds.), *Women's Movements Facing the Reconfigured State.* Cambridge: Cambridge University Press, 48–68.

della Porta, Donatella 2003b: Social Movements and Democracy at the Turn of the Millennium. In P. Ibarra (ed.), *Social Movements and Democracy*, 105–36. New York: Palgrave Macmillan Press.

della Porta, Donatella 2004b: *Europeanization and Social Movements*. In Gianfranco Bettin (ed.), *Sociology of Europe*. Bologna: Monduzzi.

della Porta, Donatella (ed.) 2004c: *Comitati di cittadini e democrazia urbana*. Cosenza: Rubbettino.

della Porta, Donatella 2004d: Démocratie en mouvement: les manifestants du Forum Social Européen, des liens aux réseaux. In *Politix*, 1.

della Porta, Donatella 2005a: Paths of Global Activism: Experiences of Political Participation and the Participant to the International Day for Peace. In D. Rucht and S. Waalgrave (eds.), *Protest Politics: Antiwar Mobilization in Advanced Industrial Democracies* (forthcoming).

della Porta, Donatella 2005b: Making the Polis: Social Forums and Democracy in the Global Justice Movement. *Mobilization*, 10.

della Porta, Donatella 2005c: From Corporatist Unions to Protest Unions? On the (Difficult) Relations between Labour and New Social Movements. In C. Crouch and W. Streek (eds.), *The Diversity of Democracy: A Tribute to Philippe C. Schmitter*, forthcoming.

della Porta, Donatella 2005d: Deliberation in Movement: Why and How to Study Deliberative Democracy and Social Movements. *Acta politica*, forthcoming.

della Porta, Donatella 2005e: Multiple Belongings, Flexible Identities and the Construction of Another Politics: Between the European Social Forum and the Local Social Fora. In D. della Porta and S. Tarrow (eds.), *Transnational Protest and Global Activism*. Lanham, MD: Rowman and Littlefield, 175–202.

della Porta, Donatella and Andretta, Massimiliano 2002: Changing Forms of Environmentalism in Italy: The Protest Campaign against the High-Speed Railway System. *Mobilization*, 1, 59–77.

della Porta, Donatella, Andretta, Massimiliano, Mosca, Lorenzo, and Reiter, Herbert 2005: *Transnational Movements*. Minneapolis, The University of Minnesota Press.

della Porta, Donatella and Caiani, Manuela 2005: Quale Europa? Discorso pubblico e europeizzazione. Bologna, il Mulino.

della Porta, Donatella and Diani, Mario 2004: *Movimenti senza protesta? L'ambientalismo in Italia*. Bologna: il Mulino (with the collaboration of Massimiliano Andretta).

della Porta, Donatella and Diani, Mario 2005: "No to the War With No Ifs or Buts": Protests Against the War in Iraq. In S. Fabbrini and V. Della Sala (eds.), *Italian Politics Yearbook 2004*. New York: Berghahn.

della Porta, Donatella and Fillieule, Olivier 2004: Policing Social Protest. In David A. Snow, Sarah H. Soule, and Hanspeter Kriesi (eds.), *The Blackwell Companion to Social Movements*. Oxford: Blackwell, 217–41.

della Porta, Donatella, Kousis, Maria, and Valiente, Celia 1996: Women and Politics in Southern Europe: Paths to Women's Rights in Italy, Greece, Spain and Portugal. Paper presented at the SSRC Conference on Democratic Consolidation and Culture in Southern Europe, Palma de Mallorca, July.

della Porta, Donatella and Kriesi, Hanspeter 1998: Social Movements in A Globalizing World: An Introduction. In D. della Porta, H. Kriesi and D. Rucht (eds.), *Social Movements in a Globalizing World*. New York/London: Macmillan.

della Porta, Donatella and Mosca, Lorenzo 2005: Global-net for Global Movements? A Network of Networks for a Movement of Movements. *Journal of Public Policy*, forthcoming.

della Porta, Donatella and Reiter, Herbert 1997: Police du gouvernement ou des citoyens? *Les Cahiers de la sécurité intérieure*, 27, 36–57.

della Porta, Donatella and Reiter, Herbert (eds.) 1998a: *Policing protest: The Control of Mass Demonstrations in Western Democracies*. Minneapolis: University of Minnesota Press.

della Porta, Donatella and Reiter, Herbert 1998b: Introduction: The Policing of Protest in Western Democracies. In D. della Porta and H. Reiter (eds.), *Policing Protest: The Control of Mass Demonstrations in Western Democracies*, 1–32. Minneapolis: University of Minnesota Press.

della Porta, Donatella and Reiter, Herbert 2004a: *Polizia e protesta*. Bologna, Il Mulino.

della Porta, Donatella and Reiter, Herbert, 2004b: *La protesta e il controllo. Movimenti e forze dell'ordine nell'era della globalizzazione*. Milano: Berti/Altreconomia, 2004.

della Porta, Donatella and Rucht, Dieter 1995: Left-libertarian Movements in Context: Comparing Italy and West Germany, 1965–1990. In J. C. Jenkins and B. Klandermans (eds.), *The Politics of Social Protest. Comparative Perspectives on States and Social Movements*, Minneapolis: University of Minnesota Press, 229–72.

della Porta, Donatella and Rucht, Dieter (eds.) 2002a: Special Issue: Comparative Environmental Campaigns. *Mobilization*, 7, 1–98.

della Porta, Donatella, and Rucht, Dieter 2002b: The Dynamics of Environmental Campaigns. *Mobilization*, 7, 1–14.

della Porta, Donatella and Tarrow, Sidney 1987: Unwanted Children: Political Violence and the Cycle of Protest in Italy, 1966–1973. *European Journal of Political Research*, 14, 607–32.

della Porta, Donatella and Tarrow, Sidney (eds.) 2005: *Transnational Protest and Global Activism*. Lanham, MD: Rowman & Littlefield.

DeNardo, James 1985: *Power in Numbers: The Political Strategy of Protest and Rebellion*. Princeton, NJ: Princeton University Press.

Derloshon, Gerald B. and Potter, James E. 1982: *The Success Merchants: A Guide to Major Influences and People in the Human Potential Movement*. Englewood Cliffs, NJ: Prentice-Hall.

Desai, Manisha 1996: Informal Organizations as Agents of Change: Notes from the Contemporary Women's Movement in India. *Mobilization*, 1, 159–74.

Desario, Jack 1988: Consumers and Health Planning: Mobilization of Bias? In J. Desario and S. Langton (eds.), *Citizen Participation in Public Decision Making*. New York/Westport, CT/London: Greenwood Press, 133–51.

Devine, Fiona 1997: *Social Class in America and Britain*. Edinburgh: Edinburgh University Press.

Di Maggio, Paul 1986: Structural Analysis of Interorganizational Fields. *Research in Organizational Behavior*, 8, 335–70.

Di Maggio, Paul and Powell, Walter 1983: The Iron Cage Revisited. International Isomorphism and Collective Rationality. *American Sociological Review*, 48, 147–60.

Di Maggio, Paul J. and Powell, Walter W. 1991: Introduction. In W. W. Powell and P. J. DiMaggio (eds.), *The New Institutionalism in Organizational Analysis*. Chicago, IL: University of Chicago Press, 1–38.

Diamanti, Ilvo 1993: *La Lega. Geografia, storia e sociologia di un nuovo soggetto politico*. Roma: Donzelli.

Diamanti, Ilvo 1994: Geopolitica del bluff federalista. *Limes*, 4, 37–44.

Diamanti, Ilvo 1996: The Northern League: From Regional Party to Party of Government. In S. Gundle, and S. Parker (eds.), *The New Italian Republic*. London / New York: Routledge, 113–29.

Diani, Mario 1984: L'area della "Nuova Coscienza" tra ricerca individuale ed impegno civile. In A. Melucci (ed.), *Altri codici*. Bologna: il Mulino, 223–66.

Diani, Mario 1986: Dimensione simbolica e dimensione sociale nelle esperienze di "Nuova Coscienza". Il caso dell'area milanese. *Rassegna italiana di sociologia*, 27, 89–115.

Diani, Mario 1988: *Isole nell'arcipelago. Il movimento ecologista in Italia*. Bologna: il Mulino.

Diani, Mario 1990: The Network Structure of the Italian Ecology Movement. *Social Science Information*, 29, 5–31.

Diani, Mario 1992a: Analysing Social Movement Networks. In M. Diani and R. Eyerman (eds.), *Studying Collective Action*. Newbury Park / London: Sage, 107–35.

Diani, Mario 1992b: Dalla ritualita' delle subculture alla liberta' dei reticoli sociali. *Democrazia e diritto*, 32, 199–221.

Diani, Mario 1992c: The Concept of Social Movement. *Sociological Review*, 40, 1–25.

Diani, Mario 1994: The Conflict over Nuclear Energy in Italy. In H. Flam (ed.), *States and Anti-nuclear Movements*. Edinburgh: Edinburgh University Press.

Diani, Mario 1995a: *Green Networks: A Structural Analysis of the Italian Environmental Movement*. Edinburgh: Edinburgh University Press.

Diani, Mario 1995b: Le reti di movimento: Prospettive di analisi. *Rassegna italiana di sociologia*, 36, 341–72.

Diani, Mario 1996: Linking Mobilization Frames and Political Opportunities: Insights from Regional Populism in Italy. *American Sociological Review*, 61, 1053–69.

Diani, Mario 1997: Social Movements and Social Capital: A Network Perspective on Movement Outcomes. *Mobilization*, 2, 129–47.

Diani, Mario 2000a: Simmel to Rokkan and Beyond: Elements for a Network Theory of (New) Social Movements. *European Journal of Social Theory*, 3, 387–406.

Diani, Mario 2000b: Social Movement Networks Virtual and Real. *Information, Communication and Society*, 3, 386–401.

Diani, Mario 2003a: Networks and Social Movements: A Research Programme. In Mario Diani and Doug McAdam (eds.), *Social Movements and Networks*. Oxford / New York: Oxford University Press, 299–318.

Diani, Mario 2003b: Leaders or Brokers? In Mario Diani and Doug McAdam (eds.), *Social Movements and Networks*. Oxford / New York: Oxford University Press, 105–22.

Diani, Mario 2004a: Do We Still Need SMOs? Paper for the ECPR Annual Sessions of Workshops, Upssala, April 13–18.

Diani, Mario 2004b: Networks and participation. In D. Snow, S. Soule, and H. Kriesi (eds.), *The Blackwell Companion to Social Movements*. Oxford: Blackwell, 339–59.

Diani, Mario 2004c: Demonstrators and Organizations in the 15th Feb. Protests. International Peace Protests Survey, unpublished report, Trento, March.

Diani, Mario 2005a: Cities in the World: Local Civil Society and Global Issues in Britain. In D. della Porta and S. Tarrow (eds.), *Transnational Protest and Global Activism*. Lanham, MD: Rowman & Littlefield, 45–67.

Diani, Mario 2005b: The Structural Bases of Movement Coalitions. Multiple Memberships and Networks in the February 15th 2003 Peace Demonstrations. Paper for the American Sociological Association Centenary Meeting, Philadelphia, August 13–16.

Diani, Mario and Bison, Ivano 2004: Organization, Coalitions, and Movements. *Theory and Society*, 33, 281–309.

Diani, Mario and Donati, Paolo R. 1984: L'Oscuro oggetto del desiderio: Leadership e potere nelle aree dil movimento. In A. Melucci (ed.), *Altri codici. Aree di movimento nella metropoli*. Bologna: il Mulino, 315–44.

Diani, Mario and Donati, Paolo R. 1996: Rappresentare l'interesse pubblico: La comunicazione dei gruppi di pressione e dei movimenti. *Quaderni di scienza politica*, 4, 1–42.

Diani, Mario and Donati, Paolo R. 1999: Organizational Change in Western European Environmental Groups: A Framework for Analysis. *Environmental Politics*, 8, 13–34.

Diani, Mario and Eyerman, Ron (eds.) 1992: *Studying Collective Action*. London/Beverly Hills: Sage.

Diani, Mario and Forno, Francesca 2003: Italy. In C. Rootes (ed.) *Environmental Protest in Western Europe*. Oxford: Oxford University Press, 135–65.

Diani, Mario and Lodi, Giovanni 1988: Three in One: Currents in the Milan Ecology Movement. In B. Klandermans, H. Kriesi, and S. Tarrow (eds.), *From Structure to Action*. Greenwich, CT: JAI Press, 103–24.

Diani, Mario and McAdam, Doug (eds.) 2003: *Social Movements and Networks*. Oxford/New York: Oxford University Press.

Diani, Mario and van der Heijden, Hein-Anton 1994: Anti-nuclear Movements across Nations: Explaining Patterns of Development. In H. Flam (ed.), *States and Anti-nuclear Movements*. Edinburgh: Edinburgh University Press, 355–82.

Diani, Mario, Rucht, Dieter, Koopmans, Ruud, Oliver, Pamela, Taylor, Verta, McAdam, Doug, and Tarrow, Sidney 2003: Book Symposium. Focus on: Dynamics of Contention. *Mobilization*, 8, 109–41.

Diez Medrano, Juan 1995: *Divided Nations: Class, Politics, and Nationalism in the Basque Country and Catalonia*. Ithaca: Cornell University Press.

Dines, Nicholas 1999: Centri sociali: occupazioni autogestite a Napoli negli omni novanta. *Quaderni di Sociologia*, 90–111.

Dixon, Marc and Roscigno, Vincent 2003: Status, Networks, and Social Movement Participation: The Case of Striking Workers. *American Journal of Sociology*, 108, 1292–1327.

Dobson, Andrew 1990: *Green Political Thought*. London: Unwin Hyman.

Doherty, Brian 1998: Opposition to Road-Building. *Parliamentary Affairs*, 51, 370–83.

Doherty, Brian 1999: Manufactured Vulnerability: Eco-Activism in Britain, *Mobilization*, 4, 75–89.

Doherty, Brian 2002: *Ideas and Action in the Green Movement*. London: Routledge.

Doherty, Brian, Plows, Alex, and Wall, Derek 2003: The Preferred Way of Doing Things: The British Direct Action Movement. *Parliamentary Affairs*, 56, 669–86.

Donati, Paolo R. 1989: Dalla politica al consumo. La questione ecologica e i movimenti degli anni settanta. *Rassegna italiana di sociologia*, 30, 321–46.

Donati, Paolo R. 1992: Political Discourse Analysis. In M. Diani and R. Eyerman (eds.), *Studying Collective Action.* Newbury Park/London: Sage, 136–67.

Donati, Paolo R. 1996: Building a Unified Movement: Resource Mobilization, Media Work, and Organizational Transformation in the Italian Environmentalist Movement. In L. Kriesberg (ed.), *Research in Social Movements, Conflict and Change,* vol. 19. Greenwich, CT: JAI Press, 125–57.

Donati, Paolo R. and Mormino, Maria 1984: Il Potere della definizione: Le forme organizzative dell'antagonismo metropolitano. In A. Melucci (ed.), *Altri codici. Aree di movimento nella metropoli.* Bologna: il Mulino, 349–84.

Donati, Pierpaolo 1993: *La cittadinanza societaria.* Roma-Bari: Laterza.

Downing, D. H. 2001: *Radical Media: Rebellious Communication and Social Movements.* London: Sage.

Downs, Anthony 1972: Up and Down with Ecology: The Issue Attention Cycle. *Public Interest,* 28, 38–50.

Downtown, James 1973: *Rebel Leadership: Commitment and Charisma in the Revolutionary Process.* New York: Free Press.

Downtown, James and Wehr, Paul Ernest 1997: *The Persistent Activist.* Boulder, CO: Westview Press.

Doyle, Timothy 2002: Environmental Campaigns against Mining in Australia and the Philippines, *Mobilization,* 7, 29–42.

Drury, John and Reicher, Steve 2000: Collective Action and Psychological Change: The Emergence of New Social Identities. *British Journal of Social Psychology,* 39, 579–604.

Drury, John, Reicher, Steve, and Stott, Clifford 2003: Transforming the Boundaries of Collective Identity: From the "Local" Anti road Campaign to "Global" Resistance? *Social Movement Studies,* 2, 191–212.

Dryzek, John S. 2000: *Deliberative Democracy and Beyond.* New York: Oxford University Press.

Duch, R. M. and Taylor, M. A. 1993: Postmaterialism and the Economic Condition. *American Journal of Political Science,* 37, 747–79.

Duffhues, Ton and Felling, Albert 1989: The Development, Change, and Decline of the Dutch Catholic Movement. In B. Klandermans (ed.), *International Social Movement Research,* Vol. 2, *Organizing for Change.* Greenwich, CT: JAI Press, 95–116.

Dunleavy, Patrick 1980: *Urban Political Analysis: The Politics of Collective Consumption.* London: Macmillan.

Duyvendak, Jan Willem 1995: *The Power of Politics: New Social Movements in an Old Polity, France 1965–1989.* Boulder, CO: Westview.

Earl, Jennifer, Martin, Andrew, McCarthy, John, and Soule, Sarah 2004: The Use of Newspaper Data in the Study of Collective Action. *Annual Review of Sociology,* 30, 65–80.

Earl, Jennifer, Soule, Sarah, and McCarthy, John 2003: Protest Under Fire? Explaining the Policing of Protest. *American Sociological Review,* 68, 581–606.

Eckstein, Susan (ed.) 2001: *Power and Popular Protest: Latin American Social Movements.* Berkeley: University of California Press.

Eder, Klaus 1985: The "New Social Movements": Moral Crusades, Political Pressure Groups, or Social Movements? *Social Research,* 52, 869–901.

Eder, Klaus 1993: *The New Politics of Class. Social Movements and Cultural Dynamics in Advanced Societies.* Newbury Park/London: Sage.

Eder, Klaus 1995: Does Social Class Matter in the Study of Social Movements? A Theory of Middle Class Radicalism. In L. Maheu (ed.), *Social Movements and Social Classes*. London/Thousand Oaks: Sage, 21–54.

Eder, Klaus 2003: Identity Mobilization and Democracy: An Ambivalent Relation. In Pedro Ibarra (ed.), *Social Movements and Democracy*. New York: Palgrave, 61–80.

Edwards, Bob and Foley, Michael 2003: Social Movement Organizations Beyond the Beltway: Understanding the Diversity of One Social Movement Industry. *Mobilization*, 8, 85–105.

Edwards, Bob and Marullo, Sam 1996: Organizational Mortality in a Declining Movement: The Demise of Peace Movement Organizations in the End of the Cold War Era. *American Sociological Review*, 60, 908–27.

Edwards, Bob and McCarthy, John 2004: Resources and Social Movement Mobilization. In David A. Snow, Sarah H. Soule, and Hanspeter Kriesi (eds.), *The Blackwell Companion to Social Movements*. Oxford: Blackwell, 116–52.

Edwards, Bob, Foley, Michael W., and Diani, Mario (eds.) 2001: *Beyond Tocqueville: Social Capital, Civil Society, and Political Process in Comparative Perspective*. Hanover: University Press of New England.

Einwohner, Rachel 2002: Bringing the Outsiders In: Opponents' Claims and the Construction of Animal Rights Activists' Identity. *Mobilization*, 7, 253–68.

Einwohner, Rachel 2003: Opportunity, Honor, and Action the Warsaw Ghetto Uprising of 1943. *American Journal of Sociology*, 109, 650–75.

Eisinger, Peter K. 1973: The Conditions of Protest Behavior in American Cities. *American Political Science Review*, 67, 11–28.

Elkington, John and Hailes, Julia 1988: *The Green Consumer Guide*. London: Gollancz.

Ellingson, Stephen 1995: Understanding the Dialectic of Discourse and Collective Action: Public Debate and Rioting in Antebellum Cincinnati. *American Journal of Sociology*, 101, 100–44.

Elster, Jon 1998: Deliberation and Constitution Making. In J. Elster (ed.), *Deliberative Democracy*. Cambridge: Cambridge University Press, 97–122.

Emirbayer, Mustafa 1997: A Manifesto for a Relational Sociology. *American Journal of Sociology*, 103, 281–317.

Emirbayer, Mustafa and Goodwin, Jeff 1994: Network Analysis, Culture, and the Problem of Agency. *American Journal of Sociology*, 99, 1411–54.

Emirbayer, Mustafa and Mische, Ann 1998: What is Agency? *American Journal of Sociology*, 103, 962–1023.

Ennis, James G. and Schreuer, Richard 1987: Mobilizing Weak Support for Social Movements: The Role of Grievance, Efficacy, and Cost. *Social Forces*, 66, 390–409.

Epstein, Barbara 1991: *Political Protest and Cultural Revolution: Nonviolent Direct Action in the 1970s and 1980s*. Berkeley: University of California.

Epstein, Barbara 2000: Not Your Parents' Protest. *Dissent*, 47 (2), 8–11.

Epstein, Barbara 2001: Anarchism and the Anti-Globalization Movement. *Monthly Review*, 53(4), 1–14.

Erickson, Bonnie 1982: Networks, Ideologies, and Belief Systems. In P. Marsden and N. Lin (eds.), *Social Structure and Network Analysis*. Beverly Hills/London: Sage, 159–72.

Escobar, Arturo and Alvarez, Sonia (eds.) 1992: *The Making of Social Movements in Latin America: Identity, Strategy, and Democracy*. Boulder, CO/Oxford: Westview Press.

Escobar, Edward, J. 1993: The Dialectic of Repression: The Los Angeles Police Department and the Chicano Movement, 1968–1971. *The Journal of American History*, March, 1483–1514.

Esping-Andersen, Gosta (ed.) 1993: *Changing Classes: Stratification and Mobility in Postindustrial Societies*. Thousand Oaks/London: Sage.

Etzioni, Amitai 1975: *A Comparative Analysis of Complex Organizations*. New York: Free Press.

Etzioni, Amitai 1985: Special Interest Groups versus Constituency Representation. In L. Kriesberg (ed.), *Research in Social Movements, Conflict and Change*, vol. 8. Greenwich, CT: JAI Press, 171–95.

Evans, Geoffrey (ed.) 1999: *The End of Class Politics?* Oxford: Oxford University Press.

Evans, Peter 2000: Fighting Marginalization with Transnational Networks. *Contemporary Sociology*, 29, 230–41.

Evans, Sara M. and Boyte, Harry C. 1986: *Free Spaces*. New York: Harper & Row.

Eyerman, Ron 1994: *Between Culture and Politics: Intellectuals and Modern Society*. Cambridge: Polity Press.

Eyerman, Ron and Jamison, Andrew 1991: *Social Movements: A Cognitive Approach*. Cambridge: Polity Press.

Eyerman, Ron and Jamison, Andrew 1994: Social Movements and Cultural Transformation: Popular Music in the 1960s. *Media, Culture and Society*, 17, 449–68.

Eyerman, Ron and Jamison, Andrew 1997: *Music and Social Movements*. Cambridge/New York: Cambridge University Press.

Fabbrini, Sergio 1986: *Neo-conservatorismo e politica americana*. Bologna: il Mulino.

Fabbrini, Sergio 1988: *Politica e mutamenti sociali*. Bologna: il Mulino.

Faber, Daniel 2004: Building a Transnational Environmental Justice Movement. In J. Bandy and J. Smith (eds.), *Coalitions Across Borders*. Lanham, MD: Rowman & Littlefield.

Fantasia, Rick 1988: *Cultures of Solidarity: Consciousness, Action, and Contemporary American Workers*. Berkeley/London: University of California Press.

Fantasia, Rick and Hirsch, Eric 1995: Culture in Rebellion: The Appropriation and Transformation of the Veil in the Algerian Revolution. In H. Johnston and B. Klandermans (eds.), *Social Movements and Culture*. Minneapolis: University of Minnesota Press, 144–59.

Fantasia, Rick and Stepan-Norris, Judith 2004: The Labor Movement in Motion. In David A. Snow, Sarah H Soule, and Hanspeter Kriesi (eds.), *The Blackwell Companion to Social Movements*. Oxford: Blackwell, 555–75.

Fantasia, Rick and Voss, Kim 2004: *Hard Work: Remaking the American Labor Movement*. Berkeley, CA: University of California Press.

Farrell, James J. 1997: *The Spirit of the Sixties: The Making of Postwar Radicalism*. New York: Routledge.

Farro, Antimo 1986: *Conflitti sociali e città*. Milano: Angeli.

Farro, Antimo 1991: *La lente verde*. Milano: Angeli.

Farro, Antimo 2003: Le tournant italien. In M. Wieviorka (ed.), *Un autre monde . . .* Paris: Balland, 177–94.

Favre Pierre (ed.) 1990: *La Manifestation*. Paris: Presses de la Fondation Nationale des Sciences Politiques.

Feagin, Joe R. and Capek, Stella M. 1991: Grassroots Movements in a Class Perspective. In P. C. Wasburn (ed.), *Research in Political Sociology*, vol. 5. Greenwich, CT: JAI Press, 27–53.

Featherstone, Mike (ed.) 1990: *Global Culture: Nationalism, Globalization and Modernity*. London: Sage.

Featherstone, Mike 1987: Lifestyle and Consumer Culture. *Theory, Culture and Society*, 4, 54–70.

Featherstone, Mike 1995: *Undoing Culture: Globalization, Postmodernism and Identity*. London/Thousand Oaks: Sage.

Fedel, Giorgio 1989: Cultura e simboli politici. In A. Panebianco (ed.), *L'Analisi della politica*. Bologna: il Mulino, 365 90.

Fernandez, Roberto and McAdam, Doug 1988: Social Networks and Social Movements: Multiorganizational Fields and Recruitment to Mississippi Freedom Summer. *Sociological Forum*, 3, 357–82.

Fernandez, Roberto and McAdam, Doug 1989: Multiorganizational Fields and Recruitment to Social Movements. In B. Klandermans (ed.), *Organizing for Change*. Greenwich, CT: JAI Press, 315–44.

Ferree, Myra Marx 1992: The Political Context of Rationality: Rational Choice Theory and Resource Mobilization. In A. Morris and C. McClurg Mueller (eds.), *Frontiers in Social Movement Theory*. New Haven: Yale University Press, 29–52.

Ferree, Myra Marx and Roth, Silke 1998: Gender, Class and the Interaction Between Social Movements. *Gender and Society*, 12, 626–48.

Ferree, Myra Marx and McClurg Mueller, Carol 2004: Feminism and the Women's Movement: A Global Perspective. In D. Snow, S. Soule, and H. Kriesi (eds.), *The Blackwell Companion to Social Movements*. Oxford: Blackwell, 576–607.

Ferree, Myra Marx, Gamson, William, Gerhards, Juergen, and Rucht, Dieter 2002: *Shaping Abortion Discourse: Democracy and the Public Sphere in Germany and the United States*. Cambridge and New York: Cambridge University Press.

Fillieule, Olivier (ed.) 1993a: Sociologie de la protestation. Les formes de l'action collective dans la France contemporaine. Paris: L'Harmattan.

Fillieule, Olivier 1993b: Conscience politique, persuasion et mobilisation des engagements. L'exemple du syndicat des chômeurs, 1983–1989. In Olivier Fillieule (ed.), *Sociologie de la protestation. Les formes de l'action collective dans la France contemporaine*. Paris: L'Harmattan, 123–55.

Fillieule, Olivier 2003: Local Environmental Politics in France: Case of the Louron Valley, 1984–1996. *French Politics*, 1, 305–30.

Fillieule, Olivier and Jobard, Fabien 1998: The Policing of Protest in France: Towards a Model of Protest Policing. In D. della Porta and H. Reiter (eds.), *Policing Protest: The Control of Mass Demonstrations in Western Democracies*. Minneapolis: The University of Minnesota Press, 70–90.

Finnegan, William 2003: Affinity Groups and the Movement Against Corporate Globalization. In J. Goodwin and J. M. Jasper (eds.), *The Social Movements Reader*. Oxford: Blackwell, 210–18.

Fireman, Bruce and Gamson, William A. 1979: Utilitarian Logic in the Resource Mobilization Perspective. In J. D. McCarthy and M. N. Zald (eds.), *The Dynamics of Social Movements*. Cambridge, MA: Winthrop, 8–44.

Flam, Helena 1990: Emotional "Man": I. The Emotional "Man" and the Problem of Collective Action. *International Sociology*, 5, 39–56.

Fischer, Frank 1993: Citizen Participation and the Democratization of Policy Expertise: From Theoretical Inquiry to Practical Cases. *Policy Sciences, 26,* 165–87.

Flam, Helena 1994a: A Theoretical Framework for the Study of Encounters between States and Anti-Nuclear Movements. In H. Flam (ed.), *States and Antinuclear Movements.* Edinburgh: Edinburgh University Press, 9–26.

Flam, Helena 1994b: Political Responses to the Anti-Nuclear Challenge: I. Standard Deliberative and Decision-Making Settings. In H. Flam (ed.), *States and Antinuclear Movements.* Edinburgh: Edinburgh University Press, 299–328.

Flam, Helena 1994c: Political Responses to the Anti-Nuclear Challenge: II. Democratic Experiences and the Use of Force. In H. Flam (ed.), *States and Antinuclear Movements.* Edinburgh: Edinburgh University Press, 329–54.

Flam, Helena (ed.) 1994d: *States and Anti-Nuclear Movements.* Edinburgh: Edinburgh University Press.

Flam, Helena 2001: *Pink, Purple, Green: Women's, Religious, Environmental and Gay/Lesbian Movements in Central Europe Today.* New York: Columbia University Press.

Follesdal, Andreas 2004: Political Consumerism as Chance and Challenge. In Michele Micheletti, Andreas Follesdal, and Dietlind Stolle (eds.), *Politics, Products and Markets: Exploring Political Consumerism Past and Present.* New Brunswick, NJ: Transaction Publishers, 3–20.

Foot, John M. 1996: The "Left Opposition" and the Crisis: Rifondazione Comunista and La Rete. In S. Gundle and S. Parker (eds.), *The New Italian Republic.* London/New York: Routledge, 173–88.

Forbes, James D. 1985: Organizational and Political Dimensions of Consumer Pressure Groups. *Journal of Consumer Policy,* 8, 133–41.

Forno, Francesca 2004: *Protest in Italy from 1988 to 1997.* Ph.D. Dissertation, Department of Government, University of Strathclyde, Glasgow.

Forno, Francesca and Ceccarini, Luigi forthcoming: Ethical Consumerism in Italy. *South European Society and Politics.*

Foucault, Michel 1977: *Discipline and Punish.* New York: Pantheon.

Foweraker, Joe 1995: *Theorizing Social Movements.* London: Pluto.

Fox, Jonathan and Brown, David L. (eds.) 1998: *The Struggle for Accountability.* Cambridge, MA: MIT Press.

Frank, Andre Gunder and Fuentes, Maria 1994: On Studying Cycles in Social Movements. *Research in Social Movements, Conflict and Change,* 17, 173–96.

Franklin, Mark, Mackie, Tom, and Valen, Henry (eds.) 1992: *Electoral Change.* Cambridge/New York: Cambridge University Press.

Franzosi, Roberto 1995: *The Puzzle of Strikes: Class and State Strategies in Postwar Italy.* Cambridge: Cambridge University Press.

Franzosi, Roberto 2004: *From Words to Numbers.* Cambridge: Cambridge University Press.

Freeman, Jo 1979: Resource Mobilization and Strategy: A Model for Analyzing Social Movement Organizations. In M. N. Zald and J. D. McCarthy (eds.), *The Dynamics of Social Movements: Resource Mobilization, Social Control, and Tactics.* Cambridge, MA: Winthrop Publishing, 167–89.

Freeman, Jo 1983a: A Model for Analyzing the Strategic Options of Social Movement Organizations. In J. Freeman (ed.), *Social Movements of the Sixties and Seventies.* London: Longman, 193–210.

Freeman, Jo 1983b: On the Origins of Social Movements. In J. Freeman (ed.), *Social Movements of the Sixties and the Seventies*. New York: Longman, 8–30.

Freeman, Linton C. 1979: Centrality in Social Networks. I. Conceptual Clarifications. *Social Networks*, 1, 215–39.

Freschi, Anna Carola 2000: Comunità virtuali e partecipazione. Dall'antagonismo ai nuovi diritti. *Quaderni di Sociologia*, 23, 85–109.

Freschi, Anna Carola 2003: Dalla rete delle reti al movimento dei movimenti. Gli hacker e l'altra comunicazione. In D. della Porta and L. Mosca (eds.), *Globalizzazione e movimenti sociali*, 49–75. Roma: Manifestolibri.

Friberg, Mats and Hettne, Bjorn 1998: Local Mobilization and World System Politics. *International Social Science Journal*, 117, 341–60.

Friedman, Debra and McAdam, Doug 1992: Collective Identity and Activism. In A. Morris and C. McClurg Mueller (eds.), *Frontiers in Social Movement Theory*. New Haven: Yale University Press, 156–73.

Fuchs, Dieter and Rucht, Dieter 1994: Support for New Social Movements in Five Western European Countries. In C. Rootes and H. Davis (eds.), *A New Europe? Social Change and Political Transformation*. London: UCL Press, 86–111.

Fung, Archon and Wright, Erik Olin 2001: Deepening Democracy: Innovations in Empowered Participatory Governance. *Politics and Society*, 29, 5–41.

Galaskiewicz, Joseph 1979: *Exchange Networks and Community Politics*. Beverly Hills/London: Sage.

Galaskiewicz, Joseph 1985: Interorganizational Relations. *Annual Review of Sociology*, 11, 281–304.

Gale, Richard P. 1986: Social Movements and the State: The Environmental Movement, Counter-movement, and Governmental Agencies. *Sociological Perspectives*, 29, 202–40.

Gallagher, John and Bull, Chris 1996: *Perfect Enemies: The Religious Right, the Gay Movement, and the Politics of the 1990s*. New York: Crown Publishers.

Gallie, Duncan 1989: Social Inequalities and Class Radicalism in France and Britain. Cambridge: Cambridge University Press.

Gallino, Luciano 1978a: Comportamento collettivo. In *Dizionario di sociologia*. Torino: UTET, 128–31.

Gallino, Luciano 1978b: Conflitto. In *Dizionario di sociologia*. Torino: UTET, 156–61.

Gamson, Josh 1989: Silence, Death, and the Invisible Enemy: AIDS Activism and Social Movement "Newness." *Social Problems*, 36, 351–67.

Gamson, Josh 1995: Must Identity Movements Self-Destruct? A Queer Dilemma. *Social Problems*, 42, 390–407.

Gamson, William 1988: Political Discourse and Collective Action. In B. Klandermans, H. Kriesi, and S. Tarrow (eds.), *From Structure to Action*. Greenwich, CT: JAI Press, 219–46.

Gamson, William 1990: *The Strategy of Social Protest* (2nd edition). Belmont, CA: Wadsworth (original edition 1975).

Gamson, William 1992a: The Social Psychology of Collective Action. In A. Morris and C. McClurg Mueller (eds.), *Frontiers in Social Movement Theory*. New Haven: Yale University Press, 53–76.

Gamson, William 1992b: *Talking Politics*. Cambridge/New York: Cambridge University Press.

Gamson, William A. 2004: Bystanders, Public opinion and the Media. In Davis A. Snow, Sarah H. Soule, and Hanspeter Kriesi (eds.), *The Blackwell Companion to Social Movements*. Oxford: Blackwell, 242–61.

Gamson, William A., Croteau, David, Hoynes, William, and Sasson, Theodore 1992: Media Images and the Social Construction of Reality. *Annual Review of Sociology*, 18, 373–93.

Gamson, William and Meyer, David S. 1996: Framing Political Opportunity. In D. McAdam, J. D. McCarthy, and M. N. Zald (eds.), *Opportunities, Mobilizing Structures, and Framing*. New York/Cambridge: Cambridge University Press, 275–90.

Gamson, William and Modigliani, André 1989: Media Discourse and Public Opinion on Nuclear Power. *American Journal of Sociology*, 95, 1–37.

Gamson, William and Wolfsfeld, Gadi 1993: Movements and Media as Interacting Systems. *The Annals of the AAPSS*, 528, 114–25.

Gamson, William, Fireman, Bruce, and Rytina, Steve 1982: *Encounters with Unjust Authority*. Homewood, IL: Dorsey Press.

Gans, Herbert 1979: Symbolic Ethnicity: The Future of Ethnic Groups and Cultures in America. *Ethnic and Racial Studies*, 2, 1–20.

Garofalo, Reebee (ed.) 1992: *Rockin' the Boat: Mass Music and Mass Movements*. Boston: South End Press.

Gaventa, John 1982: *Power and Powerlessness: Quiescence and Rebellion in an Appalachian Valley*. Champaign, IL: University of Illinois Press.

Geary, Dick 1981: *European Labour Protest 1848–1939*. New York: St Martin's Press.

Geary, Dick 1989: Introduction. In D. Geary (ed.), *Labour and Socialist Movements in Europe Before 1914*. Oxford/New York: Berg.

Gelb, Joyce 1989: *Feminism and Politics: A Comparative Perspective*. Berkeley: University of California Press.

Gelb, Joyce and Palley, Marian Lief (eds.) 1982: *Women and Public Policies*. Princeton: Princeton University Press.

Gellner, Ernest 1993: *Ragione e religione*. Milano: il Saggiatore (original edition *Postmodernism, Reason and Religion*, London: Routledge, 1992).

Gerhards, Jürgen 1991: Die Mobilisierung gegen die IWF- und Welt-banktagung in Berlin: Gruppen, Veranstaltungen, Diskurse. In Roland Roth and Dieter Rucht (eds.), *Neue soziale Bewegungen in der Bundesrepublik Deutschland*. Bonn: Bundeszentrale für politische Bildung, 213–34.

Gerhards, Jürgen 1993: *Neue Konfliktlinie in der Mobilisierung öffentlicher Meinung. Warum die IWF Tagung in Berlin 1988 zu einem öffentlichen Streitthema würde*. Berlin: Sigma.

Gerhards, Jürgen 1995: Framing-Dimensions and Framing-Strategies: Contrasting Ideal- and Real-type Frames. *Social Science Information*, 34, 225–48.

Gerhards, Jürgen and Rucht, Dieter 1992: Mesomobilization Contexts: Organizing and Framing in Two Protest Campaigns in West Germany. *American Journal of Sociology*, 98, 555–96.

Gerlach, Luther 1971: Movements of Revolutionary Change: Some Structural Characteristics. *American Behavioral Scientist*, 43, 813–36.

Gerlach, Luther 2001: The Structure of Social Movements: Environmental Activism and Its Opponents. In J. Arquilla and D. Ronfeldt (eds.), *Networks and Netwars: The Future of Terror, Crime, and Militancy*. Santa Monica, CA: Rand, 289–310.

Gerlach, Luther and Hine, Virginia 1970: *People, Power and Change*. Indianapolis: The Bobbs-Merrill Company.

Giddens, Anthony 1983: La società europea negli anni ottanta: Divisioni di classe, conflitto di classe e diritti di cittadinanza. In G. Pasquino (ed.), *Le società complesse*. Bologna: il Mulino, 153–200.

Giddens, Anthony 1990: *The Consequences of Modernity*. Cambridge/Stanford, CA: Polity Press/Stanford University Press.

Gill, Stephen 2000: Toward a Postmodern Prince? The Battle of Seattle as a Moment in the New Politics of Globalisation. *Millennium*, 29 (1), 131–40.

Ginsborg, Paul 1990: *Italy Since 1943*. London: Penguin.

Girling, John 2004: *Social Movements and Symbolic Power: Radicalism, Reform and the Trial of Democracy in France*. New York: Palgrave Macmillan Press.

Gitlin, Todd 1980: *The Whole World is Watching: Mass Media in the Making and Unmaking of the New Left*. Berkeley/Los Angeles, CA: University of California Press.

Giugni, Marco 1996: Federalismo e movimenti sociali. In *Rivista italiana di scienza politica*, 26, 147–71.

Giugni, Marco 1998: The Other Side of the Coin: Crossnational Similarities between Social Movements. *Mobilization*, 3, 89–105.

Giugni, Marco 2004: *Social Protest and Policy Change*. Lanham, MD: Rowman & Littlefield.

Giugni, Marco and Passy, Florence (eds.) 2001. *Political Altruism? Solidarity Movements in International Perspective*. Lanham, MD: Rowman and Littlefield.

Giugni, Marco and Passy, Florence 1998: Contentious Politics in Complex Societies: New Social Movements between Conflict and Cooperation. In Marco Giugni, Doug McAdam, and Charles Tilly (eds.), *From Contention to Democracy*. Lanham, MD: Rowman and Littlefield, 81–107.

Giugni, Marco, McAdam, Doug, and Tilly, Charles (eds.) 1999: *How Movements Matter*. Minneapolis: University of Minnesota Press.

Goffman, Erving 1974: *Frame Analysis*. Cambridge, MA: Harvard University Press.

Goldstein, Robert J. 1983: *Political Repression in 19th Century Europe*. London: Croom Helm.

Goldstone, Jack A. 1991: *Revolution and Rebellion in the Early Modern World*. Berkeley/Los Angeles: University of California Press.

Goldstone, Jack A. 2003: Introduction: Bridging Institutionalized and Noninstitutionalized Politics. In Jack A. Goldstone (ed.), *States, Parties and Social Movements*. New York: Cambridge University Press, 1–25.

Goldthorpe, John H. 1982: On the Service Class, Its Formation and Future. In A. Giddens and G. Mackenzie (eds.), *Social Class and the Division of Labour*. Cambridge: Cambridge University Press.

Goodwin, Jeff and Pfaff, Steven 2001: Emotion Work in High-Risk Social Movements: Managing Fear in the U.S. and East German Civil Rights Movements. In J. Goodwin, J. Jasper, and F. Polletta (eds.), *Passionate Politics: Emotions and Social Movements*. Chicago: University of Chicago Press, 282–302.

Goodwin, Jeff and Jasper, James J. 2004a: Caught in a Winding. Snarling Vine: The Structural Bias of Political Process Theory. In Jeff Goodwin and James J. Jasper (eds.), *Rethinking Social Movements. Structure, Meaning and Emotions*. Lanham, MD: Rowman and Littlefield, 3–30.

Goodwin, Jeff and Jasper, James J. 2004b, Trouble in Paradigms. In Jeff Goodwin and James J. Jasper (eds.), *Rethinking Social Movements: Structure, Meaning and Emotions*. Lanham, MD: Rowman and Littlefield, 75–93.

Goodwin, Jeff, Jasper, James M., and Polletta, Francesca (eds.) 2001: *Passionate Politics*. Chicago: University of Chicago Press.

Goodwin, Jeff, Jasper, James M., and Polletta, Francesca 2004: Emotional Dimensions of Social Movements. In D. Snow, S. Soule, and H. Kriesi (eds.), *The Blackwell Companion to Social Movements*. Oxford: Blackwell, 413–32.

Gould, Deborah 2002: Strategic Framing, Emotions, and Superbarrio – Mexico City's Masked Crusader. *Mobilization*, 7 (2), 201–16.

Gould, Roger V. 1991: Multiple Networks and Mobilization in the Paris Commune 1871. *American Sociological Review*, 56, 716–29.

Gould, Roger V. 1993a: Trade Cohesion, Class Unity, and Urban Insurrection: Artisanal Activism in the French Commune. *American Journal of Sociology*, 98, 721–54.

Gould, Roger V. 1993b: Collective Action and Network Structure. *American Sociological Review*, 58, 182–96.

Gould, Roger V. 1995: *Insurgent Identities: Class, Community, and Protest in Paris from 1848 to the Commune*. Chicago/London: University of Chicago Press.

Gould, Roger V. 2003: Why do Networks Matter? Rationalist and Structuralist Interpretations. In M. Diani and D. McAdam (eds.), *Social Movements and Networks*. Oxford/New York: Oxford University Press, 233–57.

Gouldner, Alvin 1979: *The Future of Intellectuals and the Rise of the New Class*. New York: Continuum.

Grand, Steve and Kull, Steven 2002: *Worldviews 2002: American and European Public Opinion & Foreign Policy: Final Report*. www.worldviews.org/detailreports/compreport.pdf.

Granovetter, Mark 1973: The Strength of Weak Ties. *American Journal of Sociology*, 78, 1360–80.

Granovetter, Mark 1978: Threshold Models of Collective Behavior. *American Journal of Sociology*, 83, 1420–43.

Granovetter, Mark 1985: Economic Action and Social Structure: The Problem of Embeddedness. *American Journal of Sociology*, 91, 481–510.

Grant, W., Perl, A., and Knoepfel P. (eds.) 1999. *The Politics of Improving Urban Air Quality*. Aldershot, UK: Edward Elgar.

Grazioli, Marco and Lodi, Giovanni 1984: La mobilitazione collettiva negli anni ottanta: Tra condizione e convinzione. In A. Melucci (ed.), *Altri codici*, Bologna: il Mulino, 267–313.

Gret, Marion and Sintomer, Yves 2002: *Porto Alegre. L'éspoir d'une autre démocratie*. Paris: La Découverte.

Gronmo, Sigmund 1987: The Strategic Position of Consumers in the Information Society. *Journal of Consumer Policy*, 10, 43–67.

Gulati, Ranjay and Gargiulo, Martin 1999: Where Do Interorganizational Networks Come From? *American Journal of Sociology*, 104, 1439–93.

Gundle, Stephen and Parker, Simon (eds.) 1996: *The New Italian Republic: From the Fall of the Berlin Wall to Berlusconi*. London/New York: Routledge.

Gurak, Laura J. and Logie, John 2003: Internet Protests, from Text to Web. In M. McCaughey and M. D. Ayers (eds.), *Cyberactivism. Online Activism in Theory and Practice*. London: Routledge, 25–46.

Gurr, Ted R. 1970: *Why Men Rebel*. Princeton, NJ: Princeton University Press.

Gurr, Ted R. and Harff, Barbara 1994: *Ethnic Conflict in World Politics*. Boulder, CO: Westview Press.

Gusfield, Joseph 1962: Mass Society and Extremist Politics. *American Sociological Review*, 27, 19–30.

Gusfield, Joseph 1963: *Symbolic Crusade*. Urbana, IL: University of Illinois Press.

Gusfield, Joseph 1968: The Study of Social Movements. In D. L. Sills (ed.), *International Encyclopedia of the Social Sciences*. New York: Collier & Macmillan, 445–52.

Gusfield, Joseph 1981: Social Movements and Social Change: Perspectives of Linearity and Fluidity. In L. Kriesberg (ed.), *Research in Social Movements, Conflict and Change*, Vol. 4. Greenwich, CT: JAI Press, 317–39.

Gusfield, Joseph 1989: Constructing Ownership of Social Problems: Fun and Profit in the Welfare State. *Social Problems*, 36, 431–41.

Gusfield, Joseph 1994: The Reflexivity of Social Movements: Collective Behavior and Mass Society Theory Revisited. In E. Larana, H. Johnston, and J. Gusfield (eds.), *New Social Movements: From Ideology to Identity*. Philadelphia: Temple University Press, 58–78.

Haas, Ernst B. 1964: *Beyond the Nation State: Functionalism and International Organization*. Stanford: Stanford University Press.

Haas, Peter M. 1992: Introduction: Epistemic Communities and International Policy Coordination. *International Organization*, 46, 1–37.

Habermas, Jürgen 1976: *Legitimation Crisis*. London: Heinemann.

Habermas, Jürgen 1978: *Knowledge and Human Interests*. London: Heinemann.

Habermas, Jürgen 1981: *Theorie des kommunikativen Handelns*. Frankfurt am Main: Suhrkamp.

Habermas, Jürgen 1987: *The Theory of Communicative Action*. Cambridge: Polity Press.

Habermas, Jürgen 1989: *The Structural Transformation of the Public Sphere*. Cambridge, MA: MIT Press.

Habermas, Jürgen 1996: *Between Facts and Norms: Contribution to a Discursive Theory of Law and Democracy*. Cambridge, MA: MIT Press.

Hägerstrand, Torsten 1967: *Innovation Diffusion as a Spatial Process*. Chicago: University of Chicago Press.

Haines, Herbert H. 1988: *Black Radicals and the Civil Rights Mainstream, 1954–1970*. Knoxville: University of Tennessee Press.

Hainsworth, Paul (ed.) 1992: *The Extreme Right in Europe and the USA*. London: Pinter.

Hajer, Maarten and Kesselring, Sven 1999: Democracy in the Risk Society? *Environmental Politics*, 8 (3), 1–23.

Hall, Richard 1982: *Organizations: Structure and Process*. Englewood Cliffs, NJ: Prentice-Hall.

Hampton, Keith and Wellmann, Barry 2001: Long Distance Community in the Network Society. *American Behavioral Scientist*, 45, 477–96.

Hanagan, Michael 1998a: Social Movements. Incorporation, Disengagement, and Opportunities – A Long View. In Marco Giugni, Doug McAdam, and Charles Tilly (eds.), *From Contention to Democracy*. Lanham, MD: Rowman and Littlefield, 3–31.

Hanagan, Michael 1998b: Irish Transnational Movements, Deterritorialized Migrants, and the State. *Mobilization*, 3, 107–26.

Hannigan, John 1995: *Environmental Sociology*. London / New York: Routledge.

Hargreaves Heap, Shaun, Hollis, Martin, Lyons, Bruce, Sugden, Robert, and Weale, Albert 1992: *The Theory of Choice: A Critical Guide*. Oxford/Cambridge, MA: Blackwell.

Hathaway, Will and Meyer, David S. 1993–4: Competition and Cooperation in Social Movement Coalitions: Lobbying for Peace in the 1980s. *Berkeley Journal of Sociology*, 38, 157–83.

Haunss, Sebastian and Leach, Darcy K. 2004: Scenes and Social Movements. Paper for the ECPR Annual Sessions of Workshops, Uppsala, 13–18 April.

Haydu, Jeffrey 1999: Counter Action Frames: Employer Repertoires and the Union Menace in the Late Nineteenth Century. *Social Problems*, 313–31.

Heath Anthony, Jowell, Roger, Curtice, John, Evans, Geoffrey, Field, John, and Whiterspoon, S. 1991: *Understanding Political Change: The British Voter 1946–1987*. Oxford: Pergamon Press.

Hechter, Michael 1975: *Internal Colonialism: The Celtic Fringe in British National Development, 1536–1966*. London: Routledge & Kegan Paul.

Heckathorn, Douglas D. 1989a: Collective Action and the Second-Order Free-Rider Problem. *Rationality and Society*, 1, 78–100.

Heckathorn, Douglas D. 1989b: Collective Sanctions and the Creation of Prisoner's Dilemma Norms. *American Journal of Sociology*, 94, 535–562.

Heckathorn, Douglas D. 1990: Collective Sanctions and Compliance Norms: A Formal Theory of Group-Mediated Social Control. *American Sociological Review*, 55, 366–84.

Heckathorn, Douglas D. 1991: Extensions of the Prisoner's Dilemma Paradigm: The Altruist's Dilemma and Group Solidarity. *Sociological Theory*, 9, 34–52.

Heckathorn, Douglas D. 1993: Collective Action and Group Heterogeneity: Voluntary Provision versus Selective Incentives. *American Sociological Review*, 58, 329–50.

Heckathorn, Douglas D. 1996: The Dynamics and Dilemmas of Collective Action. *American Sociological Review*, 61, 250–77.

Hedström, Peter 1994: Contagious Collectivities. On the Spatial Diffusion of Swedish Trade Unions, 1890–1940. *American Journal of Sociology*, 99, 1157–79.

Hedström, Peter and Swedberg, Richard (eds.) 1998: *Social Mechanisms: An Analytical Approach to Social Theory*. Cambridge, UK: Cambridge University Press.

Hedström, Peter, Sandell, Rickard, and Stern, Charlotta 2000: Mesolevel Networks and the Diffusion of Social Movements: The Case of the Swedish Social Democratic Party. *American Journal of Sociology*, 106, 145–72.

Heiberg, Marianne 1989: *The Making of the Basque Nation*. Cambridge/New York: Cambridge University Press.

Heirich, Max 1971: *The Spiral of Conflict: Berkeley 1964*. New York: Columbia University Press.

Held, David, and McGrew, Anthony 2000: *The Global Transformation Reader: An Introduction*. Cambridge: Polity Press.

Held, David, McGrew, Anthony, Goldblatt, David, and Perraton, Jonathan 1999: *Global Transformations*. Cambridge: Polity Press.

Hellman, Judith 1987: *Journeys among Women: Feminism in Five Italian Cities*. Oxford: Oxford University Press.

Herman, Didi 1997: *The Antigay Agenda: Orthodox Vision and the Christian Right*. Chicago: University of Chicago Press, 1997.

Hertz, Noreena 2001: *The Silent Takeover: Global Capitalism and the Death of Democracy*. London: Heinemann.

Hewitt, Lyndi and McCammon, Holly 2004: Explaining Suffrage Mobilization: Balance, Neutralization, and Range in Collective Action Frames. *Mobilization*, 9, 149–66.

Hick, Steven, and McNutt, John 2002: Communities and Advocacy on the Internet: A Conceptual Framework. In S. Hick and J. McNutt (eds.), *Advocacy, Activism and the Internet*. Chicago: Lyceum Books, 3–18.

Hilgartner, Stephen and Bosk, Charles L. 1988: The Rise and Fall of Social Problems: A Public Arenas Model. *American Journal of Sociology*, 94, 53–78.

Hinckley, Barbara 1981: *Coalitions and Politics*. New York: Harcourt Brace Jovanovich.

Hipsher, Patricia L. 1998: Democratic Transitions as Protest Cycles: Social Movement Dynamics in Democratizing Latin America. In David S. Meyer and Sidney Tarrow (eds.), *The Social Movement Society*. New York: Rowman and Littlefield, 153–72.

Hirsch, Eric L. 1990: Sacrifice for the Cause: The Impact of Group Processes on Recruitment and Commitment in Protest Movements. *American Sociological Review*, 55, 243–54.

Hirsch, Joachim 1988: The Crisis of Fordism, Transformations of The "Keynesian" Security State, and New Social Movements. *Research in Social Movements, Conflicts and Change*, 10, 43–55.

Hirschman, Albert O. 1982: *Shifting Involvements: Private Interests and Public Action*. Princeton, NJ: Princeton University Press.

Hirst, Paul 1994: *Associative Democracy: New Forms of Economic and Social Governance*. Cambridge: Polity Press.

Hobsbawm, Eric, 1952, The Machine Breakers. *Past and Present*, 1, 57–70.

Hobsbawm, Eric 1991: *Nazioni e nazionalismo dal 1780: Programma, mito, realtà*. Turin: Einaudi. (Original edition *Nations and Nationalism since 1780*, Cambridge/New York: Cambridge University Press, 1993.)

Hobsbawm, Eric 1994: *Age of Extremes: The Short Twentieth Century, 1914–1991*. London: Penguin.

Hobsbawm, Eric and Ranger, Terence (eds.) 1983: *The Invention of Tradition*. Cambridge/New York: Cambridge University Press.

Hoffman, Lily M. 1989: *The Politics of Knowledge: Activist Movements in Medicine and Planning*. Albany, NY: SUNY Press.

Horton, Lynne 2004: Constructing Conservative Identity: Peasant Mobilization Against Revolution in Nicaragua. *Mobilization*, 9, 167–80.

Hourigan, Niahm 2003: *Escaping the Global Village: Media, Language and Protest*. Lanham, MD: Lexington Books.

Howard, Judith A. 2000: Social Psychology of Identities. *Annual Review of Sociology*, 26, 367–93.

Hunt, Lynn 1984: *Politics, Culture, and Class in the French Revolution*. Berkeley, CA: University of California Press.

Hunt, Scott A. 1992: Critical Dramaturgy and Collective Rhetoric: Cognitive and Moral Order in the Communist Manifesto. *Perspectives on Social Problems*, 3, 1–18.

Hunt, Scott A. and Benford, Robert D. 1994: Identity Talk in the Peace and Justice Movement. *Journal of Contemporary Ethnography*, 22, 488–517.

Hunt, Scott A. and Benford, Robert D. 2004: Collective Identity, Solidarity, and Commitment. In D. Snow, S. Soule, and H. Kriesi (eds.), *The Blackwell Companion to Social Movements*. Oxford: Blackwell, 694–715.

Hunt, Scott A., Benford, Robert D. and Snow, David A. 1994: Identity Fields: Framing Processes and the Social Construction of Movement Identities. In E. Larana, H. Johnston, and J. R. Gusfield (eds.), *New Social Movements: From Ideology to Identity*. Philadelphia: Temple University Press, 185–208.

Hunter, Floyd 1953: *Community Power Structure: A Study of Decision Makers*. Chapel Hill: University of North Carolina Press.

Huntington, Samuel 1993: The Clash of Civilizations? *Foreign Affairs*, 72, 22–49.

Huntington, Samuel 1996: *The Clash of Civilizations and the Remaking of World Order*. New York: Simon & Schuster.

Ibarra, Pedro 1995: Nuevas Formas de Comportamiento Politico: Los Nuevos Movimientos Sociales. *Inuruak: Revista Vasca de Sociologia y Ciencias Politica*, 13, 39–60.

Ignazi, Piero 1994: *L'estrema destra in europa*. Bologna: il Mulino.

Ignazi, Piero and Ysmal, Colette 1992: New and Old Extreme Right-wing Parties: The French Front National and the Italian Movimento Sociale. *European Journal of Political Research*, 22, 101–20.

Imig, Doug and Tarrow, Sidney (eds.) 2001a: *Contentious Europeans: Protest and Politics in an Emerging Polity*. Lanham, MD: Rowman & Littlefield.

Imig, Doug, and Tarrow, Sidney 2001b: La contestation politique dans l'Europe en formation. In R. Balme, D. Chabanet, and V. Wright (eds.), *L'action collective en Europe*. Paris: Presses De Science Po, 195–223.

Inglehart, Ronald 1977: *The Silent Revolution: Changing Values and Political Styles among Western Publics*. Princeton: Princeton University Press.

Inglehart, Ronald 1985: New Perspectives on Value Change. *Comparative Political Studies*, 17, 485–532.

Inglehart, Ronald 1990a: *Culture Shift in Advanced Industrial Society*. Princeton, NJ: Princeton University Press.

Inglehart, Ronald 1990b: Values, Ideology, and Cognitive Mobilization in New Social Movements. In R. Dalton and M. Kuechler (eds.), *Challenging the Political Order*. Cambridge: Polity Press, 43–66.

Inglehart, Ronald 1997: *Modernization and Postmodernization: Cultural, Economic, and Political Change in 43 Societies*. Princeton, NJ: Princeton University Press.

Inglehart, Ronald 1999: Globalization and Postmodern Values. *The Washington Quarterly*, 23, 215–28.

Inglehart, Ronald and Abramson, Paul R. 1994: Economic Security and Value Change. *American Political Science Review*, 88, 336–54.

Inglehart, Ronald and Baker, Wayne 2000: Modernization, Globalization, and the Persistence of Tradition: Empirical Evidence from 65 Countries. *American Sociological Review*, 65, 19–55.

Inglehart, Ronald and Catterberg, Gabriela 2002: Trends in Political Action: The Developmental Trend and the Post-Honeymoon Decline, *International Journal of Comparative Sociology*, 43, 300–16.

Inglehart, Ronald and Norris, Pippa 2003: *Rising Tide: Gender Equality and Cultural Change Around the World*. New York: Cambridge University Press.

Inglehart, Ronald and Norris, Pippa 2005: *Secular and Sacred*. New York: Cambridge University Press.

Isaac, Larry and Christiansen, Lars 2002: How the Civil Rights Movement Revitalized Labor Militancy. *American Sociological Review*, 67, 722–46.

Jackson, John Harold and Morgan, C. P. 1978: *Organizational Theory: A Macroperspective for Management*. Englewood Cliffs, NJ: Prentice-Hall.

Jamison, Andrew and Eyerman, Ron 1994: *Seeds of the Sixties*. Berkeley/Los Angeles: University of California Press.

Jamison, Andrew, Eyerman, Ron, and Cramer, Jacqueline 1990: *The Making of the New Environmental Consciousness: A Comparative Study of the Environmental Movements in Sweden, Denmark and the Netherlands*. Edinburgh: Edinburgh University Press.

Janda, Kenneth 1970: *A Conceptual Framework for the Comparative Analysis of Political Parties*. Beverly Hills, CA: Sage.

Jansen, Robert 2003: Resurrection and Reappropriation: Political Uses of Historical Figures in Comparative Perspective. Unpublished paper. Los Angeles: UCLA.

Jasper, James 1997: *The Art of Moral Protest: Culture, Biography, and Creativity in Social Movements*. Chicago: University of Chicago Press.

Jasper, James M. and Nelkin, Dorothy 1992: *The Animal Rights Crusade: The Growth of a Moral Protest*. New York: Free Press.

Jasper, James M. and Poulsen, Jane 1995: Recruiting Strangers and Friends: Moral Shocks and Social Networks in Animal Right and Anti-Nuclear Protests. *Social Problems*, 42, 493–512.

Jenkins, J. Craig 1983: Resource Mobilization Theory and the Study of Social Movements. *Annual Review of Sociology*, 9, 527–53.

Jenkins, J. Craig 1985: *The Politics of Insurgency: The Farm Worker Movement in the 1960s*. New York: Columbia University Press.

Jenkins, J. Craig and Klandermans, Bert 1995: The Politics of Social Protest. In J. C. Jenkins and B. Klandermans (eds.), *The Politics of Social Protest: Comparative Perspectives on States and Social Movements*. Minneapolis: University of Minnesota Press, 3–13.

Jenkins, J. Craig and Leicht, Kevin 1997: *Class Analysis and Social Movements: A Critique and Reformulation*. In John R. Hall (ed.), *Reworking Class*. Ithaca: Cornell University Press, 369–97.

Jenkins, J. Craig and Perrow, Charles 1977: Insurgency of the Powerless: The Farm Worker Movements 1946–1972. *American Sociological Review*, 42, 249–68.

Jennings, M. Kent, van Deth, Jan, Barnes, Samuel, Fuchs, Dieter, Heunks, Felix, Inglehart, Ronald, Kaase, Max, Klingemann, Hans-Dieter, and Thomassen, Jacques 1990: *Continuities in Political Action*. Berlin/New York: Walter de Gruyter.

Jenson, Jane 1995: What's in a Name? Nationalist Movements and Public Discourse. In H. Johnston and B. Klandermans (eds.), *Social Movements and Culture*. Minneapolis/London: University of Minnesota/UCL Press, 107–26.

Johnson, Erik and McCarthy, John 2005: The Sequencing of Transnational and National Social Movement Mobilization: The Organizational Mobilization of the Global and U.S. Environmental Movements. In D. della Porta and S. Tarrow (eds.), *Transnational Protest and Global Activism*. Lanham, MD: Rowman & Littlefield, 71–93.

Johnston, Hank 1980: The Marketed Social Movement: The Case of TM. *Pacific Sociological Review*, 23, 333–54.

Johnston, Hank 1991a: Antecedents of Coalition: Frame Alignment and Utilitarian Unity in the Catalan Anti-Francoist Opposition. In L. Kriesberg (ed.), *Research in Social Movements, Conflict and Change*, vol. 13. Greenwich, CT: JAI Press, 241–59.

Johnston, Hank 1991b: *Tales of Nationalism: Catalonia, 1939–1979*. New Brunswick, NJ: Rutgers University Press.

Johnston, Hank 1994: New Social Movements and Old Regional Nationalisms. In E. Larana, H. Johnston and J. Gusfield (eds.), *New Social Movements: From Ideology to Identity*. Philadelphia: Temple University Press, 267–86.

Johnston, Hank 1995a: A Methodology for Frame Analysis: From Discourse to Cognitive Schemata. In H. Johnston and B. Klandermans (eds.), *Social Movements and Culture*. Minneapolis/London: University of Minnesota Press/UCL Press, 217–46.

Johnston, Hank 1995b: The Trajectory of Nationalist Movements: Catalan and Basque Comparisons. *Journal of Political and Military Sociology*, 23, 231–49.

Johnston, Hank 2002: Verification and Proof in Frame and Discourse Analysis. In B. Klandermans and S. Staggenborg (eds.), *Methods of Social Movement Research*. Minneapolis: University of Minnesota Press, 62–91.

Johnston, Hank and Aarelaid-Tart, Aili 2000: Generations and Collective Action in Authoritarian Regimes: the Estonian National Opposition, 1940–1990. *Sociological Perspectives*, 43, 671–98.

Johnston, Hank and Klandermans, Bert (eds.) 1995: *Social Movements and Culture*. Minneapolis/London: University of Minnesota Press/UCL Press.

Jones, Andrew, Hutchinson, Richard, van Dyke, Nella, and Gates, Leslie 2001: Coalition Form and Mobilization Effectiveness in Local Social Movements. *Sociological Spectrum*, 21, 207–31.

Joppke, Christian 1993: *Mobilizing against Nuclear Energy: A Comparison of Germany and the United States*. Berkeley/Los Angeles: University of California Press.

Joppke, Christian 1994: Revisionisms, Dissidence, Nationalism: Opposition in Leninist Regimes. *British Journal of Sociology*, 45, 543–61.

Jordan, Grant and Maloney, William 1997: *The Protest Business*. Manchester: Manchester University Press.

Jordan, John 2002: The Art of Necessity: The Subversive Imagination of Anti-Road Protests and Reclaim the Streets. In S. Duncombe (ed.), *The Cultural Resistance Reader*. London: Verso.

Jordan, Tim 1994: *Reinventing Revolution: Value and Difference in New Social Movements and the Left*. Aldershot: Avebury.

Jordan, Tim 2002: *Activism! Direct Action, Hacktivism and the Future of Society*. London: Reaktion Books.

Jünschke, Klaus 1988: *Spätlese: Texte zu Raf und Knast*. Frankfurt am Main: Neue Kritik.

Kaase, Max 1990: Social Movements and Political Innovation. In R. Dalton and M. Kuechler (eds.), *Challenging the Political Order: New Social and Political Movements in Western Democracies*. New York: Oxford University Press.

Kaldor, Mary 2000: Civilizing Globalization? The Implication of the "Battle in Seattle." *Millennium*, 29, 100–14.

Kanter, Rosabeth M. 1968: Commitment and Social Organization: A Study of Commitment Mechanisms in Utopian Communities. *American Sociological Review*, 33, 499–517.

Kanter, Rosabeth M. 1972: Commitment and the Internal Organization of Millennial Movements. *American Behavioral Scientist*, 16, 219–43.

Kaplan, Jeffrey and Lööw, Heléne (eds.) 2002: *The Cultic Milieu: Oppositional Subcultures in an Age of Globalization*. Walnut Creek, CA: Alta Mira Press.

Kaplan, Laura 1995: *The Story of Jane: The Legendary Underground Feminist Abortion Service*. Chicago: University of Chicago Press.

Karstedt-Henke, Suzanne 1980: Theorien zur Erklärung terroristischer Bewegungen. In Erhard Blankenberg (ed.), *Politik der inneren Sicherheit*. Frankfurt am Main: Suhrkamp, 198–234.

Katz, Daniel and Lazarsfeld, Paul 1955: *Personal Influence*. Glencoe, IL: Free Press.

Katzenstein, Mary 1987: Comparing the Feminist Movements of the United States and Western Europe: An Overview. In Mary Katzenstein and Carol Mueller (eds.), *The Women's Movements of the United States and Western Europe*. Philadelphia: Temple University Press, 3–20.

Katzenstein, Mary Fainsod 1998: *Faithful and Fearless: Moving Feminist Protest inside the Church and Military*. Princeton, Princeton University Press.

Katzenstein, Peter J. 1985: *Small States in the World Market*. Ithaca, NY: Cornell University Press.

Keane, John (ed.) 1988: *Democracy and Civil Society*. London: Verso.

Keating, Michael 1988: *State and Regional Nationalism: Territorial Politics and the European State*. London: Harvester-Wheatsheaf.

Keck, Margeret, and Sikkink, Kathryn 1998: *Activists Beyond Borders*. Ithaca: Cornell University Press.

Kertzer, David 1988: *Rituals, Politics, and Power*. New Haven: Yale University Press.

Kertzer, David 1996: *Politics and Symbols: The Italian Communist Party and the Fall of Communism*, New Haven and London: Yale University Press.

Khagram, Sanjeev, V. Riker, Jamev, and Sikkink, Kathryn (eds.) 2002: *Reconstructing World Politics: Transnational Social Movements, Networks and Norms*. Minneapolis: University of Minnesota Press.

Khawaja, Marwan 1994: Resource Mobilization, Hardship, and Popular Collective Action in the West Bank. *Social Forces*, 73, 191–220.

Kielbowicz, Richard B. and Scherer, Clifford 1986: The Role of the Press in the Dynamics of Social Movements. *Research in Social Movements, Conflict and Change*, 9, 71–96.

Killian, Lewis 1964: Social Movements. In Robert E. Farris (ed.), *Handbook of Modern Sociology*. Chicago: Rand McNally, 426–45.

Killian, Lewis 1984: Organization, Rationality and Spontaneity in the Civil Rights Movement. *American Sociological Review*, 49, 770–83.

Kim, Hyojoung 2002: Shame, Anger, and Love in Collective Action: Emotional Consequences of Suicide Protest in South Korea, 1991. *Mobilization*, 7, 159–76.

Kim, Hyojoung and Bearman, Peter S. 1997: The Structure and Dynamics of Movement Participation. *American Sociological Review*, 62, 70–93.

Kimeldorf, Howard and Stepan-Norris, Judith 1992: Historical Studies of Labor Movements in the United States. *Annual Review of Sociology*, 18, 495–517.

Kinnear, Ralph 1990: Visions of Europe: An Eco-Dynamic Approach to Ethno-Linguistic Conflict, Self-Organisation and the Role of the State. Unpublished paper. London School of Economics, London.

Kitschelt, Herbert 1985: New Social Movements in West Germany and the United States. *Political Power and Social Theory*, 5, 273–342.

Kitschelt, Herbert 1986: Political Opportunity Structures and Political Protest: Anti-Nuclear Movements in Four Democracies. *British Journal of Political Science*, 16, 57–85.

Kitschelt, Herbert 1989: *The Logics of Party Formation: Ecological Politics in Belgium and West Germany*. Ithaca: Cornell University Press.

Kitschelt, Herbert 1990: New Social Movements and the Decline of Party Organization. In R. J. Dalton and M. Kuechler (eds.), *Challenging the Political Order*. Cambridge: Polity Press, 179–208.

Kitschelt, Herbert 1993: Social Movements, Political Parties, and Democratic Theory. *The Annals of the AAPSS*, 528, 13–29.

Kitschelt, Herbert 1995: *The Radical Right in Western Europe: A Comparative Analysis* (in collaboration with Anthony J. McGann). Ann Arbor: University of Michigan Press.

Kitschelt, Herbert and Hellemans, Staff 1990: *Beyond the European Left: Ideology and Political Action in the Belgian Ecology Parties*. Durham NC/London: Duke University Press.

Kitts, James 2000: Mobilizing in Black Boxes: Social Networks and SMO Participation. *Mobilization*, 5, 241–57.

Klandermans, Bert (ed.) 1989: *Organizing For Change: Social Movement Organizations Across Cultures*. Greenwich, CT: JAI Press.

Klandermans, Bert 1984: Mobilization and Participation: Social-Psychological Expansions of Resource Mobilization Theory. *American Sociological Review*, 49, 583–600.

Klandermans, Bert 1988: The Formation and Mobilization of Consensus. In B. Klandermans, H. Kriesi, and S. Tarrow (eds.), *From Structure to Action*. Greenwich, CT: JAI Press, 173–96.

Klandermans, Bert 1989a: Grievance Interpretation and Success Expectations: The Social Construction of Protest. *Social Behavior*, 4, 113–25.

Klandermans, Bert 1989b: Introduction: Social Movement Organizations and the Study of Social Movements. In B. Klandermans (ed.), *Organizing for Change*. Greenwich, CT: JAI Press, 1–17.

Klandermans, Bert 1990: Linking the "Old" and "New": Movement Networks in the Netherlands. In R. Dalton and M. Kuechler (eds.), *Challenging the Political Order: New Social and Political Movements in Western Democracies*. Cambridge: Polity Press, 122–36.

Klandermans, Bert 1997: *The Social Psychology of Protest*. Oxford/Cambridge, MA: Blackwell.

Klandermans, Bert, Kriesi, Hanspeter and Tarrow, Sidney (eds.) 1988: *From Structure to Action: Comparing Social Movement Research across Cultures*. Greenwich, CT: JAI Press.

Klandermans, Bert, Roefs, Marlene, and Olivier, Johan 1998: A Movement Takes Office. In David S. Meyer and Sidney Tarrow (eds.), *The Social Movement Society*. New York, Rowman and Littlefield, 173–195.

Klandermans, Bert, and Staggenborg, Suzanne (eds.) 2002: *Methods of Social Movement Research*. Minneapolis: University of Minnesota Press.

Klandermans, Bert and Tarrow, Sidney 1988: Mobilization into Social Movements: Synthesizing European and American Approaches. In B. Klandermans, H. Kriesi, and S. Tarrow (eds.), *From Structure to Action*. Greenwich, CT: JAI Press, 1–40.

Kleidman, Robert 1993: *Organizing for Peace: Neutrality, the Test Ban, and the Freeze*. Syracuse, NY: Syracuse University Press.

Klein, Ethel 1984: *Gender Politics: From Consciousness to Mass Politics*. Cambridge, MA: Harvard University Press.

Klein, Naomi 1999: *No Logo*. New York: HarperCollins.

Klein, Naomi 2002: *Fences and Windows: Dispatches From the Front Lines of the Globalization Debate*. London: Flamingo.

Klotz, Audie 1995: *Norms in International Relations: The Struggle against Apartheid*. Ithaca: Cornell University Press.

Kniss, Fred and Burns, Gene 2004: Religious Movements. In D. Snow, S. Soule, and H. Kriesi (eds.), *The Blackwell Companion to Social Movements*. Oxford: Blackwell, 413–32.

Knoke, David 1983: Organization Sponsorship and Influence Reputation of Social Influence Associations. *Social Forces*, 61, 1065–87.

Knoke, David 1990a: *Organizing for Collective Action: The Political Economies of Associations*. New York: Aldine de Gruyter.

Knoke, David 1990b: *Political Networks*. Cambridge: Cambridge University Press.

Knoke, David 1990c: Networks of Political Action: Toward Theory Construction. *Social Forces*, 68, 1041–63.

Knoke, David and Kuklinski, James H. 1982: *Network Analysis*. London/Newbury Park, CA: Sage.

Knoke, David and Wisely, Nancy 1990: Social Movements. In D. Knoke, *Political Networks*. Cambridge/New York: Cambridge University Press, 57–84.

Knoke, David and Wood, James R. 1981: *Organized for Action: Commitment in Voluntary Associations*. New Brunswick, NJ: Rutgers University Press.

Koelble, Thomas A. 1991: *The Left Unraveled: Social Democracy and the New Left Challenge in Britain*. Durham: Duke University Press.

Koestler, Arthur 1969: *The Invisible Writing*. New York: Stein and Day.

Kolb, Felix 2005: The Impact of Transnational Protest on Social Movement Organizations: Mass Media and the Making of ATTAC. In D. della Porta and S. Tarrow (eds.), *Transnational Protest and Global Activism*. Lanham, MD: Rowman & Littlefield, 95–120.

Koopmans, Ruud 1990: Bridging the Gap: The Missing Link between Political Opportunity Structure and Movement Action. Paper presented at the Twelfth World Congress of the International Sociological Association, Madrid.

Koopmans, Ruud 1993: The Dynamics of Protest Waves: West Germany, 1965 to 1989. *American Sociological Review*, 58, 637–58.

Koopmans, Ruud 1995: *Democracy from Below: New Social Movements and the Political System in West Germany*. Boulder, CO: Westview Press.

Koopmans, Ruud 1996a: Explaining the Rise of Racist and Extreme Right Violence in Western Europe: Grievances or Opportunities? *European Journal of Political Research*, 30, 185–216.

Koopmans, Ruud 1996b: New Social Movements and Changes in Political Participation in Western Europe. *West European Politics*, 19, 28–50.

Koopmans, Ruud 1997: Dynamics of Repression and Mobilization: The German Extreme Right in the 1990s. *Mobilization*, 2, 149–65.

Koopmans, Ruud 2004: Political Opportunity Structure: Some Splitting to Balance the Lumping. In Goodwin, Jeff and James J. Jasper (eds.), *Rethinking Social Movements: Structure, Meaning and Emotions*. Lanham, MD: Rowman and Littlefield, 61–74.

Koopmans, Ruud and Duyvendak, Jan-Willem 1995: The Political Construction of the Nuclear Energy Issue and Its Impact on the Mobilization of Anti-Nuclear Movements in Western Europe. *Social Problems*, 42, 201–18.

Koopmans, Ruud and Rucht, Dieter 1995: *Social Movement Mobilization under Right and Left Governments: A Look at Four West European Countries*, Discussion Paper FS III: 95–106, Wissenschaftszentrum Berlin.

Koopmans, Ruud and Statham, Paul 1999: Ethnic and Civic Conceptions of Nationhood and the Differential Success of the Extreme Right in Germany and Italy. In M. Giugni, D. McAdam and C. Tilly (eds.), *How Movements Matter*. Minneapolis: University of Minnesota Press, 225–51.

Kornhauser, A. 1959: *The Politics of Mass Society*. Glencoe, IL: Free Press.

Kousis, Maria and Tilly, Charles 2004: Introduction: Economic and Political Contention in Comparative Perspective. In Maria Kousis and Charles Tilly (eds.), *Economic and Political Contention in Comparative Perspective*. Boulder, CO: Paradigm Publishers, 1–11.

Krackhardt, David and Porter, Lyman W. 1985: When Friends Leave: A Structural Analysis of the Relationship between Turnover and Stayer's Attitudes. *Administrative Science Quarterly*, 30, 242–61.

Krasniewicz, Louise 1992: *Nuclear Summer: The Clash of Communities at the Seneca Women's Peace Encampment*. Ithaca: Cornell University Press.

Kriesi, Hanspeter 1984: *Die Zürcher Bewegung: Bilder, Interaktionen, Zusammenhänge*. Frankfurt am Main: Campus.

Kriesi, Hanspeter 1988a: The Interdependence of Structure and Action: Some Reflections on the State of the Art. In B. Klandermans, H. Kriesi, and S. Tarrow (eds.), *From Structure to Action*. Greenwich, CT: JAI Press, 349–68.

Kriesi, Hanspeter 1988b: Local Mobilization for the People's Petition of the Dutch Peace Movement. In B. Klandermans, H. Kriesi, and S. Tarrow (eds.), *From Structure to Action*. Greenwich, CT: JAI Press, 41–82.

Kriesi, Hanspeter 1989a: The Political Opportunity Structure of the Dutch Peace Movement. *West European Politics*, 12, 295–312.

Kriesi, Hanspeter 1989b: New Social Movements and the New Class in the Netherlands. *American Journal of Sociology*, 94, 1078–1116.

Kriesi, Hanspeter 1991: *The Political Opportunity Structure of New Social Movements*, Discussion Paper FS III: 91–103. Wissenschaftszentrum Berlin.

Kriesi, Hanspeter 1992: Support and Mobilisation Potential for New Social Movements. In M. Diani and R. Eyerman (eds.), *Studying Collective Action*. Newbury Park/London: Sage, 22–54.

Kriesi, Hanspeter 1993: *Political Mobilization and Social Change: The Dutch Case in Comparative Perspective*. Aldershot: Avebury.

Kriesi, Hanspeter 1995: The Political Opportunity Structure of New Social Movements: Its Impact on Their Mobilization. In J. C. Jenkins and B. Klandermans (eds.), *The Politics of Social Protest*. Minneapolis/London: University of Minnesota Press/UCL Press, 167–98.

Kriesi, Hanspeter 1996: The Organizational Structure of New Social Movements in a Political Context. In D. McAdam, J. McCarthy, and M. N. Zald (eds.), *Comparative Perspective on Social Movements: Political Opportunities, Mobilizing Structures, and Cultural Framing*. Cambridge/New York: Cambridge University Press, 152–84.

Kriesi, Hanspeter 2003: The Transformation of the National Political Space in a Globalizing World. In P. Ibarra (ed.), *Social Movements and Democracy*. New York: Palgrave Macmillan, 195–210.

Kriesi, Hanspeter 2004: Political Context and Opportunity. In Davis A. Snow, Sarah H. Soule, and Hanspeter Kriesi (eds.), *The Blackwell Companion to Social Movements*. Oxford: Blackwell, 67–90.

Kriesi, Hanspeter, Koopmans, Ruud, Duyvendak, Jan-Willem, and Giugni, Marco 1995: *New Social Movements in Western Europe*. Minneapolis/London: University of Minnesota Press/UCL Press.

Kriesi, Hanspeter and van Praag, Philip 1987: Old and New Politics: The Dutch Peace Movement and the Traditional Political Organizations. *European Journal of Political Research*, 15, 319–46.

Kumar, Krishan 1995: *From Post-industrial to Post-modern Society*. Oxford/Cambridge, MA: Blackwell.

Kumar, Krishan 2005: *From Post-Industrial to Post-Modern Society* (2nd edition). Oxford: Blackwell.

Kurzman, Charles 2004: The Poststructuralist Consensus in Social Movement Theory. In Goodwin, Jeff and James J. Jasper (eds.), *Rethinking Social Movements: Structure, Meaning and Emotions*. Lanham, MD: Rowman and Littlefield, 111–20.

Kuumba, M. Bahati and Ajanaku, Femi 1998: Dreadlocks: Hair Aesthetics and Cultural Resistance. *Mobilization*, 3, 227–43.

Lacey, Nicola, Wells, Celia, and Meure, Dirk 1990: *Reconstructing Criminal Law: Critical Perspectives on Crime and the Criminal Process*. London: Weidenfeld & Nicolson.

Lahusen, Christian 2004: Joining the Cocktail Circuit: Social Movement Organizations at the European Union, *Mobilization*, 1, 55–71.

Lalli, Pina 1995: *L'ecologia del pensatore dilettante*. Bologna: Clueb.

Lang, Kurt and Lang, Gladys 1961: *Collective Dynamics*. New York: Thomas & Crowell.

Langman, Lauren 2004: Hegemony Lost: Understanding Islamic Fundamentalism. In T. E. Reifer (ed.), *Globalization, Hegemony and Power*. Boulder, CO: Paradigm, 181–206.

Larana, Enrique, Johnston, Hank, and Gusfield, Joe (eds.) 1994: *New Social Movements: From Ideology to Identity*. Philadelphia: Temple University Press.

Lash, Scott and Urry, John 1987: *The End of Organized Capitalism*. Cambridge: Polity.

Lash, Scott, Szerszynski, Bron, and Wynne, Brian (eds.) 1996: *Risk, Environment, and Modernity*. Thousand Oaks/London: Sage.

Latouche, Serge 1989: *L'occidentalisation du monde: Essai sur la signification, la portée et les limites de l'uniformisation planétaire*. Paris: La Découverte.

Laumann, Edward O. and Knoke, David 1987: The *Organizational State: Social Choice in National Policy Domains*. Madison, WI: University of Wisconsin Press.

Lavalette, Michael and Mooney, Gerry (eds.) 2000: *Class Struggle and Social Welfare*. London: Routledge.

Lawson, Robert 1983: A Decentralized but Moving Pyramid: The Evolution and Consequences of the Structure of the Tenant Movement. In J. Freeman (ed.), *Social Movements of the Sixties and Seventies*. London: Longman, 119–32.

Lehmbruch, Gerhard 1977: Liberal Corporatism and Party Government. *Comparative Political Studies*, 10, 91–126.

Lemert, Charles 1994: Dark Thoughts About the Self. In C. Calhoun (ed.), *Social Theory and the Politics of Identity*. Oxford/Cambridge, MA: Blackwell, 100–29.

Lémieux, Vincent 1997: Reseaux et coalitions. *L'année sociologique*, 47, 55–72.

Lémieux, Vincent 1998: *Les coalitions: Liens, transactions et contrôles*. Paris: PUF.

Lenart, Silvo 1993: *Shaping Political Attitudes: The Impact of Interpersonal Communication and Mass Media*. Thousand Oaks/London, Sage.

Lenin, Vladimir Ilich 1961 [1902]: What Is to Be Done? In *Collected Works*. Moscow: Foreign Languages Publishing House, 347–530.

Levi, Margaret, and Olson, David 2000: The Battles in Seattle. *Politics & Society*, 28 (3), 309–29.

Lewis, Tammy L. 2000: Transnational Conservation Movement Organizations. *Mobilization*, 5, 105–23.

Lichterman, Paul 1995a: *The Search for Political Community: American Activists Reinventing Commitment*. Cambridge/New York: Cambridge University Press.

Lichterman, Paul 1995b: Piecing Together Multicultural Community: Cultural Differences in Community Building among Grass-Roots Environmentalists. *Social Problems*, 42, 513–34.

Lidskog, Rolf 1996: In Science We Trust? On the Relation between Scientific Knowledge, Risk Consciousness and Public Trust. *Acta Sociologica*, 39, 31–56.

Lijphart, Arendt 1984: *Democracies*. New Haven: Yale University Press.

Lindgren, Elaine H. 1987: The Informal-Intermittent Organization: A Vehicle for Successful Citizen Protest. *Journal of Applied Behavioral Research*, 23, 397–412.

Lipset, Seymour M. and Rokkan, Stein (eds.) 1967: *Party Systems and Voter Alignments*. New York: Free Press.

Lipset, Seymour Martin 1960: *Political Man*. New York: Anchor Books.

Lipsky, Michael 1965: *Protest and City Politics*. Chicago: Rand McNally & Co.

Lipsky, Michael 1970: Introduction. In M. Lipsky (ed.), *Law and Order: Police Encounters*. New York: Aldine Publishing Company, 1–7.

Livesay, Jeff 2003: The Duality of Systems: Networks as Media and Outcomes of Movement Mobilization. *Current Perspectives in Social Theory*, 22, 185–224.

Lo, Clarence Y. H. 1982: Countermovements and Conservative Movements in the Contemporary US. *Annual Review of Sociology*, 8, 107–34.

Lo, Clarence Y. H. 1990: *Small Property, Big Government: Social Origins of the Property Tax Revolt*. Berkeley, CA: University of California Press.

Lodhi, A. Q. and Tilly, Charles 1973: Urbanization, Crime and Collective Violence in Nineteenth-Century France. *American Journal of Sociology*, 79, 296–318.

Lodi, Giovanni 1984: *Uniti e diversi: Le mobilitazioni per la pace nell'Italia degli anni ottanta*. Milano: Unicopli.

Lodi, Giovanni and Grazioli, Marco 1984: Giovani sul territorio urbano: l'Integrazione minimale. In A. Melucci (ed.), *Altri codici*. Bologna: il Mulino, 63–126.

Lofland, John 1985a: Becoming a World-Saver Revisited. In John Lofland, *Protest: Studies of Collective Behavior and Social Movements*. New Brunswick, NJ: Transaction Books, 147–57.

Lofland, John 1985b: Social Movement Culture. In J. Lofland, *Protest: Studies of Collective Behavior and Social Movements*. New Brunswick, NJ: Transaction Books, 219–39.

Lofland, John 1989: Consensus Movements: City Twinnings and Derailed Dissent in the American Eighties. *Research in Social Movements, Conflict and Change*, 11, 163–96.

Lofland, John 1995: Charting Degrees of Movement Culture: Tasks of the Cultural Cartographer. In H. Johnston and B. Klandermans (eds.), *Social Movements and Culture*. Minneapolis/London: University of Minnesota Press/UCL Press, 188–216.

Lofland, John 1996: *Social Movement Organizations*. New York: Aldine de Gruyter.

Lofland, John and Skonovd, Norman 1985: Conversion Motifs. In J. Lofland, *Protest: Studies of Collective Behavior and Social Movements*. New Brunswick, NJ: Transaction Books, 158–71.

Lovenduski, Joni and Randall, Vicky 1993: *Contemporary Feminist Politics*. Oxford/New York: Oxford University Press.

Lovendusky, Joni 1986: *Women and European Politics: Contemporary Feminism and Public Policy*. Amherst, MA: University of Massachussets Press.

Lowe, Philip D. and Goyder, Jane M. 1983: *Environmental Groups in Politics*. London: Allen & Unwin.

Lowe, Stuart 1986: *Urban Social Movements: The City after Castells*. London: Macmillan.

Lowi, Theodor 1971: *The Politics of Disorder*. New York: Norton.

Lubeck, Paul M. and Reifer, Thomas E. 2004: The Politics of Global Islam. In T.E. Reifer (ed.), *Globalization, Hegemony and Power*. Boulder, CO: Paradigm, 162–80.

Luker, Kristin 1984. *Abortion and the Politics of Motherhood*. Berkeley, CA: University of California Press.

Lumley, Robert 1990: *States of Emergency*. London: Verso.

Lyons, Matthew Nemiroff 1988: The "Grassroots" Network: Radical Nonviolence in the Federal Republic of Germany 1972–1985. *Cornell Studies In International Affairs – Western Societies Papers 20*, Ithaca: Cornell University.

Mach, Zdzislaw 1993: *Symbols, Conflict, and Identity*. Albany, NY: SUNY Press.

Macy, Michael W. 1990: Learning-Theory and the Logic of Critical Mass. *American Sociological Review*, 55, 809–26.

Macy, Michael W. 1991: Chains of Cooperation: Threshold Effects in Collective Action. *American Sociological Review*, 56, 730–47.

Macy, Michael W. 1993: Backward-Looking Social-Control. *American Sociological Review*, 58, 819–36.

Maffesoli, Michel 1995: *The Time of Tribes: The Decline of Individualism in Mass Society*. London/Thousand Oaks: Sage.

Maguire, Diarmuid 1993: Protesters, Counterprotesters, and the Authorities. *The Annals of the AAPSS*, 528, 101–13.

Maguire, Diarmuid 1995: Opposition Movements and Opposition Parties: Equal Partners or Dependent Relations in the Struggle for Power and Reform? In J. C. Jenkins and B. Klandermans (eds.), *The Politics of Social Protest: Comparative Perspectives on States and Social Movements*. Minneapolis: University of Minnesota Press.

Maheu, Louis (ed.) 1995: *Social Movements and Social Classes*. London/Thousand Oaks: Sage.

Manconi, Luigi 1990: *Solidarietà, egoismo: Movimenti, buone azioni, nuovi conflitti*. Bologna: il Mulino.

Mannheim, Karl 1946: *Ideology and Utopia*. New York: Harcourt, Brace.

Mannheimer, Renato and Sani, Giacomo 1987: *Il mercato elettorale: Identikit dell'elettore italiano*. Bologna: il Mulino.

Mansbridge, Jane 1996: Using Power/Fighting Power: The Polity. In Seyla Benhabib (ed.), *Democracy and Difference: Contesting the Boundaries of the Political*. Princeton: Princeton University Press, 46–66.

Mansbridge, Jane J. 1986: *Why We Lost the ERA*. Chicago: University of Chicago Press.

Manza, Jeff and Brooks, Clem 1996: Does Class Analysis Still Have Anything to Contribute to the Study of Politics? – Comments. *Theory and Society*, 25, 717–24.

Maraffi, Marco (ed.) 1981: *La società neo-corporativa*. Bologna: il Mulino.

Markoff, John 1996: *Waves of Democracy: Social Movements and Political Change*. London/Thousand Oaks: Sage/Pine Forge Press.

Marks, Gary 1989: *Union in Politics: Britain, Germany and the United States in the Nineteenth and Early Twentieth Century*. Princeton: Princeton University Press.

Marks, Gary and McAdam, Doug 1998: Social Movements and the Changing Political Opportunity in the European Community. In D. della Porta, H. Kriesi, and D. Rucht (eds.), *Social Movements in a Globalizing World*. New York/London: Longman.

Marks, Gary and McAdam, Doug 1999: On the Relationship of the Political Opportunities to the Form of Collective Action. In D. della Porta, H. Kriesi, and D. Rucht (eds.), *Social Movements in a Globalizing World*. New York/London: Longman, 97–111.

Marsden, Peter V. and Lin, Nan (eds.) 1982: *Social Structure and Network Analysis*. Beverly Hills/London: Sage.

Marshall, T. H. 1976: *Cittadinanza e classe sociale*. Turin: Utet. (Original edition Citizenship and Social Class. In T. H. Marshall and T. Bottomore, *Citizenship and Social Class*, London: Pluto Press, 1992 [1950], 3–51.)

Marwell, Gerald and Oliver, Pamela 1993: *The Critical Mass in Collective Action: A Micro-Social Theory*. Cambridge/New York: Cambridge University Press.

Marwell, Gerard and Ames, Ruth E. 1979: Experiments on the Provision of Public Goods, I. Resources, Interest, Group Size, and the Free Rider Problem. *American Journal of Sociology*, 84, 1335–60.

Marx Gary T. and Wood, James 1975: Strands of Theory and Research in Collective Behaviour. *Annual Review of Sociology*, 1, 363–428.

Marx, Gary T. 1979: External Efforts to Damage or Facilitate Social Movements: Some Patterns, Explanations, Outcomes and Complications. In J. McCarthy and M. N. Zald (eds.), *The Dynamics of Social Movements*. Cambridge, MA: Winthrop Publishing, 94–125.

Maurer, Sophie 2001: *Les chômeurs en action (décembre 1997–mars 1998): Mobilisation collective et ressources compensatoire*. Paris: L'Harmattan.

Maurer, Sophie et Pierru, Emmanuel 2001. Le mouvement des chômeurs de l'hiver 1997–1998: Retour sur un "miracle social." *Revue Française de Science Politique*, 512, 317–407.

Mayer, Robert N. 1989: *The Consumer Movement: Guardians of the Marketplace*. Boston: Twayne.

Mazey, Sonia and Richardson, Jeremy 1993: *Lobbying in the European Union*. Oxford: Oxford University Press.

McAdam, Doug 1982: *Political Process and the Development of Black Insurgency: 1930–1970*. Chicago: University of Chicago Press.

McAdam, Doug 1983: Tactical Innovation and the Pace of Insurgency. *American Sociological Review*, 48, 735–54.

McAdam, Doug 1986: Recruitment to High-Risk Activism: The Case of Freedom Summer. *American Journal of Sociology*, 92, 64–90.

McAdam, Doug 1988a: Micromobilization Contexts and Recruitment to Activism. In B. Klandermans, H. Kriesi, and S. Tarrow (eds.), *From Structure to Action*. Greenwich, CT: JAI Press, 125–54.

McAdam, Doug 1988b: *Freedom Summer*. New York/Oxford: Oxford University Press.

McAdam, Doug 1994: Culture and Social Movements. In E. Larana, H. Hohnston, and J. R. Gusfield (eds.), *New Social Movements: From Ideology to Identity*. Philadelphia: Temple University Press, 36–57.

McAdam, Doug 1995: "Initiator" and "Spinoff" Movements: Diffusion Processes in Protest Cycles. In M. Traugott (ed.), *Repertoires and Cycles of Collective Action*. Durham, NC: Duke University Press, 217–39.

McAdam, Doug 1996: Conceptual Origins, current Problems, Future Dimensions. In D. McAdam, J. McCarthy, and M. N. Zald (eds.), *Comparative Perspectives on Social Movements: Political Opportunities, Mobilizing Structures, and Cultural Framing*. Cambridge/New York: Cambridge University Press, 23–40.

McAdam, Doug 2003: Beyond Structural Analysis: Toward a More Dynamic Understanding of Social Movements. In M. Diani and D. McAdam (eds.), *Social Movements and Networks*. Oxford/New York: Oxford University Press, 281–98.

McAdam, Doug and Fernandez, Roberto 1990: Microstructural Bases of Recruitment to Social Movements. In L. Kriesberg (ed.), *Research In Social Movements, Conflict and Change*, vol. 12. Greenwich, CT: JAI Press, 1–33.

McAdam, Doug, McCarthy, John, and Zald, Mayer N. (eds.) 1996: *Comparative Perspective on Social Movements: Political Opportunities, Mobilizing Structures, and Cultural Framing*. Cambridge/New York: Cambridge University Press.

McAdam, Doug, McCarthy, John D., and Zald, Mayer N. 1988: Social Movements. In N. J. Smelser (ed.), *Handbook of Sociology*. Beverly Hills/London: Sage, 695–739.

McAdam, Doug and Paulsen, Ronnelle 1993: Specifying the Relationship between Social Ties and Activism. *American Journal of Sociology*, 99, 640–67.

McAdam, Doug and Rucht, Dieter 1993: The Cross-national Diffusion of Movement Ideas. *The Annals of the AAPSS*, 528, 56–74.

McAdam, Doug and Snow, David (eds.) 1996: *Social Movements: Readings on Their Emergence, Mobilization, and Dynamics*. Los Angeles: Roxbury.

McAdam, Doug and Su, Yang 2002: The War at Home: Antiwar Protests and Congressional Voting, 1965 to 1973. *American Sociological Review*, 67, 696–721.

McAdam, Doug, Tarrow, Sidney and Tilly, Charles 1996: To Map Contentious Politics. *Mobilization*, 1, 17–34.

McAdam, Doug, Tarrow, Sidney, and Tilly, Charles 2001: *Dynamics of Contention*. Cambridge: Cambridge University Press.

McAllister, Ian 1983: Social Contacts and Political Behavior in Northern Ireland, 1968–78. *Social Networks*, 5, 303–13.

McCaffrey, Dawn and Keys, Jennifer 2000: Competitive Framing Processes in the Abortion Debate: Polarization-Vilification, Frame Saving, and Frame Debunking. *Sociological Quarterly*, 41, 41–61.

McCammon, Holly 2001: Stirring Up Suffrage Sentiment: The Formation of the State Woman Suffrage Organizations, 1866–1914. *Social Forces*, 80, 449–80.

McCarthy, John D. 1994: Activists, Authorities, and Media Framing of Drunk Driving. In E. Larana, H. Johnston, and J. R. Gusfield (eds.), *New Social Movements: From Ideology to Identity*. Philadelphia: Temple University Press, 133–67.

McCarthy, John D. 1996: Constraints and Opportunities in Adopting, Adapting, and Inventing. In D. McAdam, J. McCarthy and M. N. Zald (eds.), *Comparative Perspective on Social Movements: Political Opportunities, Mobilizing Structures, and Cultural Framing*. Cambridge/New York: Cambridge University Press, 141–51.

McCarthy, John D., Britt, David W., and Wolfson, Mark 1991: The Institutional Channeling of Social Movements by the State in the United States. *Research in Social Movements, Conflict and Change*, 13, 45–76.

McCarthy, John, McPhail, Clark, and Crist, John 1998: The Emergence and Diffusion of Public Order Management System: Protest Cycles and Police Response. In D. della Porta, H. Kriesi, and D. Rucht (eds.), *Social Movements in a Globalizing World*, forthcoming, New York/London: Longman.

McCarthy, John, McPhail, Clark, and Smith, Jackie 1996: Images of Protest: Dimensions of Selection Bias in Media Coverage of Washington Demonstrations, 1982 and 1991. *American Sociological Review*, 61, 478–99.

McCarthy, John D. and Wolfson, Mark 1992: Consensus Movements, Conflict Movements, and the Cooptation of Civic and State Infrastructures. In A. Morris and C. McClurg Mueller (eds.), *Frontiers in Social Movement Theory*. New Haven: Yale University Press, 273–98.

McCarthy, John D. and Zald, Mayer N. 1977: Resource Mobilization and Social Movements: A Partial Theory. *American Journal of Sociology*, 82, 1212–41.

McCarthy, John D. and Zald, Mayer N. 1987a: The Trend of Social Movements in America: Professionalization and Resource Mobilization. In M. N. Zald and J. D. McCarthy, *Social Movements in an Organizational Society*. New Brunswick, NJ: Transaction, 1987, 337–91 (originally published as *The Trend of Social Movements in America*. Morristown: General Learning Press, 1973).

McCarthy, John D. and Zald, Mayer N. 1987b: Resource Mobilization and Social Movements: A Partial Theory. In M. N. Zald and J. D. McCarthy, *Social Movements in an Organizational Society*. New Brunswick, NJ: Transaction (originally published in *American Journal of Sociology*, 82 (1977), 1212–41).

McCrea, Frances B. and Markle, Gerald E. 1989: Atomic Scientists and Protest: The Bulletin as a Social Movement Organization. In L. Kriesberg (ed.), *Research in Social Movements, Conflict and Change*, vol. 11. Greenwich, CT: JAI Press.

McDonald, Kevin 2002: From Solidarity to Fluidarity: Social Movements Beyond "Collective Identity" – the Case of Globalization Conflicts. *Social Movement Studies*, 1, 109–28.

McFarland, Andrew 1984: *Common Cause: Lobbying in the Public Interest*. Chatham, NJ: Chatham House.

McGarry, John (ed.) 2001: *Northern Ireland and the Divided World Post-Agreement Northern Ireland in Comparative Perspective*. Oxford: Oxford University Press.

McKay, George 1996: *Senseless Acts of Beauty: Cultures of Resistance since the 1960s*. London: Verso.

McPhail, Clark 1991: *The Myth of the Madding Crowd*. New York: Aldine de Gruyter.

McPhail, Clark, Schweingruber, David, and McCarthy, John D. 1998: Policing Protest in the United States: From the 1960s to the 1990s. In D. della Porta and H. Reiter (eds.),

Policing Protest: The Control of Mass Demonstrations in Western Democracies. Minneapolis: University of Minnesota Press, 49–69.

McPherson, Miller 1983: An Ecology of Affiliation. *American Sociological Review*, 48, 519–32.

McPherson, Miller and Rotolo, Thomas 1996: Testing a Dynamic Model of Social Composition: Diversity and Change in Voluntary Groups. *American Sociological* Review, 61, 179–202.

McPherson, Miller, Popielarz, Pamela, and Drobnic, Sonja 1992: Social Networks and Organizational Dynamics. *American Sociological Review*, 57, 153–70.

McVeigh, Rory, Welch, Michael R., and Bjarnason, Thoroddur 2003: Hate crime Reporting as a Successful Social Movement. *American Sociological Review*, 68, 843–67.

Meadows, Donella H., Randers, Jorgen, and Behrens, Williams W. 1972: *The Limits to Growth*. London: Earth Island.

Melucci, Alberto 1982: *L'invenzione del presente: Movimenti, identità, bisogni individuali*. Bologna: il Mulino.

Melucci, Alberto (ed.) 1984a: *Altri codici: Aree di movimento nella metropoli*. Bologna: il Mulino.

Melucci, Alberto 1984b: Movimenti in un mondo di segni. In A. Melucci (ed.), *Altri codici*. Bologna: il Mulino, 417–48.

Melucci, Alberto 1985: The Symbolic Challenge of Contemporary Movements. *Social Research*, 52, 789–816.

Melucci, Alberto 1987: *Libertà che cambia*. Milano: Unicopli.

Melucci, Alberto 1988: Getting Involved: Identity and Mobilization in Social Movements. In B. Klandermans, H. Kriesi, and S. Tarrow (eds.), *From Structure to Action*. Greenwich, CT: JAI Press, 329–48.

Melucci, Alberto 1989: *Nomads of the Present*. London: Hutchinson Radius.

Melucci, Alberto 1990: Challenging Codes. Framing and Ambivalence. Paper presented at the workshop, Social Movements: Framing Processes and Opportunity Structure, Berlin, July.

Melucci, Alberto 1991: *L'invenzione del presente* (2nd edition). Bologna: il Mulino.

Melucci, Alberto 1994: A Strange Kind of Newness: What's "New" in New Social Movements? In E. Larana, H. Johnston, and J. Gusfield (eds.), *New Social Movements: From Ideology to Identity*. Philadelphia: Temple University Press, 101–30.

Melucci, Alberto 1995: The Process of Collective Identity. In H. Johnston and B. Klandermans (eds.), *Social Movements and Culture*. Minneapolis/London: University of Minnesota Press/UCL Press, 41–63.

Melucci, Alberto 1996: *Challenging Codes*. Cambridge/New York: Cambridge University Press.

Melucci, Alberto and Diani, Mario 1992: *Nazioni senza stato: I Movimenti etnico-nazionali in occidente* (2nd edition). Milano: Feltrinelli.

Mennell, Stephen 1994: The Formation of We-Images: A Process Theory. In C. Calhoun (ed.), *Social Theory and the Politics of Identity*. Oxford/Cambridge, MA: Blackwell, 175–97.

Merelman, R. 1984: *Making Something of Ourselves: On Culture and Politics in the United States*. Berkeley: University of California Press.

Meyer, David S. 1990: *A Winter of Discontent*. New York: Praeger.

Meyer, David S. 2004: Protest and Political Opportunities, *Annual Review of Sociology*, 30, 125–145.

Meyer, David S. and Marullo, Sam 1992: Grassroots Mobilization and International Politics: Peace Protest and the End of the Cold War. *Research in Social Movements, Conflict and Change*, 14, 99–140.

Meyer, David S. and Staggenborg, Suzanne 1996: Movements, Countermovements and the Structure of Political Opportunities. *American Journal of Sociology*, 101, 1, 628–60.

Meyer, David S. and Tarrow, Sidney (eds.) 1998b: *The Social Movement Society*. Lanham, MD: Rowman & Littledfield.

Meyer, David S. and Tarrow, Sidney 1998a: A Movement Society: Contentious Politics for the New Cantury. In David S. Meyer and Sidney Tarrow (eds.), *The Social Movement Society*. Lahman, MD: Rowman and Littlefield, 1–28.

Meyer, David S. and Whittier, Nancy 1994: Social Movements Spillover. *Social Problems*, 41, 277–98.

Meyer, John W. and Rowan, Brian 1983: Institutionalized Organizations: Formal Structure as Myth and Ceremony. In J. Mayer and W. R. Scott (eds.), *Organizational Environments: Ritual and Rationality*. Beverly Hills: Sage, 21–44.

Micheletti, Michele 2003: *Political Virtue and Shopping: Individuals, Consumerism, and Collective Action*. Palgrave: Macmillan.

Micheletti, Michele, Follesdal, Andreas, and Stolle, Dietlind 2003: *Politics, Products, and Markets: Exploring Political Consumerism Past and Present*. Rutgers, NJ: Transaction Publishers.

Michels, Robert 1915: *Political Parties: A Sociological Study of the Oligarchical Tendencies of Modern Democracy*. Glencoe, IL: Free Press.

Middendorp, C. 1992: Left–right Self-identification and (Post)materialism in the Ideological Space. *Electoral Studies*, 11, 249–60.

Mies, Maria 2002: *Globalisierung von unten: Der Kampf gegen die Herrschaft der Konzerne*. Hamburg: Europäische Verlagsanstalt.

Miliband, Ralph 1989: *Divided Societies: Class Struggle in Contemporary Capitalism*. Oxford: Clarendon Press.

Miller, David 1993: Deliberative Democracy and Social Choice. In D. Held (ed.), *Prospects for Democracy*. Cambridge: Polity Press, 74–92.

Minkoff, Debra C. 1993: The Organization of Survival: Women's and Racial-ethnic Voluntarist and Activist Organizations, 1955–1985. *Social Forces*, 71, 887–908.

Minkoff, Debra C. 1995: *Organizing for Equality: The Evolution of Women's and Racial-ethnic Organizations in America*. New Brunswick, NJ: Rutgers University Press.

Minkoff, Debra C. 1999: Bending with the Wind: Strategic Change and Adaptation by Women's and Racial Minority Organizations. *American Journal of Sociology*, 101, 1592–1627.

Mische, Ann 2003: Cross-talk in Movements: Reconceiving the Culture-Network Link. In M. Diani and D. McAdam (eds.), *Social Movements and Networks*. Oxford/New York: Oxford University Press, 258–80.

Mittdun, Atle and Rucht, Dieter 1994: Comparing Policy Outcomes of Conflicts over Nuclear Power: Description and Explanation. In H. Flam (ed.), *States and Antinuclear Movements*. Edinburgh: Edinburgh University Press, 383–415.

Mizruchi, Mark S. and Schwartz, Michael (eds.) 1987: *Intercorporate Relations: The Structural Analysis of Business*. Cambridge/New York: Cambridge University Press.

Moaddel, Mansoor 1992: Ideology as Episodic Discourse: The Case of the Iranian Revolution. *American Sociological Review*, 57, 353–79.

Moaddel, Mansoor 2002: The Study of Islamic Culture and Politics: An Overview and Assessment. *Annual Review of Sociology*, 28, 359–86.

Moody, Kim 1997: *Workers in a Lean World*. London: Verso.

Moore, Barrington, Jr. 1966: *Social Origins of Dictatorship and Democracy*. Boston: Beacon Press.

Moore, Kelly 1995: Organizing Integrity: American Science and the Creation of Public Interest Organizations, 1955–1975. *American Journal of Sociology*, 101, 1592–1627.

Moore, Kelly 1999: Political Protest and Institutional Change: The Anti-Vietnam War Movement and American Science. In M. Giugni, D. McAdam, and C. Tilly (eds.), *How Movements Matter*. Minneapolis/London: University of Minnesota Press/UCL Press.

Morgan, Jane 1987: *Conflict and Order: The Police and Labour Disputes in England and Wales: 1900–1939*. Oxford: Clarendon Press.

Morris, Aldon 1984: *The Origins of the Civil Rights Movement: Black Communities Organizing for Change*. New York: Free Press.

Morris, Aldon and Herring, Cedric 1987: Theory and Research in Social Movements: A Critical Review. *Annual Review of Political Science*, 2, 137–98.

Morris, Aldon and Mueller, Carol (eds.) 1992: *Frontiers in Social Movement Theory*. New Haven: Yale University Press.

Morris, Aldon and Staggenborg, Suzanne 2004: Leadership in Social Movements. In D. Snow, S. Soule, and H. Kriesi (eds.), *The Blackwell Companion to Social Movements*. Oxford: Blackwell, 171–96.

Morse, David 2001: Beyond the Myths of Seattle. *Dissent*, 48 (3), 39–43.

Moscovici, Serge 1979: *Psychologie des Minorités Actives*. Paris: PUF.

Moscovici, Serge 1981: On Social Representations. In J. P. Forgas (ed.), *Social Cognition*. London: Academic Press, 181–209.

Mouffe, Chantal 1996: Radical Democracy or Liberal Democracy? In D. Trend (ed.), *Radical Democracy*. London: Routledge, 19–26.

Mudu, Pierpaolo 2004: Resisting and Challenging Neoliberalism: The Development of Italian Social Centers. *Antipode*, 36 (5), 917–41.

Mueller, Carol 1994: Conflict Networks and the Origins of Women's Liberation. In E. Larana, H. Johnston, and J. Gusfield (eds.), *New Social Movements*. Philadelphia: Temple University Press, 234–63.

Müller-Rommel, Ferdinand 1985: Social Movements and the Greens: New Internal Politics in Germany. *European Journal of Political Research*, 13, 53–67.

Müller-Rommel, Ferdinand (ed.) 1989: *New Politics in Western Europe: The Rise and the Success of Green Parties and Alternative Lists*. Boulder, CO: Westview Press.

Müller-Rommel, Ferdinand 1990: New Political Movements and "New Politics" Parties in Western Europe. In R. Dalton and M. Kuechler (eds.), *Challenging the Political Order: New Social and Political Movements in Western Democracies*. Cambridge: Polity Press, 209–31.

Müller-Rommel, Ferdinand 1993: *Grüne Partein in Westeuropa: Entwicklungsphasen und Erfolgsbedingungen*. Opladen: Westdeutscher Verlag.

Mullins, Patrick 1987: Community and Urban Movements. *Sociological Review*, 35, 347–69.

Mushaben, Joyce Marie. 1989. The Struggle Within: Conflict, Consensus and Decision Making Among National Coordinators and Grass-Roots Organizers in the West German Peace Movement. In B. Klandermans (ed.), *Organizing for Change*. Greenwich, CT: JAI Press.

Myers, Daniel J and Caniglia, Beth Schaefer 2004: All the Rioting That's Fit to Print: Selection Effects in National Newspaper Coverage of Civil Disorders, 1968–1969. *American Sociological Review*, 69, 519–43.

Naples, Nancy and Desai, Manisha (eds.) 2002: *Women's Activism and Globalization: Linking Local Struggles and Transnational Politics*. New York: Routledge.

Nas, Masja 1993: Women and Classes: Gender and the Class Base of New Social Movements in the Netherlands. *European Journal of Political Research*, 23, 343–55.

Nash, Kate 2000: *Contemporary Political Sociology*. Oxford: Blackwell.

Nash, Kate 2001: Political Sociology in the Information Age. In F. Webster (ed.), *Culture and Politics in the Information Age*. London: Routledge, 81–94.

Nederveen Pieterse, Jan 2000: Globalization North and South. *Theory, Culture and Society*, 17, 129–37.

Neidhardt, Friedhelm 1981: Über Zufall, Eigendynamik und Institutionalisierbarkeit absurder Prozesse. Notizen am Beispiel der Entstehung und Einrichtung einer terroristischen Gruppe. In H. von Alemann and H. P. Thurn (eds.), *Soziologie in weltbürgerlicher Absicht*. Opladen: Westdeutscher Verlag, 243–57.

Neidhardt, Friedhelm 1989: Gewalt und Gegengewalt. Steigt die Bereitschaft zu Gewaltaktionen mit zunehmender staatlicher Kontrolle und Repression? In W. Heitmeyer, K. Möller, and H. Sünker (eds.), *Jugend-Staat-Gewalt*. Weinheim and Munich: Juventa, 233 43.

Neidhardt, Friedhelm and Rucht, Dieter 1991: The Analysis of Social Movements: The State of the Art and Some Perspectives for Further Research. In D. Rucht (ed.), *Research on Social Movements: The State of the Art in Western Europe and the USA*. Frankfurt/M and Boulder, CO: Campus and Westview Press, 421–64.

Neidhardt, Friedhelm and Rucht, Dieter 1993: Auf dem Weg in die Bewegungsgesellschaft? Ueber die Stabilisierbarkheit sozialer Bewegungen. *Soziale Welt*, 44, 305–26.

Neidhardt, Friedhelm and Rucht, Dieter 2002: Towards a "Movement Society"? On the Possibilities of Institutionalizing Social Movements. *Social Movement Studies*, 1, 7–30.

Nelkin, Dorothy and Pollack, Michael 1981: *The Atom Besieged: Extraparliamentary Dissent in France and Germany*. Cambridge, MA: MIT Press.

Nepstad, Sharon E. 2001: Creating Transnational Solidarity: The Use of Narrative in the US–Central American Peace Movement. *Mobilization*, 6, 21–36.

Nepstad, Sharon E. 2004: *Convictions of the Soul: Religion, Culture, and Agency in the Central America Solidarity Movement*. New York: Oxford University Press.

Nepstad, Sharon E. and Smith, Christian 1999: Rethinking Recruitment to High-Risk/Cost Activism: The Case of Nicaragua Exchange. *Mobilization*, 4, 25–40.

Neveau, Eric 1999: Media, mouvements sociaux, espace public. *Reseaux*, 98, 17–85.

Nevola, Gaspare 1994: *Conflitto e coercizione: Modelli di analisi e studio di casi*. Bologna: il Mulino.

Nicholson, Michael 1998: *International Relations: A Concise Introduction*. New York: New York University Press.

Nip, Joyce Y. M. 2004: The Queer Sisters and Its Electronic Bulletin Board. A Study of the Internet for Social Movement Mobilization. In W. van de Donk, B. Loader, P. Nixon, and D. Rucht (eds.), *Cyberprotest: New Media, Citizens and Social Movements*. London: Routledge, 233–58.

Noelle-Neumann, Elisabeth 1984: *The Spiral of Silence*. Chicago, IL: University of Chicago Press.

Nolan, Mary 1981: *Social Democracy and Society: Working-class Radicalism in Dusseldorf, 1890–1920*. Cambridge/New York: Cambridge University Press.

Noland, Marcus 2004: Popular Attitudes, Globalization, and Risk. Institute for International Economics Working Paper 04–02, Washington DC.

Nollert, Michael 1995: Neocorporatism and Political Protest in the Western Democracies: A Cross-National Analysis. In J. C. Jenkins and B. Klandermans (eds.), *The Politics of Social Protest: Comparative Perspectives on States and Social Movements*. Minneapolis: University of Minnesota Press, 138–64.

Noonan, Rita 1995: Women Against the State: Political Opportunities and Collective Action Frames in Chile's Transition to Democracy. *Sociological Forum*, 19, 81–111.

Norris, Pippa (ed.) 1999: *Critical Citizens*. Oxford: Oxford University Press.

Norris, Pippa 1987: *Politics and Sexual Equality: The Comparative Position of Women in Western Democracy*. Boulder, CO: Lynne Rienner.

Norris, Pippa 2002: *Democratic Phoenix: Reinventing Political Activism*. New York: Cambridge University Press.

Norris, Pippa and Inglehart, Ronald 2002: Islam and the West: Testing the "Clash of Civilizations" Thesis. Unpublished paper, Harvard University.

Notarbartolo, N. (ed.) 2001: *I giorni di Genova*. Rome: Internazionale.

Oberschall, Anthony 1973: *Social Conflict and Social Movements*. Englewood Cliffs, NJ: Prentice-Hall.

Oberschall, Anthony 1980: Loosely Structured Collective Conflict: A Theory and an Application. In L. Kriesberg (ed.), *Research in Social Movements, Conflict and Change*, Vol. 3. Greenwich, CT: JAI Press, 45–54.

Oberschall, Anthony 1993: *Social Movements: Ideologies, Interests, and Identities*. New Brunswick, NJ/London: Transaction.

Oberschall, Anthony and Kim, Hyojoung 1996: Identity and Action. *Mobilization*, 1, 63–85.

O'Brien, Robert, Goetz, Anne Marie, Scholte, Jaan Aart, and Williams, Marc 2000: *Contesting Global Governance: Multilateral Economic Institutions and Global Social Movements*. Cambridge: Cambridge University Press.

Offe, Claus 1985: New Social Movements: Changing Boundaries of the Political. *Social Research*, 52, 817–68.

Offe, Claus 1990: Reflections on the Institutional Self-transformation of Movement Politics: A Tentative Stage Model. In R. Dalton and M. Kuechler (eds.), *Challenging the Political Order: New Social and Political Movements in Western Democracies*. Cambridge: Polity Press, 232–50.

Offe, Claus 1997: *Microaspects of Democratic Theory: What Makes for the Deliberative Competence of Citizens?* In A. Hadenius (ed.), *Democracy's Victory and Crisis*. New York: Cambridge University Press, 81–104.

Ohlemacher, Thomas 1996: Bridging People and Protest: Social Relays of Protest Groups against Low-flying Military Jets in West Germany. *Social Problems*, 43, 197–218.

Okamoto, Dina 2003: Toward a Theory of Panethnicity: Explaining Asian American Collective Action, *American Sociological Review*, 68, 811–42.

Olesen, Thomas 2004: The Transnational Zapatista Solidarity Network: An Infrastructure Analysis. *Global Networks*, 4, 89–107.

Oliver, Mike and Campbell, Jane 1996: *Disability Politics: Understanding Our Past, Changing Our Future*. London: Routledge.

Oliver, Pamela 1984: "If You Don't Do It, Nobody Else Will": Active and Token Contributors to Local Collective Action. *American Sociological Review*, 49, 601–10.

Oliver, Pamela 1989: Bringing the Crowd Back In: The Nonorganizational Elements of Social Movements. In L. Kriesberg (ed.), *Research in Social Movements, Conflict and Change*, vol. 11. Greenwich, CT: JAI Press, 1–30.

Oliver, Pamela and Johnston, Hank 2000: What a Good Idea! Ideologies and Frames in Social Movement Research. *Mobilization*, 5, 37–54.

Oliver, Pamela and Marwell, Gerald 1992: Mobilizing Technologies for Collective Action. In A. Morris and C. McClurg Mueller (eds.), *Frontiers in Social Movement Theory*. New Haven: Yale University Press, 251–72.

Oliver, Pamela and Marwell, Gerald 2001: Whatever Happened to Critical Mass Theory? A Retrospective and Assessment. *Sociological Theory*, 19, 292–311.

Olson, Mancur 1963: *The Logics of Collective Action*. Cambridge, MA: Harvard University Press.

Olzak, Susan 1992: *The Dynamics of Ethnic Competition and Conflict*. Stanford, CA: Stanford University Press.

Omi, Michael and Winant, Howard 1994: *Racial Formation in the United States: From 1960s to 1990s*. New York: Routledge.

Omvedt, Gail 1993: *Reinventing Revolution: New Social Movements and the Socialist Tradition in India*. New York: M. E. Sharpe.

Opp, Karl-Dieter 1988: Community Integration and Incentives for Political Protest. In B. Klandermans, H. Kriesi, and S. Tarrow (eds.), *From Structure to Action*. Greenwich, CT: JAI Press, 83–101.

Opp, Karl-Dieter 1989: *The Rationality of Political Protest*. Boulder, CO: Westview Press.

Opp, Karl-Dieter 1990: Postmaterialism, Collective Action, and Political Protest. *American Journal of Political Science*, 34, 212–35.

Opp, Karl-Dieter and Gern, Christiane 1993: Dissident Groups, Personal Networks, and the East German Revolution of 1989. *American Sociological Review*, 58, 659–80.

Opp, Karl-Dieter, Finkel, Steve, Muller, Edward N., Wolfsfeld, Gadi, Dietz, Henty A., and Green, Jerrold D. 1995: Left–Right Ideology and Collective Political Action: A Comparative Analysis of Germany, Israel, and Peru. In J. C. Jenkins and B. Klandermans (eds.), *The Politics of Social Protest: Comparative Perspectives on States and Social Movements*. Minneapolis: University of Minnesota Press, 63–95.

Orfali, Brigitte 1990: *L'adhésion au Front Nationale*. Paris: Editions Kime.

Ortoleva, Peppino 1988: *Saggio sui movimenti del 68 in Europa e in America*. Rome: Editori Riuniti.

Osa, Maryjane 2003a: *Solidarity and Contention: Networks of Polish Opposition*. Minneapolis: University of Minnesota Press.

Osa, Maryjane 2003b: Networks in Opposition. In M. Diani and D. McAdam (eds.), *Social Movements and Networks*. Oxford: Oxford University Press, 77–104.

O'Sullivan See, Katherine 1986: *First World Nationalisms: Class and Ethnic Politics in Northern Ireland and Quebec*. Chicago: University of Chicago Press.

Otto, Karl O. 1989: *APO: Die ausserparlamentarische Opposition in Quellen und Dokumenten 1960–1970*. Köln: Pahl-Rugenstein.

Padgett, John F. and Ansell, Christopher K. 1993: Robust Action and the Rise of the Medici, 1400–1434. *American Journal of Sociology*, 98, 1259–1319.

Pagnucco, Ron 1996: Social Movement Dynamics during Democratic Transition and Consolidation: A Synthesis of Political Process and Political Interactionist Theories. *Research on Democracy and Society*, 3, 3–38.

Pakulski, Jan 1988: Social Movements in Comparative Perspective. In L. Kriesberg (ed.), *Research in Social Movements, Conflicts and Change*, vol. 10. Greenwich, CT: JAI Press, 247–67.

Pakulski, Jan 1990: *Social Movements: The Politics of Moral Protest*. London/Melbourne: Longman.

Pakulski, Jan 1995: Social Movements and Class: The Decline of the Marxist Paradigm. In L. Maheu (ed.), *Social Movements and Social Classes*. London/Thousand Oaks: Sage, 55–86.

Pakulski, Jan and Waters, Malcolm 1996: Misreading Status as Class: A Reply to Our Critics. *Theory and Society*, 25, 731–6.

Panebianco, Angelo 1988: *Political Parties: Organization and Power*. Cambridge: Cambridge University Press.

Papadakis, Elim and Taylor-Gooby, Peter 1987: Consumer Attitudes and Participation in State Welfare. *Political Studies*, 35, 467–81.

Parkin, Frank 1968: *Middle Class Radicalism*. New York: Praeger.

Passerini, Luisa 1988: *Autobiografia di gruppo*. Florence: Giunti.

Passy, Florence 1998: *L'action altruiste*. Geneve/Paris: Droz.

Passy, Florence 1999: Supranational Political Opportunities. A Channel of Globalization of Political Conflicts. The Case of the Conflict around the Rights of the Indigenous People. In D. della Porta, H. Kriesi, and D. Rucht (eds.), *Social Movements in a Globalizing World*. New York/London: Macmillan, 148–69.

Passy, Florence 2001: Socializing, Connecting, and the Structural Agency/Gap. A Specification of the Impact of Networks on Participation in Social Movements. *Mobilization*, 6, 173–92.

Passy, Florence 2003: Social Networks Matter. But How? In Mario Diani and Doug McAdam (eds.), *Social Movements and Networks*. Oxford/New York: Oxford University Press, 21–48.

Passy, Florence and Giugni, Marco 2000: Life-spheres, Networks, and Sustained Participation in Social Movements. A Phenomenological Approach to Political Commitment. *Sociological Forum*, 15, 117–44.

Pearce, Jone L. 1993: *Volunteers*. London/New York: Routledge.

Pearce, Jone. 1980. Apathy or Self-Interest? The Volunteers' Avoidance of Leadership Roles. *Journal of Voluntary Action Research*, 9, 85–94.

Peretti, Jonah (with Micheletti, Michele) 2004: The Nike Sweatshop Email: Poliical Consummerism, Internet, and Culture Jamming. In Michele Micheletti, Andreas Follesdal, and Dietlind Stolle (eds.), *Politics, Products and Markets: Exploring Political Consumerism Past and Present*. New Brunswick, NJ: Transaction Publishers, 127–42.

Perrow, Charles 1961: The Analysis of Goals in Complex Organizations. *American Sociological Review*, 26, 854–66.

Perrucci, Robert and Pilisuk, Marc 1970: Leaders and Ruling Elites: The Interorganizational Bases of Community Power. *American Sociological Review*, 35, 1040–57.

Petts, J. 1997: The Public–Expert Interface in Local Waste Management Decisions: Expertise, Credibility and Process. *Public Understanding of Science*, 6, 359–381.

Philips, Susan 1991: Meaning and Structure in Social Movements: Mapping the Network of National Canadian Women's Organizations. *Canadian Journal of Political Science*, 24, 755–82.

Pianta, Mario 2001a: Parallel Summits of Global Civil Society. In H. Anheier, M. Glasius, and M. Kaldor (eds.), *Global Civil Society 2001*. Oxford: Oxford University Press, 169–95.

Pianta, Mario 2001b: *Globalizzazione dal basso: Economia mondiale e movimenti sociali*. Roma: Manifestolibri.

Pianta, Mario 2002: Parallel Summits: an Update. In H. K. Anheier, M. Glasius, and M. Kaldor (eds.), *Global Civil Society*. Oxford: Oxford University Press, 371–7.

Pichardo, Nelson 1997: New Social Movements: A Critical Review. *Annual Review of Sociology*, 23, 411–30.

Pickerill, Jenny 2000: Environmentalism and the Net. In R. Gibson and S. Ward (eds.), *Reinvigorating Government? British Politics and the Internet*. Aldershot: Ashgate.

Pickvance, Chris 1975: On the Study of Urban Social Movements. *Sociological Review*, 23, 29–49.

Pickvance, Chris 1995: Social Movements in the Transition From State Socialism: Convergence or Divergence? In L. Maheu (ed.), *Social Movements and Social Classes*. London/Thousand Oaks: Sage, 123–150.

Pickvance, Chris G. 1977: From "Social Base" to "Social Force": Some Analytical Issues in the Study of Urban Protest. In M. Harloe (ed.), *Captive Cities*. Wiley: Chichester, 175–86.

Pickvance, Chris G. 1985: The Rise and Fall of Urban Movements and the Role of Comparative Analysis. *Society And Space*, 3, 31–53.

Pickvance, Chris G. 1986: Concepts, Contexts and Comparison in the Study of Urban Movements: A Reply to M. Castells. *Society and Space*, 4, 221–31.

Pinard, Maurice 1968: Mass Society and Political Movements: A New Formulation. *American Journal of Sociology*, 73, 682–90.

Pini, Barbara, Brown, Kerry, and Previte, Josephine 2004: Politics and Identity in Cyberspace. A Case Study of Australian Women in Agriculture Online. In W. van de Donk, B. Loader, P. Nixon, and D. Rucht (eds.), *Cyberprotest: New Media, Citizens and Social Movements*. London: Routledge, 259–75.

Pinto, Louis 1990: Le consommateur: Agent economique et acteur politique. *Revue Française de Sociologie*, 31, 179–98.

Piore, Michael and Sabel, Charles 1984: *The Second Industrial Divide: Possibilities for Prosperity*. New York: Basic Books.

Piven, Frances F. and Cloward, Richard 1977: *Poor People's Movements*. New York: Pantheon.

Piven, Frances F. and Cloward, Richard 1992: Normalizing Collective Protest. In A. Morris and C. McClurg Mueller (eds.), *Frontiers in Social Movement Theory*. New Haven: Yale University Press, 301–25.

Piven, Francis F. and Cloward, Richard A. 2000: Power Repertoires and Globalization. *Politics and Society*, 28, 413–430.

Pizzorno, Alessandro 1978: Political Exchange and Collective Identity in Industrial Conflict. In C. Crouch, and A. Pizzorno (eds.), *The Resurgence of Class Conflict in Western Europe*. New York: Holmes & Meier, 277–98.

Pizzorno, Alessandro 1981: Interests and Parties in Pluralism. In S. Berger (ed.), *Organizing Interests in Western Europe*. Cambridge: Cambridge University Press, 3–46.

Pizzorno, Alessandro 1983: Sulla razionalità della scelta democratica. *Stato e mercato*, n. 7.

Pizzorno, Alessandro 1986: Sul confronto intertemporale delle utilità. *Stato e mercato*, 16, 3–25.

Pizzorno, Alessandro 1987: Considerazioni sulle teorie dei movimenti sociali. *Problemi del socialismo*, 12, 11–27.

Pizzorno, Alessandro 1993: *Le radici della politica assoluta*. Milano: Feltrinelli.

Pizzorno, Alessandro 1996: Decisioni o interazioni? La micro-descrizione del cambiamento sociale. *Rassegna italiana di sociologia*, 37, 107–32.

Pizzorno, Alessandro 1996: Mutamenti istituzioni e sviluppo dei partiti. In P. Bairoch and E. J. Hobsbawm (eds.), *La Storia dell'Europa Contemporanea*. Torino: Einaudi, 961–1031.

Pizzorno, Alessandro, Regalia, Ida, Regini, Marino and Reyneri, Emilio 1978: *Lotte operaie e sindacato: Il ciclo di lotte 1968–1972 in Italia*. Bologna: il Mulino.

Platt, Gerald M., and Williams, Rhys 2002: Ideological Language and Social Movement Mobilization: A Sociolinguistics Analysis of Segregationists' Ideologies. *Sociological Theory*, 20, 328–59.

Plumb, Lawrence D. 1993: *A Critique of the Human Potential Movement*. New York: Garland.

Podobnik, Bruce 2004: Resistance to Globalization: Cycles and Evolutions in the Globalization Protest Movement. Paper for the ASA Annual Meeting, San Francisco, August 14–17.

Podolny, Joel and Page, Karen 1998: Network Forms of Organization. *Annual Review of Sociology*, 24, 57–76.

Poggi, Gianfranco (ed.) 1968: *L'organizzazione partitica del PCI e della DC*. Bologna: il Mulino.

Poguntke, Thomas 1993: *Alternative Politics: The German Green Party*. Edinburgh: Edinburgh University Press.

Polletta, Francesca 2002: *Freedom is an Endless Meeting: Democracy in American Social Movements*. Chicago, The University of Chicago Press.

Polletta, Francesca 1998: "It Was Like a Fever": Narrative and Identity in Social Protest. *Social Problems*, 45, 137–59.

Polletta, Francesca 1999: "Free Spaces" in Collective Action. *Theory and Society*, 28, 1–38.

Polletta, Francesca 2004: Culture Is Not Just in Your Head. In Jeff Goodwin and James J. Jasper (eds.), *Rethinking Social Movements: Structure, Meaning and Emotions*. Lanham, Rowman and Littlefield, 97–110.

Polletta, Francesca and Jasper, James M. 2001: Collective Identity and Social Movements. *Annual Review of Sociology*, 27, 283–305.

Porter, Gareth and Brown, Janet Welsh 1991: *Global Environmental Politics*. Boulder, CO/London: Westview Press.

Powell, Walter 1990: Neither Market Nor Hierarchy: Network Forms of Organization. *Research in Organizational Behavior*, 12, 295–336.

Prakash, Sanjeev and Selle, Per (eds.) 2004: *Investigating Social Capital*. New Dehli/London: Sage.

Princen, Thomas and Finger, Matthias 1994: Introduction. In T. Princen and M. Finger (eds.), *Environmental NGOs in World Politics: Linking the Local and the Global*. London: Routledge, 1–25.

Purdue, Derrik D. 2000: *Anti-GenetiX: The Emergence of the Anti-GM Movement*. Aldershot: Ashgate.

Purdue, Derrick, Diani, Mario, and Lindsay, Isobel 2004: Civic Networks in Bristol and Glasgow. *Community Development Journal*, 39, 277–88.

Rabehl, Bernd 1998: *Am Ende der Utopie: Die politische Geschichte der Freien, Universität Berlin*, Berlin: Argon Verlag.

Ranci, Costanzo 1992: La mobilitazione dell'altruismo. Condizioni e processi di diffusione dell'azione volontaria in Italia. *Polis*, 6, 467–505.

Randall, Vicky 1982: *Women and Politics*. London: Macmillan.

Rao, Hayagreeva, Morrill, Calvin, and Zald, Mayer N. 2000: Power Plays: How Social Movements and Collective Action Create New Organizational Forms. *Research in Organizational Behaviour*, 22, 239–82.

Rapoport, Anatol 1960: *Fights, Games, and Debates*. Ann Arbor: University of Michigan Press.

Raschke, Joachim 1988: *Soziale Bewegungen: Ein historisch-systematischer Grundriss*. Frankfurt am Main: Campus.

Rauch J. 2003: Rooted in Nations, Blossoming in Globalization? A Cultural Perspective on the Content of a "Northern" Mainstream and a "Southern" Alternative News Agency. *Journal of Communication Inquiry*, 27, 87–103.

Ray, Kathryn, Savage, Mike, Tampubolon, Gindo, Longhurst, Brian, Tomlison, Mark, and Warde, Alan 2000: An Exclusive Political Field? Membership Patterns and Networks in Social Movement Organizations. *Social Movement Studies*, 2, 37–60.

Ray, Raka 1999: *Fields of Protest: Women's Movements in India*. Minneapolis: University of Minnesota Press.

Redhead, Steve (ed.) 1993: *Rave Off: Politics and Deviance in Contemporary Culture*. Aldershot: Avebury.

Regalia, Ida, Regini, Marino, and Reyneri, Emilio 1978: Labor Conflicts and Industrial Relations in Italy. In C. Crouch and A. Pizzorno (eds.), *The Resurgence of Class Conflict in Western Europe since 1968*. London: Macmillan, 101–58.

Reger, Jo 2002: Organizational Dynamics and Construction of Multiple Feminist Identities in the National Organization for Women. *Gender & Society*, 16, 710–27.

Regini, Marino 1992: *Confini mobili*. Bologna: il Mulino.

Reifer, Thomas E. (ed.) 2004: *Globalization, Hegemony and Power: Antisystemic Movements and the Global System*. Boulder, CO: Paradigm Press.

Reimann, Kim D. 2001: Japanese NGO's and the Kyoto Climate Change Conference. *Mobilization*, 6, 83–100.

Reimon, Michel 2002: *Days of Action: Die neoliberale Globalisierung und ihre Gegner*. Wien: überreuter.

Reiner, Robert 1998: Policing, Protest, and Disorder in Britain. In D. della Porta and H. Reiter (eds.), *Policing Protest: The Control of Mass Demonstrations in Western Democracies*. Minneapolis: University of Minnesota Press, 35–48.

Reiter, Herbert 1998: Police and Public Order in Italy, 1944–1948. The Case of Florence. In D. della Porta and H. Reiter (eds.), *Policing Protest: The Control of Mass Demonstrations in Western Democracies*. Minneapolis: University of Minnesota Press, 143–65.

Renn, O., Webler, T. and Kastenholz, H. 1996: Procedural and Substantive Fairness in Landfill Siting: A Swiss Case Study. *Risk: Health, Safety and Environment*, 145 (Spring). (Reprinted in R. Löfstedt and L. Frewer, (eds.) (1998) *The Earthscan Reader in Risk and Modern Society*, 253–270.)

Rheingold, Howard 2002: *Smart Mobs: The Next Social Revolution*. New York: Perseus.

Richardson, Dick and Rootes, Chris (eds.) 1994: *The Green Challenge: The Development of Green Parties in Europe*. London/New York: Routledge.

Riddel-Dixon, Elizabeth 1995: Social Movements and the United Nations. *International Social Science Journal*, 144, 289–303.

Rihoux, Benoit and Walgrave, Stefaan 1997: *L'Année Blanche*. Bruxelles: EVO.

Risse, Thomas, and Sikkink, Kathryn 1999: The Socialization of International Human Rights Norms into Domestic Practices: Introduction. In T. Risse, S. Rapp, and K. Sikkink (eds.), *The Power of Human Rights International Norms and Domestic Change*. New York: Cambridge University Press, 1–38.

Ritzer, George 1996: *The McDonaldization of Society: An Investigation into the Changing Character of Contemporary Social Life*. Thousand Oaks, CA: Pine Forge Press.

Robbins, Thomas 1988: *Cults, Converts and Charisma: The Sociology of New Religious Movements*. London/Newbury Park, CA: Sage.

Robertson, Roland. 1992. *Globalization: Social Theory and Global Culture*. London: Sage Publications.

Robnett, Belinda 2002: External Political Events and Collective Identity. In D.S. Meyer, N. Whittier, and B. Robnett (eds.), *Social Movements: Identity, Culture, and the State*. New York: Oxford University Press, 287–301.

Rochford, E. Burke 1985: *Hare Krishna in America*. New Brunswick, NJ: Rutgers University Press.

Rochon, Thomas R. 1988: *Between Society and State: Mobilizing for Peace in Western Europe*. Princeton: Princeton University Press.

Rochon, Thomas R. 1998: *Culture Moves: Ideas, Activism, and Changing Values*. Princeton: Princeton University Press.

Rochon, Thomas R. and Mazmanian, Daniel A. 1993: Social Movements and the Policy Process. *The Annals of the AAPSS*, 528, 75–87.

Rochon, Thomas R. and Meyer, David S. (eds.) 1997: *Coalitions and Political Movements: The Lessons of the Nuclear Freeze*. Boulder: Lynne Rienner.

Rohrschneider, Robert 1988: Citizens' Attitudes towards Environmental Issues: Selfish or Selfless? *Comparative Political Studies*, 21, 347–67.

Rohrschneider, Robert 1990: The Roots of Public Opinion toward New Social Movements. *American Journal of Political Science*, 34, 1–30.

Rohrschneider, Robert 1993a: Impact of Social Movements on the European Party System. *The Annals of the American Academy of Political and Social Sciences*, 528 (July), 157–70.

Rohrschneider, Robert 1993b: Environmental Belief Systems in Western Europe. *Comparative Political Studies*, 26, 3–29.

Rohrschneider, Robert and Dalton, Russell 2002: A Global Network? Transnational Cooperation among Environmental Groups. *Journal of Politics*, 64, 510–33.

Rokkan, Stein 1970: *Citizens, Elections, and Parties*. Oslo: Oslo University Press.

Rolke, Lothar 1987: *Protestbewegungen in der Bundesrepublik.* Opladen: West-deutscher Verlag.

Rootes, Christopher 1992: The New Politics and the New Social Movements: Accounting for British Exceptionalism. *European Journal of Political Research,* 22, 171–91.

Rootes, Christopher 1994: Parties and Movements as Alternative Modes of Collective Action: Green Parties and Environmental Movements in Europe. Paper presented at the Thirteenth World Congress of Sociology, Bielefeld, July.

Rootes, Christopher 1995: A New Class? The Higher Educated and the New Politics. In L. Maheu (ed.), *Social Movements and Social Classes.* London/Thousand Oaks: Sage, 220–35.

Rootes, Christopher 1997: Shaping Collective Action: Structure, Contingency and Knowledge. In R. Edmonson (ed.), *The Political Context of Collective Action.* London/New York: Routledge.

Rootes, Christopher A. 2000: Environmental Protest in Britain 1988–1997. In B. Seel, M. Paterson, and B. Doherty (eds.), *Direct Action in British Environmentalism.* London: Routledge, 26–61.

Rootes, Christopher 2003: Britain. In C. Rootes (ed.), *Environmental Protest in Western Europe.* Oxford: Oxford University Press, 20–58.

Rootes, Christopher (ed.) 2003: *Environmental Protest in Western Europe.* Oxford: Oxford University Press.

Rootes, Christopher 2005: A Limited Transnationalization? The British Environmental Movement. In D. della Porta and S. Tarrow (eds.), *Transnational Protest and Global Activism.* Lanham, MD: Rowman & Littlefield, 21–43.

Rose, Fred 2000: *Coalitions Across the Class Divide: Lessons from the Labor, Peace and Environmental Movements.* Ithaca: Cornell University Press.

Rose, Richard 1988: *L'espansione della sfera pubblica.* Bologna: il Mulino. (original edition *Understanding Big Government,* London, Sage, 1984).

Roseneil, Sasha 1995: *Disarming Patriarchy.* Milton Keynes: Open University Press.

Rosenkrands, Jacob 2004: Politicising Homo Economicus: Analysis of Anticorporate Websites. In W. van de Donk, B. Loader, P. Nixon and D. Rucht (eds.), *Cyberprotest: New Media, Citizens and Social Movements.* London: Routledge, 57–76.

Rosenthal, Naomi and Schwartz, Michael 1989. Spontaneity and Democracy in Social Movements. In B. Klandermans (ed.), *Organizing For Change.* Greenwich, CT: JAI Press, 33–60.

Rosenthal, Naomi, Fingrutd, Meryl, Ethier, Michele, Karant, Roberta, and McDonald, David 1985: Social Movements and Network Analysis: A Case Study of Nineteenth-century Women's Reform in New York State. *American Journal of Sociology,* 90, 1022–54.

Rosenthal, Naomi, McDonald, David, Ethier, Michele, Fingrutd, Meryl, and Karant, Roberta 1997: Structural Tensions in the Nineteenth Century Women's Movement. *Mobilization,* 2, 21–46.

Roszak, Theodor 1969: *The Making of a Counterculture.* New York: Anchor Books.

Roth, Roland 1994: *Demokratie von unten: Neue soziale Bewegungen auf dem Wege zur politischen Institution.* Köln: Bund Verlag.

Rothenberg, Lawrence S. 1992: *Linking Citizens to Government: Interest Group Politics at Common Cause.* Cambridge/New York: Cambridge University Press.

Rothman, Franklin D. and Oliver, Pamela 1999: From Local to Global: The Anti-Dam Movement in Southern Brazil, 1979–1992. *Mobilization*, 4, 41–58.

Routledge, Paul 2003: Convergence Space: Process Geographies of Grassroots Globalization Networks. *Transactions of the Institute of British Geographers*, 28, 333–49.

Royall, Frédéric 1998: Le mouvement des chômeurs en France de l'hiver 1997–1998. *Modern and Contemporary France*, 6, 351–65.

Rubington, Earl and Weinberg, Martin S. (eds.) 2003: *The Study of Social Problems*. Oxford: Oxford University Press (6th edition).

Rucht, Dieter 1984: Zur Organisation der neuen sozialen Bewegungen. In Jürgen Falter et al., *Politische Willensbildung und Interessenvermittlung*. Opladen: Westdeutscher Verlag.

Rucht, Dieter 1989: Environmental Movement Organizations in West Germany and France: Structure and Interorganizational Relations. In B. Klandermans (ed.), *International Social Movement Research*, vol. 2, *Organizing for Change*. Greenwich, CT: JAI Press, 61–94.

Rucht, Dieter 1990a: The Strategies and Action Repertoire of New Movements. In R. J. Dalton and M. Kuechler (eds.), *Challenging the Political Order: New Social Movements in Western Democracies*. Cambridge: Polity Press, 156–75.

Rucht, Dieter 1990b: Campaigns, Skirmishes and Battles: Anti-nuclear Movements in the USA, France and West Germany. *Industrial Crisis Quarterly*, 4, 193–222.

Rucht, Dieter (ed.) 1991a: *Research in Social Movements: The State of the Art*. Frankfurt/Boulder, CO: Campus Verlag/Westview Press.

Rucht, Dieter 1991b: A Critique of Alain Touraine's *Intervention Sociologique*. In D. Rucht (ed.), *Research in Social Movements: The State of the Art*. Frankfurt/Boulder, CO: Campus Verlag/Westview Press.

Rucht, Dieter 1991c: Das Kräftefeld soziale Bewegungen, Gegenbewegungen und Staat. *Forschungsjournal Neue Soziale Bewegungen*, 2 (4), 31–42.

Rucht, Dieter 1992: *Studying the Effects of Social Movements: Conceptualization and Problems*. Paper presented at the Joint Sessions of the European Consortium for Political Research, Limerick, March 30–April 4.

Rucht, Dieter 1993: Think Globally, Act Locally? Needs, Forms and Problems of Cross-national Cooperation Among Environmental Groups. In J. D. Liefferink, P. Lowe, and A. P. J. Mol (eds.), *European Integration and Environmental Policy*. London/New York: Belhaven Press/Halsted Press, 75–95.

Rucht, Dieter 1994: *Modernisierung und Soziale Bewegungen*. Frankfurt am Main: Campus.

Rucht, Dieter 1995: The Impact of Anti-nuclear Power Movements in International Comparison. In M. Bauer (ed.), *Resistance to New Technology*. Cambridge: Cambridge University Press.

Rucht, Dieter 1996: The Impact of National Contexts on Social Movements Structure. In D. McAdam, J. McCarthy, and M. N. Zald (eds.), *Comparative Perspective on Social Movements: Political Opportunities, Mobilizing Structures, and Cultural Framing*. Cambridge/New York: Cambridge University Press, 185–204.

Rucht, Dieter 2003a: Media Strategies and Media Resonance in Transnational Protest Campaigns. Paper presented at the conference Transnational Processes and Social Movements. Bellagio, Italy.

Rucht, Dieter (ed.) 2003b: *Berlin, 1. Mai 2002: Politische Demonstrationsrituale*. Opladen: Leske + Budrich.

Rucht, Dieter 2004: The Quadruple "A": Media Strategies of Protest Movements since the 1960s. In Wim van de Donk, Brian Loader, Paul Nixon, and Dieter Rucht (eds.), *Cyberprotest: New Media, Citizens and Social Movements*. London: Routledge, 29–56.

Rüdig, Wolfgang 1990: *Anti-nuclear Movements: A World Survey*. London: Longman.

Ruggiero, Vincenzo 2000: New Social Movements and the "centri sociali" in Milan. *Sociological Review*, 48, 167–85.

Rule, James R. 1988: *Theories of Civil Violence*. Berkeley: University of California Press.

Rupp, Leila and Taylor, Verta 1987: *Survival in the Doldrums: The American Women's Rights Movement, 1945 to the 1960s*. Columbus: Ohio State University Press.

Rupp, Leila and Taylor, Verta 2003: *Drag Queens at the 801 Cabaret*. Chicago: University of Chicago Press.

Rusconi, Gian Enrico 1992: Etnia: Un costrutto polemico. *Polis*, 6, 571–87.

Rusconi, Gian Enrico 1993: *Se cessiamo di essere una nazione*. Bologna: il Mulino.

Russett, Bruce and Starr, Harvey 1996: *World Politics: The Menu for Choice*. New York: W. H. Freeman and Co.

Ruzza, Carlo 2004: *Europe and Civil Society: Movement Coalitions and European Governance*. Manchester: Manchester University Press.

Ryan, Barbara 1992: *Feminism and the Women's Movement: Dynamics of Change in Social Movements' Ideology and Activism*. New York: Routledge.

Safran, William 1989: The French State and Ethnic Minority Cultures: Policy Dimensions and Problems. In J. Rudolph and R. J. Thompson (eds.), *Ethnoterritorial Politics, Policy, and the Western World*. Boulder, CO/London: Lynne Rienner, 115–58.

Salamon, Lester M. and Anheier, Helmut (eds.) 1997: *Defining the Nonprofit Sector: A Cross National Analysis*. Manchester: Manchester University Press.

Salmon, Jean Marc 1998: *Le désir de societé: Des restaurants du coer au mouvement des chomeurs*. Paris: La découverte.

Sampson, S. 1969: Crisis in a Cloister. Unpublished Doctoral Dissertation, Cornell University.

Samuelson, Paul 1954: The Pure Theory of Public Expenditure. *Review of Economics and Statistics*, 36, 387–89.

Sanchez Jankowski, Martin 1991: *Islands in the Street: Gangs and American Urban Society*. Berkeley: University of California Press.

Sandell, Rickard 1999: Organizational Life aboard the Moving Bandwagons: A Network Analysis of Dropouts from a Swedish Temperance Organization, 1896–1937. *Acta Sociologica*, 42, 3–15.

Sandell, Rickard 2001: Organizational Growth and Ecological Constraints: The Growth of Social Movements in Sweden, 1881 to 1940. *American Sociological Review*, 66, 672–93.

Sandell, Rickard and Charlotta Stern 1998: Group Size and the Logic of Collective Action: A Network Analysis of a Swedish Temperance Movement 1896–1937. *Rationality and Society*, 10, 327–45.

Sandoval, Salvador A. M. 1998: Social Movements and Democratization. The Case of Brasil and the Latin Countries. In in Marco Giugni, Doug McAdam and Charles Tilly (eds.), *From Contention to Democracy*. Lanham, MD: Rowman and Littlefield, 169–201.

Sartori, Giovanni 1970: Concept Misformation in Comparative Politics. *American Political Science Review*, 56, 1033–53.

Sartori, Giovanni 1987: Ideologia. In *Elementi di teoria politica*. Bologna: il Mulino.

Sartori, Giovanni 1990: Comparazione e metodo comparato. *Rivista italiana di scienza politica*, 20, 397–416.

Sassen, Saskia 1998: *Globalization and Its Discontents*. New York: Norton.

Sassen, Saskia 2000: *Cities in a World Economy*. Thousand Oaks: Pine Forge Press, 117–38.

Sassoon, Joseph 1984a: Ideologia, azione simbolica e ritualità: Nuovi percorsi dei movimenti. In A. Melucci (ed.), *Altri codici*. Bologna: il Mulino, 385–415.

Sassoon, Joseph 1984b: Ideology, Symbolic Action and Rituality in Social Movements: The Effects of Organizational Forms. *Social Science Information*, 23, 861–73.

Saunders, P. 1987: Social Theory and the Urban Question. London: Unwin Hyman.

Sawer, Marian and Groves, Abigail 1994: The Women's Lobby': Networks, Coalition Building and the Women of Middle Australia. *Australian Journal of Political Science*, 29, 435–59.

Scharpf, Fritz 1999: *Governing in Europe: Effective and Democratic?* Oxford: Oxford University Press.

Scharpf, Fritz W. 1984: Economic and Institutional Constraints of Full-Employment Strategies: Sweden, Austria, and West Germany. In J. H. Goldthorpe (ed.), *Order and Conflict in Contemporary Capitalism*. Oxford: Clarendon Press, 257–90.

Scheff, Thomas 1994b. Emotions and Identity: A Theory of Ethnic Nationalism. In C. Calhoun (ed.), *Social Theory and the Politics of Identity*. Oxford/Cambridge, MA: Blackwell, 277–303.

Scheff, Thomas J. 1994a: *Bloody Revenge: Emotions, Nationalism, and War*. Boulder, CO: Westview Press.

Schlesinger, Paul 1992: *Putting "Reality" Together* (2nd edition). London: Routledge.

Schlosberg, David 2002: *Environmental Justice and the New Pluralism*. Oxford: Oxford University Press.

Schmidt, Hilmar and Take, Ingo 1997: Demokratiscer und besser? Der Beitrag von Nichtregierungsorganisationen zur Demokratisierung internationaler Politik und zu Loesung globaler Probleme. *Aus Politik und Zeitgeschichte*, 43, 12–20.

Schmitt-Beck, Rüdiger 1989: Organizational Interlocks between New Social Movements and Traditional Elites: The Case of the West German Peace Movement. *European Journal of Political Research*, 17, 583–98.

Schmitter, Philippe 1974: Still a Century of Corporatism? *Review of Politics*, 36, 85–131.

Schmitter, Philippe 1981: Interest Intermediation and Regime Governability in Contemporary Western Europe and North America. In Suzanne Berger (ed.), *Organized Interests in Western Europe: Pluralism, Corporatism, and the Transformation of Politics*. Cambridge/New York: Cambridge University Press, 287–327.

Schmitter, Philippe and Lehmbruch, Gerard (eds.) 1979: *Trends towards Corporatist Intermediation*. London/Beverly Hills: Sage.

Schneider, Volker 2000: The Global Social Capital of Human Rights Movements: A Case Study on Amnesty International. In K. Ronit and V. Schneider (eds.), *Private Organizations in Global Politics*. London: Routledge, 146–64.

Schnittker, Jason, Freese, Jeremy, and Powell, Brian 2003: Who Are Feminists and What Do They Believe? The Role of Generations, *American Sociological Review*, 68, 607–22.

Scholsberg, David 2002: *Environmental Justice and the New Pluralism: The Challenge of Difference for Environmentalism.* Oxford: Oxford University Press.

Schönleitner, Gunther 2003: World Social Forum: Making Another World Possible? In J. Clark (ed.), *Globalizing Civic Engagement: Civil Society and Transnational Action.* London: Earthscan Publications Ltd., 109–26.

Schou, Arild 1997: Elite Identification in the Palestinian Intifada. *Mobilization*, 2, 71–86.

Schudson, Michael 1989: How Culture Works: Perspectives from Media Studies on the Efficacy of Symbols. *Theory and Society*, 18, 153–80.

Schumaker, Paul D. 1975: Policy Responsiveness to Protest Group Demands. *The Journal of Politics*, 37, 488–521.

Scotch, Richard K. 1988: Disability as the Basis for a Social Movement: Advocacy and the Politics of Definition. *Journal of Social Issues*, 44, 159–72.

Scott, Alan 1990: *Ideology and the New Social Movements.* London: Unwin Hyman.

Scott, Alan (ed.) 1997: *The Limits of Globalization.* London: Routledge.

Scott, John 1992: *Social Network Analysis: A Handbook.* London/Newbury Park, CA: Sage.

Scott, W. Richard 1981: *Organizations: Rational, Natural and Open System.* Englewood Cliffs, NJ: Prentice Hall.

Seel, Bejamin, Patterson, Matthew, and Doherty, Brian (eds.) 2000: *Direct Action in British Environmentalism.* London: Routledge.

Seligman, Adam 1992: *The Idea of Civil Society.* New York: Free Press.

Sen, Amartya 2004: *La democrazia degli altri.* Milano: Mondadori.

Sewell, William H. Jr 1992: A Theory of Structure: Duality, Agency, and Transformation. *American Journal of Sociology*, 98, 1–29.

Shah, Ghanshyam 1990: *Social Movements in India: A Review of the Literature.* New Delhi/Newbury Park: Sage.

Sharpe, L. Jim 1988: The Growth and Decentralisation of the Modern Democratic State. *European Journal of Political Research*, 16, 365–80.

Shemtov, Ronit 1999: Taking Ownership of Environmental Problems. *Mobilization*, 4, 91–106.

Showstack Sassoon, A. 1987: *Women and the State. Shifting Boundaries of Public and Private.* London: Hutchinson.

Sikkink, Kathryn and Smith, Jackie 2002: Infrastructures for Change: Transnational Organizations 1953–1993. In S. Khagram, J. V. Riker, and K. Sikkink (eds.), *Reconstructing World Politics: Transnational Social Movements, Networks and Norms.* Minneapolis: University of Minnesota Press. 24–44

Sikkink, Kathryn. 2002. Reconstructing World Politics: The Limits and Asymmetries of Soft Power. In S. Khagram, J. V. Riker, and K. Sikkink (eds.), *Reconstructing World Politics: Transnational Social Movements, Networks and Norms.* Minneapolis: University of Minnesota Press, 301–17.

Siltanen, Janet and Stanworth, Michelle 1984: *Women and the Public Sphere.* London: Hutchinson.

Silver, Beverly 2003: *Forces of Labor: Workers' Movements and Globalization Since 1870.* Cambridge: Cambridge University Press.

Silver, Beverly and Slater, Eric 1999: The Social Origins of World Hegemonies. In G. Arrighi and B. Silver (eds.), *Chaos and Governance in the Modern World System*. Minneapolis: University of Minnesota Press, 175–250.

Simeant, Johanna 1998: *La cause des sans-papiers*. Paris: Presses de Sciences Po.

Simmel, Georg [1908] 1950: The Triad. In *The Sociology of Georg Simmel*, translated by K. Wolff. New York: Free Press, 145–69.

Simmel, Georg [1908] 1955: Conflict. In *Conflict and the Web of Group Affiliations*, translated by K. Wolff. New York: Free Press, 11–123. (Original edition *Die Streit in Soziologie*, München: Duncker und Humblot, 1908.)

Sklair, Laskie 1995: Social Movements and Global Capitalism. *Sociology*, 29, 495–512.

Skocpol, Theda 1979: *States and Social Revolutions*. Cambridge/New York: Cambridge University Press.

Skocpol, Theda 2003: *Diminished Democracy: From Membership to Management in American Civic Life*. Norman: Oklahoma University Press.

Smelser, Neil J. 1962: *Theory of Collective Behavior*. New York: The Free Press.

Smelser, Neil J. 1992: Culture: Coherent or Incoherent. In N. J. Smelser and R. Muench (eds.), *Theory of Culture*. Berkeley/Los Angeles: University of California Press, 3–28.

Smith, Anthony D. 1981: *The Ethnic Revival*. Cambridge: Cambridge University Press.

Smith, Anthony D. 1986: *The Ethnic Origins of Nations*. Oxford: Blackwell.

Smith, Christian (ed.) 1996: *Disruptive Religion: The Force of Faith in Social Movement Activism*. New York and London: Routledge.

Smith, Jackie 1995: Transnational Political Processes and the Human Rights Movement. In L. Kriesberg (ed.), *Research in Social Movements, Conflict and Change*, vol. 17. Greenwich, CT: JAI Press, 185–219.

Smith, Jackie 1997: Characteristics of the Modern Transnational Social Movement Sector. In J. Smith, C. Chatfield, and R. Pagnucco (eds.), *Transnational Social Movements and Global Politics*. Syracuse, NY: Syracuse University Press, 42–58.

Smith, Jackie 1998: Global Strategies of Social Protest: Transnational Social Movement Organizations in World Politics. In D. della Porta, H. Kriesi, and D. Rucht (eds.), *Social Movements in a Globalizing World*. New York/London: Macmillan, 170–88.

Smith, Jackie 1999: Transnational Organizations. In *Encyclopedia of Violence, Peace, and Conflict*, vol. 3. San Diego: Academic Publishers, 591–602.

Smith, Jackie 2001: Globalizing Resistance: The Battle of Seattle and the Future of Social Movements. *Mobilization*, 6, 1–19.

Smith, Jackie 2004a: Exploring Connections Between Global Integration and Political Mobilization. *Journal of World Systems Research*, 10, 11–34.

Smith, Jackie 2004b: Transnational Processes and Movements. In Davis A. Snow, Sarah H. Soule and Hanspeter Kriesi (eds.), *The Blackwell Companion to Social Movements*. Oxford: Blackwell, 311–35.

Smith, Jackie and Johnston, Hank (eds.) 2002: *Globalization and Resistance: Transnational Dimensions of Social Movements*. Lanham, MD: Rowman & Littlefield.

Smith, Jackie, Pagnucco, Ron and Romeril, Winnie 1994: Transnational Social Movement Organisations in the Global Political Arena. *Voluntas*, 5, 121–54.

Snow, David 2004: Framing Processes, Ideology, and Discursive Fieds. In D. Snow, S. Soule, and H. Kriesi (eds.), *The Blackwell Companion to Social Movements*. Oxford: Blackwell, 380–412.

Snow, David 2005: Social Movements as Challenges to Authority: Resistance to an Emerging Conceptual Hegemony? In D. Myers and D. Cress (eds.), *Authority in Contention*. New York: Elsevier.

Snow, David A. and Benford, Robert D. 1988: Ideology, Frame Resonance, and Participant Mobilization. In B. Klandermans, H. Kriesi, and S. Tarrow (eds.), *From Structure to Action*. Greenwich, CT: JAI Press, 197–218.

Snow, David A. and Benford, Robert D. 1992: Master Frames and Cycles of Protest. In A. Morris and C. McClurg Mueller (eds.), *Frontiers In Social Movement Theory*. New Haven: Yale University Press, 133–55.

Snow, David A. and Oliver, Pamela 1995: Social Movements and Collective Behavior: Social Psychological Dimensions and Considerations. In K. S. Cook, G. A. Fine, and J. House (eds.), *Sociological Perspectives on Social Psychology*. Boston: Allyn & Bacon, 571–99.

Snow, David A., Rochford, Burke E., Worden, Steven, and Benford, Robert 1986: Frame Alignment Processes, Micromobilization, and Movement Participation. *American Sociological Review*, 51, 464–81.

Snow, David A., Zurcher, Louis A., and Ekland-Olson, Sheldon 1980: Social Networks and Social Movements: A Microstructural Approach to Differential Recruitment. *American Sociological Review*, 45, 787–801.

Snow, David, Soule, Sarah, and Kriesi, Hanspeter (eds.) 2004a: *The Blackwell Companion to Social Movements*. Oxford: Blackwell.

Snow, David, Soule, Sarah, and Kriesi, Hanspeter 2004b: Mapping the Terrain. In D. Snow, S. Soule, and H. Kriesi (eds.), *The Blackwell Companion to Social Movements*. Oxford: Blackwell.

Snyder, David and Tilly, Charles 1972: Hardship and Collective Violence in France, 1830–1960. *American Sociological Review*, 37, 520–32.

Somers, Margaret R. 1992: Narrativity, Narrative Identity, and Social Action: Rethinking English Working-Class Formation. *Social Science History*, 16, 591–630.

Somers, Margaret R. 1993: Citizenship and the Place of the Public Sphere: Law, Community, and Political Culture in the Transition to Democracy. *American Sociological Review*, 58, 587–620.

Somers, Margaret R. 1994: The Narrative Constitution of Identity: A Relational and Network Approach. *Theory and Society*, 23, 605–49.

Sommier, Isabelle 2003: *Le renoveau des mouvements contestataires à l'heure de la mondialisation*. Paris: Flammarion.

Soule, Sarah 2004: Diffusion Process Within and Across Movements. In Davis A. Snow, Sarah H. Soule, and Hanspeter Kriesi (eds.), *The Blackwell Companion to Social Movements*. Oxford: Blackwell, 294–310.

Souza, Celina 2000: Participatory Budgeting in Brazilian Cities: Limits and Possibilities in Building Democratic Institutions. *Environment and Urbanization*, 13, 159–84.

Soysal, Yasemine N. 1994: *Limits of Citizenship: Migrants and Postnational Membership in Europe*. Chicago: Chicago University Press.

Staggenborg, Suzanne 1986: Coalition Work in the Pro-Choice Movement: Organizational and Environmental Opportunities and Constraints. *Social Problems*, 33, 623–41.

Staggenborg, Suzanne 1991: *The Pro-Choice Movement: Organization and Activism in the Abortion Conflict*. New York: Oxford University Press.

Staggenborg, Suzanne. 1988. The Consequences of Professionalization and Formalization in the Pro-Choice Movement. *American Sociological Review*, 53, 585–606.

Stamatov, Peter 2002: Interpretive Activism and the Political Uses of Verdi's Operas in the 1840s. *American Sociological Review*, 67, 345–66.

Stark, Rodney and Bainbridge, William S. 1980: Networks of Faith: Interpersonal Bonds and Recruitment to Cults and Sects. *American Journal of Sociology*, 85, 1376–95.

Steel, Brent S., Warner, Rebecca L., Stieber, Blair, and Lovrich, Nicholas P. 1992: Postmaterialist Values and Support for Feminism among Canadian and American Women and Men. *Western Political Quarterly*, 45, 339–53.

Stefancic, Jean and Delgado, Richard 1996: *No Mercy: How Conservative Think Tanks and Foundations Changed America's Social Agenda*. Philadelphia: Temple University Press.

Steinberg, Marc 1999: The Talk and Back Talk of Collective Action: A Dialogic Analysis of Repertoires of Discourse among Nineteenth Century English Cotton Spinners. *American Journal of Sociology*, 105, 736–80.

Stepan-Norris, Judith and Zeitlin, Maurice 2003: *Left Out: Reds and America's Industrial Unions*. Cambridge: Cambridge University Press.

Stoecker, Randy 1995: Community, Movement, Organization: The Problem of Identity Convergence in Collective Action. *Sociological Quarterly*, 36, 111–30.

Stokman, Frans N., Ziegler, Rolf and Scott, John (eds.) 1985: *Networks of Corporate Power: A Comparative Analysis of Ten Countries*. Cambridge: Polity Press.

Stolle, Dietlind and Hooghe, Marc 2004: Consumers as Political Participants? Shifts in Political Action Repertoires in Western Societies. In M. Micheletti, A. Follesdal, and D. Stolle (eds.), *Politics, Products and Markets: Exploring Political Consumerism Past and Present*. New Brunswick, NJ: Transaction Publishers, 265–88.

Strand, David and Meyer, John W. 1993: Institutional Conditions for Diffusion. *Theory and Society*, 22, 487–511.

Strauss, Anselm L. 1947: Research in Collective Behavior: Neglect and Need. *American Sociological Review*, 12, 352–4.

Streeck, Wolfgang 1992: *Social Institutions and Economic Performance*. Thousand Oaks/London: Sage.

Stryker, Sheldon, Owens, Timothy J., and White, Robert W. (eds.) 2000: *Self, Identity, and Social Movements*. Minneapolis: University of Minnesota Press.

Subramaniam, Mangala, Gupte, Manjusha, and Mitre, Debarashmi 2003: Local to Global: Transnational Networks and Indian Women's Grassroots Organizing. *Mobilization*, 8, 335–52.

Suh, Doowon 2004: Outcome Framing and Movement Dynamics: Korean White-Collar Unions' Political Mobilization and Interunion Solidarity, 1987–1995. *Mobilization*, 9, 17–38.

Swidler, Ann 1986: Culture in Action: Symbols and Strategies. *American Sociological Review*, 51, 273–86.

Swidler, Ann and Arditi, Jorge 1994: The New Sociology of Knowledge. *Annual Review of Sociology*, 20, 305–29.

Szasz, Andrew 1994: *EcoPopulism: Toxic Waste and the Movement for Environmental Justice*. Minneapolis/London: University of Minnesota Press/UCL Press.

Szelenyi, Sonia and Olvera, Jacqueline 1996: The Declining Significance of Class: Does Gender Complicate the Story? – Comments. *Theory and Society*, 25, 725–30.

Szerszinski, Bron 1995: Entering the Stage: Strategies of Environmental Communication in the UK. In K. Eder (ed.), *Framing and Communicating Environmental Issues*, Research Report, Commission of the European Communities, DGXII, Florence / Lancaster: European University Institute / CSEC, University of Lancaster.

Sztompka, Piotr 1993: *The Sociology of Social Change*. Oxford: Blackwell.

Taggart, Paul A. 1996: *The New Populism and the New Politics: New Protest Parties in Sweden in a Comparative Perspective*. New York: St Martin's Press.

Tarrow, Sidney 1983: Struggling to Reform: Social Movements and Policy Change during Cycles of Protest. *Western Societies Paper 15*. Ithaca: Cornell University.

Tarrow, Sidney 1989: *Democracy and Disorder: Protest and Politics in Italy, 1965–1975*. Oxford / New York: Oxford University Press.

Tarrow, Sidney 1989b. Mutamenti nella cultura di opposizione in Italia, 1965–1975. *Polis*, 3, 41–63.

Tarrow, Sidney 1990: The Phantom at the Opera: Political Parties and Social Movements of the 1960s and the 1970s in Italy. In R. J. Dalton and M. Kuechler (eds.), *Challenging the Political Order: New Social Movements in Western Democracies*. Cambridge: Polity Press, 251–73.

Tarrow, Sidney 1994: *Power in Movement: Social Movements, Collective Action and Politics*. New York / Cambridge: Cambridge University Press.

Tarrow, Sidney 1995: The Europeanization of Conflict: Reflections from a Social Movement Perspective. *West European Politics*, 18, 223–51.

Tarrow, Sidney 1998 [1994]: *Power in Movement: Social Movements, Collective Action and Politics*. New York / Cambridge: Cambridge University Press.

Tarrow, Sidney 2005: *The New Transnational Contention*. New York / Cambridge: Cambridge University Press.

Tarrow, Sidney and McAdam, Doug 2005: Scale Shift in Transnational Contention. In D. della Porta and S. Tarrow (eds.), *Transnational Protest and Global Activism*. Lanham, MD: Rowman and Littlefield, 121–49.

Taylor, Bron (ed.) 1995: *Ecological Resistance Movements*. Albany, NY: SUNY Press.

Taylor, Charles 1993: *Multiculturalismo: La politica del riconoscimento*. Milano: Anabasi (original edition *Multiculturalism and the Politics of Recognition*, Princeton, NJ, Princeton University Press, 1992).

Taylor, Ian 1996: Fear of Crime, Urban Fortunes and Suburban Social Movements: Some Reflections from Manchester. *Sociology*, 30, 317–37.

Taylor, Verta 1989: Social Movement Continuity: The Women's Movement in Abeyance. *American Sociological Review*, 54, 761–75.

Taylor, Verta 1996: *Rock-a-by Baby: Feminism, Identity, and the Post-Partum Depression*. New York: Routledge.

Taylor, Verta and Van Willigen, Marieke 1996: Women's Self-Help and the Reconstruction of Gender. *Mobilization*, 1, 123–42.

Taylor, Verta and Whittier, Nancy 1992: Collective Identity in Social Movement Communities: Lesbian Feminist Mobilization. In A. Morris and C. McClurg Mueller (eds.), *Frontiers in Social Movement Theory*. New Haven: Yale University Press, 104–32.

Taylor, Verta and Whittier, Nancy 1995: Analytical Approaches to Social Movement Culture: The Culture of the Women's Movement. In H. Johnston and B. Klandermans (eds.), *Social Movements and Culture*. Minneapolis/London: University of Minnesota Press/UCL Press, 163–87.

Taylor-Gooby, Peter 1986: Consumpion Cleavages and Welfare Politics. *Political Studies*, 34, 592–606.

Thayer, Millie 2001: Transnational Feminism: Reading Joan Scott in the Brazilian Sertão. *Ethnography*, 2, 243–71.

Thomas, Daniel C. 2001: *The Helsinki Effect: International Norms, Human Rights, and the Demise of Communism*. Princeton: Princeton University Press.

Thompson, Edward H. 1963: *The Making of the English Working Class*. London: Penguin.

Thompson, J. D. 1967: *Organizations in Action*. New York: McGraw-Hill.

Thompson, John B. 1995: *The Media and Modernity*. Cambridge: Cambridge University Press.

Tillock, Harriet M. and Morrison, Denton E. 1979: Group Size and Contribution to Collective Action: An Examination of Olson Theory Using Data from Zero Population Growth. In L. Kriesberg (ed.), *Research in Social Movements, Conflicts and Change*, vol. 2. Greenwich, CT: JAI Press, 131–52.

Tilly, Charles 1978: *From Mobilization to Revolution*. Reading, MA: Addison-Wesley.

Tilly, Charles 1984a: *Big Structures, Large Processes, Huge Comparisons*. New York: Russell Sage.

Tilly, Charles 1984b: Social Movements and National Politics. In C. Bright and S. Harding (eds.), *State-Making and Social Movements: Essays in History and Theory*. Ann Arbor: University of Michigan Press, 297–317.

Tilly, Charles 1986: *The Contentious French*. Cambridge MA: Harvard University Press.

Tilly, Charles 1987: Social Conflict. *CSSC Working Paper Series 43*. New York: New School for Social Research.

Tilly, Charles 1988: Social Movements, Old and New. In L. Kriesberg (ed.), *Research in Social Movements, Conflict and Change*, vol. 10. Greenwich, CT: JAI Press, 1–18.

Tilly, Charles 1993: *European Revolutions 1492–1992*. Oxford/Cambridge, MA: Blackwell.

Tilly, Charles 1994: Social Movements as Historically Specific Clusters of Political Performances. *Berkeley Journal of Sociology*, 38, 1–30.

Tilly, Charles 2002: *Stories, Identities, and Political Change*. Lanham, MD: Rowman & Littlefield.

Tilly, Charles 2003: *The Politics of Collective Violence*. Cambridge: Cambridge University Press.

Tilly, Charles 2004a: *Social Movements 1768–2004*. Boulder, CO: Paradigm.

Tilly, Charles 2004b: *Contention and Democracy in Europe 1650–2000*. Cambridge: Cambridge University Press.

Tilly, Charles, Tilly, Louise and Tilly, Richard 1975: *The Rebellious Century 1830–1930*. Cambridge, MA: Harvard University Press.

Tilly, Chris 2004: Living Wage Laws in the United States: The Dynamic of a Growing Movement. In Maria Kousis and Charles Tilly (eds.), *Economic and Political Contention in Comparative Perspective*. Boulder, CO: Paradigm Publishers, 143–57.

Tindall, David 2004: Social Movement Participation Over Time: An Ego-Network Approach to Micro-Mobilization. *Sociological Focus*, 37, 163–84.

Titarenko, Larissa, McCarthy, John D., McPhail, Clark, and Augustyn, Boguslaw 2001: The Interaction of State Repression, Protest Form and Protest Sponsor Strength During the Transition From Communism in Belarus, 1990–1995. *Mobilization*, 6, 129–50.

Tondeur, Alain 1997: *La crise blanche*. Brussels: Editions Luc Pire.

Touraine, Alain 1977: *The Self-Production of Society*. Chicago: University of Chicago Press.

Touraine, Alain 1981: *The Voice and the Eye: An Analysis of Social Movements*. Cambridge: Cambridge University Press.

Touraine, Alain 1984: *Le retour de l'acteur*. Paris: Fayard.

Touraine, Alain 1985: An Introduction to the Study of Social Movements. *Social Research*, 52, 749–88.

Touraine, Alain 1987: *The Workers' Movement*. Cambridge/New York: Cambridge University Press.

Touraine, Alain 1991: Commentary on Dieter Rucht's Critique. In D. Rucht (ed.), *Research in Social Movements: The State of the Art*. Frankfurt/Boulder, CO: Campus Verlag/Westview Press, 385–91.

Touraine, Alain 1992: *Critique de la modernité*. Paris: Fayard.

Touraine, Alain, Dubet, François, Hegedus, Zsuzsa, and Wieviorka, Michel 1981: *Le pays contre l'etat: Luttes occitanes*. Paris: Seuil.

Touraine, Alain, Dubet, François, Wieviorka, Michel, and Strzelecki, Jan 1983: *Solidarity: The Analysis of a Social Movement: Poland 1980–1981*. Cambridge: Cambridge University Press.

Touraine, Alain, Hegedus, Zsusza, Dubet, François, and Wieviorka, Michel 1983: *Anti-nuclear Protest: The Opposition to Nuclear Power in France*. Cambridge: Cambridge University Press.

Tranvik, Tommy 2004: Surfing for Online Connectedness: Is the Internet Helping to End Civic Engagement? In S. Prakash and P. Selle (eds.) *Investigating Social Capital*. London: Sage, 281–304.

Traugott, Mark 1995: Barricades as Repertoire: Continuities and Discontinuities in the History of French Contention. In Mark Traugott (ed.), *Repertoires and Cycles of Collective Action*. Durham: Duke University Press, 43–56.

Trigilia, Carlo 1984: *Grandi partiti e piccole imprese: Comunisti e democristiani nelle regioni a economia diffusa*. Bologna: il Mulino.

Trump, Thomas M. 1991: Value Formation and Postmaterialism: Inglehart's Theory of Value Change Reconsidered. *Comparative Political Studies*, 24, 365–90.

Turk, Herman 1977: *Organizations in Modern Life*. San Francisco: Jossey-Bass.

Turnaturi, Gabriella 1991: *Associati per amore*. Milan: Feltrinelli.

Turner, Bryan 1988: *Status*. Milton Keynes: Open University Press.

Turner, Ralph 1969: The Theme of Contemporary Social Movements. *British Journal of Sociology*, 20, 390–405.

Turner, Ralph 1994: Ideology and Utopia After Socialism. In E. Larana, H. Johnston, and J. Gusfield (eds.), *New Social Movements: From Ideology to Identity*. Philadelphia: Temple University Press, 79–100.

Turner, Ralph and Killian, Lewis 1987 [1957]: *Collective Behavior*. Englewood Cliffs, NJ: Prentice-Hall.

Urry, John 1995: Rethinking Class. In L. Maheu (ed.), *Social Movements and Social Classes*. London/Thousand Oaks: Sage, 169–81.

Useem, Bert 1980: Solidarity Model, Breakdown Model and the Boston Anti-busing Movement. *American Sociological Review*, 45, 357–69.

Valiente, Celia 2003: The Feminist Movement and the Reconfigured State in Spain (1970–2000). In Lee Ann Banaszak, Karen Beckwith, and Dieter Rucht (eds.), *Women's Movements Facing the Reconfigured State*. Cambridge: Cambridge University Press, 30–47.

Valocchi, Steve 1999: Collective Action Frames in the Gay Liberation Movement. *Mobilization*, 4, 59–74.

Van Aelst, Peter and Walgraave, Stefan 2004: New Media, New Movements? The Role of the Internet in Shaping the "Anti-globalization" Movement. In W. van de Donk, B. Loader, P. Nixon, and D. Rucht (eds.), *Cyberprotest: New Media, Citizens and Social Movements*. London: Routledge, 97–122.

van de Donk, Wim, Loader, Brian, Nixon, Paul, and Rucht, Dieter (eds.) 2004: *Cyberspace Protest*. London: Routledge.

van de Hoonaard, Will C. 1991: Numbers and "Social Forms": The Contribution of Simmel to Social Movements Theory. In L. Kriesberg (ed.), *Research In Social Movements, Conflict and Change*, vol. 13. Greenwich, CT: JAI Press, 31–43.

van der Heijden, Hein-Anton, Koopmans, Ruud, and Giugni, Marco 1992: The West European Environmental Movement. In L. Kriesberg (ed.), *Research in Social Movements, Conflict and Change. Supplement 2*. Greenwich, CT: JAI Press, 1–40.

Van Dyke, Nella, 2003: *Protest Cycles and Party Politics: The Effects of Elite Allies and Antagonists on Student Protest in the United States, 1930–1990*. In Jack A. Goldstone (ed.), *States, Parties and Social Movements*. New York: Cambridge University Press, 226–45.

van Gennep, A. 1983: *I riti di passaggio*. Torino: Boringhieri (original edition *Les rites de passage*, Paris, Nourry, 1908).

Van Zoonen, Liesbet 1996: A Dance of Death: New Social Movements and Mass Media. In D. Paletz (ed.), *Political Communication in Action*. Cress Hill, NJ: Hampton Press, 201–22.

Vegh, Sandor 2003: Classifying Forms of Online Activism. In M. McCaughey and M. D. Ayers (eds.), *Cyberactivism: Online Activism in Theory and Practice*. London: Routledge, 71–95.

Verba, Sydney, Nie, Norman H., and Kim, Jae-on 1978: *Participation and Political Equality*. Cambridge/New York: Cambridge University Press.

Vertovec, Steven and Cohen, Robin (eds.) 2003: *Conceiving Cosmopolitanism*. Oxford: Oxford University Press.

Virnoche, Mary and Marx, Gary 1997: "Only Connect": E. M. Forster in an Age of Electronic Communication: Computer-Mediated Association and Community Networks. *Sociological Inquiry*, 67, 85–100.

von Beyme, Klaus (ed.) 1988: *Right-wing Extremism in Western Europe*. London: Cass.

von Dirke, Sabine 1997: *All the Power to the Imagination! The West German Counterculture from the Student Movement to the Greens*. Lincoln/London: University of Nebraska Press.

Voss, Kim 1993: *The Making of American Exceptionalism: The Knights of Labor and Class Formation in the Nineteenth Century*. Cornell: University Press.

Wacquant, Loic J. D. 1994: The New Urban Color Line: The State and Fate of the Ghetto in Postfordist America. In C. Calhoun (ed.), *Social Theory and the Politics of Identity*. Oxford/Cambridge, MA: Blackwell, 231–76.

Waddell, Steve 2003: The Climate Action Network: Civil Society Tackling Global Negotiations, Boston, unpublished paper (www.gan-net.net/pdfs/can.pdf).

Waddington, P. A. J. 1994: *Liberty and Order: Policing Public Order in a Capital City*. London: UCL Press.

Waddington, P. A. J. 1998: Controlling Protest in Contemporary Historical and Comparative Perspectives. In D. della Porta and H. Reiter (eds.), *Policing Protest: The Control of Mass Demonstrations in Western Democracies*. Minneapolis: University of Minnesota Press, 117–40.

Walby, Sylvia 1997: *Gender Transformations*. London: Routledge.

Walgrave, Stefaan and Rucht, Dieter (eds.), forthcoming, *Protest Politics: Antiwar Mobilization in Advanced Industrial Democracies*, in preparation.

Walgrave, Stefaan and Massens, Jan 2000: The Making of the White March: The Mass Media as Mobilizing Alternative to Movement Organizations. *Mobilization*, 5, 217–39.

Walker, Jack L. 1991: *Mobilizing Interest Groups in America: Patrons, Professions, and Social Movements*. Ann Arbor: University of Michigan Press.

Wall, Derek 1999: *Earth First! and the Anti-Road Movement*. London: Routledge.

Wallace, Michael and Jenkins, J. Craig 1995: The New Class, Postindustrialism, and Neocorporatism: Three Images of Social Protest in Western Democracies. In J. C. Jenkins and B. Klandermans (eds.), *The Politics of Social Protest*. Minneapolis/London: University of Minnesota Press/UCL Press, 96–137.

Wallerstein, Immanuel 1974: *The Modern World System: Capitalist Agriculture and the Origins of the European World Economy in the Sixteenth Century*. New York: Academic Press.

Wallerstein, Immanuel 1979: *The Capitalist World Economy*. Cambridge, Cambridge University Press.

Wallerstein, Immanuel 2004: *World Systems Analysis: An Introduction*. Durham, NC: Duke University Press.

Wallis, Roy 1977: *The Road to Total Freedom*. New York: Columbia University Press.

Wallis, Roy and Bruce, Steve 1986: *Sociological Theory, Religion and Collective Action*. Belfast: Queen's University Press.

Walsh, Edward 1988: *Democracy in the Shadows: Citizens' Mobilization in the Wake of the Accident at Three Mile Island*. New York: Greenwood Press.

Walsh, Edward and Warland, Rex 1983: Social Movement Involvement in the Wake of A Nuclear Accident: Activists and Free Riders in the TMI Area. *American Sociological Review*, 48, 764–80.

Walton, John, and Seddon, David 1994: *Free Markets and Food Riots: The Politics of Global Adjustement*. Oxford: Blackwell.

Warren, Mark 2001: Power and Conflict in Social Capital: Community Organizing and Urban Policy. In Bob Edwards, Michael Foley, and Mario Diani (eds.) *Beyond Tocqueville*. Hanover: University Press of New England, 169–82.

Washbourne, Neil 2001: Information Technology and New Forms of Organising? Translocalism and Networks in Friends of the Earth. In F. Webster (ed.), *Culture and Politics in the Information Age*. London: Routledge, 129–41.

Wasko, Janet and Mosco, Vincent (eds.) 1992: *Democratic Communications in the Information Age*. Toronto/Norwood, NJ: Garamond Press/Ablex.

Wasserman, Stanley and Katherine Faust: 1995: *Social Network Analysis*. Cambridge/New York: Cambridge University Press.

Waters, Malcolm 1995: *Globalization*. London: Routledge.

Watts, Meredith W. 1997: *Xenophobia in United Germany: Generations, Modernization, and Ideology*. New York: St. Martin's Press.

Wellman, Barry 1988: Structural Analysis: From Method and Metaphor to Theory and Substance. In B. Wellman, and S. D. Berkowitz (eds.), *Social Structures: A Network Approach*. Cambridge/New York: Cambridge University Press, 19–61.

Wellman, Barry and Berkowitz, Steve D. (eds.) 1988: *Social Structures: A Network Approach*. Cambridge/New York, Cambridge University Press.

Wellman, Barry and Haythornwhyte, Carolin (eds.) 2002: *Internet and Everyday Life*. Oxford: Blackwell.

Wellman, Barry, Carrington, Peter J., and Hall, Alan 1988: Networks as Personal Communities. In B. Wellman and S. D. Berkowitz (eds.), *Social Structures: A Network Approach*. Cambridge/New York: Cambridge University Press, 130–84.

Westby, David L. 2002: Strategic Imperative, Ideology, and Frame. *Mobilization*, 7, 287–304.

Whalen, Jack and Richard Flacks 1989: *Beyond the Barricades: The Sixties Generation Grows Up*. Philadelphia: Temple University Press.

White, Harrison 1988: Varieties in Markets. In B. Wellman and S. D. Berkowitz (eds.), *Social Structures: A Network Approach*. Cambridge: Cambridge University Press, 226–60.

White, Paul E., Levine, Sol, and Vasak, George 1975: Exchange as a Conceptual Framework for Understanding Interorganizational Relationships. In R. A. R. Negandhi (ed.), *Interorganizational Theory*. Kent: Kent State University Press, 182–95.

Whittier, Nancy 1995: *Feminist Generations: The Persistence of the Radical Women's Movement*. Philadelphia: Temple University Press.

Whittier, Nancy 1997: Political Generation, Micro-Cohorts, and the Transformation of Social Movements. *American Sociological Review*, 62, 760–78.

Whittier, Nancy 2004: The Consequences of Social Movements for Each Other. In Davis A. Snow, Sarah H. Soule, and Hanspeter Kriesi (eds.), *The Blackwell Companion to Social Movements*. Oxford: Blackwell, 531–51.

Whutnow, Robert 1987: *Meaning and Moral Order: Explanations in Cultural Analysis*. Berkeley: University of California Press.

Wieviorka, Michel (ed.) 2003: *Une autre monde . . . Contestations, dérives et surprise dans l'antimondialisation*. Paris: Balland.

Wieviorka, Michel 1995: *The Arena of Racism*. London/Thousand Oaks: Sage.

Wilcox, Clyde 1996: *Onward Christian Soldiers? The Religious Right in American Politics*. Boulder, CO: Westview Press.

Willelms, Helmut, Wolf, Marianne, and Eckert, Roland 1993: *Unruhen und Politikberatung: Funktion, Arbeitweise, Ergebnisse und Auswirkung von Untersuchungskommissionen in der USA, Grossbritannien und der Bundesrepublik Deutschlands*. Opladen: Westdeutscher Verlag.

Williams, Rhys H. 1999: Visions of the Good Society and the Religious Roots of American Political Culture. *Sociology of Religion*, 60, 1–34.

Williams, Rhys H. 2002: From the "Beloved Community" to "Family Values": Religious Language, Symbolic Repertoires, and Democratic Culture. In D. S. Meyer, B. Robnett, and N. Whittier (eds.), *Social Movements: Identity, Culture, and the State*. New York: Oxford University Press.

Williams, Rhys H. 2004: The Cultural Contexts of Collective Action. In D. Snow, S. Soule, and H. Kriesi (eds.), *The Blackwell Companion to Social Movements*. Oxford: Blackwell, 91–115.

Williams, Rhys H. and Kubal, Thimoty J. 1999: Movement Frames and Cultural Environment: Resonance, Failure and Boundaries of the Legitimate. *Research in Social Movements, Conflict and Change*, 21, 225–48.

Wilson, Bryan 1982: *Religion in Sociological Perspective*. Oxford: Oxford University Press.

Wilson, Frank L. 1990: Neo-corporatism and the Rise of New Social Movements. In R. J. Dalton and M. Kuechler (eds.), *Challenging the Political Order: New Social Movements in Western Democracies*. Cambridge: Polity Press, 67–83.

Wilson, Graham K. 1990: *Interest Groups*. Oxford: Blackwell.

Wilson, James Q. 1973: *Political Organizations*. New York: Basic Books.

Wilson, John 1973: *Introduction to Social Movements*. New York: Basic Books.

Wilson, John 1976: Social Protest and Social Control. *Social Problems*, 24, 469–81.

Wilson, John 2000: Volunteering. *Annual Review of Sociology*, 26, 215–40.

Winter, Martin 1998: Protest Policing in Germany. In D. della Porta and H. Reiter (eds.), *Policing Protest: The Control of Mass Demonstrations in Western Democracies*. Minneapolis/London: The University of Minnesota Press/UCL Press, 188–212.

Wisler, Dominique and Kriesi, Hanspeter 1998: Decisionmaking and Style in Protest Policing. The Cases of Geneva and Zurich. In D. della Porta and H. Reiter (eds.), *Policing Protest: The Control of Mass Demonstrations in Western Democracies*. Minneapolis/London: University of Minnesota Press/UCL Press, 91–116.

Woliver, Laura R. 1993: *From Outrage to Action: The Politics of Grass-roots Dissent*. Urbana, IL: University of Illinois Press.

Wood, Elizabeth 2003: *Insurgent Collective Action and Civil War in El Salvador*. New York: Cambridge University Press.

Wood, Lesley 2004: Breaking the Bank and Taking to the Streets: How Protesters Target Neoliberalism. *Journal of World-Systems Research*, 10, 69–89.

Wood, Michael and Hughes, Michael 1984: The Moral Basis of Moral Reform: Status Discontent vs. Culture and Socialization as Explanations of Anti-Pornography Social Movement Adherence. *American Sociological Review*, 49, 86–99.

Woodberry, Robert D. and Smith, Christian 1998: Fundamentalism et al.: Conservative Protestants in America. *Annual Review of Sociology*, 24, 25–56.

Worster, Donald 1994: *Storia delle idee ecologiche*. Bologna: il Mulino (original edition *Nature's Economy*, Cambridge/New York, Cambridge University Press, 1985).

Wrench, John and Solomos, John (eds.) 1993: *Racism and Migration in Western Europe*. Oxford/New York: Berg.

Wright, Erik O. 1985: *Classes*. London: Verso.

Wright, Erik O. 1996: The Continuing Relevance of Class Analysis – Comments. *Theory and Society*, 25, 693–716.

Wright, Steve 2004: Informing, Communicating and ICTs in Contemporary Anti-capitalist Movements. In W. van de Donk, B. Loader, P. Nixon, and D. Rucht (eds.), *Cyberprotest: New Media, Citizens and Social Movements*. London: Routledge, 77–94.

Yashar, Deborah 1996: Contesting Citizenship: Indigenous Movements and Democracy in Latin America. *Comparative Politics*, 31, 23–42.

Yearley, Steven 1988: *Science, Technology and Social Change*. London: Unwin Hyman.

Yearley, Steven 1991: *The Green Case*. London: Routledge.

Yearley, Steven 1996: *Sociology, Environmentalism, Globalization*. London/Thousand Oaks: Sage.

Yinger, J. Milton 1982: *Countercultures*. New York: Free Press.

Young, Iris Marion 1996: Communication and The Other: Beyond Deliberative Democracy. In Seyla Benhabib (ed.), *Democracy and Difference: Contesting the Boundaries of the Political*. Princeton: Princeton University Press, 120–35.

Young, Iris Marion 2003: Activist Challenges to Deliberative Democracy. In James S. Fishkin, and Peter Laslett, eds., *Debating Deliberative Democracy*. Oxford: Blackwell, 102–20.

Young, Michael P. 2002: Confessional Protest: The Religious Birth of U.S. National Social Movements. *American Sociological Review*, 67, 660–88.

Zald, Mayer N. 1970: *Organizational Change: The Political Economy of the YMCA*. Chicago: University of Chicago Press.

Zald, Mayer N. 2000: Ideologically Structured Action: An Enlarged Agenda for Social Movement Research. *Mobilization*, 5, 1 16.

Zald, Mayer N. and Ash, Roberta 1966: Social Movement Organizations: Growth, Decay and Change. *Social Forces*, 44, 327–40.

Zald, Mayer N. and Jacobs, David 1978: Compliance/Incentive Classifications of Organizations. Underlying Dimensions. *Administration and Society*, 9, 403–24.

Zald, Mayer N. and McCarthy, John 1980: Social Movement Industries: Competition and Cooperation Among Movement Organizations. In L. Kriesberg (ed.), *Research In Social Movements, Conflict and Change*, vol. 3. Greenwich, CT: JAI Press, 1–20.

Zald, Mayer N. and McCarthy, John 1987: *Social Movements in an Organizational Society*. New Brunswick, NJ: Transaction.

Zald, Mayer N. and Useem, Bert 1987: Movement and Countermovement Interaction: Mobilization, Tactics, and State Involvement. In M. N. Zald and J. D. McCarthy (eds.), *Social Movements in an Organizational Society*. New Brunswick, NJ: Transaction Books, 247–72.

Zincone, Giovanna 1992: *Da sudditi a cittadini*. Bologna: il Mulino.

Zirakzadeh, Cyrus E. 1991: *A Rebellious People*. Reno: University of Nevada Press.

Zirakzadeh, Cyrus E. 1997: *Social Movements in Politics: A Comparative Study*. London/New York: Longman.

Zuo, Jiping and Benford, Robert D. 1994: Mobilization Processes and the 1989 Chinese Democracy Movement. *Sociological Quarterly*, 36, 801–28.

Zurcher, Louis A. and Curtis, Russel L. 1973: A Comparative Analysis of Propositions Describing Social Movement Organizations. *Sociological Quarterly*, 14, 175–88.

INDEX OF NAMES

Aarelaid-Tart, Aili, 254n1

Abramson, Paul R., 69

Agnoletto, Vittorio, 107, 141

Aguiton, Christophe, 144

Ajanaku, Femi, 109

Alberoni, Francesco, 28, 77, 83, 142

Allegretti, Giovanni, 223, 224, 225, 232

Alvarez, Sonia, 251n16

Amenta, Edwin, 203, 205, 206, 235,
251n16

Ames, Ruth E., 102

Amin, Ash, 36, 38

Aminzade, Ronald, 200

Ancelovici, Marcos, 82, 147

Anderson, Benedict, 95, 108

Andretta, Massimiliano, 2, 10, 41, 49, 60,
64, 71, 75, 76, 78, 81, 83, 84, 95, 106,
108, 109, 132, 153, 180, 185, 188, 199,
203, 214, 220, 232, 258n1

Andrews, Kenneth, 137, 152

Anheier, Helmut, 27, 64, 77, 78, 82, 118,
126, 147, 152, 154, 156, 161, 172, 250n1,
260n2

Ansell, Christopher, 159

Arditi, Jorge, 108

Armstrong, Elizabeth, 107

Arrighi, Giovanni, 2, 10

Ash, Roberta, 14, 126

Augustin, Boguslaw, 2

Auyero, Javier, 42, 107, 112, 122

Ayers, Jeffrey, 40, 60, 64

Bagguley, Paul, 40, 56, 60, 61, 159

Bainbridge, William S., 117, 123

Baiocchi, Gianpaolo, 141, 223, 224, 225,
237, 239

Baker, Wayne, 70

Balme, Richard, 19

Balser, Deborah B., 158

Bandy, Joe, 4, 89, 90, 91, 107

Barbalet, Jack, 48, 252n6

Barkan, Steven E., 159

Barker, Colin, 10, 87

Barnes, Barry, 143

Barnes, Samuel H., 56, 120, 166, 180,
256n1

Bartholomew, Amy, 9, 112, 253n12

Bartolini, Stefano, 37, 43, 58, 112, 209

Basaglia, Franco, 108

Bechofer, Frank, 253n13

Beck, John, 68

Beck, Ulrich, 43

Becker, Penny E., 125

Beer, William R., 83, 106

Behrens, William W., 3

Beissinger, Mark R., 2

Bell, Daniel, 55, 252n3

Bello, Walden, 3

Benford, Robert D., 13, 74, 79, 80, 81, 86,
91, 94

Bennani-Chraïbi, Mounia, 2, 5, 72, 174

Bennett, W. Lance, 95, 100, 132, 133, 155,
159, 170, 178, 221

Berezin, Mabel, 87, 93, 109
Berger, Peter, 17, 92, 111
Bergmann, Werner, 174
Bernstein, Mary, 93, 107, 211
Béroud, Sophie, 46
Best, Joel, 73
Bew, Paul, 97
Bianchi, Marina, 90, 92, 98, 99
Bickham-Mendez, Jennifer, 89, 90, 91, 107
Billig, Michael, 92, 98, 108
Bircham, Emma, 64
Bison, Ivano, 15, 20, 132, 136, 159
Bjarnason, Thoroddur, 227
Blee, Kathleen M., 83, 108, 111, 126
Blumer, Herbert, 12, 75, 150, 186, 250n6
Bobbio, L., 239
Bohman, James, 242
Boli, John, 15, 43, 236
Bolton, Charles D., 120, 127
Bonazzi, Tiziano, 48
Bosk, Charles, 75
Bourdieu, Pierre, 11, 49, 50, 54, 56, 66
Bourneau, François, 34
Bove, Jose, 137
Boyte, Harry C., 142
Brand, Karl-Werner, 17, 206, 212, 214, 254n2, 256n9
Brand, Ulrich, 238
Braungart, Margaret M., 57, 69, 254n1
Braungart, Richard M., 57, 69, 254n1
Brecher, Jeremy, 2, 43, 61, 236
Breiger, Ronald L., 115
Breines, Wini, 141
Breuilly, John, 61, 251n16
Brint, Steven, 252n3, 253n15
Brissette, Martha B., 46
Britt, David W., 152
Broadbent, Jeffrey, 149
Brokett, Charles D., 200
Brooks, Clem, 54, 61, 70, 254n1
Brooks, Rachelle, 143
Brown, David L., 2
Brown, Helen M., 143
Brown, Kerry, 133
Bruce, Steve, 53, 80, 83, 97

Brysk, Alison, 44
Buchanan, James, 251n10
Buechler, Steven M., 35, 250n1
Bukowski, Jeannie, 43
Burdon, Tony, 230
Burns, Gene, 83
Burstein, Paul, 140, 227, 228, 231
Button, James W., 257n5
Bystydzienski, Jill M., 4

Cadena-Roa, Jorge, 86
Caiani, Manuela, 45
Calhoun, Craig, 11, 38, 60, 62, 91, 92, 95, 98, 100, 106, 109, 117, 133, 251n16, 253n18, 255n6
Callinicos, Alex, 107
Campbell, Jane, 48
Canciani, Domenico, 106
Caniglia, Elisabeth Schafer, 15, 103, 131
Capek, Stella M., 61, 115
Cardon, Domenique, 221
Carroll, William K., 70, 128, 129
Carson, Rachel, 108
Cartuyvels, Yves, 49
Carty, Victoria, 257n4
Castells, Manuel, 10, 36, 38, 39, 40, 41, 44, 45, 61, 94, 117, 133, 159, 183, 213
Catanzaro, Raimondo, 96, 112
Ceccarini, Luigi, 3
Cerulo, Karen, 133
Cesarani, David, 48
Chabanet, Didier, 34
Chabot, Sean, 183
Chandhoke, Neera, 238
Charlton, John, 64
Chatfield, Charles, 45
Chesler, Mark, 48
Chiriboga, Manuel, 236
Chong, Dennis, 255n9
Christiansen, Lars, 154
Cinalli, Manlio, 97
Clark, Terry N., 54
Clemens, Elisabeth S., 146, 154
Cleveland, John W., 10

Cloward, Richard, 16, 18, 35, 57, 60, 121, 146, 210, 215, 227, 237, 254n6
Cohen, J., 212, 242
Cohen, Jean L., 91, 105
Cohen, Robin, 94
Cohn, Steven F., 159
Coleman, James, 12, 116
Collins, Carole J. L., 230
Connolly, Linda, 97
Connor, Walker, 61, 83
Costello, Tim, 2, 43, 61
Cotgrove, Stephen, 58, 253n15
Couldry, Nick, 221
Cramer, Jacqueline, 58
Cress, Daniel M., 61, 86, 180, 227
Cristante, Stefano, 221
Crompton, Rosemary, 45
Crook, Stephen, 57, 59, 60
Crossley, Nick, 7, 8, 11, 67, 108, 250n1, 252n5
Croteau, David, 221
Crouch, Colin, 43, 45
Curtis, Russell L., 126, 127, 151

Dale, Gareth, 10
Dalton, Russell, 24, 28, 40, 54, 58, 68, 69, 112, 159, 170, 253n13, 257n7, 259n8
Daniels, Cynthia, 143
D'Anieri, Paul, 11, 60, 251n16, 253n18
D'Anjou, Leo, 65, 219, 251n16
Davies, James, 7
de Graaf, Nan Dirk, 70
De La Pierre, Sergio, 106
Delgado, Gary, 154
della Porta, Donatella, 2, 11, 17, 18, 19, 41, 45, 46, 47, 49, 59, 71, 91, 96, 100, 111, 112, 118, 125, 132, 134, 141, 142, 147, 149, 151, 153, 158, 159, 171, 172, 174, 180, 181, 182, 184, 185, 188, 189, 191, 196, 197, 198, 199, 200, 201, 203, 205, 207, 210, 211, 214, 215, 216, 217, 218, 220, 232, 234, 236, 241, 244, 247, 251n16, 255n1, 255n4, 256n6, 258n1, 258n8
DeNardo, James, 171, 174, 255n9, 259n12

Derloshon, Gerald, 254n6
Desai, Manisha, 149
Desario, Jack, 48
Devine, Fiona, 255n2
Dhingra, Pawan, 125
Di Maggio, Paul, 104, 127
Diani, Mario, 15, 18, 20, 22, 24, 26, 31, 56, 58, 61, 80, 83, 85, 93, 98, 102, 103, 112, 116, 117, 118, 119, 123, 125, 127, 128, 129, 132, 133, 135, 136, 138, 140, 142, 143, 144, 146, 147, 151, 158, 159, 172, 181, 227, 228, 254n7, 255n4, 255n5
Dines, Nicholas, 144
Dixon, Marc, 118
Doherty, Brian, 49, 139, 149
Donati, Paolo R., 74, 103, 135, 142, 143, 146, 147, 151, 255n2
Downing, D. H., 221
Downs, Anthony, 75
Downton, James, 91, 96, 142, 143
Doyle, Timothy, 81
Drobnic, Sonja, 118
Drury, John, 92, 93, 112, 149
Dryzek, John S., 241, 242, 243
Dubet, François, 83, 250n3
Duff, Andrew, 58, 253n15
Dunleavy, Patrick, 45
Dunne, Michael, 48
Duyvendak, Jan-Willem, 24, 86, 111, 214

Earl, Jennifer, 103, 197
Eckstein, Susan, 11, 40, 42, 174, 251n16
Eder, Klaus, 49, 53, 59, 60, 245, 252n9
Edge, David, 143
Edwards, Bob, 15, 116, 137, 152
Einwohner, Rachel L., 76, 107, 140, 228
Eisinger, Peter, 16, 196, 258n4
Ekland-Olson, Sheldon, 117
Ellingson, Stephen, 86
Elliott, Brian, 253n13
Elster, Jon, 242
Emirbayer, Mustafa, 66, 116
Epstein, Barbara, 60, 148, 179
Escobar, Arturo, 251n16
Escobar, Edward J., 201

Esping-Andersen, Gosta, 39, 252n8, 255n2
Etzioni, Amitai, 25, 149
Evans, Geoffrey, 70, 255n2
Evans, Peter, 40
Evans, Sara M., 142
Everett, Kevin D.
Eyerman, Ron, 13, 31, 58, 69, 80, 84, 85, 220, 252n8

Fabbrini, Sergio, 46
Fantasia, Rick, 31, 33, 38, 40, 58, 93, 100, 102, 105, 179, 251n16
Favre, Pierre, 182
Feagin, Joe R., 61
Featherstone, Mike, 60
Fernandez, Roberto, 123, 124, 125
Ferree, Myra Marx, 16, 86, 107, 219, 251n16
Fillieule, Olivier, 2, 5, 35, 72, 174, 198, 199
Finger, Matthias, 44
Finnegan, William, 156
Fireman, Bruce, 104, 105, 112
Flacks, Richard, 142
Flam, Helena, 24, 59, 104, 206, 207, 208, 210, 246
Foley, Michael, 116, 137
Follesdal, Andreas, 3, 144, 177
Forbes, James D., 50
Forno, Francesca, 3, 22
Foucault, Michel, 77
Foweraker, Joe, 251n16
Fox, Jonathan, 2
Frank, Andre Gunder, 258n11
Franklin, Mark, 54
Franzosi, Roberto, 108, 251n16
Freese, Jeremy, 93
Freschi, Anna Carola, 133, 172, 183, 221
Friedman, Debra, 103, 141
Fuchs, Dieter, 72
Fuentes, Maria, 258n11
Fulbrick, Mary, 48
Fung, Archon, 237, 245

Galaskiewicz, Joseph, 129
Gale, Richard P., 211

Gallie, Duncan, 209
Gamson, Josh, 48
Gamson, William, 16, 18, 21, 48, 72, 75, 79, 82, 86, 87, 94, 102, 103, 104, 105, 112, 141, 142, 145, 156, 176, 178, 219, 220, 221, 226, 232, 257n5
Gans, Herbert, 109
Gargiulo, Martin, 159
Gariyo, Zie, 230
Garofalo, Reebee, 252n8
Gates, Leslie, 251n12
Gaventa, John, 75
Geary, Dick, 209
Gerhards, Jürgen, 86, 219, 256n8
Gerlach, Luther, 94, 156–7, 161
Gern, Christiane, 105, 255n1
Giddens, Anthony, 36, 48, 51, 52, 66, 94, 252n4, 253n11
Gill, Stephen, 60
Girling, John, 54
Gitlin, Todd, 103, 180, 220
Giugni, Marco, 2, 17, 19, 23, 41, 203, 227, 235
Glasius, Marlies, 64
Goetz, Anne Marie, 233, 235, 236
Goffman, Erving, 74
Goldstein, Robert J., 209
Goldstone, Jack A., 213, 251n16
Goldthorpe, John, 55, 252n3
Goodwin, Jeff, 17, 86, 87, 91, 93, 104, 109, 116, 122, 219
Gould, Deborah, 147
Gould, Roger V., 105
Gouldner, Alvin, 55, 252n3
Goyder, Jane, 158
Grand, Steve, 2
Granjou, Fabien, 221
Granovetter, Mark, 104
Grant, W., 238
Gret, Marion, 223
Gronmo, Sigmund, 50
Groves, Abigail, 159
Guiraudon, Virginie, 238
Gulati, Ranjay, 159
Gupte, Manjusha, 159

Gurak, Laura J., 173
Gurr, Ted R., 7, 250n1
Gusfield, Joseph, 7, 12, 13, 26, 60, 74, 75, 250n7

Haas, Ernst B., 204
Haas, Peter M., 28
Habermas, Jürgen, 9, 47, 241, 242, 253n11
Haines, Herbert H., 257n5
Hainsworth, Paul, 39
Hajer, Maarten, 238
Hampton, Keith, 133
Hanagan, Michael, 65, 213
Harff, Barbara, 250n1
Hargreaves Heap, Shaun, 255n9
Hathaway, Will, 159
Haunss, Sebastian, 111, 131
Haydu, Jeffrey, 76
Haythornwhyte, Carolin, 95, 117
Heath, Anthony, 54, 58
Heckathorn, Douglas D., 105
Hedström, Peter, 251n15
Hegedus, Zsuzsa, 83, 250n3
Heirich, Max, 258n9
Held, David, 43, 51
Hellemans, Staff, 253n13
Herman, Didi, 83
Herring, Cedric, 1
Hertz, Noreena, 82
Hewitt, Lyndi, 86
Hick, Steven, 170
Hilgartner, Stephen, 75
Hinckley, Barbara, 251n12
Hine, Virginia, 94, 157
Hipsher, Patricia L., 246
Hirsch, Eric, 93, 100, 105
Hirsch, Joachim, 38
Hirschman, Albert O., 179
Hirst, Paul, 260n3
Hobsbawm, Eric, 65, 108, 174, 251n16
Hoffman, Lily M., 48
Hollander, Jocelyn A., 140, 228
Hooghe, Marc, 128, 177
Horton, Lynne, 91
Howard, Judith A., 92, 106

Hoynes, William, 221
Hughes, Michael, 50, 60
Hunt, Lynn, 109
Hunt, Scott A., 74, 91, 94
Huntington, Samuel, 72
Hutchinson, Richard, 251n12

Ignazi, Piero, 251n16
Imig, Doug, 19, 45
Inglehart, Ronald, 2, 57, 68, 69, 70, 71, 72, 84, 253n13, 254n2, 254n3
Isaac, Larry, 154

Jackson, John Harold, 150
Jamison, Andrew, 13, 58, 69, 80, 84, 85, 252n8
Janda, Kenneth, 140, 142
Jansen, Robert, 85
Jasper, James, 13, 14, 16, 17, 86, 87, 91, 93, 96, 104, 121, 154, 176, 180, 181, 184, 219
Jenkins, J. Craig, 16, 146, 210, 211, 213, 215, 217, 253n13, 259n9
Jennings, M. Kent, 56, 69, 120, 253n13
Jenson, Jane, 31, 112
Jobard, Fabien, 199
Johnson, Erik, 15
Johnston, Hank, 2, 13, 31, 44, 67, 74, 85, 96, 110, 144, 254n1
Jones, Andrew, 251n12
Joppke, Christian, 213, 251n16
Jordan, Grant, 19, 62, 103
Jordan, John, 132
Jordan, Tim, 132, 172, 183, 252n8

Kaase, Max, 120
Kaldor, Mary, 64, 164
Kaplan, Jeffrey, 111
Kaplan, Laura, 143
Katz, Daniel, 221
Katzenstein, Peter J., 259n7
Keating, Michael, 43
Keck, Margaret, 28, 133, 231
Kertzer, David, 73, 109
Kesselring, Sven, 238

Keys, Jennifer, 86
Khagram, Sanjeev, 236
Khawaja, Marwan, 200
Kielbowicz, Richard B., 220
Killian, Lewis, 1, 12, 13, 25, 67, 104, 122, 129, 142, 186, 250n4
Kim, Hyojoung, 104, 105
Kimeldorf, Howard, 251n14
King, Martin Luther, 84, 108, 109, 137
Kitschelt, Herbert, 17, 26, 27, 196, 202, 203, 206, 233, 239, 244, 253n13, 258n3
Kitts, James, 118, 120, 124, 146, 255n1
Klandermans, Bert, 13, 31, 59, 72, 85, 96, 210, 211, 255n1
Kleidman, Robert, 161
Klein, Naomi, 3, 108, 156, 177
Klotz, Audie, 236
Kniss, Fred, 83
Knoepfel, P., 238
Knoke, David, 19, 118, 129, 160, 255n3
Koelble, Thomas A., 214
Kolb, Felix, 147
Koopmans, Ruud, 11, 18, 39, 86, 184, 185, 188, 214, 217, 219
Kornhauser, A., 7, 66, 68, 119
Kousis, Maria, 41
Krasniewicz, Louise, 256n6
Kriesi, Hanspeter, 2, 17, 31, 57, 58, 68, 71, 112, 123, 125, 127, 140, 143, 144, 145, 146, 173, 183, 186, 201, 202, 203, 206, 207, 208, 210, 211, 212, 214, 215, 216, 217, 218, 232, 251n13, 253n14, 253n17, 258n5, 259n6
Kubal, Timothy J., 219
Kull, Steven, 2
Kuklinski, James H., 255n3
Kumar, Krishan, 36
Kurzman, Charles, 219
Kuumba, M. Bahati, 109

Lahusen, Christian, 133, 146, 236
Laing, Ronald, 108
Lang, Gladys, 142
Lang, Kurt, 142
Langman, Lauren, 5

Lash, Scott, 36, 38, 53, 55, 252n3
Latouche, Serge, 52
Laumann, Edward O., 160
Lavalette, Michael, 10, 159
Lazarsfeld, Paul, 221
Leach, Darcy, 111, 131
Lehmbruch, Gerhard, 212
Leicht, Kevin, 213
Lemert, Charles, 98
Lémieux, Vincent, 251n12
Lenart, Silvo, 221
Lenin, Vladimir Ilich, 108
Levi, Margaret, 40
Lewis, Tammy L., 147
Lichterman, Paul, 120, 143, 149, 158
Lijphart, Arendt, 259n7
Lindgren, Elaine H., 149
Lindsay, Isobel, 136
Linton, April, 140
Lipset, Seymour M., 36, 54, 58, 119
Lipsky, Michael, 166, 167, 179, 180, 185, 197, 237
Livesay, Jeff, 11, 67, 116
Lo, Clarence Y. H., 46, 211, 251n16
Loader, Brian, 117, 254n7
Lodhi, A. Q., 38
Lodi, Giovanni, 117, 119, 123, 125, 127
Lofland, John, 25, 73, 85, 140, 141, 251n11, 255n10
Logie, John, 173
Lööw, Helène, 111
Lowe, Philip, 158
Lowe, Stuart, 45, 61
Lowi, Theodore, 111, 151
Lubeck, Paul M., 5
Luckmann, Thomas, 17, 92, 111
Luker, Kristin, 122
Lumley, Robert, 80, 97, 147, 151
Lyons, Matthew Nemiroff, 49

Mach, Zdzislaw, 91
Maguire, Diarmuid, 97, 214
Maheu, Louis, 10
Mair, Peter, 37, 58, 112

Malcolm X, 108, 109
Maloney, William, 19, 62, 103
Manconi, Luigi, 96, 112
Manin, Bernard, 217
Mannheim, Karl, 253n1, 254n5
Mansbridge, Jane J., 230, 241, 256n6
Manza, Jeff, 54, 61, 70, 254n4
Markoff, John, 252n1
Marks, Gary, 45, 207, 236
Marshall, T. H., 48
Martin, Andrew, 103
Martin, Virginie, 34
Marullo, Sam, 15
Marwell, Gerald, 102, 103, 105, 118,
    141
Marx, Gary, 133, 197
Massens, Jan, 49, 156, 220
Maurer, Sophie, 34, 35, 75
Mayer, Margit, 9, 112, 253n12
Mayer, Robert, 50
Mazey, Sonia, 236
Mazmanian, Daniel A., 239
McAdam, Doug, 15, 16, 17, 18, 19, 20, 25,
    32, 41, 45, 72, 80, 84, 96, 103, 117, 119,
    123, 124, 125, 126, 141, 173, 186, 187,
    188, 200, 212, 219, 236, 248, 255n1,
    258n2
McAllister, Ian, 97
McCaffrey, Dawn, 86
McCammon, Holly, 86
McCarthy, John, 2, 14, 15, 18, 25, 103, 119,
    129, 134, 137, 140, 145, 146, 150, 152,
    153, 155, 180, 197, 198, 251n11, 256n4,
    258n8
McClurg Mueller, Carol, 107, 251n16
McDonald, Kevin, 24, 132, 139
McFarland, Andrew, 50, 103, 152
McGarry, John, 98
McGrew, Anthony, 43
McKay, George, 252n8
McNutt, John, 170
McPhail, Clark, 2, 13, 180, 198, 199
McPherson, Miller, 118, 127
McVeigh, Rory, 227
Meadows, Donella H., 3

Melucci, Alberto, 2, 9, 13, 16, 18, 21, 22,
    24, 44, 47, 49, 51, 53, 59, 61, 67, 72, 73,
    74, 77, 83, 87, 91, 92, 93, 94, 95, 96, 98,
    99, 104, 106, 110, 117, 131, 142, 143,
    149, 171, 232, 247, 252n7, 253n11,
    255n7
Meyer, David S., 1, 2, 18, 150, 154, 159,
    196, 211
Meyer, John, 187
Micheletti, Michele, 3, 50, 144, 177, 184
Michels, Robert, 146, 150
Middendorp, C., 70, 71
Mies, Maria, 174
Miliband, Ralph, 54
Miller, David, 242, 243
Minkoff, Debra C., 15, 138, 143, 146,
    151
Mische, Ann, 66, 86, 116
Mitre, Debarashmi, 159
Mitterrand, François, 35
Mizruchi, Mark, 128
Moaddel, Mansoor, 72, 110
Modigliani, Andre, 82, 220
Moody, Kim, 10
Mooney, Gerry, 10, 159
Moore, Barrington Jr., 196
Moore, Kelly, 143
Morgan, C. P., 150
Morgan, Jane, 197
Mormino, Maria, 90, 92, 98, 99
Morrill, Calvin, 140, 145
Morris, Aldon, 1, 143, 145, 212,
    254n6
Morse, David, 164
Mosca, Lorenzo, 2, 41, 49, 172, 199, 214,
    258n1
Mosco, Vincent, 95
Moscovici, Serge, 92
Mouffe, Chantal, 260n3
Mouriaux, René, 46
Mudu, Pierpaolo, 144
Mueller, Carol, 96
Mullins, Patrick, 122
Mushaben, Joyce Marie, 143
Myers, Daniel J., 103

Nas, Masja, 253n13
Neal, Caren, 205, 206
Nederveen Pieterse, Jan, 64
Neidhardt, Friedhelm, 2, 185, 200
Nelkin, Dorothy, 154, 205
Nepstad, Sharon E., 84, 122
Neveu, Eric, 180
Nicholson, Michael, 43
Nip, Joyce Y. M., 133
Nixon, Paul, 117, 254n7
Noelle-Neumann, Elisabeth, 221
Nolan, Mary, 256n3
Noland, Marcus, 2
Nollert, Michael, 212
Noonan, Rita, 80
Norris, Pippa, 40, 56, 70, 71, 72, 84, 120,
    166, 254n3, 257n7
Notarbolo, N., 174

Oberschall, Anthony, 14, 15, 37, 50, 60, 83,
    105, 119, 120, 137, 252n2
O'Brien, Robert, 233, 235, 236
Offe, Claus, 9, 11, 59, 239, 241
Ohlemacher, Thomas, 124
Okamoto, Dina, 122
Olesen, Thomas, 22
Oliver, Mike, 48
Oliver, Pamela, 13, 25, 67, 81, 102, 103,
    105, 118, 122, 141, 159
Olson, David, 40
Olson, Mancur, 100, 102
Olvera, Jacqueline, 54
Olzak, Susan, 39
Omi, Michael, 112
Omvedt, Gail, 251n16
Opp, Karl-Dieter, 56, 101, 102, 105, 255n1
Ortoleva, Peppino, 179
Osa, Maryjane, 110, 251n16
O'Sullivan See, Catherine, 39, 97
Owens, Timothy J., 91

Page, Karen, 159
Pagnucco, Ron, 235
Pakulski, Jan, 54, 56, 251n12, 254n1,
    255n2

Panebianco, Angelo, 19, 154, 251n15,
    256n7
Papadakis, Elim, 45
Passerini, Luisa, 91, 96
Passy, Florence, 23, 41, 42, 102, 118, 119,
    120, 126, 235, 255n1
Paulsen, Ronnelle, 124
Pearce, Jone, 61, 142, 251n16
Peretti, Jonah, 221
Perl, A., 238
Perrow, Charles, 16
Petts, J., 238
Philips, Susan, 159
Pianta, Mario, 2, 4, 39, 132, 171, 179,
    187
Piattoni, Simona, 43
Pichardo, Nelson, 59
Pickerill, Jeremy, 133
Pickvance, Chris, 27, 45, 62, 120
Pierru, Emmanuel, 34, 35
Pilger, John, 3
Pinard, Maurice, 120
Pini, Barbara, 133
Pinto, Louis, 50
Piore, Michael, 252n2
Piven, Frances F., 16, 18, 35, 57, 60, 121,
    146, 210, 215, 227, 237, 254n6
Pizzorno, Alessandro, 21, 51, 91, 92, 94,
    100, 102, 179, 189, 217, 230, 232,
    251n16
Platt, Gerald M., 84
Plows, Alex, 139, 149
Plumb, Lawrence, 254n6
Podobnik, Bruce, 4
Podolny, Joel, 159
Poguntke, Thomas, 253n13
Pollack, Michael, 205
Polletta, Francesca, 86, 87, 91, 93, 131, 141
Popielarz, Pamela, 118
Potter, James, 254n6
Poulsen, Jane, 104, 121
Powell, Brian, 93
Powell, Walter, 104, 127, 159
Prakash, Sanjeev, 116
Previte, Josephine, 133

Princen, Thomas, 44
Purdue, Derrick, 136, 137, 236

Ranci, Costanzo, 50
Randers, Jorgen, 3
Ranger, Terence, 108
Rao, Hayagreeva, 140, 145
Rapoport, Anatol, 211
Raschke, Joachim, 191
Ratner, R. S., 70, 128, 129
Ray, Raka, 107, 149, 251n16
Redhead, Steve, 252n8
Reger, Jo, 98
Reicher, Steve, 92, 93
Reifer, Thomas E., 5, 10, 251n16
Reimann, Kim D., 159
Reimon, Michel, 164
Reiner, Robert, 197
Reiter, Herbert, 2, 41, 49, 185, 197, 198,
    199, 201, 207, 214, 258n1
Renn, O., 238
Rheingold, Howard, 117, 133
Richardson, Dick, 26, 153
Richardson, Jeremy, 236
Rihoux, Benoit, 49
Riker, James V., 236
Risse, Thomas, 231, 236
Ritzer, George, 52
Robbins, Thomas, 25, 97, 251n16
Robertson, Roland, 41, 52
Robnett, Belinda, 94, 96
Rochford, E. Burke, 97
Rochon, Thomas R., 13, 18, 86, 159, 173,
    178, 179, 180, 181, 182, 185, 232, 239,
    251n8
Rohrschneider, Robert, 69, 159, 253n13
Rokkan, Stein, 6, 36, 37, 58
Rootes, Christopher, 11, 22, 24, 26, 56,
    132, 148, 149, 153, 256n9
Rose, Fred, 160
Rose, Richard, 45
Roseneil, Sasha, 62, 89, 90, 254n2
Rosenkrands, Jacob, 155, 257n4
Roscigno, Vincent, 118
Rosenthal, Naomi, 130, 141, 143, 159

Roth, Roland, 233, 256n3
Roth, Silke, 107
Rothman, Franklin D., 81, 159
Routledge, Paul, 139
Rowan, Brian, 150
Roy, Arundhati, 3
Royall, Frédéric, 34
Ruane, Janet M., 133
Rubington, Earl, 75
Rucht, Dieter, 1, 2, 4, 28, 72, 86, 117,
    134, 140, 149, 152, 153, 171, 172,
    184, 186, 187, 188, 189, 196, 202,
    205, 210, 211, 215, 216, 217, 218,
    219, 221, 227, 235, 253n10, 254n7,
    255n4, 256n8
Rüdig, Wolfgang, 11, 59
Ruggiero, Vincenzo, 144
Rupp, Leila, 11, 18, 87, 91, 96, 111, 149
Russett, Bruce, 44
Ruzza, Carlo, 233, 236
Ryan, Barbara, 143
Rytina, Steve, 112

Sabel, Charles, 252n12
Safran, William, 106
Salamon, Lester M., 152
Salmon, Jean Marc, 34, 35
Samuelson, Paul, 251n10
Sandell, Rickard, 118, 251n15
Sandoval, Salvador A. M., 246
Sartori, Giovanni, 17
Sassen, Saskia, 39, 94
Sasson, Theodore, 221
Sassoon, Joseph, 74, 109, 111
Saunders, P., 45
Sawer, Marian, 159
Schacht, Steven, 4
Scharpf, Fritz, 206
Scheff, Thomas, 104
Scherer, Clifford, 220
Schlesinger, Paul, 220
Schlosberg, David, 160
Schmidt, Hilmar, 236, 238
Schmitt-Beck, Rüdiger, 130, 143
Schmitter, Philippe, 212

Schneider, Volker, 260n2
Schnittker, Jason, 93
Scholte, Jaan Aart, 233, 235, 236
Schönleitner, Gunther, 225
Schou, Arild, 131, 143
Schudson, Michael, 219
Schumaker, Paul D., 213
Schwartz, Michael, 128, 141
Schweingruber, David, 198
Scotch, Richard, 48
Scott, Alan, 55
Scott, W. Richard, 137, 138, 152
Seddon, David, 2, 42, 174
Seligman, Adam, 254n3
Selle, Per, 116
Sen, Amartya, 225
Sewell, William H. Jr., 11, 67, 116
Shah, Ghanshyam, 251n16
Shemtov, Ronit, 75
Shiva, Vandana, 137
Sikkink, Kathryn, 28, 133, 231, 236, 238
Silver, Beverly, 10, 213
Simeant, Johanna, 41
Simmel, Georg, 93, 106, 115, 118
Sintomer, Yves, 223, 239
Sklair, Laskie, 229
Skocpol, Theda, 146, 196, 199, 251n16
Smelser, Neil J., 7–8, 11
Smith, Anthony D., 42, 56, 61, 108, 251n16
Smith, Brendan, 2, 43, 236
Smith, Christian, 72, 83, 110, 122
Smith, Jackie, 2, 4, 15, 108, 132, 146, 180, 236
Smyrl, Marc, 43
Snow, David, 13, 28, 31, 61, 66, 67, 73, 74, 79, 80, 81, 82, 86, 87, 94, 97, 103, 117, 124, 125, 180, 227
Snyder, David, 38
Somers, Margaret, 86, 109, 251n16, 254n4
Sommier, Isabelle, 11, 46
Soros, George, 64
Soule, Sarah, 13, 103, 184, 197
Souza, Celina, 223, 224

Soysal, Yasemine N., 48
Staggenborg, Suzanne, 31, 143, 146, 159, 211
Stamatov, Peter, 85
Stark, Rodney, 117, 123
Starr, Harvey, 44
Statham, Paul, 18, 219
Steel, Brent S., 70
Steinberg, Marc, 86
Stepan-Norris, Judith, 33, 40, 251n16
Stern, Charlotta, 118, 251n15
Stieglitz, Josef, 3
Stoecker, Randy, 255n8
Stokman, Frans N., 128
Stolle, Dietlind, 3, 144, 177
Stott, Clifford, 93
Strand, David, 187
Streeck, Wolfgang, 252n2
Stryker, Sheldon, 91
Strzelecki, Jan, 83, 250n3
Su, Yang, 173
Subramaniam, Mangala, 159
Swidler, Ann, 67, 73, 85, 108
Szasz, Andrew, 23
Szelenyi, Sonia, 54
Sztompka, Piotr, 227

Take, Ingo, 236, 238
Tarrow, Sidney, 1, 2, 11, 16, 17, 18, 19, 20, 32, 41, 45, 59, 73, 79, 81, 102, 155, 158, 159, 169, 174, 175, 179, 188, 189, 190, 191, 196, 202, 210, 214, 217, 219, 227, 229, 246, 248, 253n18, 254n8
Taylor, Bron, 149, 160
Taylor, Ian, 144
Taylor, Verta, 11, 16, 18, 24, 49, 87, 91, 94, 96, 99, 104, 107, 110, 111, 142, 143, 144, 149, 165
Taylor-Gooby, Peter, 45
Thayer, Millie, 107
Themudo, Nuno, 147, 154, 156, 161, 172, 260n2
Thomas, Daniel, 236
Thomas, George, 15, 43,

Thompson, Edward H., 8, 38, 58, 96, 159
Thompson, John B., 52
Tilly, Charles, 6, 14, 16, 17, 18, 19, 20, 21, 25, 31, 32, 37, 38, 41, 65, 79, 81, 106, 119, 121, 133, 156, 168, 169, 182, 183, 185, 191, 197, 201, 215, 219, 245, 246, 247, 251n9, 257n2, 257n3
Tilly, Chris, 41
Tilly, Louise, 79
Tilly, Richard, 79
Tindall, David, 118, 126
Titarenko, Larissa, 2
Tocqueville, Alexis de, 201–2
Tondeur, Alain, 49
Touraine, Alain, 7, 8, 9, 21, 54, 58, 63, 83, 92, 93, 94, 106, 250n3, 251n16, 252n10, 253n10, 255n7
Tranvik, Tommy, 133
Traugott, Mark, 182
Trigilia, Carlo, 252n2
Trump, Thomas, 71
Turk, Herman, 129
Turkle, Sherry, 133
Turner, Bryan, 60
Turner, Ralph, 12, 25, 60, 67, 104, 122, 186, 250n4, 255n1

Urry, John, 36, 38, 53, 55, 58, 59, 60, 252n3
Useem, Bert, 211

Vakaloulis, Michel, 46
Valiente, Celia, 214
Van Aelst, Peter, 133, 155
Van de Donk, Wim, 117, 254n7
van Deth, Jan, 120
van Dyke, Nella, 165, 216, 251n12
van Gennep, A., 111
van Male, John, 219
van Praag, Philip, 217
van Willigen, Marieke, 144
Van Zoonen, Liesbet, 103
Vegh, Sandor, 176

Vertovec, Steven, 94
Virnoche, Mary, 133
Voss, Kim, 251n16

Waddell, Steve, 160
Waddington, P. A. J., 199
Walby, Sylvia, 39, 62
Walgrave, Stefaan, 4, 49, 133, 155, 156, 172, 205, 220, 255n4
Walker, Jack L., 146
Wall, Derek, 132, 139, 149
Wallace, Michael, 217, 253n17, 259n9
Wallerstein, Immanuel, 10, 41, 65
Wallis, Roy, 50, 83, 97, 126
Walsh, Edward, 102
Walton, John, 2, 42, 174
Warland, Rex, 102
Warren, Mark, 251n12
Washbourne, Neil, 133
Wasko, Janet, 95
Waters, Malcolm, 255n2
Wehr, Paul Ernest, 91, 96, 143
Weinberg, Martin S., 75
Welch, Michael R., 227
Wellman, Barry, 94, 95, 117, 133
Westby, David L., 78
Whalen, Jack, 142
Whitbaker, William H., 159
White, Harrison, 104
White, Robert W., 91
Whittier, Nancy, 16, 49, 89, 90, 91, 93, 94, 96, 104, 107, 110, 111, 149, 154, 178, 182, 247, 254n1
Whutnow, Robert, 109
Wieviorka, Michel, 2, 83, 250n3
Willelms, Helmut, 234, 239
Williams, Marc, 233, 235, 236
Williams, Rhys H., 79, 81, 84, 87, 219
Wilson, Bryan, 97, 251n16
Wilson, Frank L., 259n10
Wilson, James Q., 142, 256n6
Wilson, John, 19, 25, 118, 165, 168, 200, 251n16
Winant, Howard, 112
Winter, Martin, 199

Wisely, Nancy, 118, 129
Wisler, Dominique, 173, 201
Wissen, Markus, 238
Wolfsfeld, Gadi, 103, 220
Wolfson, Mark, 152, 251n11
Wood, Elizabeth, 84
Wood, Lesley, 2
Wood, Michael, 50, 60
Woodberry, Robert D., 72, 83
Wrench, John, 39
Wright, Erik, 57, 237, 245
Wright, Steve, 133, 156

X, Malcolm, 108, 109

Yinger, J. Milton, 251n16
Young, Iris Marion, 242, 243
Young, Michael P., 206

Zald, Mayer N., 14, 15, 18, 25, 67, 119, 126, 129, 134, 137, 140, 145, 146, 150, 152, 153, 155, 211, 256n4, 258n8
Zeitlin, Maurice, 251n16
Zeppetella, A., 239
Zirakzadeh, Cyrus E., 251n16
Zurcher, Louis A., 117, 126, 127, 151
Zylan, Yvonne, 251n16

INDEX OF SUBJECTS

ad hoc commissions, 238–9
advocacy networks, 236
affinity groups, 132
alliance structure, 210
allies of movements, 25, 34, 173, 179, 210–18; transnational, 227
Amnesty International, 259n2
antiglobalization, see global justice movement
antinuclear movement, 59, 205–6, 208, 210, 212, 258n3
antiracist movement, 216
antiroad movement, 49
antitoxic movement, 3, 23
ATTAC, 4, 82–3, 147, 230

Baltic countries, 110
barricades, 182
Black Bloc, 173–4, 193–4, 200
boycott, 40, 175–7, 184

campaigns of protest, 229
categories, 37
catnet, 120
celebrations, public, 169
Chicago school, 12
children's rights, 48–9
churches, as allies, 212
citizenship, citizenship rights, 48–9
civil disobedience, 177
civil rights movement, US, 72, 152, 166–7, 182, 212

class, 52–62; class conflict, 36, 38, 40; class location, 58, 120–1
Clean Clothes Campaign, 175
cleavages, 36–7; left–right, 71, 214; political, 36; center–periphery, 36, 42–3; and postmaterialism, 70
clique, 127
coalitions, political, 23–4
collective action, and the production of collective goods, 100–2; as aggregate of individual behaviors, 12; as cognitive praxis, 73–4; conflictual and consensual, 22–3; logic of, 14–15, 100–5
collective behavior, 11–13
collective identity, see identity
communist parties, as allies, 214
computer mediated communication (CMC), 132–4; and movement subcultures, 132; and organizational change, 155–6
configuration of power, 211
consensus, 242
consumerism, ethical, 50, 53, 177
conventional vs. unconventional politics, 170
conversion, 97
cooperation, competitive, 158; noncompetitive, 158
cooptation, 235
corporatism (neo), 212–13
countercultures, 49, 111, 131–4, 144
counterframing, 76

countermovement, 189–90, 205, 211, 229
countersummit, 171, 179, 195
crowd control, see protest policing
cultural change, 232–3
culture and collective action, 13–14, 65–7
cycles of protest, 188–91

decentralization, 38, 43; administrative, 234
deliberative arenas, 236
deliberative democracy, 242; empowered, 237, 241; strength of the better argument, 242–3
demands, nonnegotiable, 229
democratic theory, 239
democratization, 245–6
demonstration rights, 201
demonstrators, police image of, 199
diffusion of protest, 183; cross-national, 186–8, 258n10
direct action, 179, 183, 185
direct democracy, 234, 239–40; vs. representative democracy, 240; critique of, 244
discursive democracy, 243
discursive opportunities, 17, 47, 219–20

ecological movement, see environmental movement
economic change and collective action, 37
electoral instability, 210, 215
electronic advocacy, 170
elites, and social movement leaders, 227
emergent norm theory, 12
emotions, 13, 16, 87, 148
environmental movement, 37, 50, 58, 81, 148, 188, 233–4; in Italy, 157–8
epistemic communities, 28, 236
equality, 242
escalation, see radicalization
ethnic conflict, 39, 44, 48, 52, 56
European Social Forum, 95, 225–6
European Union, 18, 235

events, public, 169
experts, 143, 233–5, 237
expressive vs. instrumental action, 196

factionalism, 130, 157
feminist movement, see women's movement
foundations, as allies, 121
frame alignment (bridging, amplification, extension, transformation), 81–3
frame theory, critiques 85–7
frames, elements of, 74–9; changes in, 86; interpretative, 74 81; interpretative, and "empirical credibility," 81–2; interpretative, and political opportunities, 85–6; master, 79–81; realignment, 85; revitalization, 87
framing processes, 83–5
France, 33–5
Freedom Summer, 117–18, 123, 124, 167
French Revolution, 169
friendships among activists, 128
functional separation of power, 203
functionalism, 7–8
fundamentalism, 52, 87, 100, 110

gender conflict, 39, 48
Genoa, protest against G8, 193–5
Germany, 200, 216
Global Justice Movement, 2–5; and democracy, 230, 232, 240; and new social movements, 60; and organizational forms (Bristol example), 135–7; and the welfare state, 46; Genoa protests, 193; institutional control, 200–1; protest cycles, 190; repertoires, 178, 180, 182, 184–5
globalization, 44; cultural, 51–2; economic, 41–2; framing of, 64–5
goods, collective, definition of, 251n10
grassroots organizations, 149–50
green parties, 148, 247n8, 256n9
Greenpeace, 135–7, 138, 257n8

hackers, 183
historicity, 8, 54
homeless movements, 61, 86, 145
human rights movement, 231

identity, 50–2, 55, 179; and continuity of
   collective action, 95–7; and mutual
   trust, 94; and political opportunities,
   111–13; and rational action, 100–5; as
   invention, 107–11; as rediscovery,
   107–11; collective, 21; components of,
   93–4; conflicts over, 106–7; exclusive vs.
   inclusive, 98–100, 102–3; movement
   and group, 99; multiple, 98–100;
   national, 52, 107; private and public,
   90–2; self- and hetero-definition of,
   105–6; static vs. dynamic, 92–3
ideology, 66–7; versus frames, 79
immigration, 48, 112
incentives, 100
indigenous movement, 42, 44
industrial action, 37, 175
industrial conflict, see class conflict
industrial society, 8–9
Indymedia, 144, 221
interest groups, 207, 208; as allies,
   212
international governmental organizations
   (IGOs), 43–5, 146–7, 204–5, 235
Iran, 110
Islam, values in, 72
Italy, 80, 200

journalists and protest, 180
Jubilee 2000, 161, 172, 230
judiciary, 203–4

knowledge, 53, 62; and protest
   repertoires, 182

labor movement, 40–1, 183, 188, 207–10,
   217
latency, 95–6, 131, 141, 149, 247
leadership and protest, 142–3, 257n6

learning processes, 184–6
left-wing parties, 214–15, 259n11; left in
   government, 215–16
legislation, 231
lifestyles, 49–51
lobbying, 233–4
logic of bearing witness, 176; of damage,
   173–6; of numbers, 171–3

mail-bombing, 172
managers, 48, 57
marches, 171, 182
Marxism, 6, 8, 10
mass media, 167, 220; and protest, 173,
   178, 180
media activism, 221
media, movements', 181; see also mass
   media
middle class, new, 38, 55–62, 253n14;
   relationship with working class, 60;
   traditional middle class, 59
mobilization, individual and social
   networks of, 121–6; mobilization level,
   205, 208, 217; of material resources,
   103, 141–2; of participation, 103,
   141–2
moral codes, 50
moral majority, 50
moral protest, 59–60
movement associations, 143–4; strategies,
   206; success, 203, 208, 211, 218
multi-organizational field, 210; alliance
   structure, 210; opposition structure,
   210
multiple memberships, 127

nationalism, 31, 83; ethno-, 112
nationalist movements, 31, 52
nation-state, 36; crisis of the, 42–5
neocorporatism, 212
neoliberal shift, 204
neoliberalism, 43
netstriking, 172
network organizations, 159–61

networks, 15–16, 21, 37, 114–17; and
computer mediated communication,
132–4; and individual participation,
117–26; associational, 126–31;
informal movement, 131–2;
interorganizational, 157–60;
interpersonal, 117; private, 125;
subcultural, 110–11, 131–4
new politics, 1
new professions, 38, 253n14
new social conflicts, 8–11
new social movement, 61–2; and new
middle class, 8–11; ideological models
of nongovernmental organizations
(NGOs), 235, 237–8
nonviolence, 174, 179, 184–5

occupation, 179, 191
organizational change, 150–2; and
culture, 154; and computer
mediated communication, 155–6;
and institutional factors, 152–3
organizational functions, 143–4
organizational infrastructure of social
movement, 247–8
organizational models, 127–31, 145–50, 200
organizational relations, types of 157–9
organizational structure, hierarchical or
horizontal, 142–3
outcomes of social movements, 226–9;
public policy, 229–33; procedural,
223–39
overlapping memberships, 127–31
Oxfam, 135

parliamentary democracy, see
representative democracy
participation and social networks, 126–31
participation incentives, 100–5
participatory budgeting, 223–5, 228,
231–2, 237, 242–3
participatory democracy, 176, 239, 243–5,
248
participatory movement organizations,
147–50

parties, as allies, 213–18
peace movement, 172, 178, 179, 183–4,
205, 215–16, 218
petitions, 172; online, 172
political opportunities, 16–19, 196, 219,
258n2, 3, 5
political opportunity structure, 16, 196
political participation, 56–8, 166, 256n1,
257n7; education and, 56–7
political parties, transformation of,
216–17
political process theory, 16–19
poor people's movement, 33, 61
populist democracy, 246
Porto Alegre, and participatory
budgeting, 223–5, 228, 231, 240, 241;
and world social forum, 225, 227, 243
postindustrial society, 8–9
postmaterialism, 67–73
power distribution, 247
preference transformation, 242
prevailing strategies, definition, 206; and
democracy, 207; inclusionary vs.
exclusionary, 207–8
private sphere, conflict in, 47–8, 53,
252n6; vs. public sphere, 47–8, 53
procedural change, 233
protest policing, 164, 171, 173, 184–5,
190, 193–5; definition of, 197; effects
of, 200–1, 207; escalated force in, 198;
militarization of, 199; negotiated
control in, 198; strategies of,
197–8
protest, as a political resource, 29–30,
166–7; campaign, 188; definition, 165;
events, 23–4; symbolic function of,
173–4, 178–9, 181; see also cycle of
protest
public bureaucracy, 203, 206
public interest groups, 50, 123
public policies, 229–33
public sphere, 240

radicalization, 151, 174, 184, 189–90, 195,
211

rational choice theory, 14–16; critiques of, 16
realignment, political, 69, 112
recruitment, 117–21
referendum, 173, 206, 234, 238–9
reform professionals, 212
repertoire(s) of action, 168, 200, 208–9, 218; modern, 169; public acceptance of, 234; strategic dilemmas, 181–2
representative democracy, 234, 239–45
resource mobilization, 13–16, 34, 141–2
responsiveness, 231
riots, 173–4
rituals, 108–11; protest as, 182

Seattle, protest in 163–5, 185; outcomes, 232, 234–5
sect, religious, 25, 97, 117, 126–7
selective incentives, 101–2, 141; external vs. internal, 101
sense of injustice, 200
shared beliefs, 7
social change, 35–7
social classes, see class
social fragmentation, 37–41
social inequality, 39
social justice, 224
social movement organization (SMO), definition of, 140; evolution of, 150–2; professional, 25, 145–7; transnational, 146–7
social movements, and political coalitions, 23–4; and political parties, 25–7; and protest events; and public interest groups, 25–7; concept of, 20–2, 54
social problems, definition of, 74–7
social stratification and collective action, 6, 58
solidarity, 15, 95
squatters, 49
state agencies, 211
state: strong and weak, 201–2
status politics, 60
strategic options, 178

strike(s), 33, 175, 179, 183, 212, 258n11, 259n9
student movement, 188
subcultures, 110–11, 131–4, 144
success, see outcomes
symbolic conflict, 75
symbolic ethnicity, 109
symbolic vs. material resources, 54

technology, 41, 155–6, 170
territorial decentralization, 202
tertiary sector, 31
theory, American vs. European, 6–7
trade union movements, 46, 212
transnational alliances, 246
transnational campaign, 34, 40
transnationalization of protest, 42–4
transparency, 242

unemployed, movements of the, 33–5, 38, 50, 61
unions, 34, 40, 41, 46–7, 207–8; as allies, 213, grassroots, 40, 46; social movement unions, 213
united farm workers, 215
United States, 80, 83; antitoxic movement, 3, 23, homeless movements, 86; see also civil rights movement
urban conflicts, 174, 197

values, and collective action, 67–73; change, 67–73; materialist, 67–73, postmaterialist, 67–73
violence, 173–4, 184, 191, 218, 257n5, 257–8n8, 259n12
voluntary association, 19, 127

welfare state, 45–6, 252n6
women's movement: 89–91, 130, 214, 229–30, 234; internal structure of, 132
women's rights, see women's movement
World Social Forum, 4, 75, 225, 227, 243

youth movements, 49